ADVANCED

Business

Dave Needham
Rob Dransfield

TUTOR'S FILE

Edexcel
Success through qualifications

Heinemann Educational Publishers
Halley Court, Jordan Hill, Oxford OX2 8EJ
A division of Reed Educational & Professional Publishing Ltd

Heinemann is a registered trademark of Reed Educational & Professional Publishing Limited

OXFORD MELBOURNE AUCKLAND JOHANNESBURG BLANTYRE GABORONE
IBADAN PORTSMOUTH NH (USA) CHICAGO

First published 2001
2005 2004 2003 2002 2001
10 9 8 7 6 5 4 3 2 1

A catalogue record for this book is available from the British Library on request.

ISBN 0 435 45317 3

Typeset by Techtype, Abingdon, Oxfordshire.

Printed and bound in Great Britain by Athenaeum Press Ltd, Gateshead, Tyne & Wear.

Tel.: 01865 888058
Website: www.heinemann.co.uk

CONTENTS

PREFACE

This tutor's file has been designed to accompany our best-selling student textbook, *Advanced Business*. We are grateful for the help and advice we received from Edexcel in framing a coursebook designed to meet the new course specifications.

To create our new AVCE student book, we had to rewrite all our existing text and materials completely to bring it all up to date. While this involved considerable effort we are pleased with the result as we feel the post-millennium business world is considerably different from that which existed in the late twentieth century.

Our text has been designed to provide students with an up-to-date outline of how business operates in the early twenty-first century, and tutors will benefit from referring students to the numerous web links that are picked out in the text.

The tutor's file provides the sort of support our research and investigations have revealed modern AVCE tutors to be seeking:

- a series of teaching suggestions and articles outlining modern approaches and ideas for teaching the AVCE Business qualification
- suggested answers for all the case studies, discussion points and tasks. Where, in certain instances, answers have not been supplied, this is because the authors felt either that there were many answers and specifying one might be misleading, or because of the nature of the task or question, the answer would depend upon the circumstances relevant to the user of the pack
- overhead transparencies to accompany every chapter of the book. The overhead transparencies are accompanied by notes giving suggestions as to how these should be used in teaching sessions
- a set of discussion activities for each of the six units. These are intended to provide a focus for group discussion to support the Key Skill of communication
- a detailed outline of ways in which students can produce the portfolio evidence required for the assessment of Unit 1 Business at work, Unit 3 Marketing, Unit 4 Human resources and Unit 6 Business planning
- an end-of-unit test for students to practise for Unit 2 The competitive business environment and Unit 5 Business finance.

We hope tutors continue to find the text interesting and useful and that the materials provided in this tutor's file will help and support them in delivering the new AVCE in Business.

SPECIAL NOTE

Many of the OHTs in this pack have been reduced to A5 portrait size and placed two per page. Our aim has been to maximise the number of resources provided. All can be easily enlarged onto OHT film.

THE NEW AWARD

'Curriculum 2000' became the 'catch-all' buzz phrase for all that was to happen not just to GNVQs but also to other areas of post-16 education, including A levels, the new Advanced Subsidiary level and, of course, the changes to Key Skills. It meant the new millennium was, for many, celebrated, enjoyed or even suffered, not just with the accoutrements that went along with failed icons like the 'Dome' but also with attendance at meetings set up by examining bodies, at in-service courses and, inevitably, with the need to cope with changes to planning and preparation.

The changes to all the qualifications stem from the government's review of post-16 qualifications and they fall in line with the government's commitment to provide a broader and more flexible curriculum beyond the age of 16 years. The key element was that change included both GNVQs and A levels at the same time, with the hope that this would encourage more students to follow learning programmes that provided an opportunity for them to 'mix and match' both types of qualifications. In AQA speak:

> the new model AS and Advanced VCE have been designed to further enhance the motivation and achievement of Advanced VCE learners, improve the consistency and manageability of the qualifications and incorporate an improved quality assurance and assessment process.

As a result, the features of the new model AS and Advanced VCE are:

- a revised unit structure that includes clear details of learning requirements (what you need to learn), clear statements of assessment requirements (through the Assessment Evidence Grid) and teacher guidance
- revised grading criteria relating to each individual unit
- a new style of external assessment
- simplified recording
- monitoring and moderation exercises by subject moderators.

The new qualifications structure has been designed to provide a broader and more flexible curriculum beyond the age of 16 years. Feedback from pilot centres from which candidates took both a combination of GCE A levels and GNVQs showed that combining the two created a great deal of thought about how to provide choice and about how to build programmes or timetables that would meet more closely the needs of a wider range of student abilities and aspirations.

The AS and AVCE in Business have been designed to form qualifications that provide knowledge and understanding of 'business' as a vocational area. They are ideal qualifications for those students who want a broad background in business that will allow them to progress to further or higher education, training or employment.

The AS and AVCE in Business have the following objectives. They provide:

- a broad background of understanding and core knowledge while allowing some scope for candidates to focus upon a particular interest area
- a student-centred approach to learning, together with the opportunity to apply knowledge of the application of business principles in a practical way
- the opportunity for centres to forge links with industries
- cross-sector themes and approaches so that students can gain an insight into such related areas as retailing, advertising, management, marketing, finance, training, planning, communication and human resources.

An important feature of the new qualification structure for business is that students must actively experience the business environment. There are many ways in which this can be achieved through their course, not least by undertaking work experience. However, they may also wish to join a Young Enterprise group, be involved in some form of school link with employers or meet local business people when researching their work.

There are now three qualifications available in Business:

1. Advanced Subsidiary VCE – 3 units (formerly a part award)
2. Advanced VCE – 6 units (formerly a single award)
3. Advanced VCE (double award) – 12 units (formerly a full award).

Unit 1 Business at work	Unit 13 Introduction to management
Unit 2 The competitive business environment	Unit 14 Advertising and public relations
Unit 3 Marketing	Unit 15 Using sales promotion
Unit 4 Human resources	Unit 16 Using technology in retail and distribution
Unit 5 Business finance	Unit 17 Market research
Unit 6 Business planning	Unit 18 Business statistics
Unit 7 Managing production	Unit 19 Financial services
Unit 8 Business law	Unit 20 Introduction to management and accounts
Unit 9 Working in teams	Unit 21 The social costs and benefits of business activity
Unit 10 Training and development	Unit 22 Trading in international markets
Unit 11 Industrial relations	Unit 23 Business and the European Union
Unit 12 Business communications systems	Unit 24 Health and safety

The table above lists the units. Units 1–6 are compulsory for the Advanced VCE (double award).

The two externally assessed core units are:

1 The competitive business environment
2 Finance.

A key element within the new qualifications structure is to give students the opportunity to develop a broad understanding of business principles while at the same time allowing them to focus on one particular pathway, such as human resources, marketing or finance. The qualifications thus provide an opportunity for a number of progression routes:

1 *Higher education*: the units provide a sound basis for progression to a range of courses in higher education.
2 *Employment*: the units aim to maintain and support the recognised standards demanded for business education and training in a range of sectors.
3 *Related qualifications to the National Qualifications Framework*: the units enable students to progress to other related qualifications in areas such as economics, sociology and law.

The range of units on offer provides students with:

- knowledge of the key aspects of business at work, the competitive business environment and the key activities of business
- an awareness of how industry applies planning and strategy to all sectors of business activity and the role of new technology
- an opportunity to learn about the basic principles underlying business practice and to become familiar with a range of business systems
- (in the context of any commercial firm), an insight into the importance of ensuring that the various key business activities work in unison towards a common purpose.

FEDA support Learning and Skills Development Agency

When delivering the AVCE in Business, it is important to remember you are not on your own: there are many tutors around the country who need help or support of various kinds from time to time! The FEDA Support Programme, now provided by the Learning and Skills Development Agency, is designed to help tutors, whether in schools or colleges, to deliver high-quality programmes. It runs training events, produces staff development and teaching materials, funds schools and colleges for development projects, works with employers to raise awareness of the qualifications and helps to develop routes to employment.

Since 1995 the Support Programme has established itself as the national support service for GNVQs and will, of course, be doing the same for the newly structured qualifications. In fact, in recent years FEDA's energies have been geared towards helping schools and colleges cope with and plan for all the changes taking place.

For all inquiries about the AVCE, phone the FEDA Telephone Helpline on: 020-7962-1066 (between 8.30 am and 5.30 pm), or leave a message on the answer-phone at any other time.

In providing this service the Learning and Skills Development Agency aims to:

- provide an up-to-date, accurate information service about the qualifications structure
- answer queries immediately or, if it is not possible to do so, provide a response within two working days or put the tutor in touch with the organisation that can provide the answer.

For example, the FEDA Telephone Helpline could be used to answer such queries as:

1 What support materials are available for Unit 15 ('Using sales promotion')?
2 How are the new assessment arrangements likely to affect the teaching of specific units?

FEDA has a team of specially trained information officers who are able to answer questions from their bank of published information, which includes all the publications from examining bodies such as Edexcel.

It is also possible to contact FEDA by e-mail using: gnvq@feda.ac.uk or by writing to:

Learning and Skills Development Agency
Support Programme
FEDA
Citadel Place
Tinworth Street
Vauxhall
LONDON
SE11 5EH

PLANNING, CO-ORDINATING AND MANAGING AVCE BUSINESS

Planning

Probably the most difficult task for anyone trying to adapt to the changing requirements of the AVCE is to plan and develop a programme of teaching and learning that includes all aspects of each unit and that also provides assessment opportunities that successfully differentiate between students while also meeting the requirements for assessment evidence at each of the grades A to E. And with two core units now externally assessed, it is also important to prepare your students for the assessment with a range of tasks and activities that will enable them to cope with this alternative approach.

We function within an educational framework that is constantly monitored and that is replete with a range of buzz words, acronyms and phrases such as 'TQM', 'enhanced quality management' and 'benchmarking' that are used by a range of education managers to demonstrate their acumen while, at the same time, we suffer from the indignities and transparencies of all too frequent inspections. As we know, the best defence, no matter how much it baulks or fails to place sufficient emphasis upon 'good teaching', is simply to be well organised. Having paperwork in place shows that considerable thought and preparation has gone into our teaching, whatever quality it might be.

When looking at the planning framework it is possible to split it into three discrete time elements:

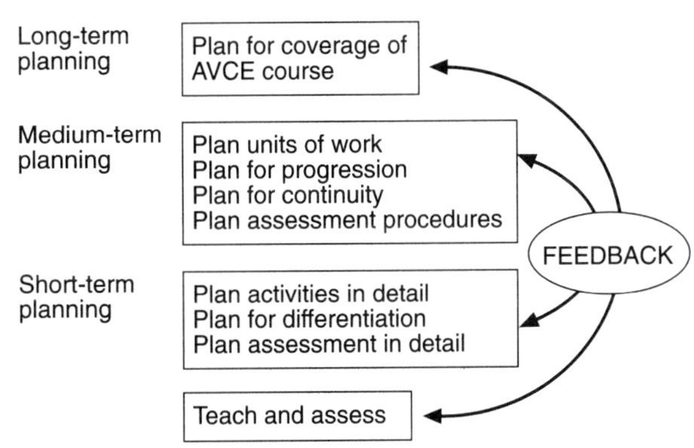

Long-term planning
This involves a department or course team discussing faculty or school or college curriculum policies. On the basis of the discussion, staff are able to identify departmental aims and policies – for example, ways of linking with other courses.

The effective delivery of each part of the course will depend on the department's plans. These plans should cover the appropriate course content, which is detailed in a scheme of work that follows the units and performance criteria. The scheme should be broad and balanced, allowing for a range and variety of experiences. It should also take into account continuity and progression by looking at the sequence of learning experiences and how learning can be reinforced and built upon.

Medium-term planning
A business studies department, faculty or school should then be able to identify units of work, topics or themes upon which to base its teaching and learning programmes. These decisions can be made only on an individual school or college basis, because each school or college will need to make use of its own local business environment. For example, you will need to use your own knowledge of local organisations to find out which employers are willing to take students for work experience, to come in to speak to your students or to be engaged in other industry/education links. At this point a range of suitable learning activities can be developed (such as local case studies, surveying local industry and visiting local organisations). It may be possible to link these contacts with the assessment programme.

Short-term planning
Short-term planning tends to be the responsibility of the individual tutor and must be placed in the context of a number of variable, but very important, factors:

- *The tutor's view of what is important about the subject.* Every tutor will have his or her own ideas about what should be taught, how it is best taught and how learners can best be supported.
- *Areas of strength and expertise.* The tutor may have particular knowledge of (or expertise in) a particular part of the course. For example, one member of staff might be more familiar with the finance area of the course, while another will be more conversant with human relations or marketing.
- *The approach of the tutor to teaching methodologies.* It would be wrong to advocate one particular approach to the teaching of the course; different groups of students have different teaching needs.
- *The needs of the learner.* Students come into the classroom with varying requirements and needs. It is important to find out what these are in order to supply the best support for each learner.
- *The requirements of the AVCE unit as expressed by the awarding body.*
- *The tutor's immediate aims.* The tutor will have the clearest picture of where the students have come from and what steps are required to take them forward.

Course management

The AVCE co-ordinator
In many institutions (particularly where a number of post-16 general vocational qualifications are taught that include vocational A levels), it is usual for one member of staff to have the responsibility of co-ordinating all the programmes. This means all the activities common to each programme can be managed centrally. For example, this member of staff could be responsible for:

- identifying and delivering staff training
- advising the senior management team (e.g. about issues concerning timetabling)
- identifying institutional resources needs
- advising curriculum teams on delivery models
- developing access and progression strategies
- induction policies
- liaising with external organisations
- developing AVCE marketing strategies
- monitoring and evaluating provision.

AVCE subject co-ordinating group
As well as having an AVCE co-ordinator, you may also have a co-ordinating group. The key purposes of such a group might be:

- timetable provision
- identifying resource requirements and staff development needs
- the co-ordination of work across the institution

- developing an overall policy for such qualifications
- establishing a strategy that both markets and promotes the qualification.

Course teams

Given the number of units within the AVCE in Business, a course team may consist of staff members with different types of expertise from across the whole institution. This is where colleges often have an advantage over schools, as their course teams usually have greater diversity. If a school department has only two or three members of staff, specialisation will obviously be much more difficult. Course teams are, of course, involved with the sharp-end of a course. Demands and course requirements change frequently, and delivering such courses often presents many challenges. For example:

- the design of learning materials and assignments
- the selection of options and their delivery alongside other core units
- the consideration of Key Skills
- assessment, recording and grading techniques
- tutoring, action planning and learning support
- the setting up of school/industry links.

And, of course, dealing with the students, including both academic and pastoral support mechanisms.

Management issues

Undoubtedly, each AVCE programme will be affected by a series of issues. Some of these may be outside the control of the institution, while others may be influenced by the factors internal to the school or college.

Selection

You will have to set minimum requirements for the course, in terms of academic background as well as personal qualities, ambitions and characteristics. Are your selection criteria going to be based upon success at GCSEs and/or GNVQ Intermediate, and where are you going to draw the boundaries? To clarify the situation, you may wish to use some form of diagnostic testing to identify whether your students can cope with the level of work, whether they are likely to be committed to the course or whether they might need specialist support.

Induction

AVCE courses are student centred, which means the students have considerable responsibility for their own learning. The course is full of terms that some might find difficult to understand, as well as paperwork that will require some demystification. Induction programmes are a useful way of getting to grips with key issues early in a course.

The design of the learning programme

There are a number of factors that might influence the design of the learning programme, and programmes will differ from school to school and college to college. Such factors might include:

- the choice of options
- term dates
- the various programmes and points of entry
- the integration of the programme with other qualifications.

The timetable

You have to decide how to allocate resources to the programme. This may be influenced by staffing, links with other courses and many other issues.

Learning and assessment activities

Are these to include workshops, classroom exercises, tasks, formal teaching or assignments based upon case analysis? Some of these activities may be designed for structured learning, while others may simply provide an opportunity for students to investigate and research their work. There are, however, a number of fundamental requirements:

- students should understand the nature and purpose of each element of their learning programme
- it is important that students can relate learning activities to learning outcomes.

Assessment issues

Assessment is at the heart of every course. Perhaps the most important issue is to make sure that staff (particularly those new to these types of programmes) understand assessment requirements.

WRITING ASSIGNMENTS FOR AVCE COURSES

One of the most important and yet probably most underestimated aspects of delivery within an AVCE course is the setting up and further development of an assignment programme, particularly for those units that are internally assessed. An assignment is an activity or linked series of activities learners undertake. It may take place in a real workplace or, more commonly, in an educational institution or in the community. Even though widespread changes have taken place within Curriculum 2000 and the re-badged qualification, assignments are still the centrepiece for supporting the delivery of courses. They also uniquely identify and differentiate one course from another. In doing so they allow each individual course to meet the needs of each set of individual local circumstances, and they represent the quality of the learning experiences for the course and its participants.

There is no doubt that writing good assignments is a skill in itself, and each course team will have its assignment-writing 'champions'. These are often individuals who enjoy writing the programme and who take some pleasure, and often some pride, in the quality of the assignments they write.

It is difficult to develop a series of guidelines that identify a 'good assignment' because, as we know, each programme is different and may consist of a range of assignment tools and methods of assessment. Also, given the range of levels at which some assignments may be focused, a style suitable for AVCE would be completely inappropriate for a group at Intermediate.

Many assignments depend upon a scenario. This may be a case study and could be a description of a setting, either real or simulated, or a sequence of events. The details should be contemporary and realistic, and therefore credible for the learners who will use it. It may be possible to use a realistic setting (such as an imaginary company or workplace) as the focus for the whole assignment programme to provide continuity for the participants.

The learners may have a realistic role to play as, for example, an 'assistant' or 'trainee' which they carry with them through the assignment. The scenario is therefore part of the learning resource and should expose individuals to a range of materials that help to develop the experience and insight of the participants. It is helpful if the role undertaken by the learner is realistic and does not change during a sequence of tasks. (In the past we have probably all seen assignments where participants have been the Chancellor of the Exchequer or the chief executive of a large corporation.) If students have part-time jobs, it may be possible to link their roles with their own experience. It may also be possible to tie an assignment in with a period of work experience.

In developing a scenario, it is useful to make the assignment work related. For example, instead of creating a list of questions, an assignment should be what the word itself implies – something for the learners to do. In undertaking the assignment, learners not only experience a range of stimulus material but also have the opportunity to use it within a realistic context. It can be argued that assignments should be sufficiently open-ended to allow students the freedom to develop their own approaches and to pursue issues as far as they may wish to.

Relevance helps students to feel the tasks they are undertaking fit with their ambitions and the realities of the workplace. In tailoring assignments to a group of students, it may be useful to provide them with a range of narratives, case studies and supporting documents. For example, these may include statistical tables, forms, newspaper cuttings, e-mails, URLs, screen dumps, etc. It may also be useful to direct them towards alternative sources, such as textbooks, newspapers, *The Times 1000*, magazines, etc.

Within the programme of assignments there should be some notion of 'fit' between each of the different units. In writing assignments, you may make assumptions about learning undertaken in other areas students have completed and build upon the knowledge and skills they have already gained.

In order to build upon their Key Skills, it may be useful to use a range of different assessment methods. For example, during a programme, you may want to provide students with an assignment requiring:

- individual research
- testing using reference sources within the classroom
- group work
- some form of discussion
- a simulation
- the writing of a report
- a closed-book examination
- a presentation to the rest of the student cohort or to a group of local business people.

Assignments should be neither too easy nor too hard. They should be posed in a way that makes completion difficult unless the students have the relevant knowledge and skills. They are also an important opportunity for you to differentiate between your students. It is no good developing an assignment the students can all do easily and where everybody gets the highest grade.

Timing is a key element in delivering assignments. For example, should an assignment be given at the beginning of a unit, in the middle of the unit or towards the end? A lot will depend upon the nature and type of assessment. For example, it could be used as an inductive device that sets out the process of learning for the unit. The development of the assignment will also reflect how the unit is delivered. For instance, the assignment could be ongoing over the whole year to reflect various knowledge points within the course.

Writing assignments is not about creating spoon-feeding devices. It is about actively engaging learners in realistic tasks that encourage them to stamp their mark upon their assessments. Good students will search for relevant materials and information, and will reflect their interests and enthusiasm for their work in the approaches they take. The key ingredient of a good assignment is not being over-directive but in allowing students the flexibility and latitude to take responsibility for their own learning in an environment in which they can expect to receive support.

Every assignment should be referenced carefully and closely to each unit. It helps if students know exactly what they are achieving, which is why assessment criteria and an action plan help them to work through the assignment process. Within an assignment, there might be opportunities for formative assessment, and it is important learners should be made aware of all the criteria and generic elements against which they are to be assessed. Also, given the construction of the grading system and the assessment requirements, it is useful to provide students with details of what you expect for each of these different levels.

You could also create a standard format for the assignments you give to your students, which will help them to know exactly what is expected of them.

1 *A title page.* This could have on it the name of the course, the number and name of the unit, the assignment title and boxes for the recording of any relevant information, dates, etc.
2 *An introduction.* This could set the scene for the assignment and might include some form of case study. It might also explain what materials or sources students should use in completing the assignment.
3 *Tasks.* These should be clear and unambiguous.
4 *Hand-in date.* The assignment might also indicate tutorial dates as well as any other special arrangements.

One concern tutors often have is whether they should create an entirely new assignment programme each new academic year. While there are always problems delivering a programme that has been used before, reinventing the wheel annually could be considered an unnecessary exercise. However, a programme of assignments should be reviewed every year, with changes being made to reflect the different external environment under which students will be examined.

It is good practice to review each assignment before it is issued to ensure it is a good test of the course outcomes. FEDA's assignment checklist is as follows.

FEDA assignment checklist

- Is it clear and readable for the group?
- Does it require knowledge, understanding and skills that students are required to demonstrate (as described in the 'What do you need to learn' section of the unit specification)?
- Does it cover the requirements of the 'What do you need to produce' section of the unit?
- Does it provide opportunities for students to meet the requirements for the higher grades?
- Have relevant opportunities to incorporate key skills been taken?
- Does it demonstrate opportunities for students to demonstrate the vocational relevance of what they have learnt?
- Is it interesting and challenging for students?

Though the writing of assignments is not easy, they help tutors to contemplate the processes course participants will go through to meet the requirements for each course of study. They can, of course, be both original and enjoyable, and they should reflect the unique relationship that exists between course tutors and students.

PERSONAL ACTION PLANNING

One way students can improve their own learning on an AVCE course is by drawing up their own personal action plans – not just for each assignment but also as part of a wider process.

An action plan will help students put their plans into motion. Therefore each student's plan will be unique and will be a very personal thing. The many benefits of an action plan include:

- helping students to identify and then develop their objectives
- helping students to organise their activities into a logical sequence
- enabling students to relate their activities to the timing of events
- helping the tutor to keep a check on the students' progress and matching their actual progress with their aims and objectives
- making sure students do not leave certain things out
- an aid to personal organisation
- enabling students to identify and then build upon their strengths.

There are a number of ways of developing action plans. Attaching an action plan to an assignment is one method of applying the plan to a specific task. Another way of developing an action plan is to create some form of booklet each student could keep. The nature of this booklet would vary from one institution to another as there may be things some tutors might want to include in their plans which other tutors might wish to leave out. Most action plans might also include some sort of diary.

From the students' point of view, action planning is a way of organising themselves so they can develop and achieve their ambitions and objectives. The whole process of action planning can be illustrated more clearly by the following diagram.

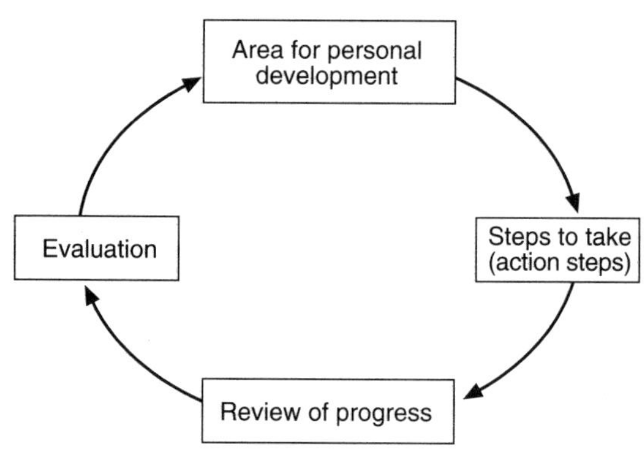

The starting point for any action plan is for each student to ask him or herself: 'Where am I now?' Once they have done this they can identify where they want to go and can think about the training and learning requirements they need to get there. In other words, they next need to ask themselves: 'Where am I going and how am I going to get there?' To be able to do this, students need to think about the course they are on (for example, why are they doing an AVCE in Business? What do they hope to learn, and how will this help them to achieve their ambitions?).

One of the great benefits of the action planning process is that it provides students with the opportunity to collate a great deal of information which might come in useful later when they apply for jobs or complete their UCAS applications. There are many different ways of constructing an action plan. The following model has six elements.

1 Personal information

The starting point for the plan is for students to think where they are. They need to think about their strengths, weaknesses, successes and achievements. There are many different ways of approaching this. For example, you might ask the students to list their hobbies and interests. It is also possible to ask them to do a personal SWOT analysis. Strengths and opportunities may open up avenues for students, while weaknesses and threats will need to be recognised so the problems they may represent can be overcome.

2 Skills evaluation

This section may help students to evaluate their own cognitive or thinking skills as well as their more traditional Key Skills. Without going into detailed reasoning, it is important for students to think about their own personal skills and abilities and to match these to their objectives. These types of skills can be extremely important as they may influence their career choices directly.

3 Objectives

It is important for the students to identify clear and well-focused objectives. In other words, they need to think about what they are trying to achieve in the short, medium and long term. Having clear objectives provides them with some form of direction for their planning. It also provides them with a mechanism which makes it possible for them to test whether these objectives are being met. For example, longer-term objectives might be obtaining a university offer or a job of some description, while shorter-term objectives might involve being punctual for taught sessions, completing assignments by the deadlines set, working hard during placements, and so on.

4 Evidence of achievements

Before reviewing their action plans, students must try to collect evidence that shows how well or how badly their personal action planning process is progressing.

5 Review of progress

From the tutor's point of view, this is probably the most important part of the personal action planning process. At this stage, the tutor reviews the student's progress against that student's action plan so both can identify what has been happening. The key issue is whether the objectives are being met and/or the nature of any problems that may have developed. It is this part of the action plan that turns it into a working document. It may be possible at this stage for the tutor to 'sign off' some of the shorter-term objectives.

6 Evaluation of the action plan

It is useful to make students aware of how successful (or not) the action planning process has been. Evaluation (so that action planning objectives and outcomes can be reviewed and fine-tuned) is important for both the tutor and student alike.

There are many different ways of introducing personal action planning. The techniques used may well depend upon how the course is structured and the nature of the timetable. Perhaps the best time to introduce the plan is during the introduction to the course, when you may want to provide each student with a personalised booklet that can then be monitored periodically. From a tutor's point of view it can be a useful way of tracking the students' progress and also for dealing with problems as and when they arise. The review with the course tutor could take place termly or half-yearly. The review should help to emphasise the importance of the process and should provide a useful way of reviewing the overall progress of each individual.

By learning about the processes of planning and evaluating their work, students will have more of an opportunity to be rewarded with better grades for their work as they will have been taught about focusing upon achieving their objectives.

WORKING IN GROUPS

Many activities and assignments on an AVCE Business course may be carried out by groups of students working together. An important part of the course, therefore, involves introducing students to teamwork skills and helping them to appreciate the benefits of teamwork.

It is helpful if a course is allocated a 'team base' the students can use right from the start. The base could then house such work resources as computers, folders, texts and business dictionaries, etc. You may wish to allocate responsibilities for the base to individual students.

What is a team?

A team is a small group of people who have developed to the stage where they are able to perform effectively together, with each member adopting a role necessary to the successful functioning of the team through the deployment of his or her own complementary skills. When forming teams, it might be useful to perform a skills audit (a record of the skills each member of the group possesses). Another useful exercise is for the students to think about other groups they belong to in order to try to draw out ways in which these groups are similar or different.

In looking at what makes a successful team, students will notice that, for a team to exist, it must *identify* itself as a team. There may also be:

- a set of written or unwritten rules which are known to the group members (e.g. an accepted way of doing things)
- some form of sanction for breaking rules (e.g. a form of pastoral sanction via reference to a tutor)
- a common aim or purpose (even if it is just to work together on assignment presentations)
- a form of communication (such as a time to meet)
- ways for team members to identify themselves as belonging to the team
- ways by which individuals can achieve their own goals as a part of the group or team.

Having established what a team is, students can go on to focus on what skills each person needs in order to work with the others as part of that team. They might refer to:

- closeness
- loyalty to the group or team
- a good knowledge of all the other team members, including their strengths and weaknesses
- accepted ways of behaving
- good time management
- high levels of communication
- freedom to express opinions and feelings
- complementary skills and roles
- group language and jargon.

If students are going to work well together as a group, they will need to develop many, if not all, of these teamwork skills. Teamwork and co-operation with others towards a common goal will help the students develop insights into such processes as conflict, co-operation and consensus. At the same time, participants may learn about leadership skills and some of the practices associated with authority.

A group activity

Many different activities can be carried out at the beginning of a course to encourage groups of students to share ideas and working practices. The following is an example.

Developing teamworking skills: an example

The business studies tutor has asked the students to work in groups of three on an assignment that will take three weeks. The assignment involves the students imagining they are going through an induction process together, each of them being a new trainee working for a local medium-sized or large business of their choice (this work is for Unit 1: 'Business at work'). At the end of the assignment the group have to make a presentation about their collective experience.

By putting the emphasis on 'collective' experience and, hence, on group responsibility and the delineation of roles, the group should provide a more detailed and professional presentation than if each individual produced a presentation of his or her own.

How well a team works together depends in some measure on the mix of the group members' personalities and abilities. If everyone wants to lead or everyone wants to follow, it is unlikely the group will interact very well together. Robert Belbin identified eight roles that may be crucial to teamwork. Of course, individuals may take on more than one of these roles at different times during a course.

- The *chairperson* presides over the group and co-ordinates team efforts.
- The *shaper* is a would-be chair of the group. He or she drives the team on to complete the task successfully.
- The *plant* may be a rather shy person who is, at the same time, successful at creating ideas and new proposals.
- The *monitor evaluator* is able to analyse a situation, to look at what is going on and to suggest ways forward. This person checks the quality of progress and makes relevant comments.
- The *resource investigator* is usually an extrovert who mixes well with other group members. He or she can bring new contracts and ideas to the team, which will need to be worked on by more methodical members of the group.
- The *company worker* is a very hard worker who can turn ideas into manageable tasks. He or she tends to be a good administrator rather than a leader.
- The *team worker* is very good at supporting the team. He or she helps by encouraging the others and by supporting and harmonising the working of the team.
- The *finisher* makes sure tasks are completed and deadlines are met. He or she does not allow unfinished business to be left hanging about.

The components of group working

Whenever groups of students work together, three strands will be involved in moving from the start to the end of the decision-making process. These strands involve the following.

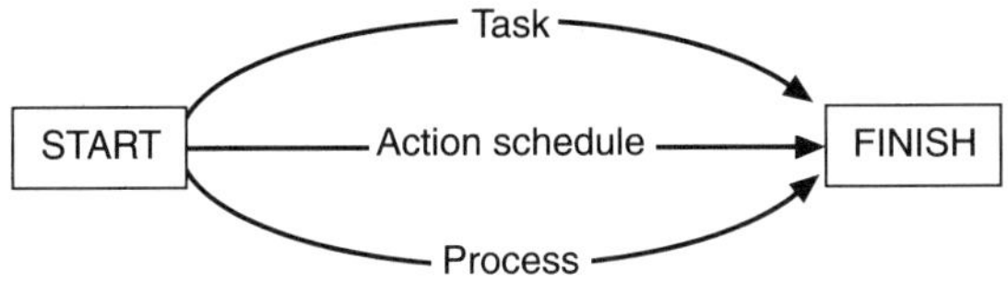

Task

The task is the content of the work – it is the conversion of information and opinions from team members into decision recommendations, reports or other outcomes. In general terms, this covers what has to be done and why. Most groups give a great deal of attention to the task.

Action schedule

The action schedule is concerned with how a group will be organised to undertake a given task. The schedule will cover such questions as who will fill the necessary roles and how progress will be checked and monitored. It will also deal with the procedures of decision-making. In general, the action schedule will cover the 'where' and 'how' of decision-making. Most groups will give some attention to their action schedule.

Process

The process is the interaction that takes place between the members of a group. It is about how people work together. It involves such interpersonal skills as listening to others and helping others to join in a discussion. It also involves expressions of feelings and the giving and receiving of feedback. In general, it covers who does what and when. Many groups get so involved in the task and action schedule strands they forget about process.

The above three strands of group working are all important in group decision-making. For example, a group that concentrates entirely upon its action schedule and its process may have a wonderful time but it may not achieve the task. In contrast, concentrating purely on the task is likely to lead to arguments about how things should be organised, and inattention to group members' thoughts and feelings will lead to mishandled resources and misunderstandings.

It is important to help learners become aware of these three elements of teamworking. This is particularly true of process, which is often neglected. Therefore students should be encouraged to consider process right from the outset by means of the tutor carrying out a number of group tasks in class at the beginning of the course.

There is no doubt that if students develop teamwork skills as part of their AVCE Business course, they will become more competent in collaborating with other people to achieve organisational goals:

- motivating others and helping them to operate as effective team members in achieving task objectives
- performing a variety of roles within a team
- appreciating that individuals and groups have differing perceptions of goals, and that there may be conflict between them.

RECRUITMENT TO THE AVCE PROGRAMME

In recent years more young people than ever have come to realise that not only have they a wide choice of courses to take after they reach the age of 16 years but also that they have an increasingly varied range of institutions to choose from. As a result, recruitment practices, marketing activities and the development of a cost-effective promotional plan that targets individuals most likely to join a course have become extremely important for schools and colleges across the UK. Of course, there may be criticisms of what seems to be public sector-funded promotional activity from organisations whose activities overlap, particularly when 'sweeteners' are provided by some colleges that are determined to stop at nothing in order to fill their courses. With any form of competition, a moral element will at some stage come into play and, whereas some education administrators know where to draw the line, some recent instances (without naming names) have shown that some do not. But then when reading this missive they might claim that 'who are we to make value judgements about them?' They are only making a fair response to market forces!

Recruitment practices will, therefore, vary from institution to institution, with tried and tested practices probably cited as the best way to proceed. The responsibility for recruitment may lie simply with one tutor (sometimes a marketing officer) or perhaps even with a whole course team. Whatever the circumstances of the school or college, the most important element within the recruitment process is to ensure that students who are most suited for AVCE courses such as that in Business, and for whom the course would be a good part of their career and academic progression, are informed about the availability of the course and advised appropriately. With the increasing complexity of post-16 education and because, for many students, an AVCE may not seem like a standard route towards higher education, students need to know about:

- how AVCEs relate to other qualifications
- the particular features of the Business course, as well as the facilities, options and choices they might have to make
- levels and entry qualifications
- study facilities and learning resources
- the role of assessment, as well as assessment practices and procedures
- developing an appropriate balance between the AVCE and AS and A levels
- what their options might be when they finish the course
- statistical information from past courses, such as numbers and progression.

As a recruitment officer, it may be possible to provide this information in a variety of ways. For example, a recruitment officer could construct specific course leaflets or, alternatively, information may be provided within a college or sixth-form prospectus. Newspaper articles or advertisements, on the other hand, are often targeted too widely, even when focused locally. It may be possible to become involved in recruitment fairs, to organise centre visits, to arrange presentations from past students or simply to have an opportunity to talk to all interested students through assemblies or class visits. Information is only part of this process, and it is important that guidance is provided not just to prospective students but also to parents and guardians.

CREATING A MEANINGFUL INDUCTION PROGRAMME

Whether students are new to the school or college or not, coming into an AVCE programme such as Business is a completely new venture as it represents new ways of working and a completely different pattern of learning from that of GCSEs or any other courses they might have previously undertaken. A good, well-constructed induction process helps students to find out about the course and the institution, makes them feel they have made an appropriate decision (or not) to take the course and enables them to settle in quickly.

A good induction programme rapidly prepares students for the course they have enrolled on. It is an important opportunity for them to learn about the ethos of the course programme and to find out about various aspects not just of the course but also of the school or college, particularly if they are attending a different institution. There are things that should be dealt with during an induction programme. For example, when finding out about the *school* or *college*:

- the induction process may include studying a map of the site as well as a guide to the specialist resources available (some form of training in the use of these resources might also be given at this stage)
- an introduction to the people connected with the course. This could include course leaders and various support staff (including administrative staff and learning centre/library staff), as well as vocational and academic tutors and student counsellors
- the various policies and practices carried out within the institution, such as equal opportunities, environmental policies and curriculum entitlement. They may also be briefed in disciplinary and appeal procedures.

Students will also need to know about the *whole curriculum*. The induction process may be used to discuss with the students what they will be studying in the first year of their AVCE in Business and the choice of units they may be provided with, as well as other activities they may wish to opt for, such as the further development of their Key Skills. They will also need to be informed of tutorial support and any other activities (such as Young Enterprise or sport and leisure activities) offered by the school or college.

Teaching AVCEs may involve delivering a course to students from a range of backgrounds and experiences, including some with work and professional experience. For many of these students, these types of qualifications will be completely new. They will need to know about the qualifications' structure as well as what distinguishes AVCEs from other courses. It may be useful to inform students about:

- the teaching and learning styles used during the course. It may be useful to provide a range of sample induction activities that introduce the students to the various elements of the course (this would also give the course team some idea of the range of student abilities and backgrounds)
- how they should manage their own learning (combined with the responsibility they should take for their own learning)
- the content of each of the units of the AVCE, focusing in particular upon what they have to learn
- other elements related to assessment procedures and practices, such as hand-in dates, the completion of action plans and other assessment literature
- the challenges that lie ahead
- the link between the AVCE course and the achievement of Key Skills qualifications.

The process of induction should help the students to find out about the course and all that is required of them, as well as meet other students and become part of the course. It should help them to confirm their own expectations and should be used as an opportunity to make friends and become motivated to learn. More importantly, however, a good induction programme will help to reassure students about the different approaches to teaching and learning they will encounter, and should help them to feel confident about their own abilities and skills.

There are a number of ways of running an induction programme. Some schools or colleges may run some form of induction prior to the GCSE results in July. Others are wedded to two weeks of induction in September. The danger with this is that the induction process may become too long at a time when the students just want to get on with some work. A more realistic approach might be to incorporate induction into the timetable and to include it as a one-hour a week exercise during the first term.

An important element of the induction process is to develop a course handbook. This handbook could be a useful source of information for students, being full of information about:

- the course and the people associated with the course
- the AVCE system
- key staff and their responsibilities
- unit specifications
- facilities (and the use of such facilities as IT areas, reprographics, etc.)
- resources and specialist teaching areas
- recreational opportunities/use of college areas such as refectory, gymnasium, etc.
- school or college policies
- learning contracts
- local facilities
- the layout of the centre
- opportunities for careers advice
- the UCAS system
- the students' charter
- important school or college/programme dates
- tips and hints
- appeals and complaints procedures.

Induction is also an important opportunity to find out about the students' strengths and weaknesses and, in so doing, about any students who may need help with their learning. A key feature of the induction process, therefore, might be to interview all students to find out about their backgrounds, to attempt to screen their basic skills and to identify if they need any learning support.

A useful way of delivering the induction process is to set up some form of assignment or project that engages the participants in some sort of learning activity. For example, for AVCE Business, the focus could be upon an investigation into the nature and types of businesses within the local community. The investigation may involve using local brochures, *Yellow Pages* and *Thomson* directories, followed by some fieldwork, or even be based upon a visit by a local business adviser or a visit to a local business organisation. The purpose should be to create a situation in which the students work collaboratively in groups, learn about the local community (as other assignments might be based upon local businesses), find out how to identify sources of information, combine these with an investigation, use information technology resources and, finally, present a report to the rest of the class.

A good induction assignment would:

- encourage students to find out about the nature of the area they are studying
- involve them purposefully in an investigation
- be both enjoyable and achievable
- help the students to understand how assignments will be assessed
- allow students to work collaboratively
- include a range of tasks, some of which will be group based while others will be focused upon individuals
- help students to understand about the crucial role of Key Skills.

Finally, it is important that the process of induction is monitored, as this allows the induction process to be adjusted from one year to the next. Monitoring also helps you as a course tutor not just to improve your planning but also to develop an induction process that prepares learners better for all they can expect to go through.

DEVELOPING QUESTIONING TECHNIQUES IN THE CLASSROOM

When we think about 'evidence' in the learning process, we tend to think about tangible evidence that can be seen and kept in a portfolio. However, we know that, as tutors, we come across evidence of learning that can guide our assessment within the everyday learning process. One technique that provides such evidence is that of questioning.

Questioning allows us to elicit information from our students in a variety of ways. It may enable us to probe the extent of our students' prior knowledge before a new area is introduced; or it may be used to consolidate and provide feedback on recent teaching and learning. When we ask questions we should be assisting students to focus and clarify their thoughts to develop their own understanding. For example, a simulated job interview could relate questions to the interviewee and the job description.

Important aspects of questioning

In asking student teachers 'What aspects are important to effective questioning?', groups of student teachers have come up with the following areas:

- clear language
- simple language
- a friendly manner
- timing
- pausing
- sequencing
- distributing questions
- open-ended questions
- accepting answers.

The following sections attempt to deal with some of these issues and also try to emphasise how questioning can become an effective (and often underestimated) classroom tool in the teaching of the AVCE in Business. The areas of concern from the above can be broadly classified under the headings 'Level' and 'Clarity'.

Level

If we look at the questions we ask our students, it is possible to categorise them into two broad types: lower-order questions (which tend to test knowledge) and higher-order questions (which create or generate new levels of understanding). The latter are usually more open-ended and require students to explore ideas.

Using Bloom's *Taxonomy of Educational Objectives* (1956), the six levels Bloom identified can provide us with practical examples of the types of questions which are lower order and higher order.

Bloom's six levels of questioning

The six levels	The student is asked to
Lower-order questions	
1 Knowledge (recall)	Remember information – 'What'
2 Comprehension	Express ideas in own words – 'Describe'
3 Application	Understand and apply to new situations – 'Classify'
Higher-order questions	
4 Analysis	Distinguish between things – 'Why'
5 Synthesis	Solve problems – 'Plan'
6 Evaluation	Make judgements – 'Appraise'

Different types of questions and the words most commonly associated with them

Type of question	Words	Examples
Recall questions	Name Recognise Define	How many partners are permitted in a limited partnership?
Comprehension	Describe Compare Contrast Explain	Describe the main principles of insurance
Application	Classify Use Choose Give examples of	Choose which methods of advertising you consider to be most appropriate for each of the following
Analysis	Why What factors Discuss	Why does a company need to measure its cash flow?
Synthesis	Plan	Plan and conduct a market research survey into an area of interest related to your school, college or work
Evaluation	Appraise	Examine the information provided on the small business, and advise the owners about a suitable course of action

In order to encourage students to focus and develop their understanding we, as tutors, need to be able to formulate questions that run through both the lower-order and the higher-order cognitive levels. The box on the previous page indicates the words most often found in the various different levels of questions. It is interesting to note that one problem with questioning is that many tutors tend to overuse questions which test knowledge and recall.

If you wish to ensure you use a range of lower-order and higher-order questioning in your teaching, try to undertake the following tasks:

1 Tape part of a lesson when you are using questioning. Play back the extract and classify the questions as: R (Recall), C (Comprehension), An (Analysis), S (Synthesis) and E (Evaluation). Look at the spread of questions you asked. How balanced was your approach?
2 Plan a questioning session as part of an introduction to a topic in order to assess the group's understanding. Ensure you use both lower- and higher-order questions.
3 For students to use their responses to questions as part of a process of assessment, you need to think about how to reward effective responses to your questions. Rather than do so on individual questions which would become mechanistic and probably spoil the effectiveness of the question-and-answer session, if a student has repeatedly answered questions with clarity and understanding, use his or her oral responses or techniques as support for his or her understanding of a written task he or she has undertaken.

Clarity

It is sometimes assumed that framing questions can be done on the spot and that the whole process comes naturally to tutors. Certainly, experienced tutors who have dealt with particular teaching areas a number of times will probably be able to frame questions effectively. When experience is lacking or a teaching area is new, however, it may be necessary to consider some of the basic skills in formulating and asking questions.

Clearly, a question is not going to be effective if it is badly expressed and therefore unintelligible to the students. Questions need to be precisely and unambiguously worded. It is often easier to ensure this when you are formulating questions and tasks for assignments, as there is usually more time for reflection. Oral questioning, on the other had, can be more problematic.

The level of the vocabulary we use is also important. We have to consider the age and ability of the class being taught. To help the students explore concepts, it may be necessary to establish that they understand the technical language involved through the use of questioning. For example, in order to meet specific information requirements, you might want to ask: 'What might be the effects of changing office technologies upon office staff?' To facilitate a discussion of the possible effects, it may be necessary to go back a step to explore the concept of 'office technologies' and to provide some examples.

Questions are an important part of the teaching and learning process, particularly on courses such as the AVCE. Creating a climate of confidence within an active classroom, with warm responses from students, allows tutors to develop a good knowledge not just of the levels of understanding of different individuals but also of the problems and difficulties they may be experiencing.

USING SIMULATION AS A TEACHING TOOL

A business simulation is a realistic model situation participants study through role play. As a result of this role play, the participants can come to understand the behaviour of the system (the situation), and they can develop strategies to control or change the system as well as to evaluate their own and the system's performance.

It is not always possible to use the 'real thing' in a chosen teaching situation. For example, in preparing students for work experience, we may want to practise a simulated job interview before the students are faced with the real thing. To help make the activity as useful as possible, the simulation could be carried out in front of a group of students. The tutor would introduce the role play and ask the students to look at particular points: body language, communication skills, questions asked and answered, social relations involved, etc. The tutor would then ask the students for feedback, and would review the activity with the group.

Even though this activity is not the 'real thing', it could be a powerful learning tool because it can be:

- introduced with clear and stated learning objectives
- stopped at any point so that processes can be scrutinised
- controlled by both learners and the tutor – the learner would be free to ask questions and to make comments.

Furthermore, outcomes can be evaluated in the light of the stated objectives. It is also possible to make a video of such a simulation. Students can observe the way in which they acted and can explore ways of improving their performance. We have found this to be a very useful vehicle for learner development. The interviewees' performance has also improved greatly as a result of the increased self-awareness that comes from evaluating a video recording critically.

A similar activity is to ask students to 'interview' a selected group of 'actors' (students from another course) for a mock job. This involves the preparation of job descriptions, letters of application, CVs, job specifications and interview criteria. The students who might be involved in this activity usually become very serious about their work. They are able to develop a clearer picture of the processes involved in the preparation for, and implementation of, the interview situation.

The examples outlined above help to support the case for the use of simulation and role play in the classroom. The lessons learnt and the process of learning can be as vivid as any experience of real working situations.

Simulation is most effective when:

- it is carefully planned, executed and debriefed
- it involves all the students in a participatory way – clearly students who observe and provide feedback are just as much participants as those involved in an acting role
- it feels real – when the students feel they are replicating a real situation rather than just playing a game.

Planning an activity

As the manager of the learning environment, the tutor needs to know in detail how the simulation is going to be developed. Introducing a business game or simulation for the first time can be daunting, particularly if it is complex. Wherever possible, it is advisable to test the materials beforehand or to run through them on your own. When you have done this you will have a clearer idea as to what will go on and when. Make sure that:

- the activity fits the objectives of the course
- you are aware of the likely outcomes and how these relate to your initial objectives (although you will always have a few surprises)
- you have identified the parts of the simulation which may need to be reinforced or for which help may be required
- you have planned for when tutor input will be required (you may need to stop the simulation at particular stages and discuss what is going on and what has been learnt)
- there are enough copies of instructions, playing materials and other resources
- you have a good idea of the timing of the various sections of the simulation
- the simulation is at an appropriate level for the students you are working with.

Running the activity

The simulation should have three main parts:

1 the briefing
2 the activity
3 the debriefing.

The briefing

The briefing is the initial explanation by the tutor of the purpose, principles and rules of the simulation. Sometimes activities are designed deliberately to encourage regular briefing sessions in order to assess progress, comment on performance and/or introduce information to change the direction of the activity. Documents read during the briefing may need to be consulted by students as part of an ongoing process.

Instructions given to students should be clear. You will need to repeat key points and to clarify objectives and time constraints (perhaps by writing them clearly on the board). You should allow the students to obtain clarification about objectives by asking questions. It is essential the briefing is clear and that it is understood. Without such an understanding, the purpose and the actual running of the activity may lose much of their value.

The activity

During the activity, the tutor becomes the controller in charge of the mechanics of the game or simulation. In this role, the tutor needs to exert tight control over such areas as time constraints, the release of information, the interaction between groups and the participation of all individuals. The beauty of such an activity is that, although the exercise is being carried out by young people who may have little experience of business activities, their thinking and their contributions to the decision-making processes are genuine and mirror reality. At times the tutor may need to advise groups on the implications of their decisions – although failure could be viewed in some circumstances as a valuable learning experience (we should be wary of activities that give a sense of personal failure).

The debriefing

In the debriefing, the controller reverts back to a teaching role. A thorough debriefing helps to bring out the lessons learnt, and participants can more fully see connections with other parts of their business education. A useful method of gaining feedback is to ask the participants to give an oral presentation to the whole group – a participant from each group can present the group's work supported by a written report or by the use of visuals, such as flip-chart illustrations. Tutors can learn about the effectiveness of the simulation from the debriefing stage. This will help you to improve your organisation and presentation the next time you run the simulation.

INTRODUCING KEY SKILLS

The government has a policy of encouraging learners to undertake programmes of study that include Key Skills. There are many reasons why Key Skills are important. Key Skills are important:

- in learning because they help students to focus on what and how they are learning so that they can get better results
- for careers because they enable people to become flexible in whatever kind of work they do. In fact, Key Skills are the sort of things employers look for when they are recruiting new staff
- in life because they help people to organise, to manage money and financial information, and to get on with others.

Although since September 2000 Key Skills have been certificated separately, this does not mean they are less important. The new specifications for AVCE in Business include a range of 'natural opportunities' for the development of Key Skills as part of the learning process.

As with the AVCE, learners embarking on a course in Key Skills will need to take in a great deal of information, structured in three main parts of the new Key Skills Units:

- Part A: What you need to know
- Part B: What you must do
- Part C: Guidance.

Learners need to develop various techniques for collecting evidence that meets the specifications for Key Skills. Your role as a tutor will be to set various tasks wherever signposted opportunities occur and also to set up some form of tutorial system that enables you to keep in touch with the students as they take personal responsibility for collecting their own Key Skills.

There is no doubt that the importance of Key Skills, even at this early phase of development, is part of what will soon become the process of lifelong learning. In the future, the abilities and techniques students use to develop their own Key Skills will become part of the way they represent their own 'progress' as employees: something students will be able to record electronically as well as display and present through some form of electronic presentational mechanism such as Powerpoint. This might include a CV, a personal action plan, monitoring and updating devices and much more. While this might still be in the future, it is probably not far away.

As a tutor it is important that, within the early phases of the course, you:

- introduce learners to the concept of Key Skills and their relevance
- discuss the range of skills they will cover during their study
- specify the evidence required for meeting the specifications
- outline the curriculum framework within which Key Skills are to be studied
- identify the assessment opportunities for your students
- confirm the tutorial and action planning procedures to support the process
- identify the roles of members of staff within the Key Skills process.

To achieve the Key Skills qualifications or individual units in application of number, communication or information technology, candidates must pass an external assessment and produce a portfolio of evidence for each Key Skills unit, demonstrating they can apply the skills in a range of contexts. Each piece of evidence should be assessed by an assessor, who will indicate how each piece of evidence has met the requirements and who will supply the candidates with clear feedback. Where the evidence is not paper-based, there should be assessor observation records or other records that enable some form of assessment to take place. For example, evidence may come from:

- the main programme of study, such as the AVCE
- enhancement programmes, such as Young Enterprise
- other diplomas of achievement
- the candidate's paid employment, whether full or part time
- other activities, such as charity work, involvement with a club or society or arranged activities such as Camp America.

Tutorial support is essential to this process of Key Skills development. When learners meet tutors, this provides them with the opportunity to review their progress and to collect evidence. It also enables both to discuss the gaps students have in the achievement of such skills and enables an action plan to be developed that allows such gaps to be filled. The tutorial system also enables the essential process of providing feedback. Where business tutors are responsible for co-ordinating the whole of the Key Skills process, or for students who are studying across a range of areas of study, the use of tracking documentation will help to identify from which areas Key Skills are being developed.

A recent UCAS survey (2000) has identified that more than half of schools and colleges will teach the AVCE, with 86% offering at least one unit of Key Skills. Key Skills will be taught in over 90% of colleges. UCAS has announced that achievements in Key Skills will be awarded as follows:

- each unit passed at Level 4 will score 30 points
- each unit passed at Level 3 will score 20 points
- each unit passed at Level 2 will score 10 points.

WORK EXPERIENCE

Planned work experience is an essential part of any AVCE course in Business. During work experience, a student visits a workplace both to watch and to work alongside people who are earning their living. This provides an essential opportunity to develop and enhance Key Skills first hand. At the same time, it provides the students with a valuable context in which to carry out research and investigations for some of their coursework. Some of the benefits of work experience are as follows:

1 The learner gets inside a workplace and has a feel of what it is like at work.
2 He or she develops cross-transferable general competences relevant to any work situation (e.g. time management, dress code, teamwork, communication skills, decision-making, and so on).
3 The learner can collect and experience real data that can have considerable value for his or her AVCE course.
4 He or she finds out more about his or her own personal likes and dislikes. For example, the student might find out more about his or her suitability for different types of employment.
5 By going through the procedures of applying for the placement and being interviewed, the learner undergoes good experience for the 'real thing'.
6 Through work experience the learner could develop a clearer understanding of

the inter-relationship between the theoretical and practical aspects of the course.

7 The learner benefits from experiencing the independence and responsibility of working life.
8 The learner can ask questions at work of people who have practical experience.
9 He or she is able to develop new skills and to use equipment and resources that are not available in a school or college environment.

Developing the necessary criteria for work experience

It is necessary to develop objectives and criteria so the work experience can be planned and evaluated in a clear way. The development of criteria should be seen as an ongoing exercise involving all parties (student, tutor and employer). Clearly, the work experience available in a particular area will depend on the characteristics of the local economy.

As with many elements of an AVCE course in Business, students need to be able to negotiate and discuss the expected outcomes of work experience with the tutors involved. A placement supervisor should visit the placement prior to the work experience commencing. Regular visits should then be made by the placement supervisor to discuss the learner's performance, both with the learners' representative and with the learner him- or herself. Because of the sheer quantity of work involved with the AVCE course, it may be necessary for the employer to take over some of the monitoring process, which makes the student feel like a real employee.

Preparation for work experience

An important purpose of work experience is to help students to prepare for the transition to full-time employment. One emphasis, therefore, will be on a careers element of work experience: developing skills, attitudes and understanding about different work situations to provide a general preparation for working life. Students will need to be aware of their objectives. Most, if not all, working environments provide opportunities for reflection about the nature of working life. These opportunities need to be drawn out. Students will need to be fully prepared and briefed so they can make the most of their work experience.

Work experience is a useful opportunity to integrate some element of the coursework with a range of learning objectives for the course that are both achievable and flexible. The following is just one model for preparing for the work experience process.

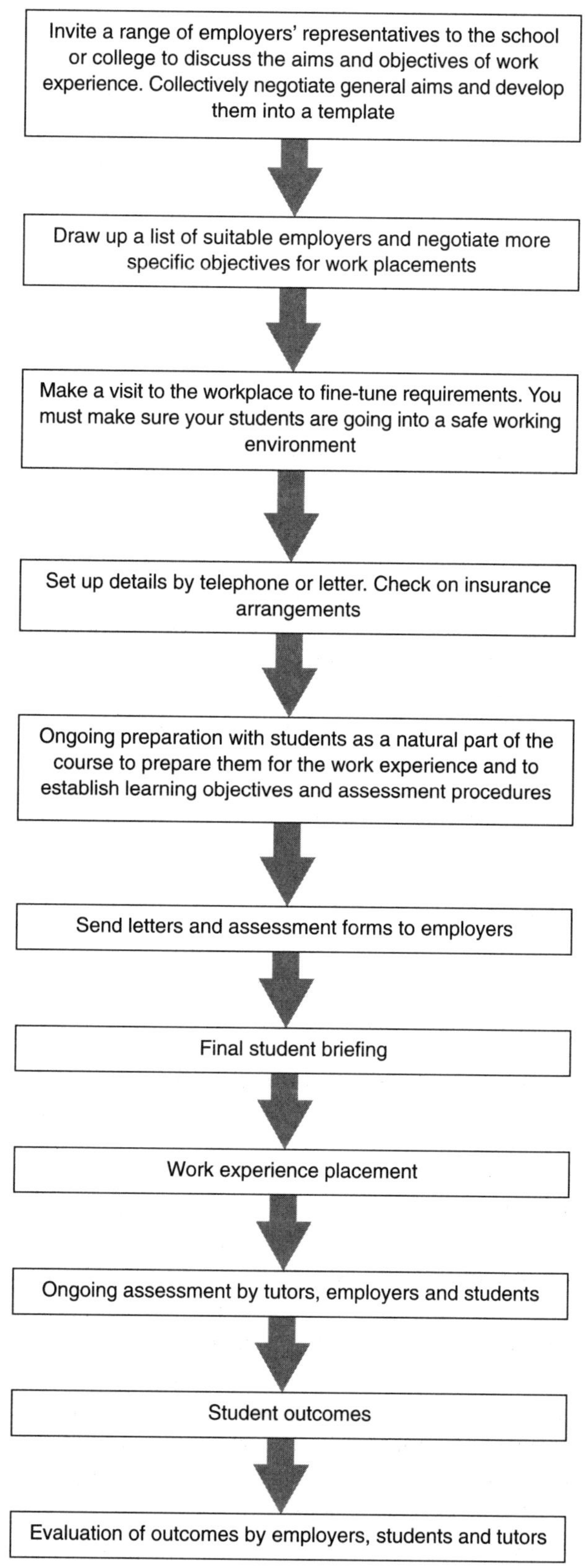

Student preparation for work experience

Preparation for work experience is not a five-minute operation. It is a lengthy, practical and natural part of a course, involving preparation for interviews, discussion of work-based competencies, study of application techniques and many other elements.

Students need to evaluate and, if necessary, improve on their production of a CV and job application. As part of work experience, students are normally expected to write a letter of application and then attend an interview for a work experience placement. The employer will normally have the right to reject unsuitable applications. The student's letter of application should be addressed to the personnel manager, who will be looking for candidates:

- with the necessary attributes for that workplace
- who express themselves clearly and in an organised way
- who show an enthusiastic interest in the work offered
- who have taken the trouble to find out what the work entails, and also something about the organisation itself.

Once personnel managers have selected whom to interview, they may send for references. It is therefore essential that students first seek permission from referees.

Students will need to be aware there will be other applicants going for the work experience placement and that they will need to promote themselves as someone keen to fill the vacancy.

In preparation for the work experience, it may be helpful for all students to fill in a sheet giving clear details of the location and details of the people involved with the placement.

Name of organisation: ....

Address of employer: ....

Telephone number of employer and contact name: ....

....

Person to whom responsible at work: ....

Date for reporting at placement: ....

Hours of work: ....

Map to show place of work

Performance at work

Students are expected to perform to certain standards at work in order to show general work proficiencies. These can be detailed in terms of outcomes, and students must be informed of the nature of the expected proficiencies at different levels of performance.

Indicators need to be established in order to record and assess performance. For example, a student may be involved in filing, invoicing, recording, using accounting packages and answering the phone, in which case the possible indicators are:

- recording transactions in a clear, correct and well-organised fashion
- showing initiative in handling incoming phone messages, etc.

Students will also be expected to meet established standards in coursework related to the work experience. For example, they should:

- meet their aims and objectives
- interview appropriate people and obtain relevant data
- record findings in an organised way
- draw clear conclusions related to the learning outcomes.

The model for student work experience should fit the following pattern.

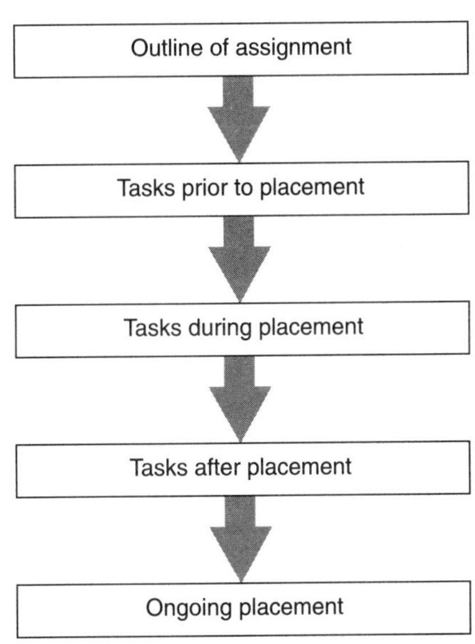

Monitoring and assessment

The tasks students are asked to carry out before the placement act as monitoring devices, ensuring they know something about the organisation before the initial contact. The requirement to draw up a checklist and questions ensures they have done some preparation for the work ahead.

From these specific tasks, students should be able to gather suitable material to use later. If the employer is already aware of these tasks, this will assist the student. Students are often required to keep a daily diary or log of their activities on work experience. This can be useful practice in logging information and can be submitted as evidence of the work experience. It may be helpful for schools or colleges to produce a structured log-book for their students.

You may ask students to collect artefacts and information related to their work experience in order to assist them should they make a presentation to the rest of their group after their placement is completed.

There is sometimes a moral element to the work experience process. For example, you may have to make decisions about whether you wish to allow students to work for organisations that make cigarettes, alcohol or condoms, or work for a book-maker or casino. Clearly, although this sort of decision will depend upon circumstances, dealing with some issues will require a certain amount of sensitivity.

Finally, it is essential students are clear about how their work is to be assessed, what work they need to submit, when they need to submit the work and the criteria against which their work will be judged.

THE IMPORTANCE OF INTELLIGENCE

The nature of applied education (as in the case of AVCEs) is that it prepares individuals for adult roles – it is about developing their capabilities to make the most of opportunities in modern society. Applied education is therefore not just about vocationalism; it is about the development of the whole person. In particular, AVCEs are about enabling people – to become more confident, to accept responsibilities willingly and to have a belief in their own abilities. Applied education is all about helping young people to develop their intelligence (where intelligence refers to a range of intellectual and social skills and processes) and to have confidence they can use this intelligence to make things happen. As such it provides them with an ideal preparation for life in the twenty-first century.

In post-industrial Britain, service industries now account for the majority of employment opportunities, and the current strength of the British economy rests upon flexible working practices employed within service and knowledge-based industries (e.g. hospitality, leisure and tourism, media and communications, science and technology). For example, computer software, music, fashion, design, film, broadcasting, publishing and the performing arts are sectors of creativity which, in 1999, accounted for some £50 billion of economic activity and more than a million jobs (interestingly the word 'imagineer' has recently entered the *Oxford Dictionary* along with the term 'knowledge worker'. An imagineer is a person who devises a highly imaginative concept or technology, especially the attractions in Walt Disney theme parks!).

At the end of the twentieth century, people and human intelligence were able to reclaim their rightful place as the dominant wealth-creating factors in society. Their role had been usurped by physical capital – buildings and machinery – during the Industrial Age which saw some of the most destructive (yet highly productive) forces set loose on human relationships – not least of which was the creation of industrial systems. Of course, the remnants of the Industrial Age – Fordism, Taylorism, etc. – are still with us but the influence of top-down mechanism hierarchies is less prevalent.

Intelligent organisations today recognise that their strength (and the strength of their balance sheets) rests in intellectual capital rather than physical capital. In the Industrial Age machinery, plant and other items of physical capital drove the industrial process. Today, it is the brain power of people that is at the forefront. It is brain power that enables an organisation to identify customer needs and requirements; it is brain power that enables an organisation to engage in product research and development; it is brain power that enables the organisation to develop the most effective quality systems; and it is brain power that enables the organisation to come up with the most appropriate promotional activities.

In 1998 this transformation in society was symbolised by the arrival of Microsoft as the most valuable company in the USA. On 13 September 1998, Microsoft toppled General Electric as the highest-valued company. However, GE is still overwhelmingly an industrial manufacturer providing big-ticket items such as large domestic appliances, from washing machines to cookers, as well as aircraft engines. The company continues to be successful but not as successful as Microsoft.

While GE represents the Industrial Age, Microsoft represents the Information Age with its dominating presence in providing software systems to personal computers and its success in exploiting the explosion of the Internet. Microsoft is a company which is very much based on the knowledge and expertise of its employees. The generosity of the company in distributing shares to employees has created no fewer than 4,000 millionaires around its Redmond, Washington, base – the so-called Microsoft Millionaires.

Intelligent organisations like Microsoft recognise that knowledge workers need to be valued because they add the most value to products. In recent years we have seen striking examples of the ways in which knowledge workers create value to all sorts of organisations. For example, the small group of creatives who came up with the Levis in the laundrette advertisement added millions of dollars to the value of the brand, and the group of researchers working for Mars who developed Mars ice-cream created a new product concept that has not only led to millions of pounds of extra profits for Mars, but also for rival producers of confectionery and sweet-based ice-creams.

In western society, the impact of the knowledge-based revolution has led to a driving forward of living standards for large swathes of the population at a much faster rate than ever before. For example, one of the explanations given for Bill Clinton's popularity in the USA at the end of the 1990s was the fact that the US economy had boomed more or less continually throughout the decade. GNP increased at dizzying levels and, of course, GNP told only a small part of the story. Consumers were able to enjoy an increasing variety of new and better-quality goods fuelled by a spiral of technological advances – for example, the digital revolution which is revolutionising home entertainment and which will help the development of a raft of interactive technology-led development during the early part of this century, interactive banking, shopping, and so on.

In the USA business analysts have been talking about a new paradigm of economic thinking, sometimes referred to as the New Economy which purports to explain the American 'miracle' of the 1990s. On 20 May 1999, Alan Blinder outlined the nature of the New Economy in a daily briefing published by the Group of Seven. He showed that the ideas of the New Economy are based on two key ingredients:

1 the fact that the economy can sustain a much lower level of unemployment than in the past, without this leading to an acceleration in inflation (from 6% in the late 1970s to about 4.3% today). This is partly as a result of increasing competition in both national and international markets, not least in the labour market

2 the underlying growth rate of productivity in the US economy rose sharply in the 1990s, largely as a result of globalisation and information technology.

At the end of May 1999, a meeting of OECD ministers gave priority to a year-long study to explore in depth the degree of substance to the notion of the New Economy to see whether other nations such as Britain could learn from the American success story.

Of course, there are serious reservations about the coherence of the notion of the New Economy, particularly among academic economists (although they also took a long time to recognise the validity of what Keynes and Hayek had to say). However, it is clear that many business corporations recognise and reward the contributions made by their knowledge workers, particularly in the USA.

The intelligent organisation seeks to hang on to its intelligent people because they are worth it. Many knowledge workers also realise they can use their knowledge to best effect by working with or for dynamic asset-rich companies which are able to provide the knowledge worker with the means to add exponential value to knowledge (e.g. through links and connections, through marketing expertise, through access to scarce and expensive resources, etc.). Companies like Nestlé (the world food company) are driven by a science and technology base which has accumulated over time and which gives the organisation and the people who work for it an immense resource. Over a long period of time, Nestlé has been able to build up core competences based on research, science and technology which enables the company to ally intelligence with capital. Of course, workers can and sometimes do drift away and set up their own companies – for example, in recent years we have seen the creation of new biotechnology companies – but these new ventures are relatively small when compared with Nestlé, Microsoft, and so on.

However, today's successful companies need to reward and maintain their people if they are to be able to continue their success story into the future. These rewards need to be in a range of forms. Clearly, it is helpful if you can offer a high salary, but it is also important to meet people's higher-order needs for self-fulfilment and responsibility. Modern organisations therefore need continually to find ways of empowering people – i.e. by creating semi-autonomous units within the company. Recently, I wrote a case study for GEC-Marconi which showed that with the arrival of the 'Peace Dividend' the company suddenly found it was no longer working with the security of Ministry of Defence contracts. Instead, it was having to be far more competitive. This required the company to change working practices within the organisation in order to increase productivity. The way this was carried out was through empowering the workforce. Traditionally, engineering workers had been told what to do, and had worked on specialised jobs – each specialist would take a job out of the work-in-progress store, add value to a designated job and then return the product to the work-in-progress store. The net effect was that the workforce was not highly motivated and tended to blame other people when completed jobs did not meet required quality standards. In order to transform the company it was decided to transform working practices and organise employees into small self-managing teams (cells), each with responsibility for seeing jobs through from start to finish. The cells would research their own practice in order to identify improvements they could make. The project has been an outright success. Initially there were few volunteers for the project, and then when a pilot cell was created and was shown to be successful, everyone wanted to buy in to the new approach to working. Employees were responding to a new way of working which unleashed the intelligence of all individuals. It is this step forward to the intelligent organisation and the recognition of the intelligent worker that have the potential to create world-class companies.

The GEC-Marconi story and others like it point the way forward to the future. Intelligent organisations require employees who are used to a way of working which is based on self-management and self-confidence in their own abilities. AVCEs prepare students to take on responsibility – to manage their own time, to work with others, to communicate effectively, to take responsibility, to solve problems and not to be frightened of technological change. Of course, intelligence also requires a great deal of hard work and this is why AVCEs require a strong knowledge-based component from a broad range of fields. Competent AVCE students need to feel they know something as well as knowing how to use the knowledge and other skills they have acquired. Being knowledgeable also comes with a lot of responsibility – students need to be able to appreciate that the knowledge they hold, and their understanding of how to use it, gives them privilege in a knowledge-based society. Privilege comes with responsibility – including the responsibility to help others develop their own intelligence. Intelligence is not something you should use against other people – it is a gift to be shared.

And, of course, operating in an intelligence-based society creates considerable stresses for those in most demand. Intelligent people need to be tough – they need to be able to handle pressure – and this is something that needs to be built into AVCE courses. The nature of modern work is such that employees are often expected to do lots of different things in a relatively short space of time. This brings with it considerable benefits in terms of variety, but it may also create unbearable pressures, particularly when combined with the complexities of modern family and home life. Youngsters need to be able to learn to compartmentalise aspects of work projects, and often to push through work assignments rather than letting them linger and add to the burden of stress. AVCE students also need to learn to make things happen, to lead rather than follow and not to wait for instructions from someone else. The good thing about AVCEs today is that they set out requirements in relatively clear specifications. Students need to appreciate quickly their own responsibility for turning specifications into finished learning outputs, and to use their intelligence to make the process successful. This is what they will need to do in the world of work. AVCEs, therefore, have tremendous potential to unleash intelligent and critical people who will be best placed to make a positive contribution to the development of society. It is hoped, too, that a new generation of intelligent knowledge workers will have the critical skills to rebel against the current work order and to help engineer organisations which are more humane and which recognise that work is only one component of the route to individual fulfilment.

DEVELOPING AUTONOMOUS LEARNERS

What is the best way to support AVCE Business students to become autonomous learners? At what point do you say to the learners – here are the learning objectives, it is up to you to make sure you meet the criteria in your own way?

Some people would argue that you naturally give students this sort of freedom from day one, while others are far more cautious – autonomy is something you need to work towards over a period of time.

Theories of teaching

In an interesting article by Dennis Fox ('Personal theories of teaching') which appeared in *Studies in Higher Education* (Vol. 8, no. 2, 1983), the author identified four basic theories of 'teaching'. There is the transfer theory which treats knowledge as a commodity to be transferred from one vessel to another. There is the shaping theory which treats teaching as a process of shaping or moulding students to a predetermined pattern. Thirdly, there is the travelling theory which treats a subject as a terrain to be explored with hills to be climbed for better viewpoints and with the teacher as the travelling companion or expert guide. Finally, there is the growing theory which focuses more attention on the intellectual and emotional development of the learner. These theories are reflected by, and interact with, the views students have of the process of learning. Whichever theory a tutor uses to help him or her think about the process, it will affect the strategies she or he uses and it will colour his or her attitudes to students and to any training programme that he or she undertakes.

On reflection, individual AVCE Business tutors will be able to identify their own position in relation to these various approaches. A number will worry that the nature of the way in which their courses are structured may push them in the direction of shaping rather than travelling or growing. Others will argue we must be careful not to expect learners to take on too much responsibility too early in a course. Lack of structure on some AVCE Business programmes can lead students to feel they are being dropped in at the deep end, with not enough guidance to make their own way. At the other extreme, those students who are taught on the baby food manufacturing process where the tutor sees his or her job as one of processing very tough material into more easily digestible nutrients for rather simple minds may develop an over-dependency on their tutors. Where, then, does the balance lie between too little support and too much?

The transition to self-managed learning

Talk to any group of AVCE students who have made the transition to self-managed learning and you will find most are firm believers in autonomy. They will be able to provide numerous examples of situations in which they have been able to engage in deep as opposed to surface learning by taking direct responsibility for their own learning. By engaging in critical inquiry, they will have developed new skills and knowledge with understanding that takes them forward and enables them to learn more for themselves.

The benefits of self-managed learning

In supporting self-managed learning it is important to think carefully about how we create the right sorts of conditions for learning. In particular, we need to look at what motivates students. Neil Moonie has shown that learning depends on four key issues, and that course design and teaching should be evaluated in terms of these issues. These are:

1 wanting
2 doing
3 feedback
4 digesting.

Motivation or 'wanting' to develop yourself is essential if you are going to invest time and energy and stick at something. Things are often learnt when you can put them into practice. Practice, trial and error and experimenting with ideas create an opportunity for active learning. Most people find it difficult to learn and to develop without feedback on how they are progressing. For many people, learning requires a social context; and the views and opinions of others are important. Finally, most people find it difficult to remember things which do not seem meaningful, or things that 'don't make sense'. We can remember things more easily if they click into place with what we already know. Reflection is a term which many theorists use to explain the learning process of linking new ideas or information with past experience. The metaphor of digesting information is a helpful one.

Learning styles

The tutor needs to have a good feel for the different learning styles students may be orientated towards (please see page 29, 'What style of learner am I?'). Some students are happier to go out to find things for themselves, others prefer discussions, while there is quite a sizeable number of students who prefer structured inputs. At the end of the day there will never be an exact match between preferred teaching and learning styles, so tutors and learners will always feel a degree of frustration with teaching and learning situations. The sensible tutor will look to vary approaches to learning in order to provide the best mix of opportunities for students.

The problem with learning objectives

As AVCE courses have increasingly been moved towards a learning objectives model, tutors and students have become more familiar with establishing and meeting learning objectives which are set out in defined criteria. There are many benefits to this process. Importantly, students often have a clear sense of direction. They know what is expected of them and can work systematically to meeting the required criteria (assuming they have enough time, which is not always the case).

However, there is a sense in which criteria are illusory in the impact they have on student learning. A student of mine recently carried out a work placement in which she was given responsibility for recruiting a new director to a theatre company. She went through a detailed set of procedures to create all the right sorts of recruitment and selection documents and the briefing of key personnel as to how to engage in the procedure in the spirit of equal opportunities. Finally, they interviewed the candidates, having first made sure the candidates had a good understanding of the criteria to be used in the selection process. Of course, as the job was involved in the theatre, one of the applicants had learnt his part excellently – he gave a first-class performance of someone who met all the required criteria. He was duly appointed. However, the reality was that he could not meet the requirements of the job on an ongoing basis. He was fine for a one-off interview performance.

It is possible we are teaching some AVCE students to be good actors. They are learning to be able to provide evidence they can meet selected performance criteria. However, with the nature of courses today, once they have completed a specific unit, they may then move on rapidly to another, quickly forgetting the skills and knowledge they have provided evidence for. I am not sure the process of providing evidence of performance is a true measure of actual performance – in a range of contexts over a period of time. I am not convinced the evidence which students present in their portfolios always reflects real understanding. This is why some Higher Awards students complete courses with fragmented parcels of knowledge which do not hold together particularly well. We need to devise better methods of checking on real understanding than the portfolio of evidence.

Back to self-managed learning

Self-managed learning which is rigorous and meaningful is a desired goal. However, this self-managed learning needs to be genuine. Tutors can support students to become self-managed learners only if they have a very good grasp of their own particular field, and if they know how to create effective structures to support students in the learning process.

When we tell students to find out something for themselves, we should have a good idea of the procedures students should engage in as part of their inquiry. For example, there is no point in sending a student to the library to seek information unless we are clear about whereabouts in the library the students should be looking. There is no point in telling a student to search the Internet unless we are sure the student is able to use the Internet or knows who will give him or her guidance as to procedures he or she should follow. If we tell a student to carry out some primary research, the student should be familiar with the research tools and how to make contacts. If students need to look at current publications and periodicals, these should be readily available. If you want a student to write a report, why not show the student a well-written report, perhaps by one of last year's students, etc.?

My view is that when you start with a new group of students (at whatever level), it is important to give them tightly structured guidance in the first few weeks of the course. The first inquiry they carry out could be a guided inquiry where you are fairly sure of key aspects of expected outcomes. Students should be presented with a study guide. Once students are more confident, you can let them engage in increasingly open inquiries. Of course, this will be restrictive for the extrovert who wants to find things out for him or herself from day one, but it should prevent the students from worrying unduly about the directions, boundaries and approaches that will be employed in their course of study. The objectives should be to move students forward from being dependent on the tutor to becoming independent learners. It is how we go about this process that is of fundamental importance. It is essential we are not dogmatic in our approach – too structured or too *laissez-faire*. Providing the mechanisms for autonomous learning is a very hard process. It requires detailed and systematic work by the tutor – to identify the best methods to build up the confidence and ability of the learners to do things for themselves.

PITCHING AVCE TEACHING AT AN APPROPRIATE LEVEL

The following are some suggestions about an overarching approach to facilitating learning for tutors introducing AVCE units for the first time.

Teachers have traditionally worked with the ACME approach to setting out schemes of work and lesson plans (i.e. setting out their *Aims*, deciding on the *Content* that needs to be covered, choosing the most appropriate *Methods*, and using *Evaluation* as an ongoing tool to improve the teaching and learning process).

Clearly, the starting point for such a process is to identify the needs of the learner and then to create courses which best meet these needs. Aims and objectives will then be focused on achieving this end result. Content and methods will be selected which are most appropriate to meeting desired objectives successfully. Within this pattern there is considerable room for variety. Some tutors focus very heavily on content and are continually absorbed in ensuring they are covering 'the course content'. Other tutors place more emphasis on 'methods' – they feel that if the methodology is right and that it suits the students, the 'motivational drive' will enable students to seize the knowledge more readily themselves.

Ultimately most, if not all, tutors will seek judiciously to create a suitable balance of content and process. Their choice of where the balance lies will be strongly influenced by the tutors' personalities, the nature of the groups being taught, pressure exerted by external assessment arrangements and the tutors' perceptions of what is 'educational'.

Planning for AVCE 'delivery'

One difficulty facing AVCE tutors is that they are presented with detailed course outlines which stem from a competence approach to AVCE. An AVCE is divided up into a number of units. Students need to show evidence they can match listed performance criteria in terms of their subject knowledge and capabilities within a general vocational field. This presents a considerable challenge to the tutor. The challenge is to make sure the learner is able to meet defined standards of performance as a result of his or her period of study. The problem here is that the learners' needs are being carefully defined in terms of 'should know' and 'should be able to do' standards. This creates a dilemma for the tutor – should our starting point be the learners' perceived needs at the start of the course, or should the starting point be the requirement that the learner should go on to be able to meet the standards which are established nationally for a specific vocational area?

A major criticism of GNVQs was that of poor completion rates. It seems likely that one of the causes of this poor completion rate has been the way in which the courses were focused on the emphasis on meeting standards, rather than on meeting the needs of the learner.

Work I have carried out at Nottingham Trent University looking at ways in which GNVQ courses in Business ran in local schools and colleges supported the contention that the way in which course outlines had been set out has led to many tutors focusing more attention on the need to 'deliver' a course, rather than matching a course to the learners' needs. Of course, the word 'deliver' exposes the likelihood of this happening. It was common practice to speak of 'delivering GNVQs'. They were often delivered in a systematic way, piece by piece, as set out in national guidelines. For example, in teaching 'Business in the economy' (the old GNVQ Advanced unit), tutors would often routinely work through some highly complex concepts in a way which is closely related to the documentation provided by awarding bodies. Tutors' justifications for this approach often followed the line that 'we've got little choice; there is so much to get through. Of course, there are large chunks which many students fail to understand, quite a few give up'.

Educational theory

There is a strong body of educational theory and research that would appear to question the narrow 'delivery approach' to tutoring. For example, Asubel states that:

> If I had to reduce all of educational psychology to just one principle, I would say this: The most important single factor influencing learning is what the learner already knows. Ascertain this and teach him/her accordingly.

The work of the celebrated Russian psychologist, Vigotsky, provides us with a simple yet useful method for tutoring. It indicates the importance of working from the known to the unknown. Vigotsky identifies three areas of learning. The zone of current development is where the learner is 'already at' – what he or she already knows. The zone of proximal development contains the sphere of new knowledge the learner is able to acquire with the help and guidance of a 'good' tutor. Beyond this lies a 'Badlands' area of confusion.

The implication is that the learner needs to be led gently through an incremental process of knowledge acquisition from the zone of current development to the zone of proximal development. The experienced tutor will probe and question students to find out what they already know before sensibly moving them forward. The 'deliverer', on the other hand, may rush students forward into the 'Badlands' ('because there is not the time available to do anything else!'). In contrast, the sensitive tutor will develop a blend of aims, content and methods which are suited to the learners' needs and which at the same time enable the learner to meet the required standards for a particular vocational area such as health and social care, leisure and tourism, or business.

Starting out

What, then, are the implications for the tutor designing and teaching a successful AVCE course? Perhaps the most obvious implication is that you need to give primacy to educational objectives which place the learner first. AVCE course specifications are very helpful in outlining the standards learners are expected to attain and the evidence they need to accumulate. However, they are more concerned with the end results rather than the teaching processes. While a framework is provided setting out the broad approaches students will need to follow to build up their understanding (e.g. through the creation of action plans and ongoing assignment work), little attention is given to how students will build progression into the work in the acquisition, for example, of conceptual understanding. This is an area which requires detailed thought. Experienced practitioners are only too aware that youngsters starting an AVCE course are more comfortable with descriptive work that relates to their existing background experience rather than to abstract theory. As a tutor, therefore, you could plan to start out individual units or groups of units by working from the descriptive and the familiar before progressively layering in more complex ideas. You need to decide which areas of content can safely be taught to students starting out on a course, and which ones need to be held back while the student builds up a more sophisticated thinking base. The reality is that you will rarely be able to teach AVCE units in the apparent sequences set out in course documents. For example, in the new AVCE Advanced Business course Unit 2, the course outline is concerned with the 'Competitive business environment'. The course was constructed in this way in order to emphasise the importance of economic relationships, including competition in determining business activity. However, a number of economic relationships which are set out in the standards are highly complex. It might therefore be advisable to decide which parts of these units could sensibly be taught to 'beginners' and which ones can be held back while students develop their capability in the vocational area. The tutor who states 'I am covering Unit 1 in its entirety in the first term of the course because I have to' is storing up trouble for him or herself – he or she will end up with confused and unmotivated students. (Of course, students may well achieve successful grades in units in which they have little understanding. However, they will have little confidence in a system that rewards them for what they do not know under an assessment system that allows them to produce someone else's words and explanations as evidence of their own understanding.)

In planning AVCE courses, then, tutors must first look at the course outline and decide *what the starting point should be for their students*. Education should be a student-focused activity rather than one which sets out mechanistically to train students to meet prescribed performance standards.

The great thing about AVCEs is that they have tremendous potential to motivate students by enabling them to see the value and purpose of their learning. However, for this to happen, tutors need to use the right approaches. Tutors often complain that AVCE course outlines are too mechanistic. However, as a tutor you do not have to operate in a mechanistic way. The guidance provided in the specification make it easy for us to outline clear objectives. How we enable students to achieve these objectives depends on our own ability to identify the learning needs of our students and to help them meet these needs in a creative way. The intelligent tutor does not simply blame 'the system' for leading his or her students into the 'Badlands'; rather, he or she negotiates the framework for learning with his or her students in a way that creates exciting progression from their zone of current development to a rapidly expanding zone of proximal development.

In essence, as tutors, we need to develop a clearer understanding of what exactly progression means for our students. Ultimately it is the tutor who will be the best judge of this – through intelligent evaluation and reflection on his or her own teaching and learning strategies and through careful monitoring of ongoing student development.

WHAT STYLE OF LEARNER AM I?

Psychologists have analysed the way we learn into four broad types. Do not worry if you do not fit neatly into any one type. Lots of people have a mix of two or three styles.

Activist – do it

You are open-minded and enthusiastic about new things. You'll try anything once. Your days are filled with activities. You tackle problems by brainstorming. Once an excitement has died down, you are looking for the next. You are outgoing and like to be the centre of attention.

Pragmatist – try it

You love new ideas and ways of doing things. You're keen to see if theories work in practice. You get impatient if people talk too much rather than getting on with things. You are very practical and down to earth. You see problems as a challenge. You're sure there's always a better way to do things. If something works, it must be good.

Theorist – test it

You are analytical and love detail. You take a logical, structured approach to everything you do. You're hardworking and a perfectionist. You enjoy theories and concepts and are quick at pulling together odd bits of information into rational arguments. You don't like uncertainty and you don't like anyone being flippant about serious things.

Reflector – think it

You like to stand back and think before you act. You're a people person and enjoy watching and listening to others. You're quiet and thoughtful and like harmony. You like to have a good feel for a subject before talking about it. You look at the big picture of any topic and you're very ordered, calm and thorough.

The following are guidelines as to which ways of learning suit different people.

Activists
Probably enjoy
- Active sessions
- Project work
- Group activities and brainstorming
- Trips and visits
- Role play

May want help with
- Listening to lectures
- Background reading on a subject
- Writing up projects
- Analysing research

Pragmatists
Probably enjoy
- Examples relating theory to real life
- Role play
- Trips and visits
- Presenting ideas
- Practical group work
- Writing up projects
- Using research findings

May want help with
- Group discussion on abstract ideas
- Listening to theory
- Background reading

Theorists
Probably enjoy
- Lectures with lots of theory
- Background reading
- Writing up notes
- Research
- Analytical exercises

May want help with
- Group discussion – especially talking about feelings and emotions
- Presenting ideas to groups

Reflectors
Probably enjoy
- Thinking about what they've learnt before discussing it
- Listening to experts
- Trips and visits
- Gathering views and opinions
- Background reading
- Doing and using their own research

May want help with
- Seeing the big picture before they've got the detail
- Role play
- Presenting ideas to a group

The following is a quiz to help you find out what your learning style is (based on work by Peter Honey and Alan Mumford). There is no time limit, but it will probably take you about 10 to 15 minutes. The accuracy of the results depends on how honest you are. There are no right or wrong answers. Tick the box next to the statements you agree with. Also tick the boxes where you *mostly* agree with the answers.

1 I like to be absolutely correct about things ☐ ***

2 I quite like taking risks ☐ *

3 I prefer solving problems step by step rather than guessing ☐ ***

4 I prefer simple, straightforward things to something complex ☐ ****

5 I often do things 'just because I like it' rather than thinking about them first ☐ *

6 I don't often take things for granted. I like to check things for myself ☐ ***

7 The most important thing about what you learn is if it works in practice ☐ ****

8 I'm always looking for new things to do ☐ *

9 When I hear a new idea, I immediately start thinking how I can work it out ☐ ****

10 I am keen on fixed routines and timetables ☐ ***

11 I take great care to work things out. I don't like jumping to conclusions ☐ **

12 I make decisions very carefully. I look at all the possibilities first ☐ **

13 I don't like 'loose ends'. I prefer things to fit into a kind of pattern ☐ ***

14 I get straight to the point in discussions ☐ ****

15 I like the challenge of new and direct things ☐ *

16 I prefer thinking things through before coming to a conclusion ☐ **

17 I don't find it easy to think of wild ideas off the top of my head ☐ ***

18 I love lots of information – the more I have to sift through the better ☐ **

19 I prefer jumping in and doing things than planning ahead ☐ *

20 I tend to judge other people's ideas on how well they will work in practice ☐ ****

21 You can't make a decision just because it feels right. You have to think about all the facts ☐ **

22 I'm fussy about how I do things – a bit of a perfectionist ☐ ***

23 I usually come up with lots of unusual ideas in discussions ☐ *

24 In discussions, I put forward only ideas I know will work ☐ ****

25 I look at problems from as many angles as possible before starting to solve them ☐ **

26 Usually I talk more than I listen ☐ *

27 Quite often I work out more practical ways of doing things ☐ ****

28 I believe that careful, logical thinking is the key to getting things done ☐ ***

29 If I'm writing a formal letter, I try out several drafts first ☐ **

30 I like to consider all my options before making up my mind ☐ **

31 I don't like creative ideas. They aren't very practical ☐ ****

32 It's best to look before you leap ☐ **

33 I usually do more listening than talking ☐ **

34 I can't be bothered with rules and plans. They take all the fun away ☐ ****

35 It doesn't matter how you do something so long as it works ☐ *

36 I'm usually the life and soul of the party ☐ *

37 I do whatever I need to do to get the job done ☐ ****

38 I like to find out how things work ☐ ***

39 I like meetings or discussion to follow a pattern and timetable ☐ ***

40 I don't mind in the least if things get out of hand ☐ *

Add up the number of ticks for each of the categories (i.e. one star, two stars, three stars and four stars):

*	represents activist responses
**	represents reflector responses
***	represents theorist responses
****	represents pragmatist responses.

The category with the highest number of ticks is the way you prefer to learn. If you have high scores in two categories, you are probably happy with both these ways of learning. If your score is fairly evenly spread, you are probably happy learning in several different ways.

THE USE OF VIDEO ON AN AVCE BUSINESS COURSE

There are some excellent videos available to support an AVCE Business course. The following are all produced by TV Choice, except where stated. TV Choice can be contacted at 22 Charing Cross Rd, London WC2H 0HR. For more details ring (020) 7379 0873. The videos are referenced below to the units and chapters of the student book.

Unit 1: Business at work

Chapter 3: Organisational functions

What is a Business? (28 minutes – support booklet available)

A clear and simple explanation of the features common to every business. Using toy manufacturer Rose Toys, it looks at the key departments, including marketing, production, finance and personnel. It explains their function and how they work. This video provides a sraightforward, realistic introduction to the business world.

Chapter 4: Organisational structures

Flattening the Organisation (42 minutes – support booklet available)

Follows Lloyd's Bank IT department to Camelot to get staff used to working with a new structure of 'matrix management', flattening the hierarchy and introducing teamworking and empowerment. They dress in medieval costume and act out scenarios to help prepare them for their new roles in the department. But getting staff to accept more responsibility is harder than expected.

Unit 2: The competitive business environment

Chapter 7: How competition in the market affects business

Business in the Economy (35 minutes – support booklet available)

A basic introduction to how the economy works and the part played by businesses and government. The basis types of economic activity are explained (primary, secondary and tertiary); how the market economy works; and the impact of historical change and efforts at regeneration. Such issues are explained with case studies from South Wales, where economic decline and attempts to regenerate are powerful factors in people's lives.

Chapter 8: How business is affected by government policy

End of Enterprise (28 minutes – support booklet available)

A look at the effects of government policy in the 1980s on the economy of Chesterfield. The 'enterprise' culture promised much, but seems to have worsened the lives of people in this area. Owners of a small business, a large manufacturer and redundant workers explain what recession has meant to them.

Unit 3: Marketing

Chapter 10: The principles of marketing

Marketing a Theme Park (35 minutes – support booklet available)

Looks at all the key aspects of how Alton Towers markets itself. Promotional offers through newspapers, PR work, direct mail and 'pester power' all play a part. Also, we see how the marketing team came up with a TV ad for their new ride, called 'Oblivion'. The idea is to win back their thrill-seeking teenage market. But in the process, do they risk alienating the young family customers?

Chapter 11: Establishing customer needs

Marketing Research in Action (25 minutes – support booklet available)

A detailed study of how one company, a US marketing research company, undertakes research for its customers in the car-dealership business. The video follows every stage of the process, from constructing the survey through to the presentation and analysis of the results. Such information, claims the company, allows the car dealers to target their advertising far more effectively.

Chapter 12: Methods of analysing marketing opportunities

The Green Marketing Gamble (25 minutes – support booklet available)

The environment is a major selling point in business, but should a firm really gamble its future on a new 'green' product and scrap a market-leading brand? Swiss glue-maker, Ebnother, did just this. This shows the risks and benefits of 'going green'. There was much internal resistance to the new product, as well as from customers, but chief executive Gerry Leuman was determined to push it through.

Chapter 13: Developing strategies to meet customer needs: the marketing mix

The Marketing Mix in Action (36 minutes – support booklet available)

Looks at the battle for prominence among the big names in the high street, including the multi-million-pound TV advertising campaigns of Müller Yoghurt and the Prudential. The video also looks at the role of marketing research in developing new ideas for products. Also featured is a company bypassing supermarkets to deliver organic vegetables direct to customers. Finally, a look into the future and the 'virtual supermarket'.

Unit 4: Human resources

Chapter 14: Human resource planning

Empowering the People (25 minutes – support booklet available)

Japanese-style working practices applied to a UK firm. Unipart makes great claims for a policy of 'empowering' its workforce, replacing 'them and us' with harmony and commitment. Clocking-in and supervisors are out: teamworking and quality circles are in. But how real are the benefits? Some dissenting voices put a counterview.

Chapter 15: Recruitment and selection

Recruitment in Action (32 minutes – support booklet available)

Blow-by-blow account of how a travel company sets about advertising for, and recruiting, a marketing assistant. We see how they define the job description and eavesdrop on the recruitment interviews. We also witness the meetings of the managers as they try to decide on the most suitable candidate. The viewers are invited to make their choice before the decision is made. It also covers equal opportunities. The film then follows the story on. Did the managers make the right choice?

Chapter 16: Training and development

A Practical Guide to Management Self-Development (25 minutes – support booklet available)

To manage efficiently, you need to understand people and communicate with them, but these skills are hard to acquire through conventional training. It looks at a powerful alternative approach: self-development, which means learning through personal experience. We follow a group of managers who experiment with self-development, the exercises they have to do and how they monitor their progress.

Chapter 17: Performance management

What is Motivation? (27 minutes – support material available)

Comprehensive guide to the essentials of motivation theory and practice. Using a wealth of interviews and case study material, this video offers a clear introduction to this central business issue. It explains and illustrates the classic theories of Taylor, Maslow and McGregor. Companies promoting 'teamworking' and 'empowerment' as the key to motivation are illustrated. Outdoor 'adventure' courses are supposed to motivate teams, but what's the reality behind the hype?

Unit 5: Business finance

Chapter 19: Constructing accounts

Managing the Money (32 minutes – support material available)

This video explains in clear and simple terms how a financial manager plans and monitors a firm's finances. Topics covered include: sources of finance, financial forecasting (profit and loss, and cash flow) and financial monitoring. The use of the balance sheet is also explained.

Chapter 20: Interpreting financial information

A step-by-step, comprehensive guide through the main parts of this key business document. Concepts such as assets and liabilities are explained; also gearing, solvency and liquidity. The relationship between the balance sheet and profit and loss is also explained.

Unit 6: Business planning

An excellent video covering all aspects of business planning, called *Minding Your Own Business*, is available from Shell Education Service, Shell International Ltd, Shell Centre, London SE1 7NA, tel: 020 7934 3149 (30 minutes and support booklet).

Other useful business planning videos available from TV Choice are as follows.

Starting a Business: The Café Bar (30 minutes with support booklet)

Running your own restaurant may be many people's dream but it's also many people's nightmare – 80% of such start-ups fail in the early stages. This is the story of how David set up his own café bar, the 'Tin Drum', in Brighton, with four partners. They first had to choose the location, get planning permission and a licence. Then they designed and refurbished the premises.

Although it's very popular, six months after opening the new café bar comes close to bankruptcy. Too much of the revenue is just 'leaking away'. They simply don't know how much money they're making – or losing. The answer is much tighter controls – on staff and stock. They bring in a new till system which gives them the stock control they need. But the staff are unhappy and many resign – including the manager and the head chef!

A business can seem successful, with many happy customers, but can, in fact, be doing badly financially. A lesson for all business start-ups; it's always harder than you think.

How to Do a Business Plan (28 minutes with support booklet)

Jay is a fashion designer, Robin is a tree surgeon. Two very different firms but with one thing in common: they both had to write a business plan. How did they do it? This film is a detailed, step-by-step account of how Jay and Robin went about the task. Covers key sections of a business plan, including 'Objectives', 'Marketing plan', 'Production' and the 'Financial plan'.

KEY SKILLS AS A NATURAL PART OF THE BUSINESS AVCE

Business tutors should have no fear of Key Skills as part of the Business course. The six core units of the Business AVCE lend themselves naturally to Key Skill development.

Communication skills

Communication is an everyday feature of business life. At all but the very lowest levels of an organisation, individuals will be expected to carry out research to provide evidence to write up in reports, to read and understand extended documents, to make presentations to others, to discuss issues in small groups and in larger forums, to send communications and to give information to customers, etc.

The tutor therefore needs to plan a series of opportunities which appear naturally in the course to enable students to practise and develop their Key Skills.

- Opportunities for extended report writing will include the assessments for 'Business at work' and 'Human resources'. In addition, students will need to set out a business plan for the 'Business planning' unit and to create a marketing strategy for the 'Marketing' unit.

- Students will have the opportunity to carry out detailed research, and to analyse complex information in creating their business plans and their marketing strategies. Similarly, when they create a human resource plan for an organisation, they will need to analyse labour market information to identify an appropriate plan for an organisation.
- The tutor will want to provide a series of ongoing opportunities for discussion during the course. This will typically involve the tutor in providing students with pre-reading materials and then, perhaps, asking them to play a role or take a stance in discussing a particular issue – for example, the case for and against rail privatisation (the 'Competitive business environment'), the costs and benefits of empowerment in the workplace ('Business at work'), the most appropriate marketing mix for a new product ('Marketing'), etc.
- Presentation skills are a very important communication skill. The best way to start with students is on the basis of short and frequent presentations in the early parts of the course – building up to longer and more detailed presentations. The more opportunities the students have to stand in front of a class, the less self-conscious they will become. Early presentations should involve just a few visual aids – e.g. the use of overhead transparencies. Later on, students can work with more detailed Powerpoint presentations. However, the tutor needs to be aware that the students' presentation skills can be held back by over-reliance on Powerpoint. Students need to learn to speak confidently rather than to hide behind a number of elaborate illustrations. As students gain more confidence in giving presentations, they can be encouraged to make presentations to an outside audience (e.g. a member of a local company).

Application of number skills

Practice in the application of number will be most frequently carried out in relation to 'The competitive business environment' and 'Business finance' units. A number of students following GNVQ courses have struggled with the numerical aspects of the course, leading to the highest failure rates in these units. Tutors need to recognise students may have real difficulties in these areas (e.g. in the calculation of %s and % changes as they are used in accounting ratios and calculations of elasticity of demand). The sensitive tutor will, therefore, seek to discover areas of difficulty students have and then to work from very simple examples to more complex calculations. Failure to meet student needs in this area will leave a considerable gap in the students' knowledge and understanding.

Information technology skills

Students' abilities to work with information technology have increased extensively in recent times. At the start of the student book we provide some useful guidance on using the Internet, and the book provides a host of website addresses for students to use.

Opportunities to practise information technology skills are particularly significant in the units on 'Marketing' (e.g. market research), 'Business finance' (e.g. profit calculations) and 'Business planning' (e.g. market research and financial information).

The tutor needs to build in opportunities for students to work with spreadsheet applications (e.g. in working out changes in profit and loss accounts, and setting out budgets) and databases (e.g. in examining data for the labour market, or extracting economic data related, for example, to interest rates and inflation).

Improving the students' own learning and performance

The nature of an AVCE course is that it encourages a process of self-managed learning. The development and monitoring of action plans are a particularly important part of this process and this area is covered on pages v–vii of the student book. Tutors and students need to identify learning objectives and targets, particularly in relation to assignment work. Students need to be encouraged to reflect on how they have learnt and on the improvements they are making over time to the process of learning.

Working with others

In the 'Business at work' and 'Human resources' units, we outline the benefits of teamworking in organisations. Students should appreciate that working with others is desirable and that they need to develop this vocational skill in preparation for their working lives. There are many opportunities for students to work with others:

- with tutors in establishing action plans and learning targets, and then monitoring and evaluating these plans
- with contacts at business organisations as part of research and assessment work
- with other students to manage group projects and presentations.

A key part of learning to work with others is a reflection on the process of teamworking and liaising and planning with others. Students need to be encouraged to think about what went well and what went badly in working with others in order to outline ongoing steps for improvements.

Conclusion

The development of key skills is an essential part of the Business course and is also a natural part of the course. At the end of each unit in the student book we have outlined opportunities to develop core skills. Tutors should develop a grid outlining the opportunities they are presenting to students to develop key skills during their course. By mapping out the key skills in this way, tutors will be able to help students to build the skills over time and to make sure that all the key skills are given adequate coverage.

SECTION A DISCUSSION POINT

BOSS TYPES: HOW TO IDENTIFY THEM – AND HOW TO COPE WITH THEM

In November 2000, the Institute of Management produced a guide outlining a number of management types and ways in which employees can cope with them.

1 Dictatorial type

In charge for a reason – they are the best person for the job – and must therefore tell everyone else what to do and how to do it. They are motivated by the need to win every argument. They rely on reward and punishment.

How to cope with them

Always ask their permission before doing anything and demonstrate you are fulfilling their orders with enthusiasm.

2 Bureaucratic type

These people got where they are today by following the rules and see no reason to change now. They lack the ability to take risks and are law-abiding citizens who take responsibility seriously. Problems are dealt with by referring to the rule book.

How to cope with them

By giving them the rules when a discussion is necessary and submitting any requests in writing.

3 Charismatic type

This type motivates staff by inspiring them to achieve the company's goals rather than their own. They lead by personal example and they inspire loyalty. They are driven by the need to act for the company's greater good at the expense of personal desires.

How to cope with them

Be enthusiastic about their dreams and show that you, too, put the company first.

4 Consultative type

These people are highly concerned about establishing and keeping close personal and emotional relationships. Likely to consult staff at every turn. Afraid of making solo decisions and prefer to share the burden of power.

How to cope with them

By not being afraid to give an opinion, and to involve them by taking them out to lunch or to the pub after work.

5 *Laissez-faire* (leave it alone)

This type makes a conscious decision to leave the staff to get on with it, having observed they are working well on their own. Probably assume people are working because they want to, and are self-motivated.

How to cope with them

By showing you can be trusted to get on with it and by sending regular progress memos. Don't bother them with trivia.

6 Abdicatorial

These people do not care enough to get involved with the staff. They leave them to it because difficult positions have to be avoided. Staff have to make decisions and must confront and handle problems that are the bosses' responsibility.

How to cope with them

By asking for formal meetings to discuss issues and getting permissions for projects where possible.

POINTS FOR DISCUSSION

1 Drawing on your own experience of working in organisations, which of these types have you most frequently come across?
2 Describe a manager you are familiar with who fits one of these types.
3 How did you deal with the manager you have described? How different was your approach from that suggested by the Institute of Management?
4 What do you think would be the best type of manager to work for? Why?

SECTION B SUGGESTED ANSWERS

CHAPTER 1 BUSINESS OBJECTIVES

Case study: Nottingham Forest in March 1998 (page 7)

1 The key difference between a Premier League club and a First Division one is in its ability to generate much larger revenues, both through on-the-field and off-the-field activities. Premier clubs are likely to be able to sell all their seats to season ticket holders, and are likely to play in larger stadiums. Today, much of the revenue comes from television broadcasts and the sale of club strips, souvenirs and a range of other club-related merchandise. However, for Premier teams, there is an additional problem of higher costs – particularly in relation to players' salaries and other additional costs, such as the increased costs of policing matches, etc. A number of Premier teams do make losses and some First Division clubs make profits. It is all about matching costs with revenues.

2 Some Premier clubs will make losses because their playing and non-playing activities do not generate enough revenue to cover operating costs. Only the most successful clubs make the very high revenues and have a global following (e.g. Manchester United). Less successful clubs have a smaller ground capacity and receive lower revenues from the sale of merchandise because of their smaller fan base. Also, television revenues are related to the number of times a team's matches are broadcast.

3 Nottingham Forest were prepared to make a loss in the short term in the hope of making large profits in the longer term. The key cost that was leading to the loss were the very high wages that were being paid to star players. In the long term, these high costs could be justified if Nottingham Forest were to regain Premier status, which would give them access to the vast television revenues and other benefits that come from playing at the higher level.

4 If Nottingham Forest had failed to be promoted, their costs would have been much higher than their revenues for the following season as well. The club could not have afforded such a drain on resources and would have had to sell players to cut costs. Other costs they could have cut would be that of their manager – replacing him with a cheaper one – cutting the training budget, cutting the number of ancillary employees at the club and cutting expenditure on equipment (e.g. maintenance, repairs, replacement of existing items, etc.).

5 Terms mentioned in the case study:

- *Expenses* – expenditures required for the day-to-day running of the club (e.g. players' salaries, groundstaff wages, expenditure on sporting equipment and materials, etc.).
- *Cost base* – the costs of running the club on an ongoing basis.
- *Revenues* – the receipts the club takes in from its activities (e.g. gate receipts, sale of replica shirts, etc.).
- *Loss* – a situation where costs are higher than revenues – the extent of the difference between costs and revenues.
- *Operations* – the key day-to-day activities of the club.

6 They were promoted at the end of the season, giving them access to the benefits of being in the Premier Division. Unfortunately, they were then relegated the following season.

7 Because Nottingham Forest were successful in gaining promotion in 1998, they were able to claim a share of the much higher revenues available to Premier clubs. Unfortunately, they finished the following season at the foot of the Premier League. Their lack of success on the field meant they were not able to achieve the sorts of revenues they desired – and thus they finished the season in a loss-making position.

8 Business organisations like Nottingham Forest can make a profit by achieving revenues that are higher than costs. Making a profit enables a business to invest for the future. For example, clubs like Manchester United have been able to invest in their stadiums, in their teams

and in their merchandising activities to secure long-term benefits.

Check your understanding (page 9)

If Melchester Rovers are promoted to the Conference League and are able to charge £7.50 per spectator, their revenue will rise from £25,000 per match to £37,500 per match. Assuming their costs stay at £25,000 per match, they will make a profit of £12,500 per game.

However, their costs will probably rise because they will need to pay higher wage bills to better-quality players. The management costs will also probably rise, as will those of the coaches. They may also need to employ more stewards at matches. They may also have to pay for ground improvements.

Their revenues will rise from more sponsorship of the club, the higher gate fees and more additional revenues (e.g. from television rights, etc.).

Check your understanding (page 10)

Students should study a quality newspaper, looking at the business pages over a week. They should then highlight stories where a headline relates to the profit or loss made by the company. They should then explain in their own words what has happened to the profit or loss, and also explain who stands to lose or gain from the situation.

Case study: Laura Ashley (page 10)

1 A business like Laura Ashley will make a loss if its costs are higher than revenues. This may be because costs of production are too high – perhaps because of inefficient production methods. The business's revenues may be too low because it is not able to sell enough items at high enough prices. By lowering prices it is less able to cover costs.
2 When a company makes a loss, shareholders will lose confidence in the business. As part owners of a company, what they make in profit – the dividend – will be low as a result of the loss made. Shareholders may then be inclined to sell their shares and switch over to companies that make better profits.
3 It is not just the shareholders who lose out when a company makes a loss. Employees may lose their jobs or have their salaries cut. Suppliers may lose contracts to supply the firm. People who have lent the company money will worry about being paid back, and so on.

Case study: increasing the market share of BSkyB (page 11)

1 BSkyB was able to build up an initial lead over rivals and then to secure this advantage by coming up with new ideas. It has been particularly successful in its use of sport to win subscribers by gaining a monopoly of key sporting events. BSkyB has built up a presence in people's homes (e.g. by offering free set-top boxes for digital services).
2 By gaining the lion's share of the market, BSkyB is able to make more profit than its rivals and then to plough back these profits into further investments that maintain its lead. As it has the largest share of the market, rivals are able only to win a proportionately smaller section of the market.
3 By losing market share to rivals the rivals are able to spread their costs over a larger output, reducing BSkyB's initial advantage.

Case study: supermarket wars (page 12)

1 Market dominance enables a business to have a bigger share of sales than rivals. Larger sales enable a business to benefit from all sorts of economies that help to slash costs – for example, bulk purchasing, bulk distribution, etc. Market domination gives the sort of cost domination that enables a firm to undercut rival offers while offering a wider variety of goods and quality advantages.
2 The firm with the biggest market share is able to drive down prices and push up quality, while at the same time spending more on advertising, promotion and investment in new innovations that win customer loyalty. The leading supermarket

is able progressively to wrest market share from its rivals.

Case study: ICI (page 14)

1 In the modern world, many businesses aim to 'survive' in a competitive world. ICI were operating in a world of considerable risk, faced by large-scale overseas producers in Germany and the USA while, at the same time, facing the 'threat' of not being seen as environmentally sound. The company needed to make a radical shift in strategy. It was already a very successful company but it needed to refocus its billions of pounds of resources into new lines that would enable it to survive.
2 Students need to examine examples in the quality press (or by using the Internet) of organisations that are having to restructure in order to survive (e.g. organisations which are seeking to develop more sustainable environmental policies).

Check your understanding (page 15)

In a rapidly changing business environment, organisations can be successful simply by continuing to exist – to survive. Profits are very important in that they can be ploughed back into securing the long-term survival of a company and into investments that enable a company to develop a competitive advantage over rivals. Because of the dynamic nature of the modern business environment, survival is a key objective enabling an organisation to build into the future.

Case study: Barclays and the New Economy (page 16)

1 Students should look at the two sides to the argument. On the one hand, Barclays might be seen to be taking a sound business decision. The organisation needs to be competitive and, in a world of Internet and telephone banking, Barclays are not in a position to subsidise branches which are a drain on resources. However, students may also feel that Barclays are being disingenuous in that they are ignoring local communities they purport to be serving.
2 Barclays might argue that their decision is in the long-term interest of all their customers. While they might be withdrawing a face-to-face service with customers in certain localities, this is being replaced by one-to-one Internet and telephone links, enabling customers to deal directly with a member of Barclays' staff.
3 Students will need to support their arguments with valid reasons. They might, for example, argue that shareholders must receive a fair return on their investments or they would switch their funds elsewhere. Alternatively, they may feel local interests should be served because businesses are there to meet customer needs. Other interested stakeholders include Barclays' suppliers, Barclays' account holders in other parts of the UK, Barclays' employees, etc.

Check your understanding (page 16)

Examples of situations where business activity is driven by community service include providing post and ferry services to out-of-the-way areas where there is little demand and services provided for the elderly, such as 'meals on wheels'. The BBC provides public broadcasting services for the nation, which are not always profit driven. Some football clubs offer free entry to schoolchildren to encourage sport in the community, etc.

Case study: the objectives of War Child (pages 17–18)

1 Not-for-profit organisations have a central objective which focuses on providing a service or meeting a need that is not profit driven – e.g. helping children in war zones, providing famine relief to the needy, etc. Not-for-profit organisations recognise that their objectives will usually best be met by subsidies and donations rather than through commercial activities. Profit-based organisations are more concerned with carrying out activities that enable them to make more revenue than they pay out in costs.
2 Any organisation needs to have a clear sense of direction so that it can tailor its activities towards meeting its objectives and so it can measure its success in meeting these objectives. The organisation that does not have this clear direction will

waste scarce resources and will fail to secure its objectives effectively.

3 Not-for-profit organisations can measure their success against clearly stated objectives. If these objectives can be quantified, it is possible to measure performance.

Check your understanding (page 18)

Students should choose an environmental charity or group such as Friends of the Earth, Greenpeace, etc., and then carry out a newspaper or Internet search to find the organisation's objectives. These objectives can then either be directly contrasted with a specific for-profit organisation or, generally, with profit-based organisations.

Check your understanding (page 19)

Many educational organisations have received Investors in People awards. Students could therefore examine how their own educational institution went about securing this award. Alternatively, students could examine an organisation one of the students works for that has received or is working towards IiP.

Case study: how IKEA aims to give people high-quality products (pages 20–21)

A high-quality product is one that is 'fit for the purpose' it is intended for. IKEA specifically set out to provide good-quality furniture and other goods at low prices to ordinary people. The quality of its products, therefore, should be judged in terms of its ability to meet this need.

Check your understanding (page 21)

Students should define high quality in terms of a product's ability to meet the needs for which it is required. Students' perceptions of high-quality products will be based on their own perceptions of what they see as being good products. However, more importantly, students need to identify high-quality goods and services as being ones that meet the needs of the targeted market. A product that I perceive to be 'not very good' may be a high-quality product in terms of its ability to meet the needs of its targeted customers.

Case study: BT staff to strike over 'dictatorial' management (page 22)

The case study shows only one aspect of culture at BT – i.e. in respect to call centres. In the case study, BT is seen as operating in a dictatorial way in its call centres, with employees having little scope for personal initiative. This is in clear contrast with the earlier notes in the student book (pages 20–21) in which IKEA is seen to have a democratic way of working.

Check your understanding (page 24)

Students need to outline what they see as being the strengths and weaknesses of a power culture in their own terms. Typical strength factors include the consistency with which decisions can be made, the speed of decision-making, the lack of disagreement, etc. Weaknesses include the potential tyranny of the decision-maker, the lack of questioning and discussion of decisions, etc.

Students should point out that the strengths or weaknesses of a power culture depend on the individual concerned and the context in which he or she is operating.

Check your understanding (page 25, a)

As part of their work experience or their part-time work, students may have worked in a bureaucratic-type organisation. Students should discuss how such a role culture enables the organisation to meet its objectives (e.g. by enabling members of the organisation to focus on tasks designed to meet organisational objectives). However, they should also point out weaknesses, such as how red tape restricts the organisation in meeting its objectives speedily.

Check your understanding (page 25, b)

Students should focus on a situation in which individuals work in teams to perform given tasks. In particular, they should focus on situations in which, as part of their course, they are operating as team members. They should look at how the task culture enables the team, and hence the larger organisation, to meet objectives.

Check your understanding (page 26)

Students will need to contrast an organisation that is very 'history' bound (continually looking to the past and to tradition to make decisions) with an organisation that is continually making new decisions and frameworks for decision-making that seek to secure success in the future. Having identified two organisations to look at, they can list the key distinctive features and differences between the two organisations that have been chosen.

Check your understanding (page 28)

This task is set out as a clear and simple set of questions asking students to explore a recent change that has taken place in an organisation they are familiar with – whether it be the educational institution they attend or their place of work. They need briefly to explain what the change was and the processes by which the change was brought about. They need to examine whether the change was imposed on the individuals involved or whether the individuals felt 'ownership' of the change. If students work in twos or threes on the task, they can brief the rest of the class on the change process they examined. It should then be possible to draw out some general conclusions as to the best way of managing change in an organisation.

Check your understanding (page 29)

1 Most organisations today have to develop policies and procedures with an environmental consideration. Students should comment on how such awareness in an organisation they are familiar with impacts on culture.
2 They should do the same for a particular social issue that affects an organisation.

Check your understanding (page 30)

Students need to examine the feedback between culture and the structure and objectives of an organisation. For example, an organisation with a democratic and caring culture may have a more democratic structure and objectives. Students need to tease out this relationship by using actual case examples they are familiar with.

CHAPTER 2 TYPES OF BUSINESS

Case study: Jenny's Sandwich Bar (pages 32–33)

Advantages	Disadvantages
Makes own decisions	Long hours
Works for herself	Must sort out own problems
Good personal relationship with customers	Will have to sell off own property if business falls into debt
Takes all the profits	Has to be a 'jack of all trades'
Business affairs are kept private	Problems if sick
Easy to file tax returns	Had to raise all the finance needed
	Small business cannot obtain bulk discounts

Check your understanding (page 33)

The students should arrange an interview at a time when the person being interviewed is not busy or in after-work hours. This task will be easier to arrange with a relative or family friend. The students should ask the sole trader to identify a list of advantages of being a sole trader and then a list of disadvantages.

Check your understanding (page 34)

Working in groups of two or three, students should find out information about a partnership by interviewing one of the partners or an employee who works for the partnership (e.g. a dentists' practice, doctors' surgery, solicitors, accountants, etc.).

Case study: Patak's (page 35)

1 The business has moved on from being a small business operating from home to a nationally recognised business supplying all the major supermarket chains. In order to finance this expansion, the company needed an injection of capital – from shareholders and also from financial institutions. This would be much easier to obtain by becoming a company.
2 a Company status provides the owners with limited liability so their personal possessions are protected should the company run into difficulties. b Outside investors are far more likely to commit their capital to an organisation which has company status. c Having company status creates far more credibility with suppliers and other organisations with which the business comes into contact.
3 As a company, the profits will need to be shared out amongst shareholders rather than being retained by the sole owner. Also, the company will require far more administration work in terms of filing company records, tax returns, etc.

Check your understanding (page 36)

Working in groups of two or three, students should research a local private company – indicated by having 'Ltd' after its name. Students may work for such a company or have parents or relatives working for such an organisation. They should then arrange a short 30-minute interview to find out the relevant details of company organisation.

Case study: reading share prices in a national newspaper (page 37)

1 Black Arrow has gone up by 1p since the previous day.
2 Lonmin fell by 25p.
3 The highest yield is 8.3 – for Black Arrow.
4 A shareholder may be attracted to Lonmin by the yield of 3.2 and the P/E ratio of 33.3. However, the fall in 25p since the previous day might make the shareholder wary. The shareholder would need to find out what had caused the fall and see whether this was part of a trend – the shares have fallen from a high for the year of 662p.

Case study: welcome to Webvan (pages 39–40)

1 Webvan had to become a public company as this was the best possible route to raising the large amounts of capital required to get such a massive enterprise up and running in a relatively short period.
2 Investors are looking at the long-term possibilities for Internet trading. They saw Webvan as the sort of organisation that would have a major long-term impact on the market. Shareholders were also confident about the sorts of credentials people involved with the company had.
3 Webvan anticipated that the Internet would become a major way of buying goods in the early twenty-first century. The company was prepared to take a risk and create a major investment strategy that was forward looking rather than being primarily based on what had come before.

Check your understanding (page 44, a)

Co-operatives exist in a range of forms. However, the easiest forms of co-operatives to investigate are farming co-operatives in rural areas and retail co-operatives in urban areas.

Check your understanding (page 44, b)

Not all McDonald's are operated under a franchise arrangement. If students live in urban areas, there are a range of other franchises they can investigate if there is not a franchised McDonald's available. Many pizza chains operate the franchise system, as do Benetton and Body Shop stores.

Case study: taking out a delivery franchise (page 45)

1 The franchisee would be working for him- or herself. He or she could then decide how hard he or she wanted to work. The harder the franchisee worked at delivering goods, the greater the profits he or she would make. The franchisee would need to be somebody who enjoyed driving and working for him- or herself. He or she would benefit from trading under a well-known name and being supplied with equipment, training and expertise from the franchisor.
2 Disadvantages of taking out a delivery franchise would be the high initial start-up fee and the working capital required to keep the business running. The franchisee also has to share profits with the franchisor and is often tied to buying parts and supplies. The franchisee may feel he or she is working for him- or herself in name only.
3 Someone taking out such a franchise would need to be well organised and highly motivated. He or she would need to be able to stand on his or her own feet and work long hours. He or she would also need to be able to build up contacts and good relationships with customers over a long period of time.

Check your understanding (page 46)

Students might find this task easier if they concentrate on a local not-for-profit organisation or a local branch of a not-for-profit organisation, such as a high-street charity shop, a local charity or a fund-raising organisation.

Check your understanding (page 48)

Limited liability	Unlimited liability
Private company	Sole trader
Public company	Partnership
Registered charity	

Check your understanding (page 49)

A plc is able to raise more finance than a sole trader or a co-operative because it has access to funds by selling shares to shareholders who can then trade their shares on the Stock Exchange. A large public company with plc after its name is able to generate public confidence – particularly as investors can track the fortunes of the company through the Stock Exchange pages of national newspapers.

Case study: trouble at Somerfield (page 50)

1 The share price of Somerfield had fallen because of poor trading results. Its sales had fallen dramatically, leading to cuts in profits. Somerfield were losing market share to more dynamic competitors.
2 Shareholders may have felt the company needed to make changes in its style of operating in order to improve sales and profits. They might have associated David Simons with the company's poor trading record. This case study shows the influence shareholders can have over business decision-making.
3 The new strategy is to make deliveries of groceries and fresh produce to rural stores.
4 Students can come up with their own ideas, for example concentrating on niche lines.

Check your understanding (page 51)

Someone setting up a co-operative may have a range of objectives. He or she may want to set up a business organisation that is ethical and fair in its trading. He or she may want to make sure all co-operators are treated equally and fairly. The co-operative may be less concerned with profit than with social considerations. In contrast, it is more likely the driving concern of the private company will be to make good sales and healthy profits – although this does not preclude a concern for social issues.

Check your understanding (page 53)

While the responsibilities and paperwork of setting up a plc are considerably more extensive than for setting up a sole trader business (e.g. memorandum and articles to fill in, more detailed tax returns, etc.), the burden is likely to be lighter than for the sole trader. The sole trader will need to carry out all or most of the legal responsibilities him- or herself. The public company is much more likely to have specialists whose sole responsibility is to handle the legal side of the company's affairs.

In order to find about the contractual arrangements involved in franchising, the student should interview a franchisee of a specific organisation (e.g. a fast-food outlet). This task does not require finding out lots of detailed information, just the broad outlines (e.g. how long the franchise agreement is for, what the main clauses in the contract are, etc.).

CHAPTER 3 ORGANISATIONAL FUNCTIONS

Check your understanding (page 55)

Land	Labour	Capital	Enterprise
Fish in sea	Brain power	Buildings and machinery	Shareholders
Factory area	Inter-personal skills	Maintenance equipment	Anita Roddick's enterprise

Case study: Harry Ramsden's (pages 55–56)

Land	Labour	Capital	Enterprise
Sites on which built	Waiters/ waitresses Cooks Accountants Marketers, etc.	'Huts' Car parks	Harry Ramsden's initiative Shareholders

Check your understanding (page 59)

Financial accounting	Management accounting
Recording day-to-day transactions	Suggesting expenditure limits
End of year P & L accounts	Information to managers

Check your understanding (page 60)

This activity is best organised by the tutor. The tutor should use local industrial links with a manufacturing company, working with the production manager of the company. The production manager could visit the school or college to outline key areas of the production subsystem. This could then be followed up with an industrial visit to the plant. Students should word process their work and samples of the best work could be shown to the company to build up an ongoing relationship.

Check your understanding (page 62, a)

Again, this activity is best organised by the course tutor. A local human resource manager could be invited in to the school or college to give a brief outline (a 30-minute talk followed by questions) setting out the key responsibilities and divisions of HRM in his or her organisation.

Check your understanding (page 62, b)

The man is giving a sales view – assuming it is the offer made by the company that will attract customers. The woman is giving the marketing view – saying you need to find out what customers' wants and expectations are first.

Check your understanding (page 64, a)

The most accessible source of information to students for answering this task is to interview an appropriate member of staff in the administration department of a school or college. In the case of an educational institution, it would make sense to look at how the administration department supports teaching and learning activities, or how administrators take a responsibility for financial affairs. Administrators will also be able to point out some of the 'red tape' involved with their work and how at times this can hinder rather than help organisational efficiency.

Check your understanding (page 64, b)

An R&D function is most likely to exist in a large manufacturing company that is at the forefront of pioneering work involving specific forms of technology (e.g. ICI, Shell, BP, Cadbury, Nestlé, etc.).

Case study: R&D at Glaxo (page 65)

1 The pharmaceutical industry is a very competitive one in which people are constantly seeking new innovations and ideas to cure medical conditions and to make people's lives easier. It is an industry involving constant change. Coming up with new medicines and drugs may take many years of research. Large budgets, therefore, need to be allocated to keeping your company ahead of rivals.
2 Glaxo had invested considerable sums into providing what they saw as being the best way of dealing with flu. The research and development programme would have cost billions of pounds. The company felt the government was being short-sighted in going for the cheapest solution.
3 Glaxo might have wanted to move overseas (e.g. to the USA) where the government might have been more encouraging of their R&D efforts. There are many other reasons for switching location overseas, including to lower production costs, to benefit from lower tax regimes, etc.

Discussion point (page 66)

The point here is that, if you have clear, focused objectives, it becomes possible for all parts of an organisation to pull in the same direction. If the organisation is clear about serving the customer and getting quality right, it will make sure that, for example, the bills sent out to customers are clear, accurate, informative and polite – which serves the public relations function of presenting a strong positive image of the company. By focusing on serving the internal customer, each section of the organisation will focus on serving other parts rather than obstructing or competing with them.

CHAPTER 4 ORGANISATIONAL STRUCTURES

Check your understanding (page 70)

- Formal relations clearly set out the structure of the organisation, as well as helping to create the culture.
- Informal patterns help to create the culture of the organisation, as well as influencing the procedures and processes that are actually employed.
- Agreed methods of communication are part of the structure, systems and procedures adopted by the organisation.
- An agreed pattern for prioritising consumer complaints is clearly a procedure that determines how a process will be carried out.
- The way in which organisational members defer is something that has become part of the culture of the organisation, which determines how processes are carried out.

Case study: the growth of outsourcing (page 71)

1 All the activities are typically non-core activities. They are additional activities/processes that enable an organisation to run smoothly. However, they lend themselves to outsourcing so that organisations can focus on what they do best.
2 Outsourcing these activities enables the organisation to slim down its core activities. It can become leaner and fitter and less hierarchical. It will simply need to have an administrative function that makes sure contracted activities are carried out effectively in addition to its central structure.
3 By restructuring in this way, the

organisation can slash its costs while increasing its operational efficiency. It is no longer responsible for carrying out peripheral tasks that are not at the core of the organisation and its central purpose.

Case study: organisational chart for Melchester Football Club (page 74)

1 The groundsmen.
2 The team manager and players.
3 Coaching, and perhaps team management.
4 The accounts clerk.
5 The structure as set out in the diagram is too much based on separate functions. It tends to preclude the links between the various elements in the organisation (e.g. the administration department may serve each of the other functions).

Check your understanding (page 75)

These organisations may already have documents setting out this information. If this is the case, students should comment on the extent to which organisational charts are an accurate reflection of the structure and relationships within the organisation. Otherwise, the students need to create their own organisation chart by interviewing relevant staff in the key departments of the organisation. This needs to be organised by the tutor.

Case study: the organisation of an American city council (page 76)

1 The City Manager is responsible for overseeing the work of seven departments. The Director of Public Utilities is responsible for six departments. The extent of their responsibility may make it difficult to oversee the work of each of these departments effectively. Responsibility lies with the person at the top of the tree – so difficulties might arise if individual departments are not run smoothly.
2 The City Clerk/Treasurer is responsible for the business office and for data processing, personnel, purchasing and accounting.
3 The organisation is relatively tall, with five or six layers in some areas.
4 In the public works department, the chain of command is from the City Manager to the Public Works Manager, to the administrative and supply department which is then broken down into three main departments – streets, sanitation and maintenance/garage. Each of these departments has a number of subfunctions.
5 The City Council is elected by voters. The City Council consists of a number of officials and bodies, including the City Manager, the City Attorney, judges, the Hospital Board, etc.

Check your understanding (page 77)

Students simply need to refer to two organisations with which they are familiar. They do not need to draw a detailed outline of these two organisations – simply to know that one is tall and hierarchical and that the other is much flatter. They should then discuss the advantages and disadvantages of the two forms of structure.

Case study: Better Foods plc (page 79)

1 It could cut out the Hull factory and, by finding out which products sell best, concentrate on niche lines.
2 A matrix could be created based on product lines, for example soups, canned vegetables.

Check your understanding (page 81)

This activity is similar to that on page 77. Indeed, the two tasks can be done in conjunction.

Check your understanding (page 82)

In a dynamic marketplace, many organisations are having to restructure. Some of the details of changes taking place are provided in newspaper coverage. Closer to home, many of the organisations students work for are faced with restructuring plans. Students simply need to identify major changes and why these have come about.

Check your understanding (page 83)

Students may want to draw on personal experience to highlight situations in which an autocratic style of management has positive benefits (e.g. when decisions needed making quickly, or where there were a range of different views as to how to deal with a situation and someone needed to make a clear decision quickly).

Similarly for democratic situations, students can pinpoint times when this approach has been effective in an organisation they worked for (e.g. when it was important to win support and commitment from across the organisation).

Case study: teamworking at Jaguar (page 84)

1 The Jaguar situation appears to be on the right-hand side of the continuum, somewhere between 'manager defines limits' and 'manager permits subordinates to function within defined limits'.
2 Advantages of this approach are that it creates a committed workforce who feel they are involved in decision-making. Expert workers are able to contribute good ideas that improve the quality of decision-making and they help to improve the quality of production processes.
3 The team may spend too much time discussing decisions, and they may be inclined to try out impractical solutions which have been suggested. Too much time may be spent on talk and not enough on practical action.

Check your understanding (page 85)

Students could compare a work placement situation with the educational organisation they are studying in. Students need to identify: **a** the structure; and **b** the culture. They should then set out a list of relationships between the structure and the culture. For example, in a flat structure in which people work in teams, there may be a very democratic culture. This could be contrasted with a tall, hierarchical organisation in which relations are 'colder'.

CHAPTER 5 COMMUNICATION

Case study: E-business (pages 88–89)

1 Companies that do not join together with others will lose all the cost advantages associated with working together (e.g. in ordering supplies, in developing shared systems, etc.). Large firms realise that if they do not join with others in a networked relationship, they will quickly be left behind in the race for global domination.
2 ICT makes it possible for people working for organisations to have instant access to up-to-the-minute information, to place orders, to find out about stock items, etc. This enables just-in-time decision-making. ICT provides the means to supply organisations with vast quantities of information required for business decision-making, including database and ordering systems.
3 No. The organisation that fails to take advantage of the e-business revolution will rapidly lose competitive advantage. However, organisations must make sure they invest in the right systems that are appropriate for their industry and line of business.

Check your understanding (page 92)

Students are provided with a choice of communications activity. In the first option, they could, for example, set out a clear set of instructions for a person to make a cup of tea, or to hand in an assignment on time, or to wrap a present, etc.

In the second option, students need to focus on the effectiveness of oral instructions – how clear are they? Are they easy to understand? Do they contain all the essential information? Would anyone be able to understand them? etc.

Case study: setting out clear instructions at Fenland Foods (page 93)

1 The instructions are numbered and set out in flow chart form to make them easy to understand and to follow. There is a clear sequence of operations employees need to follow in preparing for work. It is

essential they carry out the instructions in the order provided and that no steps are left out.

2 Students need to make up their own minds about this, but the instructions do appear to be clear and well set out. Students might like to suggest improvements.

Case study: meetings (pages 95–97)

1 In the past tense.
2 To examine the discrepancy in the money being received in the bar.
3 Jane Hopkins (President).
4 The meetings will be kept on file and will be used to refer to in making future decisions. At some stage in the future, it may be necessary to refer back to an agreement made at the meeting and recorded in the minutes. The minutes will be read at the start of the next meeting to check an accurate record was kept.

Check your understanding (page 98)

Internal communication	Strengths	Weaknesses
Memo	Brief and to the point	May be misunderstood
Report	Gives detailed account/ discussion	May be over-length
Phone	Quick/easy/ convenient	No record of communication
e-mail	Quick/cheap	Leads to junk mail – some not read
Notice-board	Clear and visual	May not be read
Meetings	Issues can be discussed and grievances aired	May waste time

Case study: making an art form of external communications (pages 99–100)

1 Students need to examine a public relations campaign that has been featured on the television or in the press and to comment on how effective they feel it has been. Are there any statistics that indicate how successful the campaign has been? For example, when Levi's launched their 'Levi's in a laundrette' advertising campaign, this not only increased the sales of Levi's but also all other brands of jeans.
2 Again, students need to keep an eye on the press to identify situations where poor PR has backfired – for example, when Gerald Ratner said his jewellery was 'crap' it led to a massive loss in confidence in his jewellery chain. Other examples include where advertising campaigns have caused offence with sizeable sections of the buying population (e.g. adverts that show women in a poor light).
3 Students need to select a well-known organisation and then identify steps in a PR activity designed to enhance the image and perception of the product. They should justify the approach they have taken.

Check your understanding (page 103)

Students need to choose one sector (e.g. music and video) and identify the methods of external communication that will be most appropriate for firms in this sector. The most suitable answers are likely to focus on communications involving the Internet (e.g. through dedicated interactive websites) or promotions and PR activities that publicise the website. Clearly, the main point of difference with previous forms of communication is the emphasis on electronic ICT communications.

Case study: Iceland.co.uk (page 104)

1 Students will need to voice their own opinions on this. Clearly, Iceland.co.uk is a snappy and easy-to-remember name that is easily recognisable with the brand.
2 The change in name may cause a problem, as some people become confused as to the relationship between Iceland and Iceland.co.uk. For example, elderly people may be frightened away from a brand which, they feel, might be moving into the high-tech field, one which they are unwilling to penetrate.

Check your understanding (page 105, a)

Students need to identify the formal channels

(such as noticeboards, newsletters, meetings, memos, reports, etc.) and the informal ones (informal gossip, person-to-person e-mail, etc.). They should comment on the extent to which the informal channels support or work against the recognised channels of communication.

Check your understanding (page 105, b)

Students can use their own work experience to identify downward communications (e.g. when they have received orders from a superior) and upward communications (e.g. when they have passed information upwards). They should comment on the extent to which the organisation uses and benefits from upward communication. They should also comment on the balance between upward and downward communication – is this balance right? They should then evaluate communication patterns in order to identify ways of improving them.

Case study: communication networks (pages 106–107)

1 Students should identify situations in which they have come across communication networks that fit the patterns of wheel, chain, circle and completely connected networks.
2 They should then evaluate these networks in the light of their own experience of working with them. For example, which forms are best at communicating information, which forms keep everyone involved and motivated, which forms lead to the greatest breakdown in communications, etc.?

Check your understanding (page 108)

Using examples they are familiar with, students should identify situations in which communication channels have been restricted and ones in which there has been open access to information and communications.

Check your understanding (page 109)

Modern service organisations are extremely customer focused. In order to give full attention to customers, it is essential that customer service staff are empowered to make decisions at the interface with customers. In such organisations it would be inappropriate to use slow-moving communication channels which involve passing decisions downwards or in a chain. Students, therefore, need to show how a service organisation they work for or are familiar with enables open channel communications.

Case study: working on a customer's account (page 110)

1 Business processes are the steps involved in turning inputs to outputs. A number of individuals working in a bank can work collaboratively on such a process.
2 ICT enables everyone involved with processing the account to have instant access to details of the account. Details are recorded on screen so there is less room for clerical error in transferring information from one paper record to another. By processing information on screen, many handling costs are cut out.
3 Customers benefit from having instant access to information about their accounts at low cost. The bank benefits from reducing its costs and, hence, raising its profits. Businesses benefit from the use of ICT in handling business accounts.

Case study: the development of the Internet (pages 111–112)

1 Students need to provide justifications as to why the Internet has been so successful as a form of business communication. Obvious reasons are the ease with which it can be accessed globally, its low cost of operation, speed and accuracy of information recorded and communicated, etc.
2 Many different types of businesses will benefit from using the Internet. Some of these are new businesses offering e-commerce (e.g. new booksellers like Amazon and holiday companies). Others will be old companies (such as the supermarket chains) and Waterstone's the booksellers, who have transferred some or large parts of their business activity to e-commerce. Businesses that benefit most will be those seeking supplies from across the globe in large quantities, and firms which can place products on to a global marketplace.

3 The Internet poses all sorts of problems for organisations – the danger of competitors building a better Internet presence, the cost of setting up an effective website, the problems of Internet fraud, etc.

Case study: demise of the print industry in the USA (page 112)

1 The USA has tended to be the leader in Internet activity, with the UK and other nations following behind. However, many of the trends in the USA are being followed in the UK, and many business people have woken up to the importance of developing an appropriate and strong Internet presence.
2 In America (particularly in Silicon Valley), a very high percentage of people 'read' the Internet. However, it seems likely that, while there may be a fall in demand for some forms of printed materials (e.g. conventional newspapers), there will continue to be a rise in demand for other printed materials (e.g. magazines targeted at Internet users).

Check your understanding (page 115)

Students need to carry out an audit of a specific organisation, or part of such an organisation, listing all the ways in which ICT is used to help the organisation to run smoothly. By interviewing someone with a key position in the organisation, they should be able to identify the strengths and weaknesses of ICT in helping the organisation.

CHAPTER 6 PRODUCTION AND QUALITY

Check your understanding (page 118)

	Transforming resources	Transformed resources
Bank	Employees Cashpoints Desks and equipment	Customer accounts Customer records
Shoe factory	Employees Machinery	Leather/plastic/rubber Glue and binding material
Public house	Publican/bar staff Pumps/other equipment	Beer/spirits/foodstuffs

Case study: adding value to products (page 119)

1 Adding value is concerned with improving a product in terms of the customers' perception of that product and what they are prepared to pay for it. Value is added in the case of Lovehearts by the message people are prepared to pay for, or the combination of the simple ingredients in a sherbet dab.
2 Students will be able to think of many examples (e.g. Polo's selling of the holes, coloured Smarties, etc.).

Check your understanding (page 121)

- Top left: batch production.
- Top right: job production.
- Bottom left: continuous flow.
- Bottom right: project production.

Case study: Coca-Cola (page 121)

1 Coca-Cola add value in the production process by taking in inputs (such as sugar, water and caramel) and then blending them, bottling them, packaging them, and advertising and promoting them to create a product people are prepared to pay a much higher price for than the sum of the constituent parts. Coca-Cola engages in a lot of processes, such as advertising and promotion, which make the product more valuable to the final consumer.
2 Business organisations can and do add value in a variety of ways. However, there are not many that have been as successful in branding their product as Coca-Cola. Coca-Cola have been particularly effective in creating a distinctive logo and successive advertising campaigns that

make Coca-Cola a premium brand. Brands take a long time to build.

Check your understanding (page 122)

Good examples are the iMac, Parker pens, the Volkswagen Beetle, Nike shoes, etc.

Case study: Sony's Art Couture range of personal cinema entertainment (pages 122–123)

1 In many parts of the world, people have the disposable income to be able to afford cinema-quality entertainment in their own homes. Home entertainment gives far more choice than going to the cinema. Increasingly, tastes are moving in favour of such lavish consumerism.
2 Sony have been able to gain such a competitive advantage by continued expenditure on research and development into state-of-the-art electronics technologies and also by focusing on providing customers with a luxury home entertainment environment based on market research to find out what customers want.
3 In this case study, customers are looking for the sort of finish and entertainment environment Sony are offering. Design is the key differentiating feature that enables Sony to tap into the customers' desire for well-designed products.

Case study: JIT at Jaguar (pages 124–125)

1 By using the JIT system, Jaguar are able to operate in a clean and uncluttered working environment in which there is no call for surplus stock. This cuts down costs and increases the efficiency of production. Jaguar will not build up a stockpile of unsold cars, which would result in costs being incurred from damages and from having to store items.
2 **a** Cell production involves teams of workers working as a group to produce all or part of a product – they see it through from start to finish; **b** Lean production involves stripping out inessential operations, activities, storepiles, etc., to focus on smarter working.
3 Japanese working techniques can be applied to a range of manufacturing and service industries. From the 1990s onwards, they became particularly popular, with increased emphasis on teamwork, cellular working, cutting out waste, an emphasis on quality at every stage in production, etc.

Case study: automation in a modern brewery (pages 126–127)

1 The beer and lager market is based on the high-volume production of standardised products, enabling mass production.
2 Anything for which there is a large demand for standardised products (e.g. biscuits, confectionery, bottled water, newspapers, computers, pens, etc.).
3 Automation is not suitable where there is only a limited demand for a product, or where customers want a craft finish to a product.
4 Customers benefit from automation in lower prices; manufacturers benefit in lower costs.
5 Employees may lose out if automation removes the skill and variety elements from their work to replace them with standardised operations. Competitors who do not automate may also lose out.

Check your understanding (page 129)

This task will require considerable tutor direction. It will probably require the tutor to prepare the ground for the student investigation by briefing the production manager of a company (with which the school or college has an industrial link) as to the areas students need to find information about.

Check your understanding (page 131, a)

This task requires the students to consider a service organisation they come into contact with daily to assess how that organisation uses people, information and communications technology to add value. In the case of a supermarket, for example, this might involve the way in which customers are greeted at the door, how they are shown to products they are searching for, how ICT can be used to check whether an item is in stock, etc.

Check your understanding (page 131, b)

Students need to identify a company whose products seek to meet customer requirements and to explain how the company achieves this. They then need to focus on a product that is making a comeback because people in the organisation are beginning to listen to customer requirements. This sort of information can be obtained either from the marketing press or from the students' own knowledge: 'this product has improved out of all recognition recently. It seems as if someone is finally listening to us, the consumers.'

Case study: Xerox (page 132)

1 Xerox realised that, without customers, they would have no business. The document-processing business is highly competitive and involves frequent contact between the supplier and the customer. Xerox realised they had to get close to the customer.
2 In the modern world, all organisations have to build 'one-to-one' relationships with their customer base. Customer focus enables the organisation to provide the solutions for customers that lead to long-term relationships.

Check your understanding (page 134, a)

Students need to demonstrate an understanding of the TQM process and to show how an educational establishment would apply this to all aspects of teaching and assessment. For example, this would involve making sure that all students are aware of criteria and that students are regularly counselled about their performance in relation to criteria.

A TQM approach would involve checking quality at every stage in the teaching and assessment process rather than waiting until it was too late – for example, to tell students they were failing.

Check your understanding (page 134, b)

Students need to identify the strengths of the quality circle approach (e.g. in placing the emphasis on high quality, in everyone taking responsibility for quality issues and in involving people from across the organisation in quality circles). They also need to identify some of the potential problems (e.g. people not used to making decisions may resent being asked to take on responsibility, particularly if no extra pay is involved).

Check your understanding (page 135, a)

This activity simply involves the students interviewing the tutor and listing what they see as being the strengths and weaknesses of self-checking in comparison to inspection.

Check your understanding (page 135, b)

Students working in groups of three or four should carry out research into a local organisation which is employing the ISO9000 approach.

Check your understanding (page 136)

Students should examine the practices of a major retailer (e.g. a supermarket chain or a high-street retailer such as WH Smith) to identify practices which put that retailer ahead of the rest of the field.

Check your understanding (page 137)

Students could examine training and development activities in an organisation where they are working part time. Alternatively, they could look at the training and development policies of their own school or college.

Case study: Xerox and training (page 137)

1 Organisations which depend on the knowledge, skills and competence of their people to gain competitive edge must invest heavily in training these key knowledge workers. This is particularly true where employees interface directly with customers.
2 Managers who are used to telling people what to do are often uncomfortable when they have to share decision-making with others. Their style of management may be inappropriate for this new type of organisation, where they are expected to work with others in a collaborative way.

SECTION C OHTs

NOTES

OHT 1.1.1: business objectives

This OHT reproduces the newspaper headlines that appear in the early part of Chapter 1 of the student book. In introducing business objectives, the tutor could ask students to identify what they see as being the key business objectives as set out in the headlines. The tutor may like to write in an additional *Daily News* headline into the final square based on a current news story. Students should be encouraged to examine the business pages of a quality newspaper in their school or college library to identify headlines that point to the current objectives of a well-known organisation.

OHT 1.1.2: breaking even at Melchester Rovers

This OHT is based on Figure 1.3 from page 8 of the student book. The tutor needs to explain the key parts of the diagram.

The total revenue line is a straight line going up at £5 per spectator – because we are assuming each spectator pays a standard ground entrance fee. Total fixed costs are at £20,000. The total variable cost line is also a straight line rising at £1 per spectator. The break-even point is thus at 5,000 spectators where total cost = total revenue.

The tutor can draw on to the OHT an additional line for total revenue, which rises at a steeper gradient (i.e. £7.50 per spectator). At 5,000 spectators, this line would now reach £37,500, showing that Melchester Rovers are now making a profit of £12,500 if they get into the Conference League.

OHT 1.1.3a: the link between market share and profits (%); 1.1.3b: the experience curve

These two diagrams are to be used together. The table shown in OHT 1.1.3a is taken from Figure 1.4 on page 12 of the student book. The tutor should show the students this table and ask them to interpret it and to try to explain why profitability is likely to increase with market share.

Once students have outlined their views on this, the tutor can disclose OHT 1.1.3b, which shows how the average cost per unit will fall dramatically with output. There are all sorts of reasons for this, which are only in part related to production efficiencies. Another reason is the ability to spread the marketing and distribution activities over a larger output.

OHT 1.1.4: organisational cultures

These two illustrations relate to two well-known organisational culture types. The power culture diagram is taken from Figure 1.7 on page 23 of the student book and refers to a situation where one individual dominates the organisation from the centre. Students should be asked why they think the power culture is well illustrated by means of a spider's web.

The role culture illustration is taken from Figure 1.8 on page 24 of the student book. It shows a typical hierarchical structure that is divided into a set of functions. The tutor could use this diagram while describing the typical functional divisions of an old-fashioned organisation and/or how a bureaucracy works in practice.

OHT 1.2.1: the different types of private and public sector enterprises

This illustration is taken from Figure 2.1 on page 31 of the student book and outlines the various types of organisation in the public and private sectors. This OHT is designed to be revisited several times. The tutor can use the OHT to show the difference between the private and public sectors (i.e. the notes on the OHT in italics). The tutor could then spend time working down the private sector column, giving suitable examples of businesses that would fit into each of the categories.

Later, the tutor could examine key types of public sector organisations. On another occasion, the tutor could use the OHT to explain the processes of privatisation and nationalisation.

The tutor may want to make copies of this OHT so the students can keep it as a ready guide when they are covering the section on types of business.

OHT 1.2.2: share prices, 11 September 2000

This OHT provides material additional to that already in the student book. It has been designed to complement the work on page 37 where students are shown how to read share prices. Showing the OHT, the tutor can explain how the share price page of a national newspaper is divided into industrial sectors (e.g. banks, chemicals, etc.). Where this OHT differs from Figure 2.4 in the student book is that the OHT shows a week's change in share prices.

Students can be asked:

- Which share prices did best in the week shown? Why might this have been the case (e.g. a good set of trading results)?
- Which share prices performed worst? Why might this have been the case (e.g. problems in trading with the strength of the pound)?
- Which shares would make the best buys? (The students should consider this in terms of price changes, yield and P/E.)

OHT 1.2.3: multinationals

This OHT is divided into a number of sections. The top part provides tutors/students with a definition of a multinational. Students are then shown the logos of some well-known multinationals. They could be asked to supply additional examples of their own. Finally, the students are shown that the world's multinationals are concentrated in the 'triad' of the USA, the European Union and Japan. This material supports the notes on pages 40–41 of the student book.

OHT 1.2.4: charities

This OHT supports page 46 of the student book. It provides some key details about the nature and organisation of charities. The OHT provides the tutor with the opportunity to describe an organisation like Oxfam and enables the students to take down some key notes.

OHT 1.3.1: inputs – process – outputs

This OHT supports the text on page 57 of the student book and is based on Figure 3.3. It presents a typical inputs – process – outputs diagram. The tutor should work through the OHT from left to right.

The left-hand side indicates the key factors of production that are used in producing goods and services. Within the organisation, there then needs to be a system (the centre of the diagram) that is responsible for adding value to products. The system includes a number of functions that carry out the processes (e.g. marketing and production). The final result of processing (the right-hand side of the diagram) is to create goods or services that are the outputs of industry. However, the tutor must not forget waste. Please note it is not suggested that waste just flows from the administrative system – it flows from the total system!

OHT 1.3.2: the functions of the marketing department

This OHT is designed to outline the activities of one of the key functions in a modern consumer-focused business organisation. It complements the notes on page 62 of the student book.

Many students are not clear about the difference between sales and marketing. This OHT helps to clarify the key purposes of marketing – identifying, anticipating and satisfying consumer requirements. Students could be asked to explain how a marketing department can do this (e.g. through market research activities, by ensuring a close relationship between marketing activities and production, etc.).

OHT 1.3.3: sales and marketing

This OHT is based on Figures 3.9 and 3.10 from page 62 of the student book. This

OHT should be used in conjunction with OHT 1.3.2.

The tutor should first disclose the top part of the OHT and ask the students to suggest which of the two people shown is in marketing and which is in sales. Students will need to justify their answers. The tutor should then disclose the lower part of the OHT to identify the difference between marketing and sales.

OHT 1.3.4: organisational objectives

This OHT has been designed to complement pages 65 and 66 of the student book. The top part of the OHT shows that an organisation creates a corporate-wide objective – or mission – in this case, 'to be the world's number 1 airline'. The corporate objective then needs to be translated down a series of functional objectives that are in line with the corporate objective. If objectives are aligned, it is much easier for an organisation to pull together to achieve a common objective. The tutor might ask the students to identify other objectives for an airline company (e.g. for the sales department, for aircrews, etc.).

OHT 1.4.1: the 'new look' organisation

This OHT is based on Figure 4.1 from page 70 of the student book. It will help the tutor to describe how organisations have been turned on their heads so that empowered front-line workers are sometimes seen as the most important organisational resource. Intelligence-based knowledge workers have to interface with the organisation's customers. These intelligent employees, therefore, are seen as being of prime importance, and they are given considerable decision-making powers to interface with customers. They are able to do so because of the ICT support systems they work with today.

In this new organisational structure, the general managers take more of a back-seat role, creating the structures and systems that enable the organisation to function.

OHT 1.4.2: the shrinking core

This OHT focuses on the changes that were taking place in many large organisations, particularly from the 1990s onwards. The tutor needs to talk through this OHT in conjunction with the notes on pages 70–72 of the student book. The tutor could reveal the left-hand side of the diagram first and then work over to the right-hand side. The left-hand side shows a traditional organisation with a large, core workforce. The late 1980s saw the delayering of many organisations, with the contracting out of many activities that were no longer seen as central to the organisation. Companies like Boots, Shell, BP and many others experienced these changes. Students may be able to furnish anecdotal evidence of these changes based on their own and relatives' and friends' personal experiences.

OHT 1.4.3: activities commonly outsourced by companies, 2000

This table is taken from Figure 4.3 on page 71 of the student book. It complements the previous OHT and indicates some of the activities that have been shed from the core in many companies. The table indicates the sorts of activities that are being outsourced.

The students should be asked to explain why these activities have lent themselves to outsourcing.

OHT 1.4.4: the management grid

This OHT is based on the management grid shown in Figure 4.15 on page 83 of the student book. The tutor should outline the features of the key points on the grid – 'country club', 'team', 'impoverished', 'task' and 'middle of the road'.

The students should then be asked to consider organisations they have worked for and where these stand in relation to these points. For example, a student may have worked for an organisation where the emphasis is purely on meeting production targets with little thought for the people working in the organisation – 'task management', etc.

OHT 1.5.1: problems of communication

This OHT combines the two diagrams on page 87 of the student book. The tutor could first reveal the top half of the illustration and take the students through the key points of getting a message from the transmitter to the receiver.

When this has been effectively explained, the tutor could transfer the focus to examine the problem of noise (by using the leaky bucket theory). Students should outline all the reasons why messages are often inaccurately transmitted and received.

OHT 1.5.2: internal and external communications

This OHT is taken from Figure 5.2 on page 88 of the student book. It gives the tutor the opportunity to describe a range of internal and external communications within an organisation. This is designed to help the tutor give a broad-brush approach, rather than detailed notes. It makes sense to start off at the centre of the diagram and to describe a range of internal communications that are used in a specific organisation (e.g. the school or college). The tutor could then examine the external communications.

OHT 1.5.3: examples of external communications

This OHT could be used in conjunction with OHT 1.5.2 when the tutor is examining external communications. The OHT outlines the various stakeholder groupings that external communications would be sent to. Students should simply make notes from the OHT.

OHT 1.5.4: communication networks

The networks shown in this OHT are taken from the case study on pages 106–107 of the student book. The tutor could examine each of these networks in turn. As the tutor works through these, he or she should ask the students to describe actual situations they have been in which fit closely with the patterns the tutor has described. The students should then be asked to comment on how effective these networks proved to be.

OHT 1.6.1: operations management: the transformation of resources

The key operations of different organisations will vary – for example, in a hairdressing business, operations will be concerned with washing, cutting and styling hair. In a bank, the operations will be concerned with processing transactions, granting loans, etc. In a chocolate factory, they will be concerned with mixing ingredients, shaping the chocolate, packing finished chocolate products, etc. However, all these operations involve the transformation of inputs to create finished outputs in the form of goods and services.

This OHT is based on Figure 6.5 from page 118 of the student book. While working through the OHT, the students should be asked to provide actual examples (e.g. 'explain how a product you are familiar with involves transformation processes that turn inputs into final outputs').

OHT 1.6.2: which type of production?

This OHT outlines the four drawings presented in Figure 6.6 on page 121 of the student book. Students simply need to state which type of production is involved in each case (i.e. batches in the bakery, job production in hairdressing, continuous flow in bottling and project production in creating the nature film).

OHT 1.6.3: changing to the JIT system

This OHT complements the notes on JIT on pages 123–124 of the student book. Students should note that, instead of machines being grouped together, they are now grouped in cells in which employees can carry out a complete job.

Students could be shown the OHT and asked how the new situation varies from the old one, and to describe what they consider to be the benefits (and drawbacks) of the change.

OHT 1.6.4: moving to total quality management

This OHT outlines the changes that have taken place in the quality management process. The tutor should start from the left-hand side of the OHT and work towards the right, explaining improvements that have taken place over time. This OHT complements the notes in the student book on pages 132–134 and is taken from Figure 6.11 on page 133.

OHT 1.1.1. BUSINESS OBJECTIVES

Daily News

15 JULY 2000

Airtours share prices tumble with fall in profits warning

Daily News

14 JULY 2000

Boehringer may gain market share at expense of Glaxo

Daily News

16 JULY 2000

The Day Chocolate Company wins Business in the Community's Award for Excellence

Daily News

18 JULY 2000

Quality Award for Black Pudding Producer

David Hirst's of Barnsley have won another prestigious quality award for their finest Barnsley Black Pudding.

Daily News

OHT 1.1.2 BREAKING EVEN AT MELCHESTER ROVERS

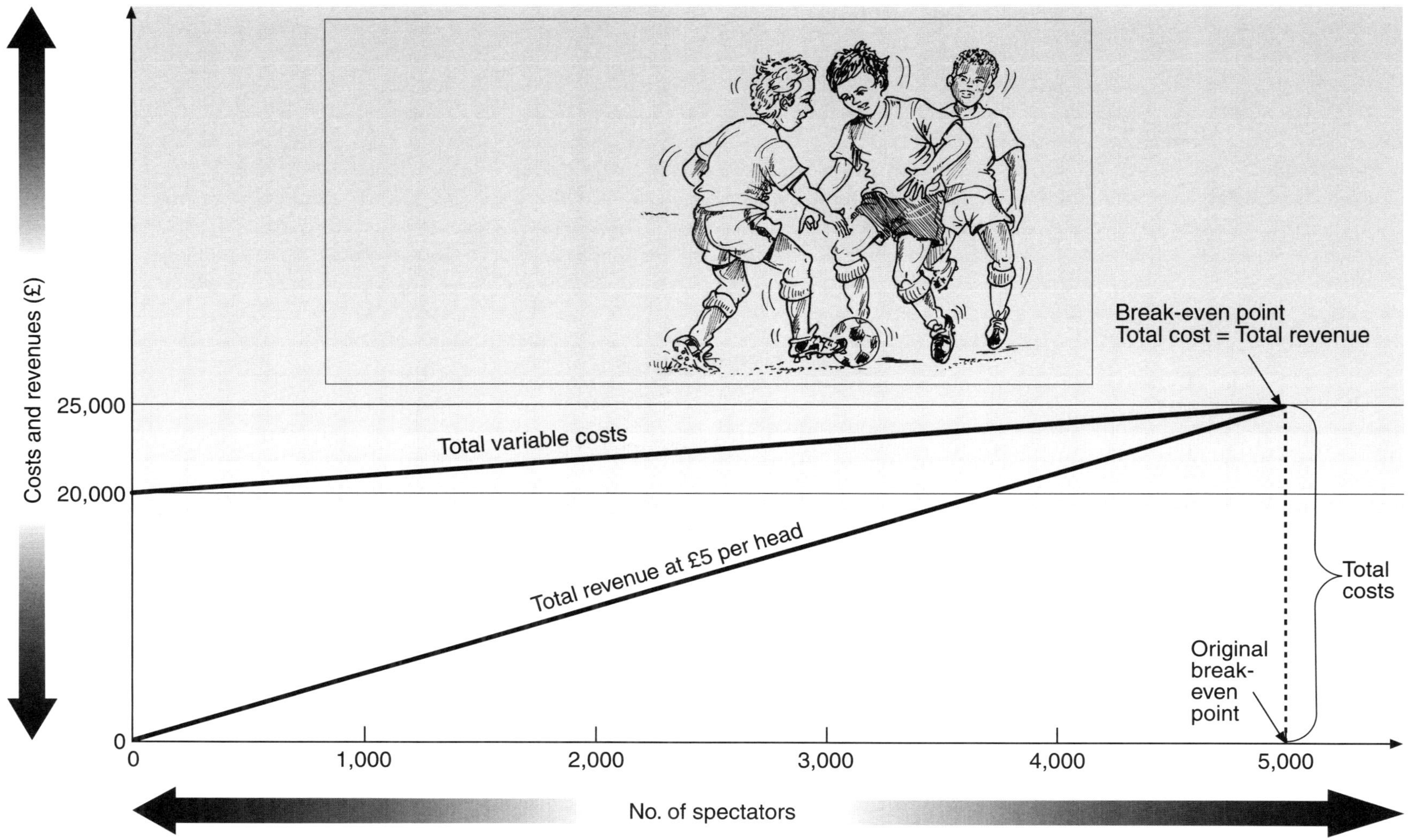

OHT 1.1.3A THE LINK BETWEEN MARKET SHARE AND PROFITS (%)

Market share (%)	Profitability (%)
Under 7	9.6
7 – 14	12.0
14 – 22	13.5
22 – 36	17.9
Over 36	30.2

OHT 1.1.3B THE EXPERIENCE CURVE

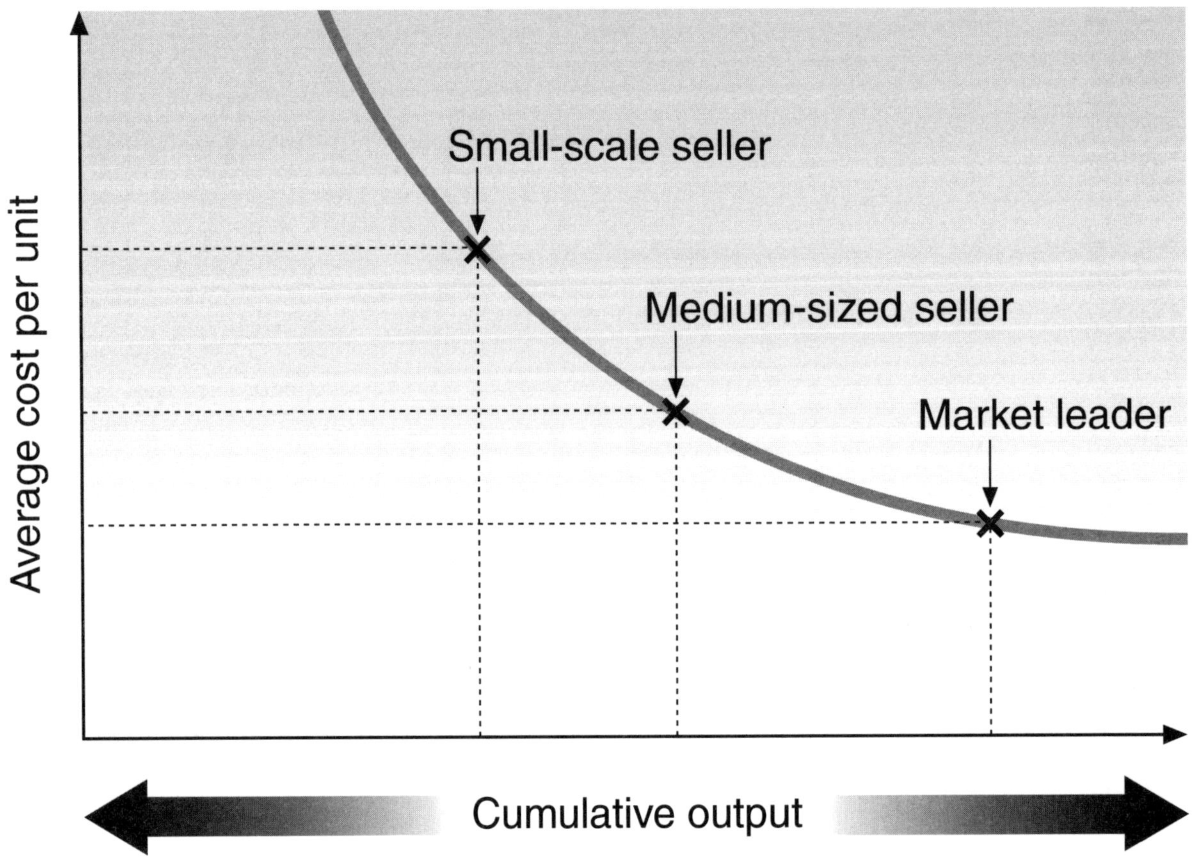

OHT 1.1.4 ORGANISATIONAL CULTURES

The power culture

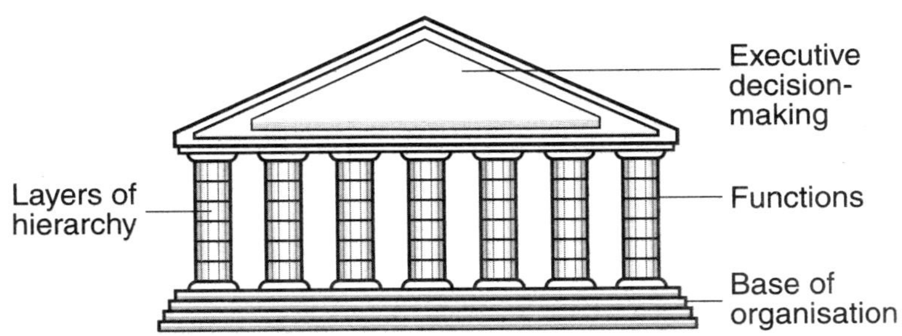

The role culture

OHT 1.2.1 THE DIFFERENT TYPES OF PRIVATE AND PUBLIC SECTOR

Private sector *(Owned by individuals and private organisations)*	Public sector *(Owned by the state)*
• Sole trader (1 owner)	• Public corporations and other government enterprises (owned by the government)
• Partnerships (2–20 owners)	• Municipal undertakings (owned by local government)
• Private limited companies (Ltd) (2–unlimited number of shareholders)	
• Public limited companies (plc) (2–unlimited number of shareholders)	
• Co-operatives (owned by 2 or more co-operators)	
• Franchises (owned by one or more franchisees)	

Nationalisation →

← Privatisation

OHT 1.2.2 SHARE PRICES, 11 SEPTEMBER 2000

Stock	Price	Yield	Change	P/E
Banks				
Abbey National	842.5	20.5	5.5	9.8
Woolwich	358.0	2.0	3.9	15.9
Chemicals				
BOC	949.0	-51.0	4.1	18.5
ICI	438.0	-26.0	8.1	27.2
Food and drug retailers				
Iceland	315.0	20.0	2.3	15.1
Tesco	215.8	-1.5	2.3	21.4
Oil and gas				
BP Amoco	652.5	6.0	2.3	21.3
Shell	609.5	5.5	2.6	28.5

OHT 1.2.3 MULTINATIONALS

Headquarters in one country – operations in a number of others

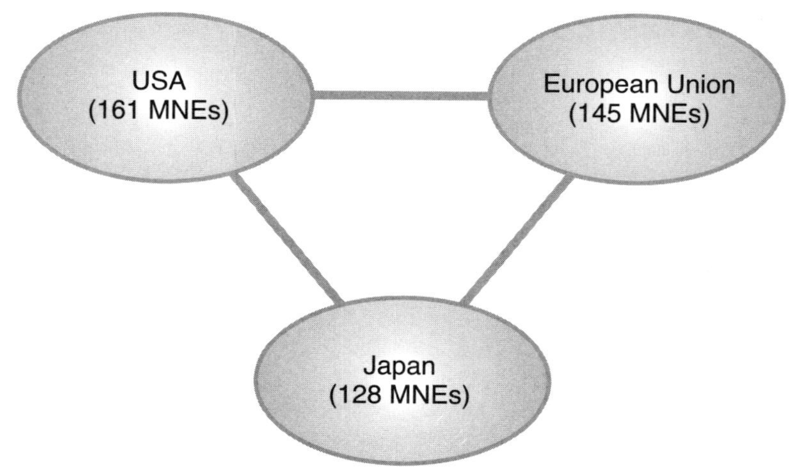

OHT 1.2.4 CHARITIES

Charities like Oxfam raise funds to help others/needy cases:

- The surplus is the balance after costs are paid.
- A group of trustees oversees the work of the charity.
- Charities must be registered and must produce an annual set of accounts.
- Charities employ paid managers.

OHT 1.3.1 INPUTS – PROCESS – OUTPUTS

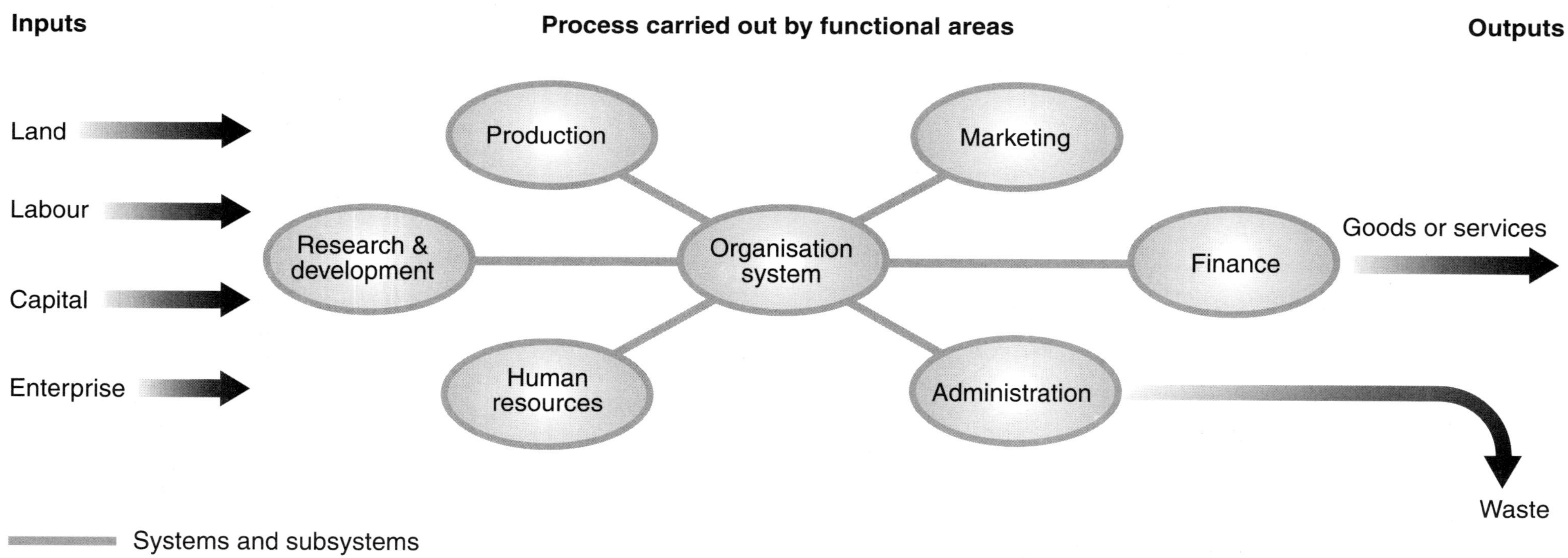

OHT 1.3.2 THE FUNCTIONS OF THE MARKETING DEPARTMENT

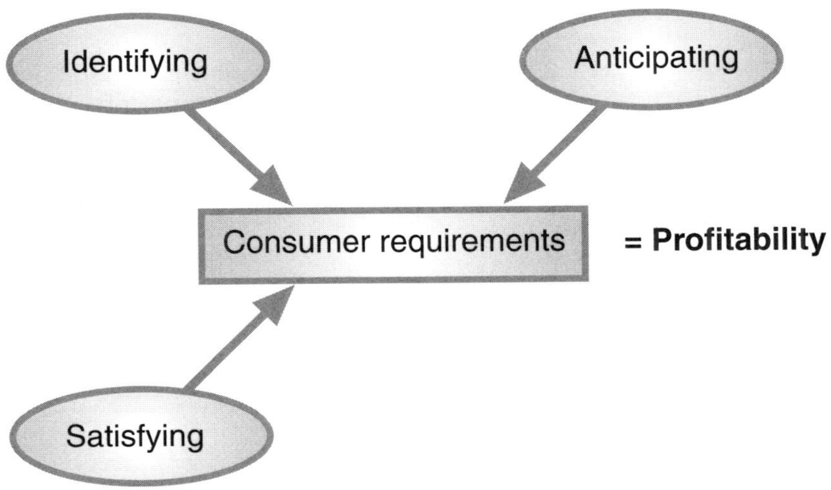

OHT 1.3.3 SALES AND MARKETING

Marketing

Getting the company to produce what the customer wants

Sales

Getting the customer to want what the company produces

OHT 1.3.4 ORGANISATIONAL OBJECTIVES

Corporate objective:
to be the world's number 1 airline

Marketing objective:
To identify and meet customer requirements of the number 1 airline

Finance objective:
To yield a high rate of return on investment

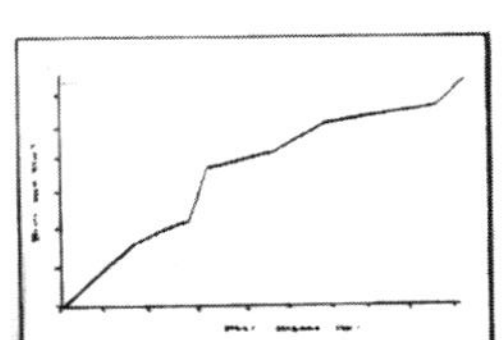

Administration objective:
To run the most efficient airline

OHT 1.4.1 THE 'NEW LOOK' ORGANISATION

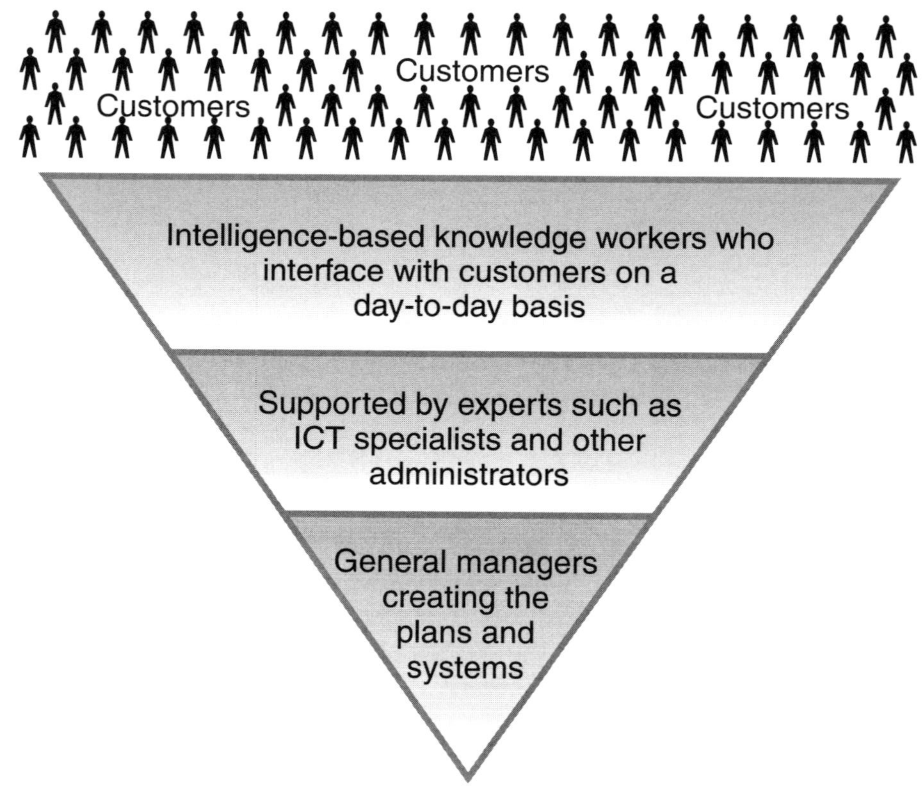

OHT 1.4.2 THE SHRINKING CORE

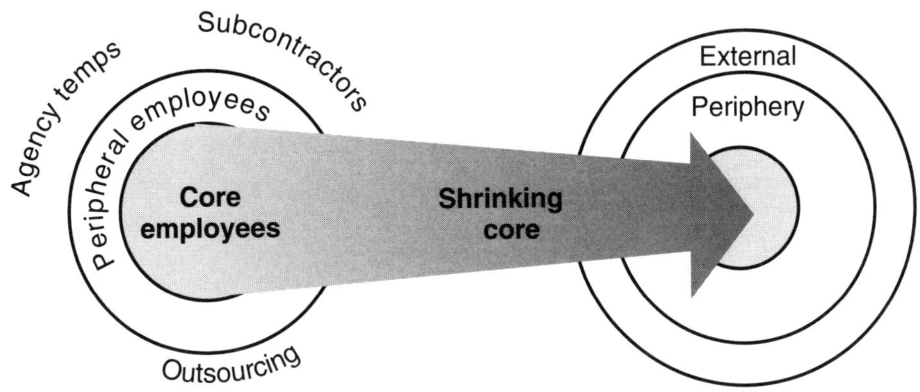

OHT 1.4.3 ACTIVITIES COMMONLY OUTSOURCED BY COMPANIES, 2000

Activities	Companies outsourcing (%)
Information and communications technology	30
Catering and cleaning	25
Facilities management	14
Advertising and PR	12
Security	10
Transport/logistics	10
Training and recruitment	9
Payroll and pensions	9
Others	9

OHT 1.4.4 THE MANAGEMENT GRID

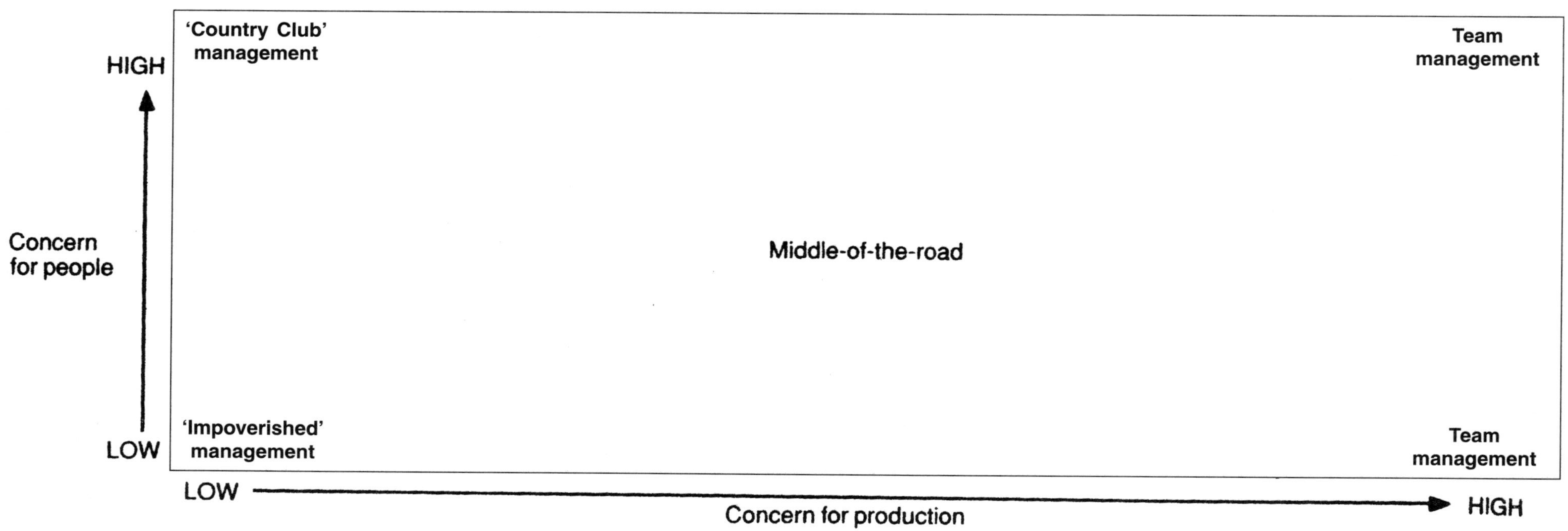

OHT 1.5.1 PROBLEMS OF COMMUNICATION

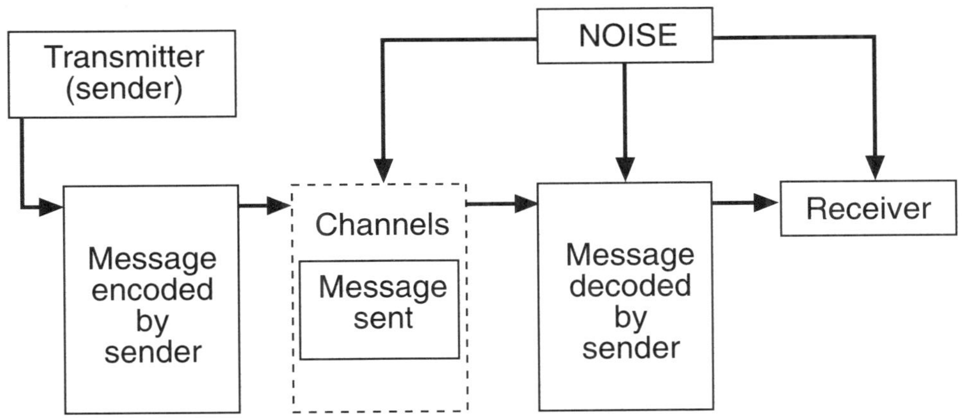

OHT 1.5.2 INTERNAL AND EXTERNAL COMMUNICATIONS

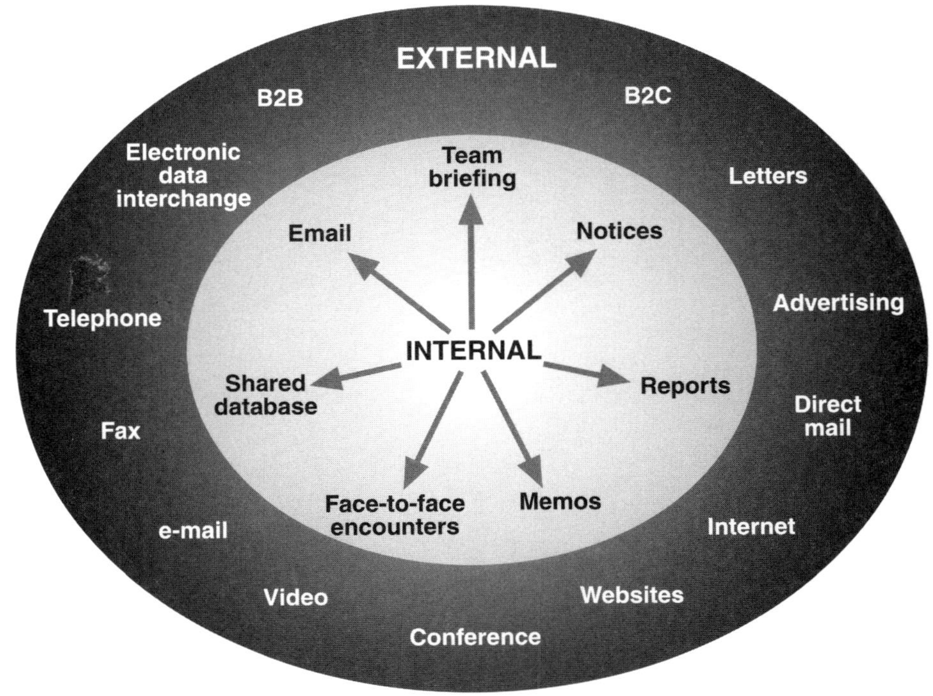

OHT 1.5.3 EXAMPLES OF EXTERNAL COMMUNICATIONS

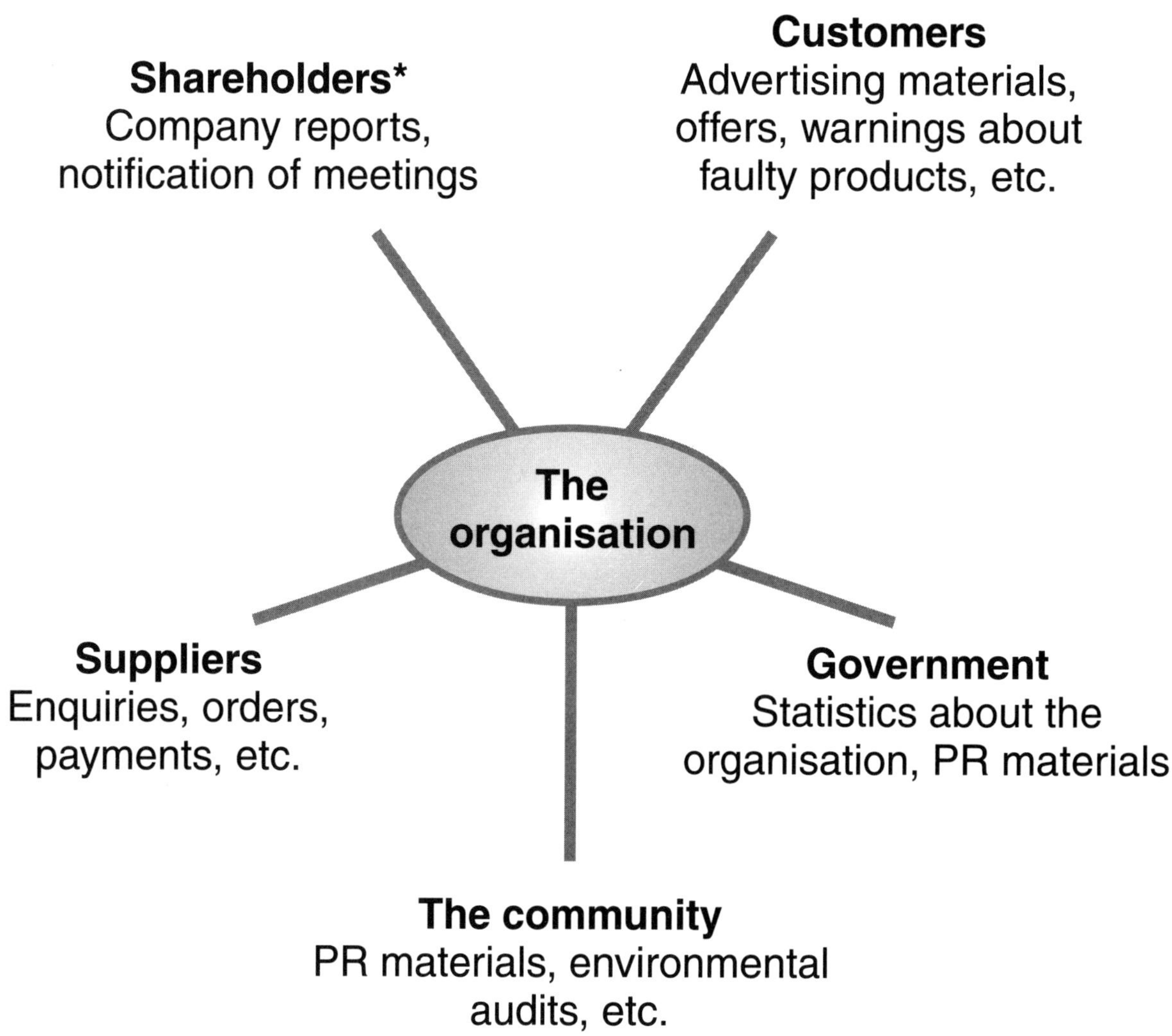

* Shareholders are really part of the organisation – they are the owners.

OHT 1.5.4 COMMUNICATION NETWORKS

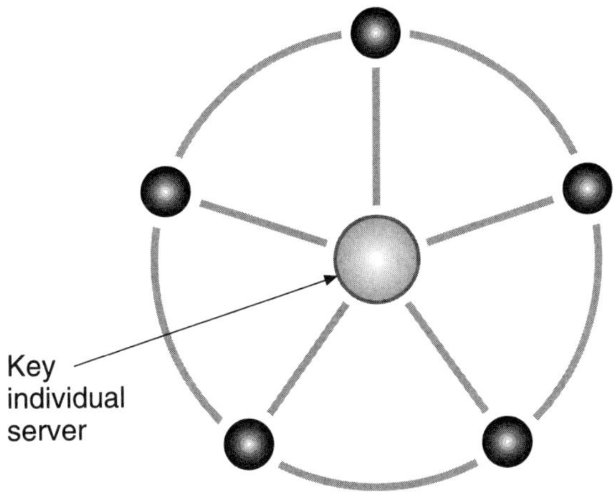

The wheel network

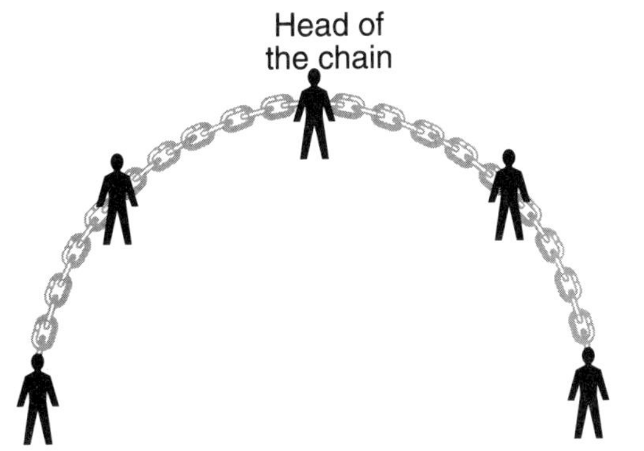

The chain network

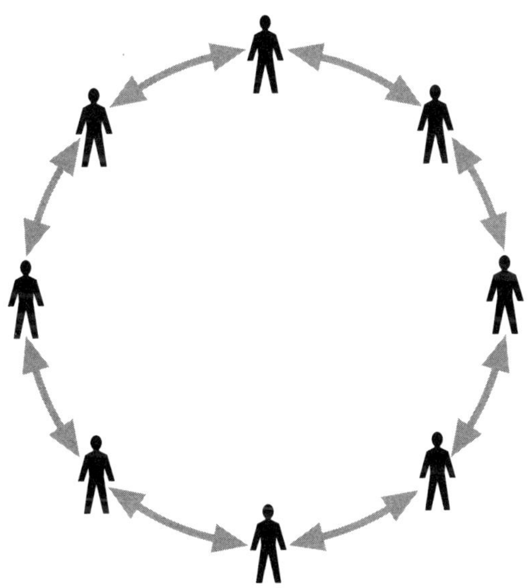

The circle network

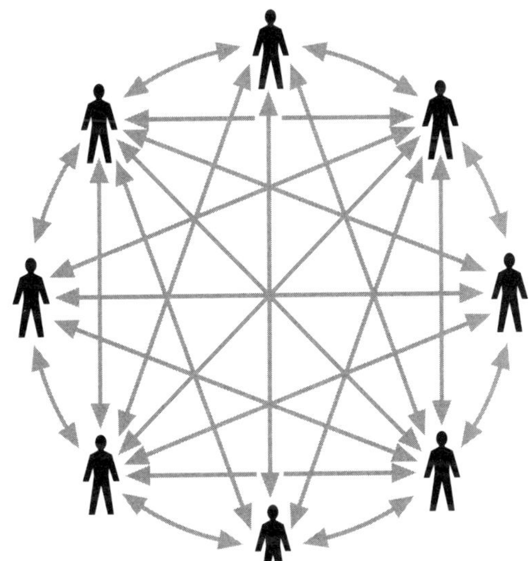

The completely connected network

OHT 1.6.1 OPERATIONS MANAGEMENT: THE TRANSFORMATION OF RESOURCES

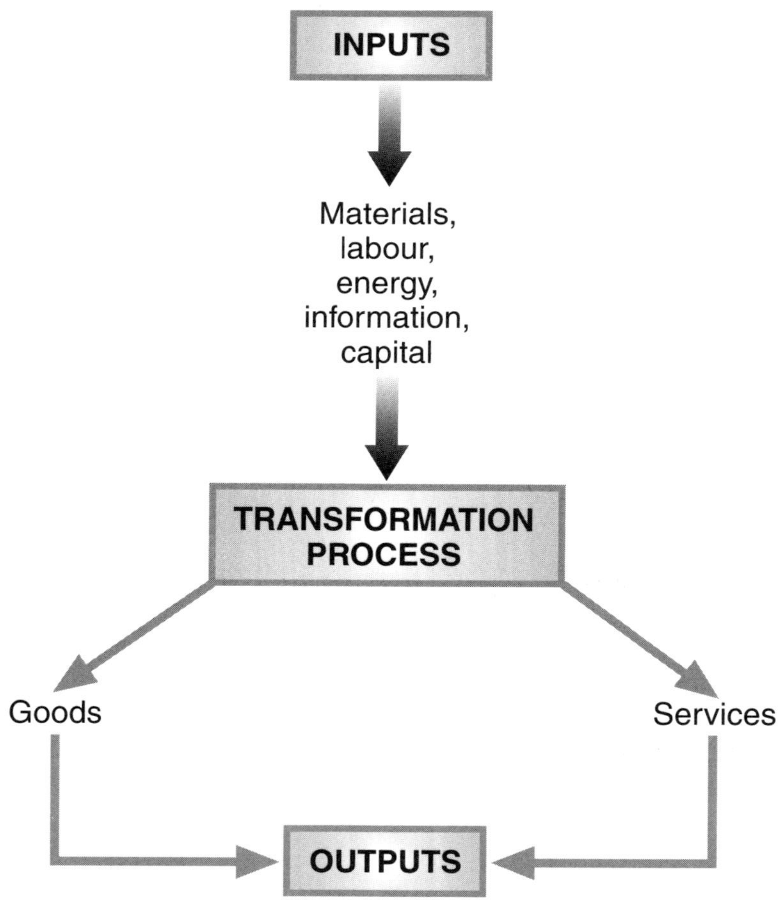

OHT 1.6.2 WHICH TYPE OF PRODUCTION?

OHT 1.6.3 CHANGING TO THE JIT SYSTEM

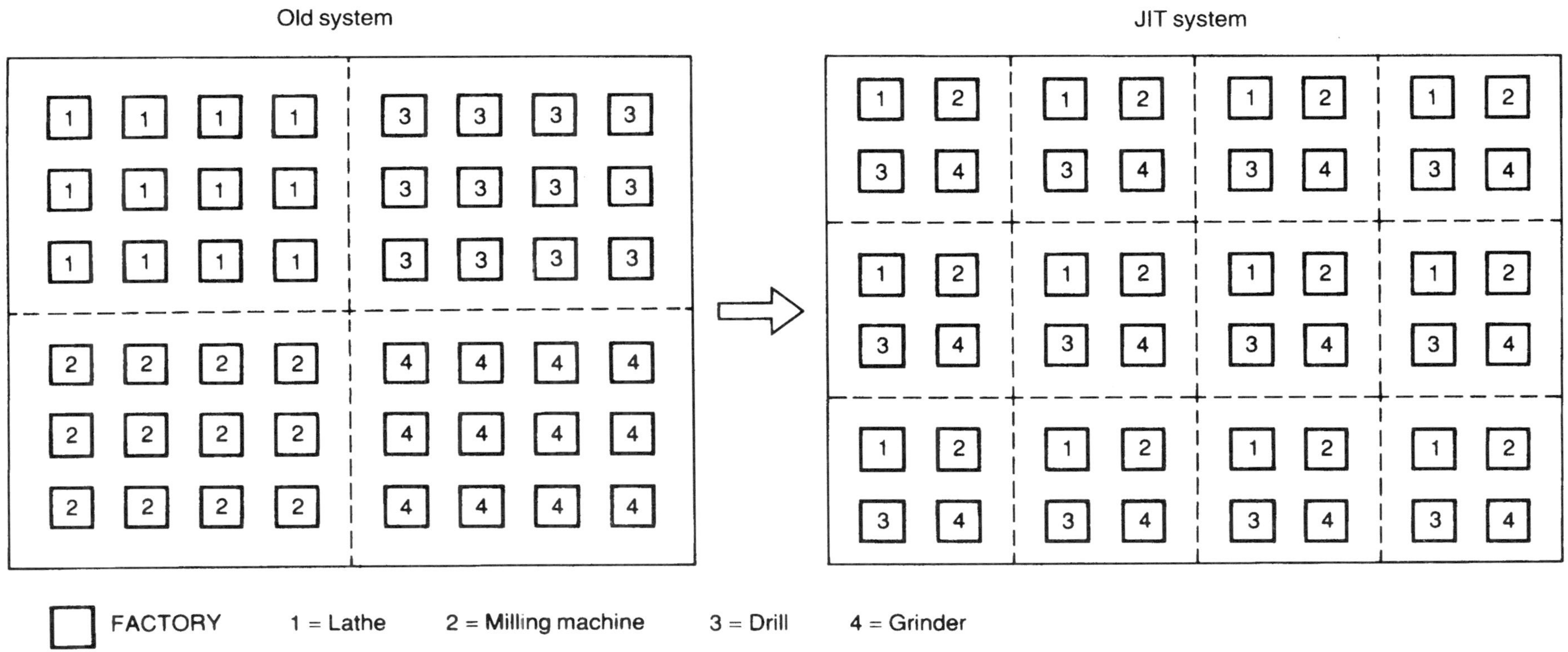

OHT 1.6.4 MOVING TO TOTAL QUALITY MANAGEMENT

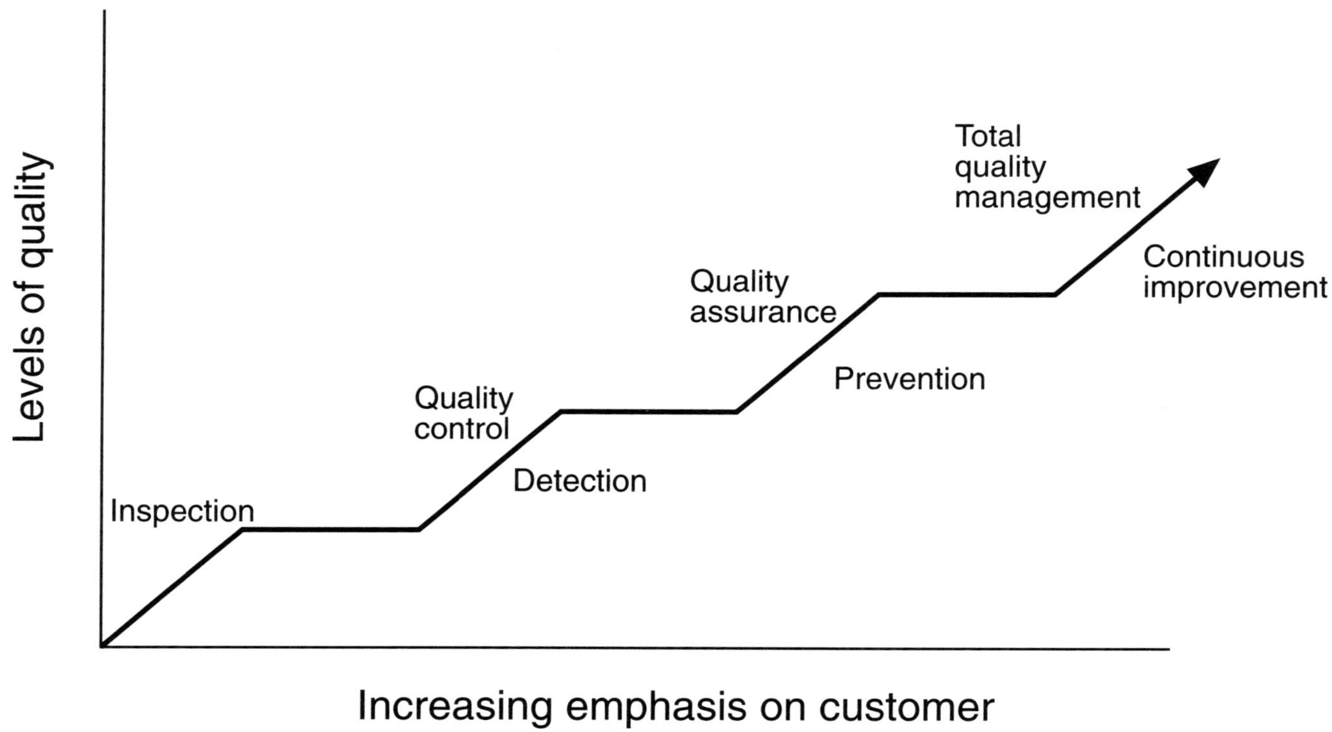

SECTION D ASSESSMENT

EXAMINING A MEDIUM-SIZED OR LARGE BUSINESS

This assessment should be carried out using the report format described in the student book on page viii.

1 Classifying the business according to its ownership

The business you study is likely to have one of the following forms of ownership:

- partnership
- private company
- public company
- franchise
- charity or voluntary organisation.

In a partnership, you should interview one of the partners. In a company, interview the company secretary or a senior manager. In a franchise organisation, interview the franchisee. In a voluntary organisation, interview one of the senior volunteers or a manager in a charity organisation.

Find out why the organisation has chosen the form of ownership it has. You could list the advantages of the particular form of ownership using the knowledge you have gained from the student book, but it would be better if you asked the person you were interviewing to list the advantages and disadvantages for the specific organisation you are investigating.

2 Describing and explaining the objectives of the business

All businesses need to have objectives. Many larger organisations have what is called a mission statement, which describes the general aim of the organisation. The organisation will then have a number of sub-objectives to support the mission statement. The objectives set out what the organisation is trying to achieve. Find out what these objectives are. For example, in a company there will be corporate objectives for the whole organisation. These will then be broken down into sub-objectives for the different parts of the organisation.

For a grade C you need to be able to make judgements about how successfully the business is meeting its objectives. For example, if it has an objective to win 20% of the local market, is it meeting that objective? If it has an objective to satisfy customers, how many customer complaints has it received? etc.

3 Describing the functional areas of the business

The business will be divided up into a number of parts (e.g. marketing, production, administration, finance and accounts, etc.). Draw a diagram to show the various functional areas. These will vary from one business to another (e.g. a college might be split up into administration, academic, financial, etc.). You will need to make some judgements about how effective the functional organisation of the organisation is. Could it be improved by dividing it up in another way? Talk to people who work in the various functional areas.

4 Describing the management style and culture of the business

Different managers operate in different ways. Some of them are very authoritarian, wanting to oversee all decisions and processes. Other managers are more democratic and encourage employees to make decisions for themselves. Some managers encourage their employees to take risks, while others want to control everything that is taking place in the organisation.

The culture of the organisation is the typical pattern of doing things and the set of values in the organisation. The student book describes a range of cultures – the role culture, the power culture, the task culture and the person culture. Which of these cultures is most typical of the organisation you are studying? If you interview a senior manager in the organisation, he or she will be able to describe the typical culture. If you work for the organisation you are studying, you will already have a good idea of its culture.

To achieve a grade C, you will need to analyse how the organisational structure, culture and management style of the business affect its performance and operation and help it to meet objectives.

To achieve a grade A, you will need to explain how the organisational structure, culture and management style inter-relate in the business and will also need to evaluate their impact (and that of ICT) on the business's performance.

To obtain the higher grades, you will not only be able to draw organisational charts, describe the main functions of the organisation, explain the management style and the typical culture of the organisation but you will also need to show how the effectiveness of these things help your organisation to perform at a high level.

A high-performance company will need to have:

- a clear and easy-to-understand structure
- a structure that motivates people who are working for the organisation
- functions that are appropriate to the business and which are easy to understand and welcomed by employees
- a management style that encourages employees and enables the organisation to meet its objectives
- a position culture which people who work for the organisation feel comfortable with.

5 Describing the use of ICT for internal and external business communication

You will need to investigate and then describe the key methods the organisation uses for internal communications (e.g. e-mail, memos, phone links, company noticeboards, etc.). You will also need to explain all the major forms of external communications (e.g. a website for dealing with customers, the telephone, direct mail, etc.).

To gain a grade A, you will have to identify the strengths and weaknesses of existing communication systems and point out any improvements that could be made. For example, the business may not use some of the modern forms of electronic communication, such as the Internet, which are being successfully used by rivals.

6 Explaining the production process and quality assurance/control system used by the business help it to add value to its product or service

Here you will need to find out how the major production process the organisation is involved in works. Identify the key inputs, processes and outputs involved in production. Show how each stage of production adds value to the product (i.e. makes the product more desirable to customers). You will also need to investigate quality processes employed by the organisation. To gain a grade A, you should show how the organisation can improve its quality control or quality assurance and how this might help the organisation to achieve its objectives better and to improve the performance of its functions.

CHECKLIST FOR CARRYING OUT YOUR ASSIGNMENT TO A HIGH STANDARD

Tick the boxes

1 I have classified the business according to ownership. ☐

2 I have identified the benefits of the pattern of ownership to the business studied. ☐

3 I have described the objectives of the business. ☐

4 I have weighed up how successful the business is in meeting its objectives. ☐

5 I have described the key functional areas of the business. ☐

6 I have explained how the functional areas help the business to meet its objectives. ☐

7 I have shown how the organisation structure affects the performance of the business. ☐

8 I have described management styles within the organisation. ☐

9 I have shown how the management style affects the performance of the business. ☐

10 I have described the culture of the business. ☐

11 I have shown how the culture of the business affects its performance. ☐

12 I have described the use of ICT for internal and external communications in the business. ☐

13 I have evaluated the effectiveness of the communications systems used. ☐

14 I have explained the main production processes in the organisation. ☐

15 I have shown how the production processes help the organisation to add value to products or services. ☐

16 I have explained the quality assurance/control systems used by the business. ☐

17 I have evaluated the effectiveness of the quality assurance/control systems. ☐

18 I have examined the impact of quality assurance/control systems on the business's ability to meet its objectives and the ability of the functions to operate well. ☐

HOW YOU CAN USE KEY SKILLS WHILE WORKING ON THIS ASSESSMENT

Communication skills

- *Producing the report itself.* Use the report format suggested on page viii of the student book.
- *Making a group presentation.* If a group of you carry out this investigation, you can prepare a Powerpoint presentation to the managers of the organisation you have studied. Alternatively, you could make your presentation to your AVCE class. The presentation could include all the areas covered in your assessment. Alternatively, it may cover selected parts of your assessment (e.g. a presentation on the structure of the organisation studied, a presentation on the management styles and culture of the organisation, etc.).
- *Group discussions.* After researching the management styles and cultures of different organisations, you and your tutor could discuss different cultures and management styles and how effective they appear to be.
- *Researching information.* As part of your investigation for the assessment, you should be able to show you have researched complex documents. For example, you may examine company reports setting out organisation structures and functions.

Information technology skills

- *Planning to use and researching information from the Internet.* There is a good chance the company you choose to investigate has an Internet presence (e.g. a website setting out the organisation structure and functions).
- *Using information technology skills to present information.* You may want to use a graphics package to help you to create organisational charts, or to set out diagrams to illustrate production and quality control processes in the organisation you are studying (e.g. a chart to show the key inputs, processes and outputs).

Improving your own learning and performance

- *Developing independent study skills.* Working with your tutor, you should be able to develop and then carry out a plan which enables you to carry out research independently and with other students. By setting targets and clear action steps, you will be able to improve the management of your own learning. For example, you should set out a plan to interview people in the organisation you are studying (developing clear sets of questions to ask) and follow-up procedures to clarify information.

Working with others

- *Liaising with members of the organisation you are studying.* The organisation you are working with will want to help you – but will want to feel you are organised and are working in a constructive way. This places considerable responsibility on you to make sure you work in a reliable manner.

- *Reporting to the organisation you are studying.* It is important you give feedback to the organisation you are studying on the progress you are making. It is helpful to send a copy of your final report to the organisation which has helped you – or even to make a Powerpoint presentation.
- *Working with others to review performance.* You can learn from constructive feedback about your performance by listening carefully to the judgements of others.

SECTION A DISCUSSION POINT

Daily News

6 JULY 2000

Retailers feel the pinch

Sales growth in Britain's shops fell last month, according to the Confederation of British Industry. Together with figures indicating the boom in house prices is over, the survey prompted renewed calls from industry and homeowners for the Bank of England to leave interest rates on hold.

As the bank's monetary policy committee began its deliberations yesterday morning, the latest snapshot of the retail sector published by the CBI showed that sales growth in June was at its lowest for more than a year. The balance of retailers reporting increased sales volumes last month dropped to a +15% from +45% the previous month – the second largest fall in the survey's 17-year history.

A spokesperson from the CBI states that: 'There is no sign of a consumer boom, so interest rates can be safely left on hold.'

The news of a slowdown on the high streets came as separate data showed that the growth in the services sector, of which retailing is part, had eased to a five-month low. Over the past four years, the services sector has been the main engine of growth in the economy, outpacing the flagging manufacturing sector.

All the main subsectors of service economy reported slower growth, according to recent figures. Firms have also reported a marked downturn in plans to take on new workers.

If the bank leaves interest rates on hold today at 6%, as is widely expected, it will be the fifth consecutive month it has made no change. As each month passes, commentators are becoming increasingly confident in their prediction that the next move by the MPC will be downwards.

Expectations that interest rates have peaked helped to send sterling sliding against other major currencies yesterday. The pound fell to $1.5105, after having peaked at $1.5166, while against the euro it slipped to 0.6327p from 0.6278p earlier.

POINTS FOR DISCUSSION

1 Why does the article suggest there were no grounds for raising interest rates at the time?

2 What might have been the impact of a rise in interest rates on business?

3 Why do you think the service sector of the economy had been doing much better than the manufacturing sector?

4 Why did expectations that interest rates had peaked help to send sterling sliding?

5 Why might the fall in the pound have helped UK businesses?

SECTION B SUGGESTED ANSWERS

CHAPTER 7 HOW COMPETITION IN THE MARKET AFFECTS BUSINESS

Case study: agricultural prices in June 2000 (page 145)

1 Coffee is the most expensive commodity per tonne and barley is the cheapest. This results largely from coffee's scarcity value. Coffee can be grown only in limited geographical areas, whereas barley can be grown in much wider areas of the world due to the climatic and soil factors associated with this crop's growth. The demand for coffee is also more intense – perhaps because of the caffeine content – so coffee is seen as a necessity with no very close substitutes.

2 Typically, as we move into the future, we expect futures prices to rise. This is because of the uncertainty associated with moving into the future. For example, a poor harvest next year may push up prices. In order to anticipate this, traders are prepared to pay a higher price for future trades. This is not always the case, however, because another factor to consider for agricultural commodities is when the harvest is due.

Check your understanding (page 145)

Students are asked to carry out an Internet search using www.bloomberg, which provides a host of information about commodity trading and share dealing.

Check your understanding (page 146)

1 Tea, coffee, sugar, chocolate bars, bread, rice, syrup, cake mixture, breakfast cereals, fresh orange juice, etc.

2 Luxuries and necessities:

Luxuries	Necessities
Caviar	Bread
Videos	Rice
Cream cakes	Cereals
Bottled water, etc.	Milk, etc.

3 Clearly, the list is open to what the student considers to be a luxury or a necessity. For example, deodorant may be regarded as a luxury by some and a necessity by others. Students should identify consumer durables such as television sets, computers, washing machines, cars, etc. They should discuss the extent to which price was a determinant in the buying decision.

Check your understanding (page 147)

The first part of this task is quite easy – simply to list the items of capital employed by an organisation (e.g. in a supermarket it would include the shopping trolleys, computer systems, etc.).

More significantly, the student needs to find out about the sorts of factors which determine the level of investment in the organisation (e.g. level of optimism about future sales, sales growth patterns, profitability, etc.). Although detailed information about this is best prised from the head office of an organisation, it should be possible to glean general information from someone who works for the organisation and who has a feel for how the business works.

Check your understanding (page 148)

The students are required to interview a buyer or salesperson in a manufacturing firm to find out how he or she is involved in buying and selling. The sorts of questions to ask are how the buyer or salesperson develops leads, whether he or she deals with a small or large number of contacts, how he or she nurtures these contacts over time, the extent to which he or she shops around, etc.

Check your understanding (page 149)

Service areas students might be familiar with include retailing, hairdressing, education, banking and insurance. They should outline the nature of the contact that takes place between the customer and the service provider. They could discuss the way the quality of this contact has changed in recent times and, possibly, outline ways in which organisations could improve these contacts.

Case study: demand and supply for 'Sweet Pastilles' (page 152)

1

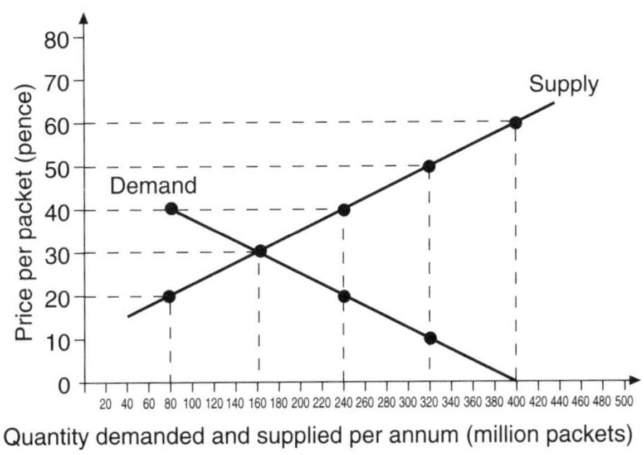

2 The equilibrium price is 30p. This is where the quantity supplied to the market is equal to the quantity consumers are prepared to purchase. Some 160 million packets will be supplied per year at this price.

3 At 10p, buyers will want to buy 320 million packets. However, suppliers are not prepared to supply the market at this price because they would be unable to cover their costs of production. Price, therefore, has to rise, which will cut back demand. Equilibrium will be restored when the price has risen to 30p. At 40p, customers demand 80 million packets per year. Not many would buy at this price because of the high price. However, suppliers would be prepared to supply 240 million packets. This would lead to unsold stocks, forcing producers to cut supply until equilibrium was restored again at 30p.

Check your understanding (page 152)

Students should choose a market they are familiar with (e.g. cosmetics, newspapers, toys, foodstuffs, computers, etc.). The suppliers will be the firms that produce these products (e.g. Nestlé in the case of coffee, Cadbury-Schweppes in the case of confectionery and soft drinks, etc.). However, it is not just the manufacturer involved in the supply process: the students also need to consider the retailer. The end consumer will be the person who ultimately purchases a finished product. However, intermediaries are also customers for manufacturers.

Over time, demand for a product will increase if it becomes more popular, if incomes of the relevant population increase, if people become more aware of the product, if the relevant population increases in size, if rival products become more expensive and if complementary products become cheaper.

Check your understanding (page 153)

Although we do not know Fred, we might assume he would see:

Normal goods	**Inferior goods**
Digital sound system	Skegness holiday
Armani suit	Black and white television
World cruise	Boiler suit
A Rolls-Royce	Ford Ka

Check your understanding (page 155)

Students should choose a good to examine (e.g. set-top boxes for digital televisions). Increased incomes have made these more affordable (demand shifts to the right), and advertising has made consumers increasingly aware of this option (demand shifts to the right).

Check your understanding (page 156)

- Prices of computer chips to temporarily rise – this is likely to lead to a rise in production costs of all products that use computer chips, leading to a slight reduction in the supply of these goods.
- If wages fall in the printing industry, this could lead to a fall in the production costs of printing and therefore an increase in supply (although other factors may be working against this).

- Good growing conditions for French wines may mean an increase in the supply of these wines.
- New subsidies for start-up businesses in high-tech industries would encourage supply in these industries, as the subsidy effectively reduces production costs.
- The bad coffee harvest in Brazil would lead to a fall in the supply of coffee, as less is produced.
- By raising taxes on smoking, the government would discourage the supply of cigarettes, as the tax would increase costs of production.
- Earthquakes in South East Asia would disturb the supply of products from this geographical region – although they might encourage suppliers of competing products in the west to increase supplies.

Case study: retailing in the UK (page 157)

1 Competition in the retailing sector helped to drive down profits. More and more firms were offering similar goods and services. At the same time, competition from e-commerce was driving down costs because retailing over the Internet requires much less retail outlet space and incurs far fewer costs than running a conventional retailing outlet.

2 E-commerce has been significant in that it has developed so quickly. Initially, we saw a range of specialist firms (such as Amazon) develop an e-commerce presence. Perhaps a more significant step was when existing businesses began to develop e-commerce initiatives of their own.

3 Industries where competition increases will be ones where there are more competitors (e.g. telephony), where rival firms begin to offer more and more similar products and services (e.g. banking and insurance) and where e-commerce is beginning to take a hold (e.g. sale of flight tickets).

Case study: singing socks (pages 158–159)

1 Sound Tactics are able to make healthy profits because of the way the product is differentiated from rivals. First of all came the good idea, which created value by combining the novelty of the music with the sock product. The company then spent time and money on research to make the product better than rival offerings. The socks are sold through upmarket distribution channels.

2 In the longer period, if abnormal profits are initially being made, this will attract new competitors to enter the market, who will then compete over price to win market share.

Case study: restricting access to the Internet (page 160)

1 Companies which invest a great deal in developing new leading-edge technologies often feel they have a right to protect their own ideas and innovations against others, who may use their new developments as a means to develop complementary products. Companies like Microsoft may feel they are developing products and technologies which benefit the wider consumer in both the long and short run, and that others are jumping on the bandwagon of their ideas.

2 Restrictive practices are harmful to consumers when they prevent new firms from entering the market. When new firms enter the market, this not only creates a more competitive environment (driving down prices) but also leads to more innovations and ideas because there are fresh minds tackling problems and new companies injecting innovation into an existing marketplace.

Check your understanding (page 161)

The students need to contrast two markets:

1 a highly competitive one (e.g. service stations in a busy town, rival providers of mobile phones, tabloid newspapers, etc.)

2 a market where there is little competition (e.g. a service station on a motorway where there are no others nearby, the provision of emergency plumbing services outside the 9–5 slot, etc.).

They should compare these markets in terms of such features as profit potential, the relative power of consumers and suppliers, etc.

Check your understanding (page 162)

The tutor may need to provide guidance to students on this task by keeping a record of articles covering this topic (e.g. the impact of the spread of the textile industry to low-cost locations, the globalisation of motor vehicle production, etc.). If the tutor keeps a record of when suitable articles appear in the quality press, he or she can refer the students to such articles on Internet or CD-ROM copies of these newspapers.

Check your understanding (page 163)

1 The text refers to Microsoft as having considerable influence because of its market domination. Other examples could be Nestlé in the coffee market, Coca-Cola in the cola market, Heinz in the production of baked beans, etc.
2 Small firms that take up only a very small section of a total market will have a lot less influence. Examples might include a small-scale provider of cheese or a small farmer producing onions or potatoes.

Check your understanding (page 164)

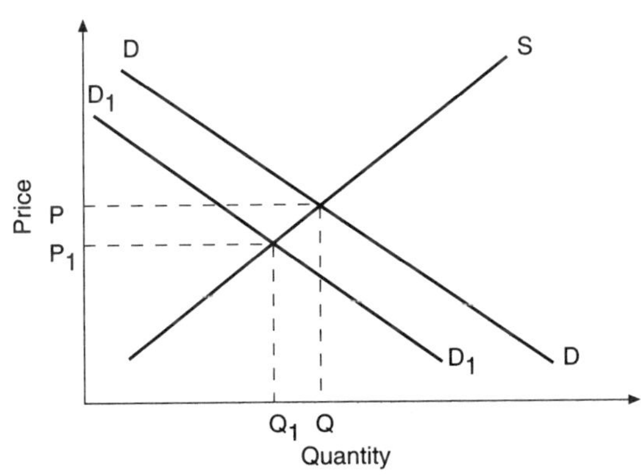

Demand shifts to left from D to D_1

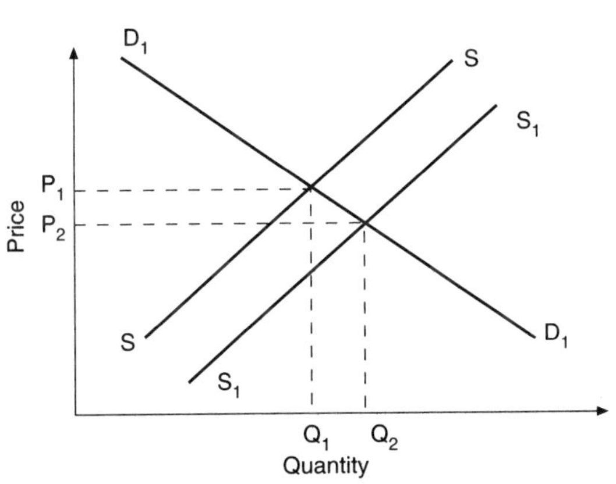

New technology pushes supply curve to right

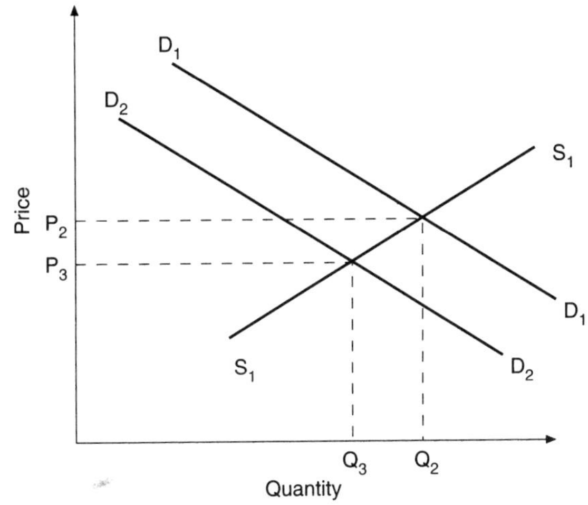

Teenagers cut cigarette smoking so demand shifts to left again

Case study: Tesco and Sainsbury's battle for the home-shopping market (page 165)

1 Providing direct home shopping adds value by providing a more desirable service for consumers. Consumers have to do less of the work themselves and the supermarket chains, in some ways, have to do more. Consumers who have opted to buy into this service feel they are getting more value for their money.
2 Adding value is perhaps the prime way of driving competitive advantage by increasingly differentiating one product from another. The consumer will tend to opt for goods and services that offer more value per pence spent.

Check your understanding (page 166)

Students need to show how specific adverts enabled producers to differentiate the products from rival offerings and to make them more desirable. For example, many people want to feel sexy. Advertising that makes the consumption of a product more sexy will increase the value of that product. For example, the 'Levi's in a laundrette' advert featuring Nick Kamen stripping down to his boxer shorts to wash his Levi's had that sort of impact.

Check your understanding (page 167)

Students could compare two supermarket groups, two confectionery firms, two cosmetic firms, etc. For example, in the supermarket example, they could show how firms have added value by providing longer opening hours, more friendly staff and a wider selection of goods; how they have improved quality by ensuring staff are fully trained to deal with all consumer queries; that they have differentiated their product by offering organic/'green' products; that they advertise on television; and that they are seeking to undercut rivals' prices for many items.

Case study: demerger (page 169)

1 From the 1990s onwards, in business there was an increasing emphasis on businesses focusing on their core lines – what they were best at. In a globalised international marketplace, it was widely recognised you could not be the best at producing 200 different products. It was more sensible to identify categories of products that were related and that you were the best at producing. The next step was to channel your resources into gaining global domination in these best lines.
2 Students should identify firms that still have a very wide portfolio (e.g. Nestlé, which purports to be the world food company). Although companies like Nestlé do have a wide spread of products, there are often clear synergies and relationships between these products. Large cash-rich companies like Virgin also tend to diversify when they have spare resources and when they can see attractive opportunities where the return on capital may be high.

Check your understanding (page 170, a)

This task will need to be based on what is happening in the economy at the time. Students need to scour the newspaper headlines in the business sections to find examples of actual or potential merger situations. Who are the players involved in the merger? What is the attraction of the merger? Having investigated a particular sector (e.g. travel agents, sports clubs, media groups, etc.), the students need to identify a business that has not taken the merger route but instead is seeking to gain advantage from a differentiation policy.

Check your understanding (page 170, b)

Shareholders would experience a fall in the value of their shares, probably coupled with a fall in the dividend they received. Suppliers might find that Hazlewood were putting pressure on them to lower their prices. Managers at Hazlewood would find increasing pressure placed on them to cut costs and to create higher levels of productivity in the organisation. Employees might find they were expected to work harder for the same money. The end consumers would be the people who bought from the supermarkets at the end of the process – they would benefit from lower prices.

Check your understanding (page 172)

The figures show a decline in primary and secondary industries. The main beneficiaries are in the service sector, with increases in the numbers employed in banking, insurance and business services, health and education, and public administration. At the same time, there was some growth in construction and distribution.

CHAPTER 8 HOW BUSINESS IS AFFECTED BY GOVERNMENT POLICY

Check your understanding (page 174)

Examples of anti-social business practice that could be controlled by government legislation include:

- waste emission
- traffic pollution caused, for example, by heavy lorries
- noise pollution.

Check your understanding (page 179)

1 Within the law – simple supply contract.
2 Illegal – a supplier cannot restrict particular retailers. This is an anti-competitive restriction.
3 This contravenes the social legislation of

the European Union. The government has a responsibility to protect children.

4 This contravenes consumer protection law because the items are potentially dangerous. The government is there to protect the safety of consumers.
5 Weighing scales must provide accurate measurements. Weights and Measures Inspectors have a responsibility to ensure the public receive fair weights and measures.
6 The firm is in a monopoly position but is not necessarily behaving in an illegal manner. The case could be referred to the Competition Commission, which would investigate to find out if the monopoly works against the public interest.
7 This is anti-competitive because it involves collusion between firms against the interests of the consumer.

Case study: drug firms to face price probe (page 180)

1 There is no hard evidence the market was becoming less competitive. However, the rise in prices might not simply have been caused by genuine supply problems. There was a possibility that some of the middlemen were hoarding generics to push up their prices.
2 The reduction in competition (if it existed) could have come about as a result of some firms having developed sufficient scale that they were able to withdraw considerable supplies from the marketplace. Firms may have come to voluntary agreements to push up prices.
3 Such a development takes power away from consumers and their protector, the government. This could raise prices and mean shortages for needy patients, leading to higher rates of death and/or medical problems.
4 The government is there to make sure fair trading takes place, to protect the customer and to punish (if needs be) those firms that are exploiting their position of strength.

Case study: driving out road congestion (page 181)

1 London is heavily congested at peak times. This leads to considerable loss of economic value, as hold-ups cost money.
2 Students should identify the costs and benefits of such a scheme. Costs would include the increased cost to users of driving cars in London and the increase in the production costs of running a business, particularly a business heavily dependent on motor transport. Benefits would include the reduction in congestion, the reduction in pollution and the increased speed of transport, as there would be fewer vehicles on the road.
3 Students need to weigh up the relative benefits of push and pull. Clearly, there is little point in pushing too many people off the roads if you do not create the public transport system to get them in and out of the city.

Case study: child labour (pages 182–183)

1 This case involves moral principles – issues of what is right and wrong. It is not just a business or legal issue.
2 Again, this is a matter of opinion. The government, however, must establish a framework based on a moral as well as a legal code. The government needs to be representative of people's views, and of higher moral codes, if it is to be fit to govern.
3 The students should be encouraged to debate Clare Short's view.

Check your understanding (page 187)

1 An appeals side has been added to the work of the Competition Commission.
2 Article 81 (1) prohibits agreements and joint practices that might adversely affect trade between member states and which seek to reduce competition.
3 Mergers involving a combined worldwide turnover of 5 billion ecu, where the EC turnover of each business is greater than 25 million ecu (and where the businesses do not have at least two-thirds of their EC turnover from the same member state).
4 They are subject to national competition law – hence the UK Competition Commission is responsible.
5 The Secretary of State for Trade and Industry.
6 The students need to follow a specific case over a period of time, particularly by accessing Internet sites.

Check your understanding (page 195)

Students should record GDP information from the website suggested and illustrate this on graph paper. Similar statistics could be recorded by collecting them from the statistics section of business reports in a quality newspaper such as the *Guardian* or *The Independent*, which should be available in a local library.

Check your understanding (page 198)

Students can record unemployment figures from a national newspaper or from the sites listed in the box on page 198 of the student book. Again, these figures should be recorded on a graph.

Check your understanding (page 200)

Weights:

Wine – 7
Bread – 2
Cheese – 1

1995 all items = 100

2001:

Wine	= 50 × 7	= 350
Bread	= 200 × 2	= 400
Cheese	= 400 × 1	= 400

$$\textit{Total} = \frac{1{,}150}{10} = 115$$

1 The new index is 115.
2 It has risen by 15% since 1995.
3 The weighting might need to be altered if:
- people have changed the proportion of their income spent on the three items
- new items have entered into household budgets in a major way
- the original calculation of weightings had been wrong.

Case study: an error that makes us better off than we thought (pages 200–201)

1 The way the RPI had been calculated failed to take account of changes that were taking place in expenditure items so that the RPI was outdated. It also failed to take account of improvements in the quality of goods, which was the equivalent of a reduction in price.
2 This could be remedied by adjusting items in the basket more frequently and by developing an indicator to translate improvements in quality into price changes.
3 People whose incomes were determined partially by the RPI benefited (e.g. pensioners and people whose wage increases were related to the RPI).

Check your understanding (page 203)

Using a quality newspaper, students should monitor interest rate changes and changes in the quantity of money. They should record this information on a graph. They should then pick out stories from the press outlining the views of business people about the impact monetary policy (in particular interest rates) is having on their business. They should focus on particular companies.

Case study: a low-inflation economy? (page 204)

1 The case refers to a recovery in production and thus in GDP while, at the same time, prices are stable or rising at a very slow rate.
2 A budget surplus is where the government takes in more revenue in taxes than it spends. This surplus therefore gives the government a bonus of built-up reserves, which it can then spend in an appropriate way when it chooses (although it must be careful not to cause inflationary pressures to build up in the economy).
3 It suggested interest rates should be increased because this would make it more expensive for people to borrow, which would then discourage spending, helping to prevent inflation.
4 The danger of increasing government spending and lowering taxes is that this might lead to too rapid an expansion in demand in the economy, which can quickly create inflation.
5 Businesses would have been pleased about the optimistic nature of the report. This might have encouraged them to put into

place investment plans they might have been holding back on.

Check your understanding (page 207)

Students need to look for reports in the quality press about the way in which GDP is changing. Articles that examine the state of the British economy will furnish this information. They should also look for reports on the level of business optimism. Armed with this information, they should be able to predict whether business is likely to be investing or holding back on investment plans.

Check your understanding (page 209)

There has been a great deal of coverage in the press (particularly in *The Independent* – see articles by Diane Coyle) on this issue. Students should record figures for unemployment and GDP and examine these in conjunction with articles about the impact the new economy is having.

Case study: taxes and the supply curve (page 211)

1 4,000 bottles of whisky.
2 The new equilibrium price is £22.
3 The price has risen by £2 from the old equilibrium of £20.
4 The price has risen by less than the tax – tax of £5/price rise of £2. The producer has therefore paid £3 of the tax and the consumer £2.
5 Producers are able to pass some of the tax on to consumers when they are in a strong position to do so (i.e. when demand for the product is inelastic). The more inelastic the demand for the product, the easier it is for producers to pass on the price increase to consumers.

Check your understanding (page 212)

A number of national newspapers provide Internet coverage of the budget. Students simply need to carry out a search using the words 'Budget 2000', 'Budget 2001', etc. The students should simply read through the budget report until they find a tax change for business which interests them and which is spelt out clearly. They should find the rationale for the tax change and then follow this up with some newspaper articles examining the impact of the change.

Check your understanding (page 213, a)

Students can find out about grants and subsidies by talking to farmers and other business people. They could interview the business development officer from the local council.

Check your understanding (page 213, b)

Students can gather this information by looking at the tourist exchange rates in the business pages of *The Independent*. They need to follow this up by looking at editorial comments and features articles about the impact of the price of the currency on the business sector.

Check your understanding (page 214)

There is a range of services the students can refer to:

- education – helping to create a skilled labour force
- health – helping to create a healthy workforce
- public transport networks – helping to bring people to work, etc.

Students should then explain how businesses contribute to these services through the payment of business taxes (such as corporation tax and employers' national insurance contributions).

Case study: rail privatisation (page 215)

1 Students should set out some of the arguments for and against rail privatisation in order to come to a balanced conclusion. For example:

For	Against
Leads to more competition and more efficiency	Could lead to corners being cut (e.g. in safety initiatives)
Gives the customers more control over the services they receive	Public transport and essential services should be run for the people and owned by the public rather than private shareholders
Privatised concerns have to stand on their own two feet, rather than be subsidised from the public purse	Can lead to unprofitable lines and services being closed down

2 Maintaining the safety and standard of the rail infrastructure is a very important task that needs to be handled separately from the running of trains. You could not have infrastructure being created in different ways in different parts of the country. Running the trains and the railway network could lead to a lack of focus, leading to inefficiencies.

Check your understanding (page 216)

Students should simply do an Internet search using the words 'Royal Mail' to get to the latest stories covering the changes taking place.

Check your understanding (page 217)

Students should interview a family member or friend who runs or owns his or her own business to find out about the impact of interest rate changes on the business.

Case study: the EU directive on parental leave (page 217)

1 Students might mention social reasons, such as the fact that parents do not have the double stress of holding down a job and looking after a new child. This applies both to men and women. Employees know their jobs are safe. They may also mention economic reasons, such as the security of employment and job guarantees.
2 Some employers will see this initiative as an additional cost. An increase in the wage bill may lead to redundancies. Of course, many employers will welcome this because it creates a level playing field within the European Union. However, they may be less happy if a great deal of the competition is from outside the EU where this directive does not apply.

Check your understanding (page 218)

Students can carry out an Internet search by keying in 'EU environmental policy' or 'EU social policy'.

CHAPTER 9 HOW BUSINESSES ARE AFFECTED BY INTERNATIONAL COMPETITORS

Case study: the impact of the information revolution on costs (page 222)

1 The notion of the 'weightless economy' is that products are becoming physically lighter. In a weightless economy, ideas and intelligence are exchanged for money rather than physical goods like steel girders or bales of wheat. In the weightless economy, goods are easier to transport (and hence distribution costs are pared to the bone).
2 The trend to globalisation has been fuelled by the rapid development of communication links (transport and telecommunications). Increasingly, products are being made which are lighter, to make them easier to transport, and which use fewer raw materials. Also, many of the products and services that are valued today involve services based on intelligence. These services do not involve large physical items. The development of a weightless economy means the goods and services people desire can be moved much more rapidly from one country to another – hence supporting globalisation.

Case study: Heinz' Project Millennia (pages 224–225)

1 Heinz originally set about improving their global presence by setting up manufacturing and distribution centres in more and more countries, as well as by increasing the range of products they sold. They moved on to operating at 150 locations in six continents. They built up an organisational structure that would support this international presence.
2 Like many other companies, Heinz realised the folly of spreading their resources too thinly over too many separate products. They have decided to focus on those areas where they have the greatest competitive advantage and, therefore, where they are able to make the highest possible return on capital employed. The focus, therefore, is on six key product areas.
3 They can build competitive advantage in these categories by being the best in everything they do in these areas. By generating profits, they can plough part of this profit back into further investment in capital projects and marketing initiatives to keep them ahead of the field.

Check your understanding (page 225)

There are many definitions of globalisation. Some see it as a process through which the experiences of people on the globe are becoming more similar in terms of the development of a shared common language, shared cultural patterns, common products on the shelves, etc. Others emphasise the economic aspects of globalisation – the way in which capital flows from one continent and country to another, the way in which transport links and ICT links are so rapid, etc. Others look at globalisation in a business sense – in the way businesses see the globe as being their marketplace, as opposed to national and regional markets.

Students will have different perspectives on globalisation, depending on whether they see the benefits of economic development to be progressive and shared. Others will have negative views of globalisation, pointing to the destruction of traditional ways of doing things and local cultures, the environmental impact of rapid industrialisation and the destruction of variety.

Case study: Unilever swallows up French mustard maker (page 229)

1 Like many other companies, Unilever are focusing their assets on what they see as being their best lines. Companies like Amora-Maille are seen as fitting in with Unilever's core strengths, enabling them to become the global leader in these types of products.
2 By focusing on their best lines, Unilever are able to allocate resources to gaining competitive advantage in a smaller rather than a larger range of product lines. They are thus able to plough back investment into the research, product development, marketing, etc., of their chosen lines of strength.
3 Students should follow this up either through Unilever's Internet site or by simply pulling down the address from the site and writing to ask for an annual report.

Check your understanding (page 231)

This information is normally contained in the early pages of a company's annual report. Most companies provide a map indicating the locations where they operate, plus information about the range of products they produce and their current strategy. The chairman's report typically sets out the new markets and the new products the company has produced in the year.

Check your understanding (page 234)

Useful UK companies to investigate would include Manchester United plc, Marks & Spencer, Unilever (Anglo-Dutch), Cadbury-Schweppes, Dyson, Shell (Anglo-Dutch) and BP. Again, students should seek to obtain either a company report or information from the Internet setting out the fortunes of the selected company.

Check your understanding (page 236)

Students should select a business that is involved in exporting or whose products are affected by competition from imports (e.g. a textile business, a shoe manufacturer, a steel manufacturer, a farmer, etc.).

Case study: different interest groups at the Seattle Conference (page 237)

1 There are so many viewpoints because the freeing of world trade impacts on so many people. Many manufacturers, for example, will benefit from being able to sell into more markets. However, some manufacturers will lose out – for example, small-scale producers who find it difficult to compete with the giant multinationals. Others are opposed to Seattle and the development of world trade because it threatens their traditional way of life. Environmentalists fear the expansion of world trade will cause a massive increase in the level of global pollution.

2 Students will voice all sorts of opinions about Seattle, depending on whether they are in favour of the expansion of the world economy along current lines or whether they see dangers for developing countries and for the ecosphere of overfast development patterns.

Check your understanding (page 239)

Students should study business reports in quality newspapers to find this information. A quicker route is to search the Internet using the word 'quota'. This will quickly yield a range of stories about quotas facing UK firms and quotas protecting UK firms. Students may want to use a more specific search (e.g. 'steel quota', etc.).

Check your understanding (page 242)

Students can interview friends/relatives who are involved in businesses with a 'Euro dimension'. Alternatively, they may arrange to interview a manager with responsibility for trading in a local company with which the school or college has an industrial link.

Check your understanding (page 243)

1 Students should simply refer to an example where a business (e.g. Amazon or Iceland.com) has exploited e-commerce to boost demand.

2 Students should identify an example of ways in which a well-known organisation has improved its supply chain by careful use of the Internet (e.g. lastminute.com, which is able to provide last-minute holidays and many other 'last-minute' items).

3 Students can refer to a host of Internet-related benefits (e.g. communications to sort out misunderstandings in trading, financial dealings over the Internet, etc.).

SECTION C OHTs

NOTES

OHT 2.7.1: demand for old tennis balls

This OHT is based on the table on page 149 of the student book and Figure 7.6 from page 150 of the student book showing the demand curve for old Wimbledon tennis balls. The figures from the table have been used to plot the demand curve.

The tutor could use these illustrations to show why a demand curve will slope down from left to right. The tutor can ask the students to explain why fewer buyers would be prepared to buy the second-hand tennis balls at higher prices than at lower ones.

OHT 2.7.2a: supply of old tennis balls

This OHT is based on Figure 7.9 on page 151 of the student book. It shows Wimbledon would be prepared to make available to the public more of its old balls at higher rather than lower prices. This OHT complements OHT 2.7.1 and 2.7.2b.

OHT 2.7.2b: old tennis balls – market equilibrium

This illustration brings together the demand and supply curves for old tennis balls from the previous illustrations. The tutor may ask the students to draw the illustration from the OHT. However, it is more likely the tutor will ask students to construct this diagram from tables for demand and supply at different prices.

Once students have drawn the diagram, the tutor could explain the nature of market equilibrium. The tutor should then choose the disequilibrium position (e.g. at £2.50 and £1.00) and show how these are not equilibrium positions and how the market will return to the equilibrium position of £2.00.

OHT 2.7.3: newspaper headlines

This OHT is based on the newspaper headlines in Figure 7.17 on page 156 of the student book. Working with a class group, the tutor should ask the students to identify in each case what happens to supply in the markets indicated, using the diagram at the foot of the OHT.

Answers:

- Prices of computer chips to temporarily rise – this will, in the short period, lead to an increase in the production costs of computers, so the supply curve shifts to the left from SS to S_1S_1, leading to at least a temporary increase in the prices of computers (if this is not offset by other factors).
- Wages to fall in the printing industry – the supply of printing products shifts to the right from SS to S_2S_2, leading to falling prices for printing products.
- Good growing conditions for French wines – supply of such wines shifts to the right from SS to S_2S_2, leading to a fall in the price for the wines from the year in question.
- New subsidies for start-up business in high-tech industries – again, this encourages an increase in supply because this lowers production costs – a shift in supply from SS to S_2S_2, lowering the prices of high-tech products.
- Bad coffee harvest in Brazil – leads to a reduction in the supply of coffee – supply shifts from SS to S_1S_1 and price rises.
- Government raises taxes on smoking – this increases the production costs of cigarettes, causing the supply curve to shift to the left – SS to S_1S_1 – leading to an increase in the price of cigarettes.
- Earthquake in South East Asia – if this leads to a disruption in production, it could raise production costs for many products, forcing the supply curve to the left from SS to S_1S_1 and pushing up lots of prices.

OHT 2.7.4: the changing market for hockey boots

This set of OHTs is based on the changes in the hockey boot industry described on pages 163–164 of the student book. The tutor should talk students through these changes, which illustrate dynamic market conditions. The first one shows a shift to the right in the demand curve for hockey boots. This will help to push up prices and hence the quantity of boots manufacturers are prepared to supply to the market.

The second illustration shows the situation following a change in hockey boot technology, which leads the supply curve to shift to the right. Because hockey boots can now be produced more cheaply, it is possible to sell a greater quantity of boots at lower prices.

The final illustration shows a subsequent increase in demand for hockey boots, which leads to more being supplied to the market while, at the same time, enabling manufacturers to raise prices.

These OHTs enable the tutor to show the students how dynamic markets are.

OHT 2.8.1a: the relationship between total demand and supply

This OHT has been designed to enable the tutor to explain the relationship between national output, national income and national expenditure, where the economy is divided into firms and households. The tutor needs to emphasise that the value of national output is shared out in the form of national income, which is then returned into the circular flow through the expenditure process.

OHT 2.8.1b: the circular flow of income

This diagram is to be used in conjunction with OHT 2.8.1a. However, it goes further to include the financial, governmental and foreign trade sectors of the economy. The diagram illustrates the nature of the complex circular flow, and shows how leakages can sap demand from the economy. However, these leakages are returned back into the circular flow in the form of injections.

OHT 2.8.2: examples of aggregate demand

The problem with terms like consumption, investment, etc., is that, for many students, they are difficult to visualise. This set of diagrams, therefore, is designed to enable the students to see economic aggregates in terms of concrete examples. The OHT is based on Figure 8.10 on page 193 of the student book.

The five elements of demand – consumption, investment, government, exports and imports – need to be aggregated to get the figure for aggregate demand, which is shown by the demand curve in the top centre of the illustration. Using this approach, the tutor should be best placed to enable the students to see aggregate demand as consisting of:

$$C + I + G + X - M$$

OHT 2.8.3a: changes in GDP in the UK economy since 1981

This OHT is to be used in conjunction with OHT 2.8.3b and is based on the notes and illustration on page 194 of the student book. By studying this illustration, students can see a general increase in the level of GDP in the UK economy over time.

OHT 2.8.3b: the business cycle

In many ways this illustration is more useful than the one shown in OHT 2.8.3a because it shows changes in economic activity over time. What it shows is that GDP is growing faster in some periods than in other – giving rise to the trade cycle. Students should be asked to comment on why these changes arise.

OHT 2.8.4a: unemployment in the economy

This OHT is based on Figure 8.17 on page 197 of the student book. The illustration points to Keynes' idea that the economy is not always at the full employment point. Indeed, the economy can be in equilibrium at any level of employment. In this case, aggregate demand lies well short of the full employment point in the economy.

OHT 2.8.4b: too much demand causes inflation

This OHT is based on Figure 8.20 on

page 201 of the student book. This diagram can be contrasted with OHT 2.8.4a. Here, demand starts from a position at the full employment point and then rises through two inflationary situations. Note that employment cannot go beyond the full employment point.

OHT 2.9.1: the characteristics of globalisation

The nature of globalisation is discussed on pages 219–226 of the student book. The illustration on this OHT outlines some of the key features and contributory factors to globalisation. The tutor should work round the OHT, describing each of these features. Students can be asked to discuss which of the factors listed they believe to have been most important in contributing to globalisation.

OHT 2.9.2: why businesses internationalise

This OHT is based on the notes provided on pages 228–229 of the student book. Tutors need to familiarise themselves with these notes and should also seek to provide recent examples (gleaned from news coverage) of some of these reasons for internationalising (e.g. many companies are internationalising for defensive reasons in a globalised marketplace).

OHT 2.9.3: Seattle Conference – differing views

This OHT is based on the case study on page 237 of the student book and provides an excellent focus for discussion activity.

Students can be asked:

1 Why are there so many different viewpoints about the direction forward for the WTO?
2 Which of the arguments put forward do you sympathise with most? Why?

A possible activity for the tutor is to group members of the class into syndicates representing each of the different viewpoints, and to hold a conference to discuss the way forward for liberalising world trade.

OHT 2.9.4: for and against the euro

This OHT is based on the table on page 242 of the student book, which outlines a series of arguments for and against the euro. This OHT would be best used in conjunction with a recent newspaper article, chosen by the tutor, outlining recent views from one side or another. Students should discuss whether it is the arguments for or against the euro which seem to be the stronger.

OHT 2.7.1 DEMAND FOR OLD TENNIS BALLS

Price of balls (£)	Quantity demanded per month
2.50	200
2.00	400
1.50	600
1.00	800
0.50	1,000

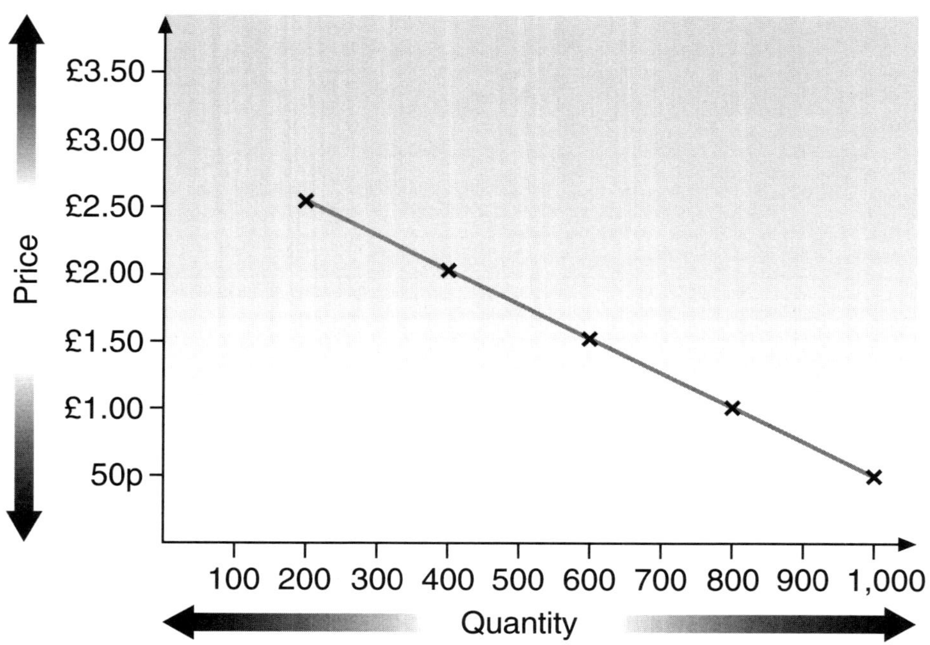

OHT 2.7.2A SUPPLY OF OLD TENNIS BALLS

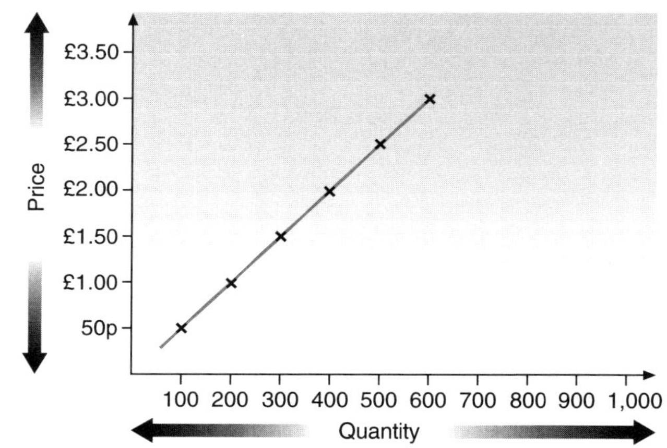

OHT 2.7.2B OLD TENNIS BALLS – MARKET EQUILIBRIUM

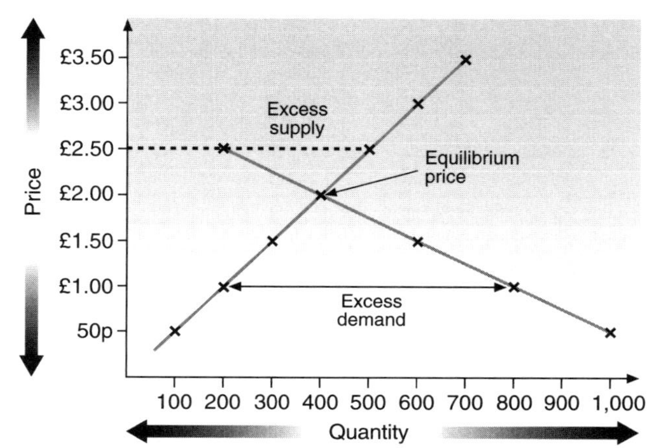

OHT 2.7.3 NEWSPAPER HEADLINES

WAGES TO FALL IN THE PRINTING INDUSTRY

PRICES OF COMPUTER CHIPS TO TEMPORARILY RISE

GOOD GROWING CONDITIONS FOR FRENCH WINES

NEW SUBSIDIES FOR START-UP BUSINESS IN HIGH-TECH INDUSTRIES

BAD COFFEE HARVEST IN BRAZIL

GOVERNMENT RAISES TAXES ON SMOKING

EARTHQUAKE IN SOUTH-EAST ASIA

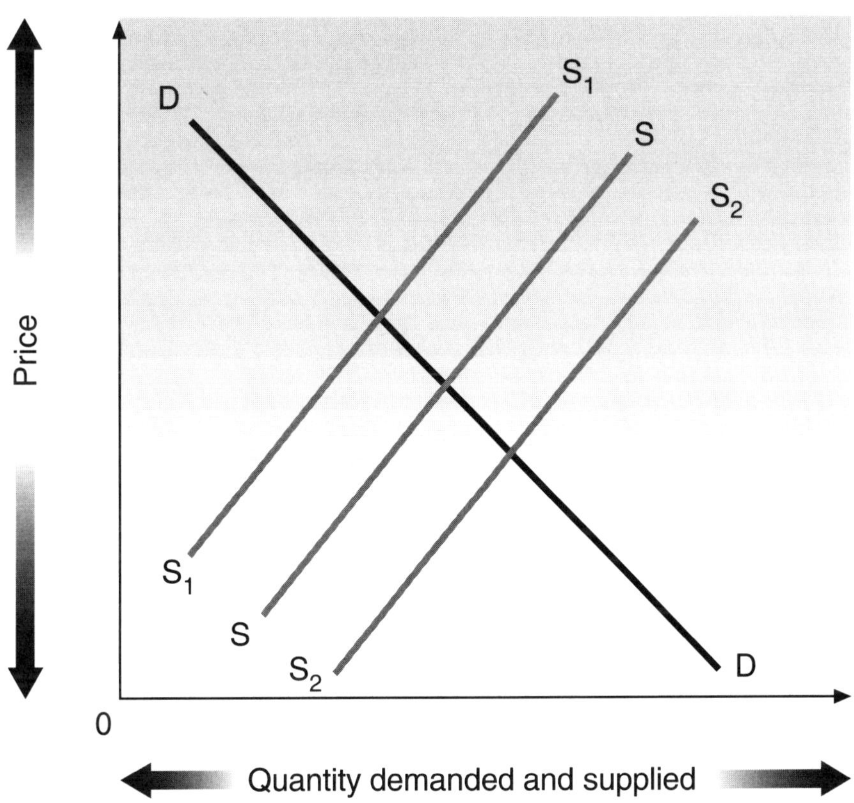

OHT 2.7.4 THE CHANGING MARKET FOR HOCKEY BOOTS

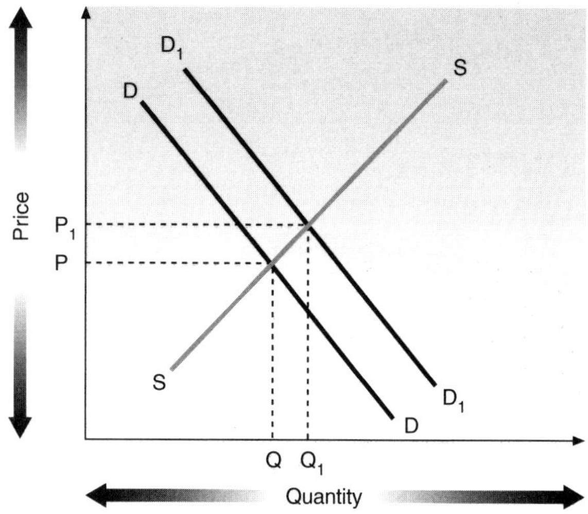

Increasing demand for hockey boots

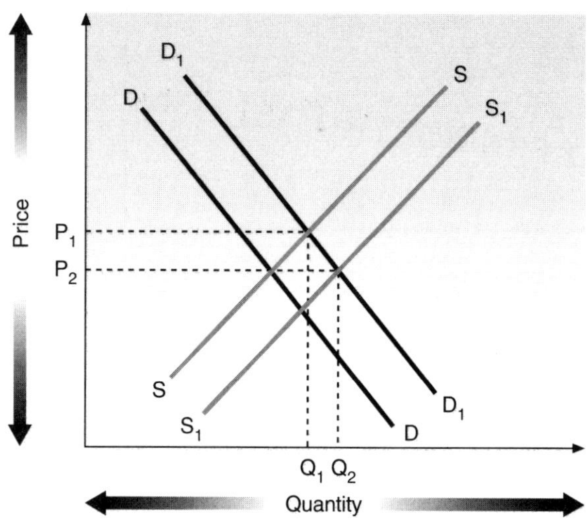

Improvement in hockey boot production technology

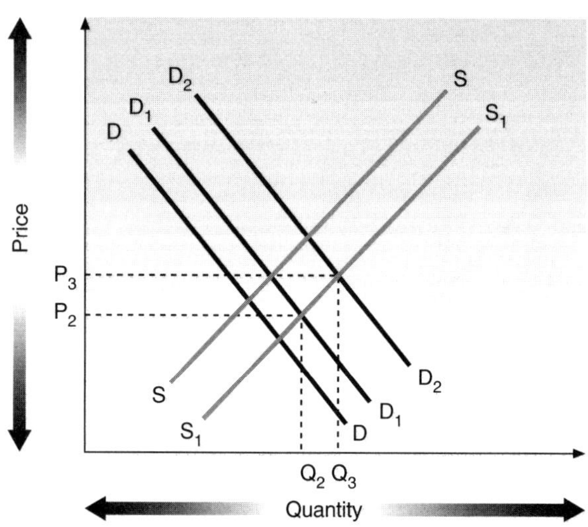

Further increase in demand for hockey boots

OHT 2.8.1A THE RELATIONSHIP BETWEEN TOTAL DEMAND AND SUPPLY

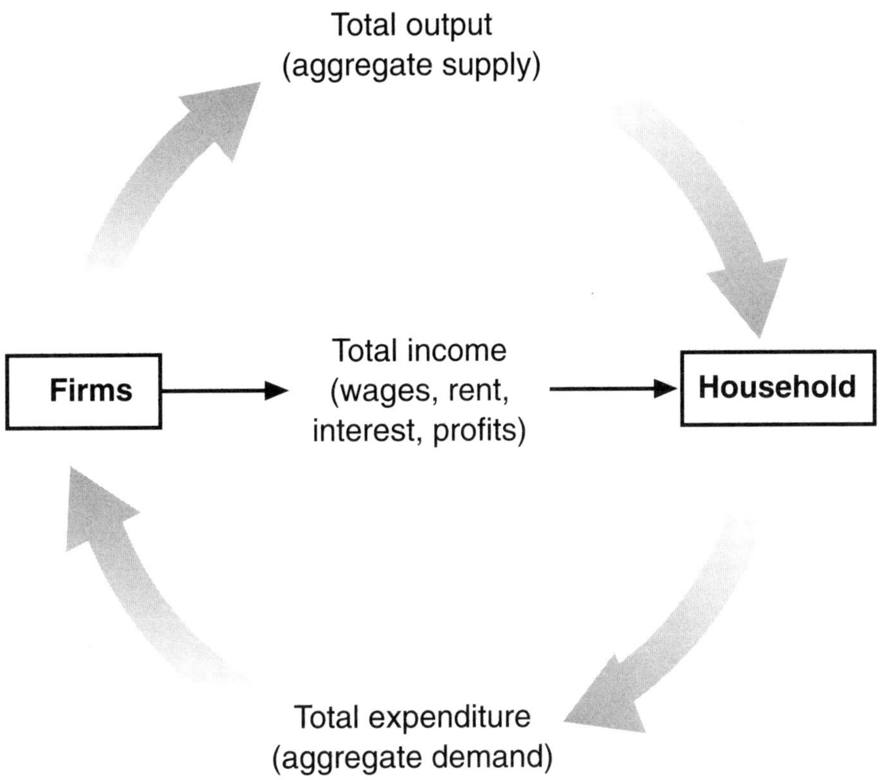

OHT 2.8.1B THE CIRCULAR FLOW OF INCOME

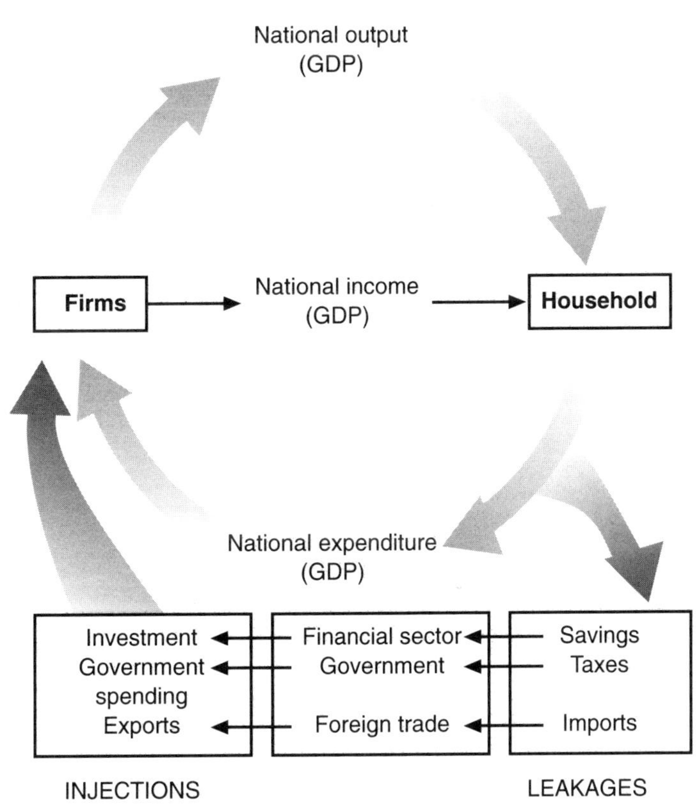

OHT 2.8.2 EXAMPLES OF AGGREGATE DEMAND

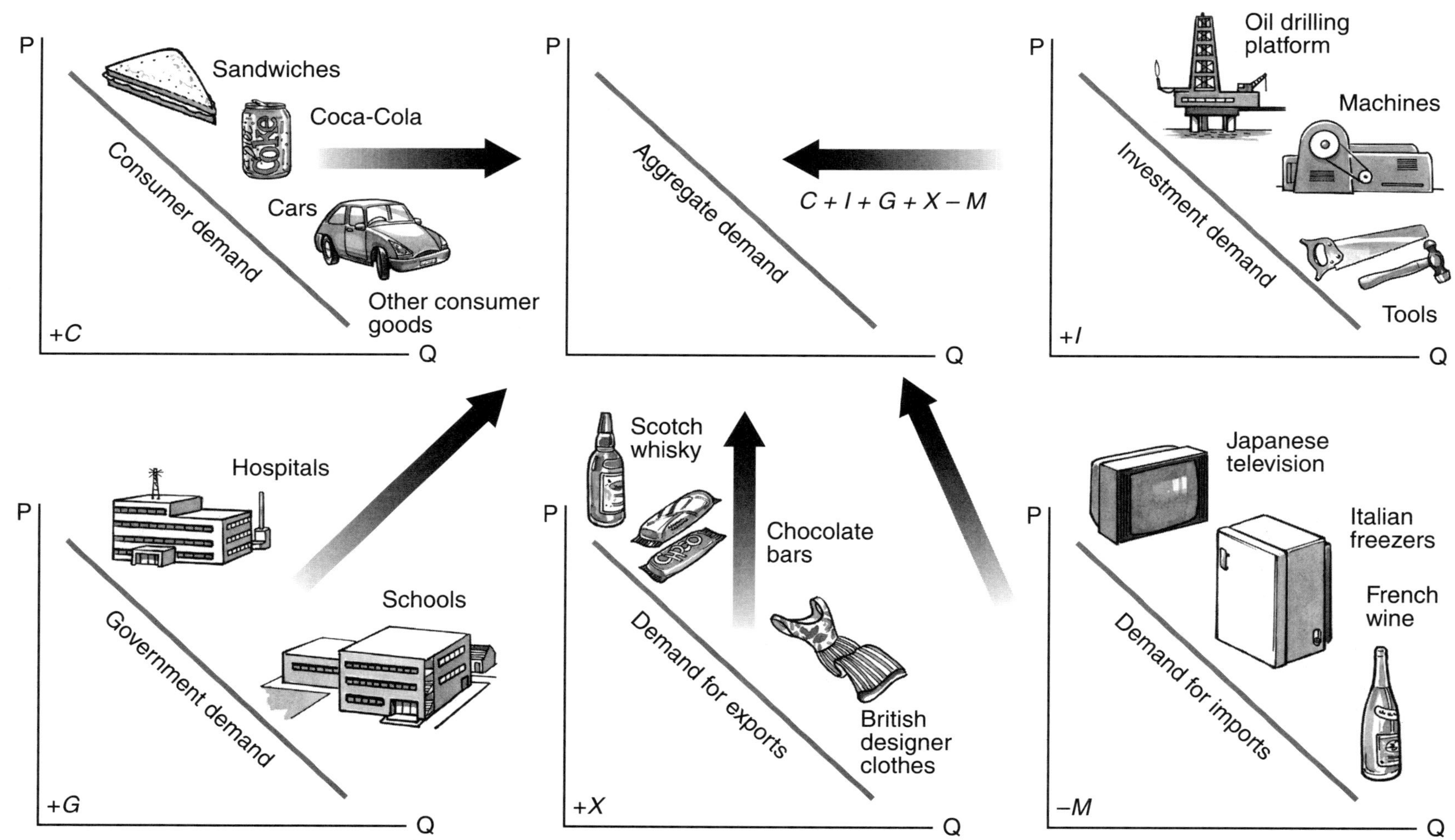

OHT 2.8.3A CHANGES IN GDP IN THE UK ECONOMY SINCE 1981

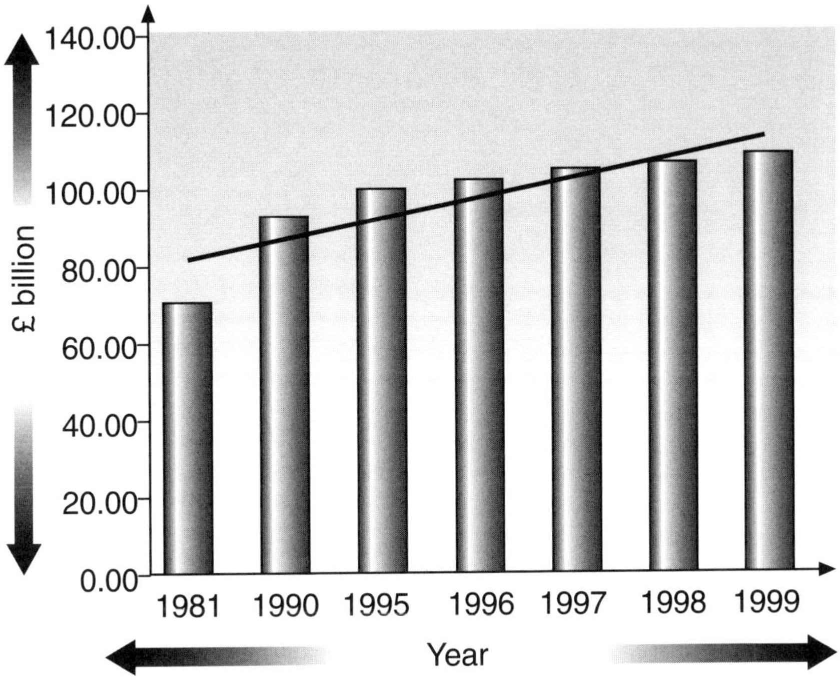

OHT 2.8.3B THE BUSINESS CYCLE

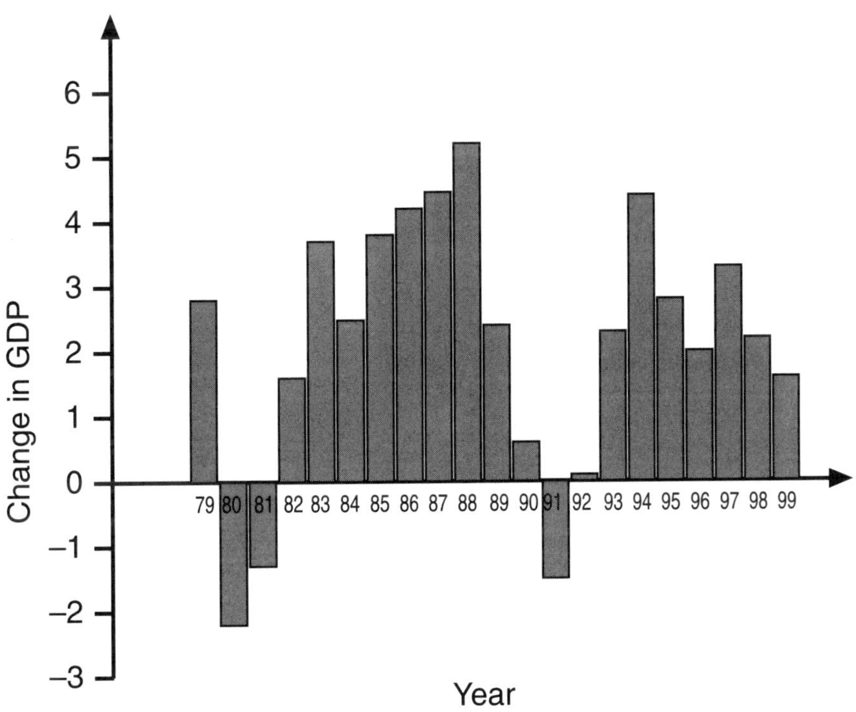

OHT 2.8.4A UNEMPLOYMENT IN THE ECONOMY

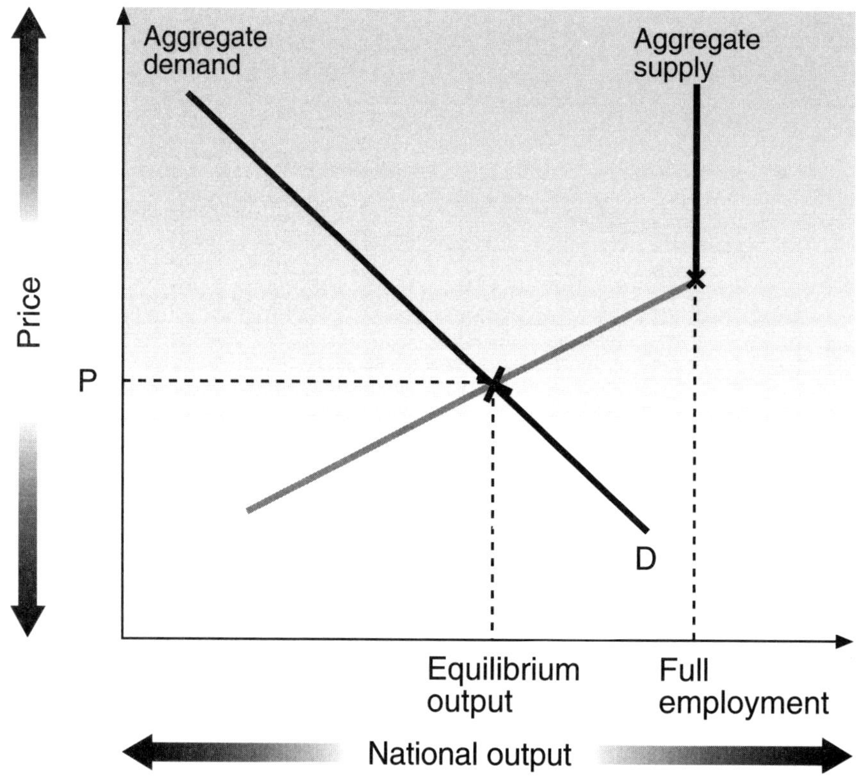

OHT 2.8.4B TOO MUCH DEMAND CAUSES INFLATION

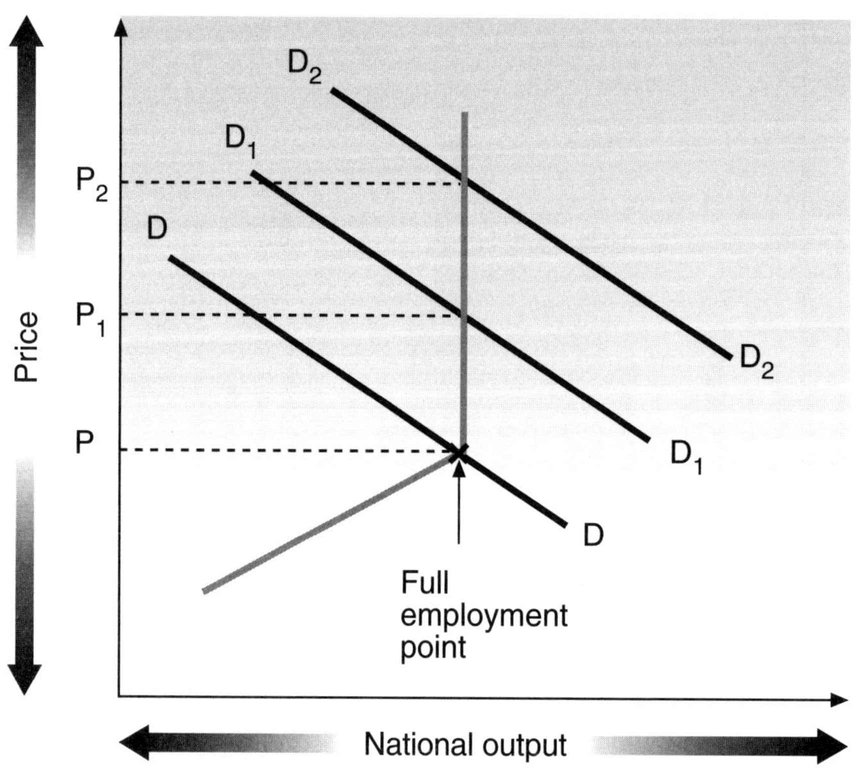

OHT 2.9.1 THE CHARACTERISTICS OF GLOBALISATION

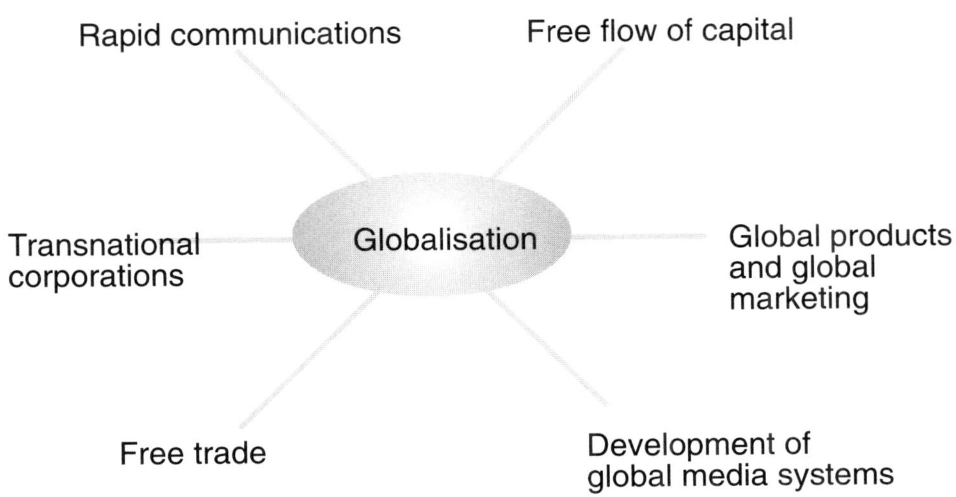

OHT 2.9.2 WHY BUSINESSES INTERNATIONALISE

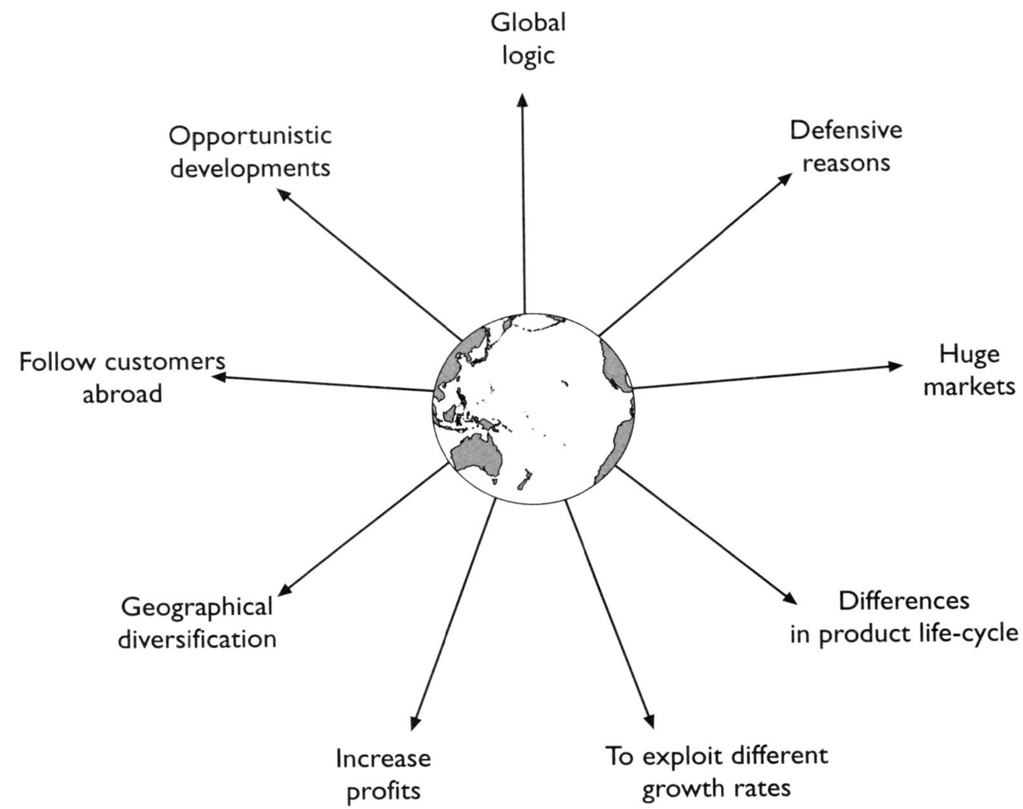

OHT 2.9.3 SEATTLE CONFERENCE – DIFFERING VIEWS

SEATTLE '99

America

Wanted to reduce farm trade barriers, clear the way for global e-commerce and establish rules for labour standards

India

Sought to resist the extension of environmental and labour standards, which it saw as thinly veiled protectionism. Also pressured developed countries to open their markets to textiles more

European Union

Tried to beat off pressure to abolish its support to agriculture, claiming it was already committed to substantial action under its Agenda 2000 programme

Japan

Sought to force the USA to ease back on its use of anti-dumping duties to keep out imports

The protest lobby

Intent on protesting that free trade is not fair trade: free trade harms the environment and poorer nations

Cairns Group

Group of 15 farm-exporting nations (Argentina, Australia, Brazil, Canada, Chile, Colombia, Fiji, Indonesia, Malaysia, New Zealand, Paraguay, Philippines, South Africa, Thailand and Uruguay) founded in Cairns, Australia. Want the EU to agree to set in train the end of all farm subsidies

OHT 2.9.4 FOR AND AGAINST THE EURO

For	Against
A fixed exchange rate will end currency instability in Europe	National government will have less control over monetary policy
Unstable markets have caused economic crises in the past, forcing governments to choose between high interest rates (leading to unemployment) and currency devaluation (leading to high inflation)	Global economic shocks are likely to affect member states in different ways
Low interest rates and a fixed exchange rate will encourage more progressive and long-term government domestic policies and boost trade and investment	Unemployment could increase, at least in the short term, if a government comes under pressure to cut public expenditure owing to restrictions relating to the requirement to limit its deficit
No one member of the EU will be able to dictate monetary policy	Critics fear that the German central bank (the Bundesbank) will dominate proceedings
The euro should be strong enough to compete against the dollar and the yen on world markets	The European Monetary Institute and European Central Bank might not look beyond the issue of price stability and might ignore the knock-on social and political effects of monetary policy

SECTION D TEST

Note: Questions 1–4 relate to the data given below.

Research has shown that almost half of Britons are cutting back on meat or going vegetarian in the wake of BSE and other food scares. The switch away from meat has been leapt on by the food industry, which has developed a huge range of meat lookalikes ranging from bacon to fillet steak. Figures show the value of the market has increased by 67% in the last five years alone, up from £255 million to £428 million.

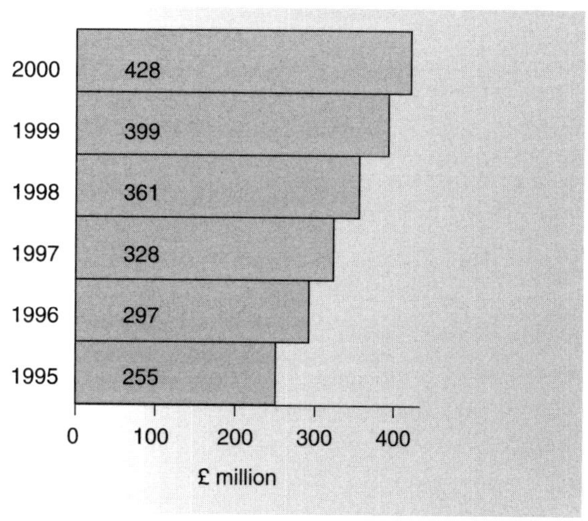

Value of the market

1 Draw a fully labelled diagram to show the impact of the change in demand for vegetarian meat lookalike products. (*4 marks*)

2 Explain how this change in demand for meat lookalike products is likely to have affected the supply of such products. (*3 marks*)

3 Why might meat producers' profits have declined as a result of this trend to vegetarianism? (*4 marks*)

4 How can producers of meat and meat substitute products be said to be in competition with each other? (*4 marks*)

5 Beef farmers take out insurance for their herds from insurance companies in the tertiary sector of the economy. What sector of the economy are:

a beef farmers in? (*1 mark*)
b producers of meat substitutes in? (*1 mark*)

a

b

6 Why is the service sector of the economy so important in the UK economy today? (*8 marks*)

7 The table below shows the results of a survey by the Vegetarian Society in the autumn of 2000 into what people think of vegetarian food. All figures shown are percentages.

	Enjoy it	Don't like it	Forced to eat it	Regularly eat it
All	49	23	15	12
Men	52	27	12	9
Women	47	20	18	15
Age 15–19	35	45	12	11
20–24	42	30	17	11
25–34	46	21	20	14
35–44	48	23	15	15
45–54	48	21	17	14
55–64	54	20	15	11
65+	61	19	10	10

Using figures from the table, identify a market segment that it might be worth while targeting a new vegetarian product at. (*4 marks*)

8 A friend has suggested to you that, if you want to launch a new meat-free product into the vegetarian market, it is best to use a penetration pricing strategy. What would be the advantages and disadvantages of using a penetration pricing strategy? (*6 marks*)

9 The meat substitute Quorn (from Marlow Foods) had sales worth £100 million in the UK in 2000. At the time it had few direct competitors. What advantages can a company benefit from when it has few direct competitors? (*4 marks*)

10 Why is Quorn likely to attract more competitors in the next few years? (*5 marks*)

11 Why might the fact that the Bank of England's Monetary Policy Committee is considering raising interest rates be a cause for concern for Marlow Foods? (*3 marks*)

12 If the government was to subsidise the production of meat substitute products in the European Union, how would this affect the supply of these products? Draw a diagram to illustrate your answer (*8 marks*)

13 Marlow Foods would like to export Quorn to France. How might the fall in the value of the euro encourage this

move into France? How might it discourage the move? (*6 marks*)

14 You have been examining some economic statistics relating to gross domestic product in the UK. These show that GDP is currently increasing (at over 3% for the year), and is likely to increase in the near future.

What is gross domestic product a measure of, and what do these statistics tell you about the stage of the trade cycle the UK is currently in? (*4 marks*)

15 An economist has warned the economy is in danger of 'overheating', leading to an inflationary situation. Why is inflation bad for business? (*6 marks*)

16 Companies producing vegetarian products in the UK are increasingly looking to the European Union as their home market. What are the benefits of seeing the EU as their home market? (*8 marks*)

17 Many large UK and European Union food companies are in favour of the single European currency, the euro. Why might large UK and European food companies be in favour of the euro? (*6 marks*)

18 In recent years, many multinational companies have benefited from the World Trade Organisation (WTO): **a** What is a multinational? (*2 marks*); **b** Explain one way multinationals can benefit from the development of the World Trade Organisation. (*5 marks*)

a

b

Total mark for Unit 2: 92 marks.

MARKING SCHEME FOR THE TEST

1 Two marks for correct labelling of axes (price on the vertical, quantity demanded on the horizontal). One mark for showing shift in the demand curve to the right. One mark for labelling old and new demand curves. Total four marks.

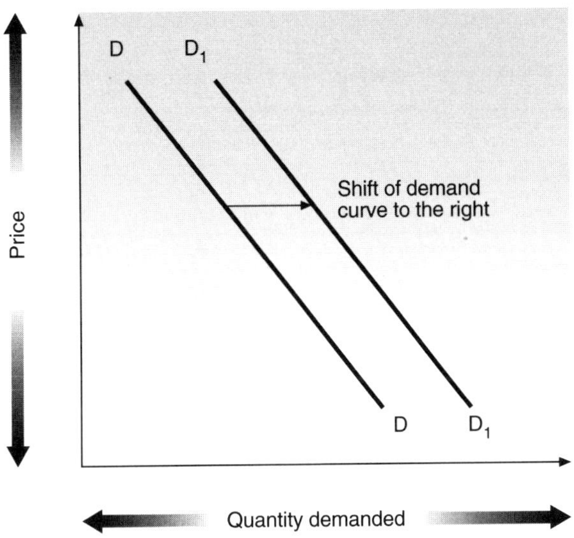

Demand for meat lookalike products

2 One mark for stating that supply is likely to increase, one mark for stating this will be in response to increased demand or increase in price, one mark for other appropriate reason, such as increase in demand enables producers to produce larger quantities at lower unit costs. Maximum three marks.

3 Up to two marks for explaining factors likely to have led to an increase in costs (e.g. farmers will have to reduce the size of their herds, raising unit costs or rearing individual animals). Up to two marks for explaining factors leading to a fall in revenues (e.g. fall in demand reduces sales made and thus receipts taken by farmers). Total four marks.

4 Up to two marks for each developed point (e.g. meat substitutes are seen by some consumers as fairly direct substitutes and will compare prices and offers of these substitutes). A relative fall in the price of one product will encourage buyers to switch purchases. Total four marks.

5 a Beef farmers are involved with the primary sector (one mark).
b Meat substitute producers are in the secondary (manufacturing) sector (one mark).

6 Up to three marks for each developed argument. Maximum of eight marks. For example: the service sector is the largest sector by employment – including industries such as insurance, banking, leisure and tourism – which are prominent in a developed economy. Many of the UK's most successful businesses in recent years have been in this sector (e.g. Prudential, Halifax, Center Parcs, etc.), providing high-quality value-added services. Services are also important to the UK's overseas trade – in invisibles – bringing in currency to this country. While manufacturing has been in decline, new jobs have been created in services (such as retailing, catering and personal services).

7 Up to two marks for each developed argument that draws on data from the table. Maximum four marks. Older people, particularly over the age of 55 years, where over 50% state they enjoy eating vegetarian food. Males also provide a potential market with 52% enjoying it, although more women eat it regularly.

8 One mark for explaining that penetration pricing involves charging a relatively low initial price to enter a market. Two marks for describing an effective advantage of penetration pricing (e.g. penetration pricing enables a firm to gain a foothold in a market, which can then be built on using sales to generate revenues for further expansion). Up to three marks for explaining a disadvantage of penetration pricing (e.g. the low initial price means the firm is taking quite low receipts relative to costs, which could lead to a loss-making situation). Total six marks.

9 Two marks for each advantage developed. Total four marks. For example: having few direct competitors gives a firm elements of a monopoly situation, enabling it to charge relatively high prices. The firm is able to make higher than normal profits in the short term, which can be ploughed back into the business.

10 Two marks for each developed point. Maximum five marks. For example: the excess profits will attract competitors who want to take a share of the profits.

Because of the increasing demand for meat substitute products, other firms will spot the profit opportunity. In the longer term, it is easy for new firms to enter an existing market.

11 Up to three marks for each developed point. For example: rising interest rates will increase the cost of borrowing, leading to a rising cost structure and reducing profit potential. Total three marks.

12 Two marks for correct labelling of diagram – vertical axis price of meat substitutes, horizontal axis quantity of meat substitutes. One mark for showing supply curve shifting to right. One mark for correct labelling of supply curve.

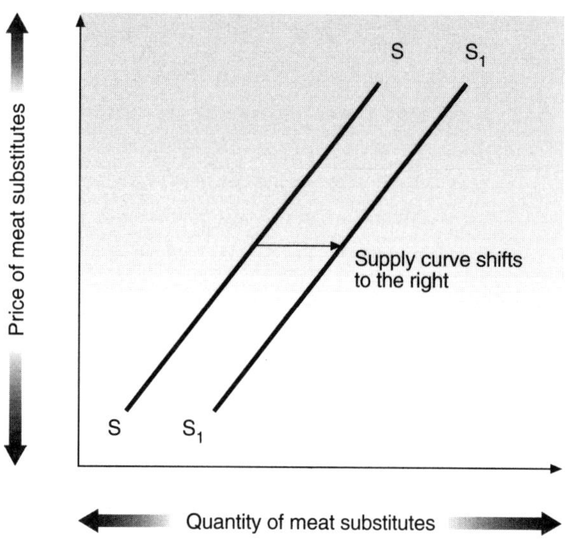

The impact of a subsidy

Two further marks for each developed point, up to a maximum of four. For example: the subsidy effectively reduces costs of production, enabling businesses to increase supply at each and every price. The subsidy encourages producers to make more of the product because the subsidy is similar to an increase in demand for the product. Total eight marks.

13 Up to three marks for explaining how the fall in the value of the euro might encourage the move to France. For example: a fall in the euro reduces the cost of UK exports in France, encouraging the French to buy more British products and thus adding to total sales of the company. Up to three marks for explaining how the fall in the value of the euro might discourage the move to France. For example: a fall in the euro means each unit sold to France is worth less in revenue terms, so that more products have to be sold than before to gain the same amount of currency. Total six marks.

14 One mark for explaining that GDP is either a measure of national income/national output or national expenditure. Up to three marks for explaining the stage in the trade cycle. For example: the trade cycle is on the upturn (perhaps in a boom or recovery stage) with increases in output/income/expenditure. Total four marks.

15 Up to three marks for each developed explanation of why inflation is bad for business. Maximum six marks. For example: inflation creates uncertainty, which means businesses are unsure about the environment in which they operate (e.g. how much they will receive when credit payments become due). Inflation can add to business costs (e.g. costs of raw materials, wage costs, etc.), which cut into profit margins.

16 Up to three marks for each developed benefit of the EU as a home market for business. Maximum eight marks. For example: the EU is a market of 380 million people – considerably more than the UK's 60 million – enabling much larger sales. Economies of scale (resulting from operating within a mass market) enable the lowering of average unit costs. Some products that have only a limited demand in the UK (e.g. black pudding and tomato sauce) may have much larger markets in the European Union because of differing tastes and customs.

17 Up to three marks for each developed argument for large firms' support for the euro. For example: the euro provides a common currency for trading, thus eliminating some transaction and exchange costs and helping to increase profits. Large multinationals operate and trade across borders, seeing the EU as their home market and finding any lack of uniformity a costly inconvenience. Total six marks.

18 **a** Up to two marks for definition of multinational (e.g. corporation operating in many countries, with head office in another country). **b** Up to three marks

for each developed point showing how multinationals can benefit from the WTO. Total five marks. For example: the WTO has removed many barriers and restrictions to trade, vastly freeing up and increasing world trade and reducing tariffs and other costs to traders. The WTO has progressively sought to increase the volume of world trade by creating agreements between member countries to cut down and eliminate trade restrictions.

Total mark for Unit 2: 92 marks.

UNIT 3 – MARKETING

SECTION A DISCUSSION POINT

MCDONALD'S CHANGES THE HAMBURGER MARKET WITH 'MARKETING'

They may be easy to criticise. You might not like their products. But we have to admit McDonald's is a well-marketed, consumer-orientated organisation. The company has more than 14,000 outlets in 73 countries with double the sales of its nearest rival, Burger King, and triple those of third-place Wendy's. Nineteen million customers pass through the McDonald's golden arches every day, and more than 96% of Americans eat at McDonald's. It is claimed credit for the success of the company is simply down to market orientation.

Before McDonald's set standards for the burger business, Americans could get hamburgers in diners and restaurants, and people from many parts of the world had never even experienced a burger. Consumers in the USA were often confronted with poor-quality service, poor décor, unclean restaurants and a noisy, busy atmosphere. In 1952, Ray Kroc, a 52-year-old salesperson of milkshake-mixing machines, noticed the work of Richard and Maurice McDonald, who had seven restaurants, and he bought the chain. He expanded the chain by selling franchises and then introduced:

- expanded seating areas
- better décor
- a breakfast menu
- new food items
- new outlets.

Kroc's ideas were captured in his philosophy of 'quality, service, cleanliness and value' or 'Q, S, C & V'. In terms of marketing orientation, it means customers enter a clean restaurant, are served by a friendly salesperson, are served quickly and receive a basic meal that is priced competitively and targeted at particular audience groups, and which they can eat there or take out. There are no jukeboxes or cigarette machines and McDonald's are clearly aimed to appeal to family groups.

The arts of servicing customers are taught to employees and franchisees, and each McDonald's aims to become part of a neighbourhood through community involvement. As it does this, McDonald's continue to pursue business opportunities around the globe. Its focus upon consumers has made it into the world's largest food-service organisation.

POINTS FOR DISCUSSION

1. Focusing upon your own experiences of McDonald's, describe the market-orientating factors that have helped to make it such a huge success.
2. Briefly describe each of the elements of McDonald's marketing mix.
3. In what ways do these factors provide McDonald's with a clear advantage over many of its competitors?
4. What are the problems with sustaining marketing focus in the light of previous marketing successes?

SECTION B SUGGESTED ANSWERS

CHAPTER 10 THE PRINCIPLES OF MARKETING

Case study: shopping without stress for fun (pages 248–249)

1 Shopping habits have changed fundamentally in recent years, with an increasing focus upon meeting customer needs in many more different ways. The environment in which we shop has changed, with more precincts, better shopping centres and better-focused customer-shopping environments. The experience not only includes the shop but also customer service and even peripherals such as the quality of the plastic bag. Recent changes have seen a movement towards shopping over the Internet, more mail order, out-of-town centres and much more focus upon targeting and needs.

2 There are many ways in which shopping has become more focused upon customer needs in recent years. Students may draw extensively upon their own personal experiences as they discuss these changes. For example, these include:

- use of technologies
- a better customer environment
- shops focusing upon customer segments
- improved targeting
- locating retail outlets that are designed to meet customer needs and requirements more carefully
- better-trained staff offering a consistent service
- the use of the Internet, etc.

3 The answer to this question should draw from students the difference between a customer-focused experience and one that is not. The likelihood is many will refer to both good and bad experiences, with good experiences providing a range of benefits and bad experiences discouraging customers from visiting particular outlets again.

Discussion point (page 250)

The organisation chart on page 250 of the student book clearly indicates that, for Starbucks, the most important people of all are its customers. It shows that everybody in the organisation, including the resources they control, are focused upon customers.

Case study: Virgin Holidays (page 251)

1 This is a question that places great emphasis upon the students' observations. It also asks a rather 'loaded' question by asking why many of the business strategies adopted by Virgin have been successful. Students may identify a number of factors that could be used as a basis for discussion. For example:

- entrepreneurial vision
- a good brand name
- products focused upon customer needs
- a reputation and brand heritage, etc.

2 Online holidays help users to browse and discover more about places and facilities before they book their holidays. They can be accessed in the home, be based upon the use of a PC or laptop, enable customers to look at specific holidays and also enable customers to make comparisons, judgements and decisions in the environment of their own homes.

Check your understanding (page 251)

In this exercise, students are asked to describe how an organisation known to them anticipates market needs and opportunities. It is not easy to understand and anticipate market needs. In order to do this, organisations will frequently use market research as a focus for understanding the behaviour of different groups of customers, and then build a strategy that directly targets them in a variety of ways. Given the broad nature of this exercise, students could use their own knowledge of the organisation – but also be creative. It is clear that organisations that do well and that are successfully marketing are more likely to be those that have anticipated market needs and opportunities closely.

Discussion point (page 252)

This is a different statement from that of the Chartered Institute of Marketing and, as a result, it tries out different points that broaden the students' understanding of marketing principles and practices. For example, it is clear to see this statement emphasises the reduction of risk. It also, in its own way, highlights the role of marketing research by emphasising the process (formal techniques) marketing uses to assess the situation before applying the response through the adjustment of the ingredients of the marketing mix.

Check your understanding (page 252)

As a data interpretation exercise, this is designed to encourage the students to interrogate figures for trends and developments. For example, aerobics, badminton and swimming are popular sports amongst females, particularly those under 24 years of age. As a starting point for product development, this clearly indicates that the markets aimed at such demographic groups could have a high potential. This is, however, fairly basic trend information, so students might pose other questions or refer to the need for other data. It is important to draw out points that describe how manufacturers would use this information. For example, would they use it to predict sales, develop more new products on the basis of trends, ascertain other data, such as market share information, etc.?

Case study: falling behind the needs of the customer (page 254)

1 It could be argued that M&S have not so much encountered problems in recent years as created them. They were originally supported by the blind faith of customers and products were concerned with rather archaic values such as 'dependable'; they were also regarded as dull, and M&S were considered to be out of touch with fashions because of their emphasis upon value. As customers became disaffected, this spread across all their sales and started to become a major problem for the organisation.

2 Marketers failed to keep up with customer needs by ignoring customer trends, focusing instead upon products rather than the market, by becoming embroiled in increasingly M&S-dominant supply chains and by selling dull, unfashionable products.

3 The consequences for M&S have been vast. The company has seen a fall in turnover across all sectors. Consumer disaffection also has longer-term financial ramifications.

Case study: an online rival to Dixons (page 255)

1 Shoppers for electrical products either buy from the high street or from an out-of-town shopping mall. Some purchases may take place at specialist retailers, as well as an increasing amount through mail order (particularly the Internet).

2 Although present patterns of shopping are not illustrated in this study, there are many different types of customers who may be targeted by an electrical retailer. There are also many different ways of breaking them down. For example, customers may be broken down according to age, income, socioeconomic profiles, lifestyle, customs, etc.

3 Dixons clearly need to undertake some form of strategic review to assess their market position if they wish to remain the largest electrical retailer in the UK. Given the changing nature of the market, clearly the use of the Internet is likely to become more widespread as people buy more products online. They may also look for forms of relationship marketing, perhaps through mail order and catalogues.

4 Failing to respond to the competitive threat would mean that, over the longer period, Dixons would lose market share and their role as the largest retailer would be threatened.

Check your understanding (page 256)

The purpose of this activity is to encourage the students to identify two market-leading products in the same market segment. It is helpful if students analyse two products that compete directly each other, as this can make it easier to compare the subtleties behind two different marketing strategies (e.g. own-brand tomato soup and Heinz or *The Mirror* and *The Sun*). The matrix on page 256 of the student book illustrating comparisons between the marketing mix of two products should serve as the model upon which the student can base his or her analysis.

Check your understanding (page 257, a)

This question expects the students to think carefully about the nature and characteristics of products in similar markets, and to make observations as to whether they are:

- product orientated – for example, the students may refer to gadgets, electronic devices or other products that have a high technical input. They might also mention organisations that are very product focused. In each case, product-focused organisations are unlikely to serve large markets. For example, it could be argued that a Rolls-Royce or another motor car with a high product specification is product orientated.
- market orientated – students may refer to products or organisations that attempt, through their market focus, to reach mass markets. For example, *The Times* has had circulation increases in recent years. With both price cuts and the development of popular elements, the whole newspaper has become much more centred upon the requirements of a larger market.
- sales orientated – this orientation is about 'piling it high and selling it cheap'. Boyes is a popular store in the north east of England that appeals to mass consumer markets by selling products cheap in high streets. There are many other examples of shops that are as sales orientated. It is also possible to argue about the fine distinction between sales and market orientation. For example, given the intense competition between supermarkets, have some become more sales orientated as they search for better market shares?

As students discuss these different orientations, the tutor should try to encourage them to think about which sort of orientation is more likely to be successful.

Check your understanding (page 257, b)

This exercise is designed to encourage the students to visit a site that provides a valuable source of secondary data. Although there are other sites, students may wish to bookmark this site or combine their use of it with a search for other websites that may provide them with the sort of data they could use in their studies of this area.

Check your understanding (page 258)

The lists show the top radio stations by breakfast-time advertising revenue as well as the top advertisers on breakfast radio. There are many reasons why advertisers target breakfast radio. For example, these might include:

- earlier in the day, consumers are more receptive to advertising messages
- breakfast radio is perceived to be fun and lively. Radio stations usually have their best staff working at this time of day
- viewing figures for local radio stations are high
- they provide a perfect opportunity to target specific demographic groups and audiences in a region.

Students might want to look at one or two of the advertisers before commenting upon what they are looking for. For example, Coldseal double-glazing may want to introduce a new promotional campaign in a particular area. Advertising on radio may be part of that promotion. Mobile phone companies may be seeking to compete with each other on the radio by increasing brand awareness and through emphasising differences between products and deals, perhaps as part of a seasonal campaign. Students may want to discuss their own views of the effectiveness of such messages on local radio. They may say that although, on the one hand, they may detract from listening, others may be perceived as fun and wacky, in tune with the programmes themselves.

Case study: interactive advertising (pages 259–260)

1 Interactive advertising involves viewers having the opportunity to follow up advertisements as and when they appear on their screens. So, as advertising takes place, the viewer could respond in a variety of ways.
2 At this stage this would have appeal only to particular groups of consumers, at first

those who are either cable subscribers or who have Sky Digital. And, even then, it would appeal only to particular groups of individuals who use each of these services. For example, it might appeal to young individuals, those who want to purchase from home and save the bother of using the high street, discerning consumers who want to find out a great deal about products before making decisions, etc.

3 There may be many different product categories that can be developed through this medium, including cars, health-related products and white goods, such as dishwashers and fridges. Products are more likely to be durable rather than consumable, so consumers would want to see more information before making any decision.
4 Real-time involves an advertisement interacting during a commercial, during which time consumers respond to the messages. Non-real-time involves the viewer making a conscious decision to press an icon, either after an advertisement or in his or her own time.
5 Advantages for TV viewers:

   - they can follow up advertisements
   - enables comparisons to be made between products
   - puts the viewers in more control of what they see.

   For the advertiser, it:

   - enables leads to be followed up
   - allows an element of relationship marketing to develop
   - allows the advertiser to interact further only with those customers who are interested in the product and so helps to increase the advert's effectiveness.

Check your understanding (page 261)

The purpose of this exercise is to encourage the students to be creative, using a mouse without a roller-ball as a starting point for their ideas. It is important they think about who the target market is likely to be for their mouse, as well as the competition for this type of mouse in that market. These products already exist in a variety of forms across a range of users, and are particularly targeted at gamers. However, they might want to consider the alternative market segments as well as the ease with which a 'smart' mouse might be put to other uses.

Check your understanding (page 263)

The umbrella could probably be described as a mature product. It has been around for a long time and, although from time to time there have been design improvements and changes, they can retail from as little as a couple of pounds. It could be argued this market is in such a state of maturity and decline it would be impossible to revive it, but how creative are the students? Do they think there are any possibilities with this product or the markets it serves? The purpose of this activity is for the students to use market research techniques to find out. These techniques may be based upon the use of their ideas, as well as a careful analysis of the market, to see if the umbrella could appeal to different demographic groups.

Case study: becoming millionaires! (page 264)

1 There are a number of internal constraints to the activities of Dan and Ron. For example, the first clear constraint is having enough cash to buy either the videos or the quick-boiling kettles. There are a number of other internal constraints affecting their internal capability to store, distribute, market and sell them. As well as such internal constraints, there are also external factors limiting their ability to undertake these transactions. For example, there seem to be question marks over the 'pedigree' of the products and they may be breaking the law. Similarly, they have to decide if it is the right time to release such products and how they will relate to their competitors in the markets they use.
2 Such constraints clearly limit their ability, first, to enter the market for each of their product areas and, secondly, to buy and sell goods. Having said this, as market traders, they are in an area where it is easy to set up a business, but also one where it is possible to make expensive mistakes.
3 In order to deal with their constraints, the priority seems to be to obtain some

finance and pursue the options necessary to buy the products. At the same time, they must examine questions concerned with the legality of the products and, if they feel the products are a good option, then attempt to find out if they might sell by undertaking some basic market research.

Check your understanding (page 265)

There are many stakeholder groups for a school or college, each of which may be affected in a number of ways by the actions of managers in the organisation. For example, these may include:

- the students – the students will be affected in a number of ways, such as for timetabling and the distribution of resources
- the local community – will be affected by the out-of-school hours use of the facilities, perhaps for sport or night classes
- teachers, cleaners, support staff and others – who may depend upon the school or college for employment
- suppliers of educational materials, such as books – depend upon such institutions to buy goods or services from them
- local education authority – whose reputation will depend upon the performance of individual schools
- the government – whose actions affecting schools and influencing examination results will impact on the ways in which their education policies are perceived
- the environment – the way the school or college looks, and how it is managed or maintained, will influence how the institution's environment is perceived
- parents – will clearly want the school or college to work in the best interests of their sons or daughters.

Check your understanding (page 266)

There are many situations over which stakeholders may disagree. For example:

- meeting environmental standards may reduce profits for shareholders
- reducing the number of staff in an organisation may reduce its effectiveness in meeting the needs of customers
- keeping paperwork up to date for the government may make the business more unmanageable, and make it more difficult to satisfy customers
- giving wage rises to managers would reduce profits.

Case study: stakeholder interests (pages 266–267)

1 In each of the following instances the stakeholders are:

- Barmac – employees and the local economy
- Halifax – investors and customers
- Microsoft – competitors, customers and society
- European regulations – part-time workers and small businesses
- BT – competitors and customers
- DTI – taxpayers, Post Office employees.

2 In resolving each of these issues, each would have to be deal with in turn:

- Barmac – difficult to resolve unless investment comes in from another source
- Halifax – could be resolved with better security
- Microsoft – could be resolved by dividing up the corporation
- European regulations – could be resolved with more help for small businesses
- BT – could be resolved if BT got rid of its dirty-tricks campaign
- DTI – other options could be open for Post Offices, such as privatisation.

3 For this answer the students have to choose one of the instances and discuss realistic options for dealing with the dispute. For example, in the first instance, central intervention from government or from EU sources may help to keep the yards open in the north of Scotland.

CHAPTER 11 ESTABLISHING CUSTOMER NEEDS

Discussion point (page 269)

In the context of market research, this means that, if a problem has been analysed and recognised, a solution can be applied. Market research is there to help to solve problems by providing the data that enables realistic solutions to be developed. Where marketing disasters such as the Millennium Dome have taken place, it could be argued that insufficient data from research had been generated. Market research does not take away risk, but it does help to reduce it.

Case study: connecting the washer to the web (pages 269–270)

1 Although the innovations reflect sound product research, such developments would not be acceptable to customers unless they are linked with effective processes of market research. Market research ensures customers want such products, will be helped by the new range of machines and will make purchasing decisions at the price points indicated.
2 Market research might aim to find out: how much customers are willing to pay; the uses customers might make of such machines; the nature and types of customers willing to purchase these machines; the sort of customer service package they might require; other product features customers might want; etc.
3 At this stage this is clearly a premium entry product skimming the market at a high price. The range of products is innovative, with an appeal to high-income 'tech' customers.

Check your understanding (page 271)

In finding out what courses might encourage new students to enter the school or college, or to persuade existing students to stay longer, the students may wish to talk to a number of other students or tutors. The sort of information that would be useful would include:

- information about the nature and types of courses offered by different examining bodies – data about results is available over the Web
- data from other educational institutions
- data from local authorities.

Check your understanding (page 272)

Although to some extent the distinction between proactive and reactive organisations is a matter of perception, working in groups will help to identify the real differences between organisations that seem to respond and those that seem to follow. For example, many might claim Virgin as a proactive organisation, or events during the winter of 2000/2001 would support the view that Railtrack is reactive.

Case study: using focus groups in the car industry (page 274)

1 Focus groups or clinics allow potential customers to react at a very early stage to new concepts.
2 A variety of issues would be dealt with by such groups, such as product concepts and features, names, services, prices, etc.
3 Preselecting the right people for the focus groups is clearly important. It would involve people wishing to trade down or trade up as well as other carefully identified discerning motorists and customers.
4 Information would be linked to market research data already gathered and this could be used with other data, such as costing information, design data and product development data.

Check your understanding (page 276)

The purpose of this task is to encourage the students to learn about some of the issues when setting up a consumer discussion panel. The starting point would be for members of the panel to record data over a two-week period. They should then be prepared to answer questions about this data. It might be sensible to narrow this data down into some form of product or service area. For example, the students could be asked to collect information related to their use of public transport, entertainment or convenience food.

Case study: waving the wand (pages 276–277)

1 Being a member of a Homescan panel would involve using the wand and other information associated with it to record purchases.
2 The information is considered valuable as it provides a precise record of purchasing

data, and this would relate to promotional offers, price changes and any other changes in the market.

3 Companies and marketers managing products in each market would use the information. This would give them a better understanding of the market, particularly when various changes take place.

Check your understanding (page 280)

We are probably all fooled in some instance by examples of suggers and fuggers, thinking they are real market researchers. One of the tests is to ask the researcher for some form of identification. If their ID relates to the charity or fund-raising body or to the company they are selling for, they are unlikely to be real market researchers. Real market researchers will be working for an agency and will have a range of professional experience in collecting data.

Discussion point (page 280)

The process of 'Internet relationships' is still in its infancy. An online relationship does, however, open up a range of new possibilities for developing new avenues with groups of consumers. For example, it may be possible to set up consumer groups via the Web through chat rooms/cafés; similarly, customer service could be improved through a responsive e-mail facility.

Check your understanding (page 281)

Questionnaires are often much more difficult to write than many think. The purpose of this exercise is to give the students basic experience in writing their own questionnaires and in developing their interview techniques. The starting point for the activity is for them to write a basic questionnaire that would enable them both to find out and to record the hobbies and leisure pursuits of respondents they may interview. The students should jot down any problems they may have had when conducting their interviews. For example, they might not have had enough space to take notes, or not have asked clear questions respondents understood. The other market research methods they might identify could include observation, Internet questionnaires or postal questionnaires.

Discussion point (page 282)

Students may debate the pros and cons of some form of mystery shopping extensively. On the positive side, it may keep staff on their toes, encourage them to treat everybody as if they are an inspector and ensure continuity of service. However, on the negative side, it could be considered to be a form of spying on employees and could discourage employees from relaxing. This may have a negative effect upon customer relationships.

Check your understanding (page 285)

The tutor should encourage the students to think about the nature and purpose of a questionnaire they have recently used. They should be asked to evaluate the questionnaire critically as respondents. For example, how could it have been improved? They also need to think about the purpose of the questionnaire and what it was trying to find out. Were there any issues surrounding the questionnaire about which they felt uncomfortable or any questions they did not understand? The students should be asked to identify any issues with the questionnaire they felt uncomfortable with.

Case study: your opinion about the performance of a product you regularly purchase (page 286)

1 This is a simple questionnaire designed to find out how the performance of a product can be improved to meet customer needs more closely. The responses from the questionnaire may be presented to product developers or marketers for further discussion, or even be used to glean more information from a focus group.

2 The questionnaire attempts to find out if a consumer is satisfied with a product and to analyse whether satisfaction levels have improved or got worse over a time period. It also looks for reasons for any changes that have occurred.

3 The questions start with a scale and are then open-ended.
4 The first two questions are quantitative and easy to analyse. The final two questions are designed to evoke a more qualitative response, and would be more difficult to interpret.

Check your understanding (page 288)

For this question, students need to think further about how they would undertake a research process for this area, related to a product that is familiar to them such as those suggested. The important element in their answer is how well they justify their choice of sampling method. For example, they may go for convenience sampling because a product has a broad market, and this is a cheap and easy method of sampling to use.

Check your understanding (page 289)

Nearly all products go through extensive field trials of one form or another before use, particularly cosmetics and pharmaceuticals.

Case study: the Electricity Generating Company (page 290)

1 The answers to these questions help marketers in the company to know more about the nature and type of customers in each of the markets it serves. Such questions would help them to develop and target appropriate products at customers in specified market segments. They would also help the company develop a strategy to target the most profitable customers. Answers would also help them to develop the most appropriate methods of operation which, on the one hand, would be low cost while, on the other hand, providing the best customer service.
2 Other questions might include:

- What size and types of business use electricity and other services?
- How effective are company strategies in encouraging peak-rate and economy-rate use?
- How effective are company strategies in influencing the market?
- What changes are taking place in payment methods?
- Which types of customers find different forms of payment most appropriate for their needs? etc.

Check your understanding (page 291)

For the owner or manager of a small shop, the information that might provide a better understanding of decisions might be:

- demographic information about customer groupings
- consumer information about consumption habits and changes
- competitor information about the actions of other organisations serving the market
- product information.

Discussion point (page 291)

Population projections such as those provided by census information are valuable because they provide:

- a breakdown of age profiles
- information about which groups are getting larger/smaller
- the basis for forecasts about product or service changes.

Further demographic information could include:

- birth and death rates
- demographic statistics by region
- links between demographic information and socioeconomic considerations.

Check your understanding (page 293)

Examining the external environment of a product or industry is significantly easier to undertake than in the past, mainly because of access to, and availability of, technology. The purpose of this activity is for students to identify sources for their research, such as Mintel reports, newspapers, etc., as well as appropriate Internet sites. Final analysis would provide a summary of the external environment for the product or industry.

Case study: applying to be a market researcher (pages 294–295)

1 The person specification would include:

Attributes	Essential	Desirable	How identified
Skills	Good research skills	Previous experience	CV
	Knowledge of statistics	Degree or other higher level qualification	Certificates

2 The purpose of this part of the question is for the students to think about how well or otherwise they might fit the specification for this post, particularly given they will have drawn this up. Having done this, they will then have to draft a letter of application for the post. The tutor may wish to refer them to pages 397–400 of the student book in order to help them draft their letter. The tutor may also wish to integrate this process more closely with recruitment and selection, and arrange or stage some videotaped interviews.

Discussion point (page 296)

Even though we live in days where there are claims for freedom of information, there is a strong argument that access to databases should be limited to prevent people using information against others; to keep sensitive information confidential; to provide fair competition between organisations; etc.

Check your understanding (page 297)

Students may identify a number of different product markets they feel have potential for growth. For example, these may include electronic or entertainment products, new food products or lifestyle commodities. In their chosen area, they need to think about the sort of information that would help them to analyse changes in each marketplace. For example, this might include demographic information, consumer data from different market research agencies, information from other commercial sources, as well as first-hand primary data.

Check your understanding (page 299)

The purpose of this activity is for the students to analyse the competitive activity of organisations in a specified market. They may wish to do this by analysing changes over a period of 3 or 4 weeks. The tutor should encourage them to think about changes from the viewpoint of decision-takers in each market. They may discover some of the decisions that have recently been made, such as product launches, promotional campaigns, re-imaging of brands, etc. They also need to think about the sort of information that would have justified such decisions, such as information relating to product life-cycle positions, etc.

CHAPTER 12 METHODS OF ANALYSING MARKETING OPPORTUNITIES

Check your understanding (page 301)

In this exercise, students are to think about many of the changes that are taking place in the environment of a business with which they are familiar. For example, it could be a small business or a large business one or more of their relatives works for. Rapid changes in the environment might include a need for re-imaging, for new products or a requirement for changing corporate strategies as many new competitors enter the market, etc. Slow changes may be imperceptible but could include a static market for products, few product changes, consumers with few discerning tastes, etc. In summarising their answers, the students should be encouraged to think about some of the things decision-takers can do to anticipate and respond to such changes.

Discussion point (page 302)

Where competition within markets is intense, consumers will periodically switch from one product or brand to another. Within these markets, it is imperative that organisations get their 'product offer' right. If they do not, given the elasticities within the market, consumers will switch to other products. For example, in recent years consumers have been far more likely to switch makes of motor cars or retailing habits. On the other hand, it could be argued that a business is not only as good as its next product, if there is little competition affecting consumer choice.

Case study: washing clothes (pages 302–303)

1 During the past 25 years the detergent market has undergone huge change as a result of:

- changes in the ownership of automatic washing machines
- the halving of the cotton content of fabric
- changes in social patterns
- the need to develop products that wash at lower temperatures.

2 The market, although dominated by two companies, has a clear emphasis upon various brands and products, each of which is designed to match customer needs closely.

3 A business that failed to move as quickly as its competitors would lose customer support and sales, particularly by adopters of new products.

Case study: rapid change in an expanding marketplace (pages 304–305)

1 The telecoms industry has become deregulated. This has increased consumer choice and helped to lead to the rapid expansion of a wide range of services.

2 Marconi Communications, formerly GEC, has invested heavily in research and development for solutions designed to meet the needs of this massively expanding market and product area. It has been proactive in meeting market changes, with a rapid response to the needs of consumers and organisations in this market.

Check your understanding (page 307)

The PEST analysis may include a range of different features and characteristics as exemplified by the elements identified on pages 306–307 of the student book. When presenting their PEST to other students, it is important the points are supported in a rational and theoretical way.

Case study: developing the portable DVD player (pages 308–311)

1 The advertisement for the newspaper or magazine should be focused and relevant. It should also emphasise clearly the support or use it makes of branding.

2 The tutor should ask the students to check their totals. The tutor may also wish the students to check each other's totals.

3 The presentation should be both creative and theoretical. The tutor should encourage the students to use marketing/advertising-related words.

Check your understanding (page 313)

This activity is largely anecdotal. From time to time problems do develop with products or the provision of services, but what was the best way to deal with such issues? This activity enables the students to recount such events and also to discuss what should or should not constrain the activities of organisations.

Case study: Toyota (GB) Ltd (page 314)

1 It is argued advertisers should take into account the views and sensitivities of individuals as the last thing they want to do is to start some form of consumer boycott. Similarly, it is claimed it is ten times more expensive to attract new customers as retain old customers, so by damaging goodwill with customers, a company could be incurring considerable expense.

2 The complainant was unhappy that the advertisement showed the car in a setting that was illegal for motorists and, thus, might lead to irresponsible behaviour.

3 The ASA's decision was that this was a minority view. It was felt many others would not share the complainant's interpretation.

Check your understanding (page 315)

This activity should encourage students to keep a file of advertisements, identifying those that fall into the categories of not being altogether 'legal', 'decent', 'honest' or 'truthful'. They should be encouraged to write a short summary for each advertisement, explaining why they have identified it in that particular way.

Discussion point (page 315)

Students may have difficulty interpreting this discussion point. There is no doubt consumers want low prices and high-quality goods, but has consumerism passed or just begun? Students may argue that consumerism has become a product of the movement away from product centredness, towards market orientation, and that as markets become more focused upon the consumer, the consumer has developed more power and better opportunities to take decisions that meet his or her needs more closely. On the other hand, it could be argued that if markets are more consumer orientated, consumers have less of a need to be 'consumerist' about the products they buy.

Case study: eating GM convenience foods (page 316)

1 There are a number of arguments for informing consumers about the specific details of the products they are consuming. For example, some consumers may have allergies, others may have principles or practices they may want to follow (i.e. certain countries they may not wish to buy from, etc.) or they may simply want to know more about the composition of the products they use.
2 Changing negative to positive perceptions is not an easy process and may take considerable time. As a public relations exercise, it would involve considerable thought with many subtle processes.
3 There may be a number of areas where it could be argued labelling should change. For example, statements about sources of ingredients could be included, etc.

Check your understanding (page 317)

Stakeholders for a school or college could include teachers, other staff (including support staff and managers), local residents, students, the local authority, suppliers of equipment and books for the school or college, local shops, etc.

Discussion point (page 317)

If a company was downsized, the proposition might be supported by creditors and shareholders but opposed by employees and managers.

Check your understanding (page 318, a)

The purpose of this activity is to encourage students to broach issues that deal directly with their own consumer interests. The important ingredient for each group is to identify its own objectives and standards, before seeing if the service or products they are monitoring come up to such standards.

Discussion point (page 318)

It could be argued that restricting the access of specific products (such as cigarettes and tobacco products) is an infringement of the rights of each individual, as well as a way of distorting the market mechanism. On the other hand, as the consumption of these products is against the health interests of the individuals who use them, it could be argued less exposure to them would reduce consumption.

Check your understanding (page 318, b)

In answering this question, students should consider whether the advertisements they watch are legal, decent, honest and truthful, comply with the law, apply to the spirit of the law and meet various codes and pieces of legislation.

Discussion point (page 321)

There are almost no markets where segmentation does not take place. Even salt comes in different forms geared for different groups of consumers. It may be better for the students to refer to industrial markets where, with a limited consumer base, goods are less segmented (e.g. iron ore or sugar).

Check your understanding (page 322, a)

For example, in the popular segment of the tea market, advertising would be national, prices would depend upon the strength of the brand, the product would be high quality and the goods would be available in all outlets. In contrast, in the economy segment, products would be cheap, the product would be available only in certain low-cost or budget outlets and the quality and integrity of the brand would not be so high; the advertising and other promotional methods would also be limited.

Check your understanding (page 322, b)

The key element in this exercise is for the students to contrast the marketing mixes of two similar products in order to identify different positioning strategies. The tutor should try to encourage them to think about how each of the products is perceived by consumers across a range of areas, such as price, value, brand image, etc.

Case study: is the replica football shirt dead? (page 323)

1 Wearing replica football shirts has become unfashionable in recent years. Fashion markets change quickly, and brands other than 'football clubs' have become much more desirable because they are more aspirational and individualistic.
2 It has not been easy for football clubs to avoid such changes in tastes. There are, however, a number of avenues, one of which is to focus upon alternative types of clothes, other than football shirts, and either to join with other brands or to reposition their own brands through these clothes.
3 Repositioning to meet aspirational needs would inevitably involve a partner in the fashion industry, rather like the partnership between George and Asda Wal-Mart.

Case study: the PIMS study (page 324)

1 The evidence demonstrates there is a direct relationship between market share and profits, showing that organisations with a bigger market share are going to be more profitable. The results help to illustrate why market share is such an important business objective.
2 In rapidly changing markets, a proactive business is much more likely to be able to build and develop its market share than in relatively static markets. Static markets are characterised by several large organisations that retain market share.
3 Any reasonable examples for an appropriate industry would suffice. For example, it could be claimed that two organisations that have improved their market share in recent years are Tesco in the supermarket grocery sector and Virgin Atlantic in the area of air travel.

Discussion point (page 324)

It is wrong to assume that large organisations with a large market share are profitable. They may be inefficient, suffer from diseconomies of scale or be tied with costs related to size and other activities. A small niche organisation with a small market share may be efficient, responsive to consumer demand and successfully develop a market share that yields better profits than those of the large organisation. For example, one or two entrepreneurial snack food producers have been incredibly successful in serving small parts of the larger market with high-value premium branded products.

Case study: X1 Button radio (page 327)

1 The features and benefits of a radio that fits into an ear include portability, use of advanced technologies, few competitors (if any), inexpensive, etc.
2 Sinclair research might target teenagers, commuters, school students, etc.
3 The purpose of this question is to provide a creative opportunity for students to suggest ways in which the market penetration of this radio could be developed. As they do so, it is important they refer to the marketing mix.

Check your understanding (page 329)

This exercise is designed to encourage students to think about the sort of product portfolio developed by any large organisation, the life-cycle of products in a portfolio and the relationship between the marketing mix and time, as well as to think about how such a portfolio reaches different segments in a market. Cars are usually an easy example to use, but students may wish to focus upon some other type of organisation providing a broad and diverse range of products.

Check your understanding (page 330)

Again, it is difficult to provide answers for this question because they need to relate to timings and portfolio stages. A problem child would be a newly launched product; a star would be a product that had expanded and done well in a market but needed constant financial support; while a cash cow would be a successful product in a static market.

CHAPTER 13 DEVELOPING STRATEGIES TO MEET CUSTOMER NEEDS: THE MARKETING MIX

Case study: creating attention-grabbing websites (pages 334–335)

1 **a** The price would depend upon the nature and type of service provided for each customer as well as the complexity involved in developing its website. The number of hours allocated to each client might be used as a base to cost the activity or, alternatively, the various levels of service provided. **b** Given the nature and type of the industry, there would be many ways of communicating with customers. However, given the complexity of the service and the different levels offered, having a salesforce would clearly be an important ingredient. **c** Customer service would be an important element. Some customers may want whole-business solutions, while others may simply want a website. The nature and type of service would depend upon the customer. However, given the customised nature of the service for each customer, keeping in contact with them through some element of relationship marketing would be important. **d** Other product elements could include secure methods of buying and selling, chat-room facilities, e-mail returns, customer service pages, etc.

2 A company operating in such a proactive market will be successful, first, if it develops good customer relationships and, secondly, if it successfully broaches technological developments.

Check your understanding (page 335)

The purpose of this activity is for the students to study a particular product area in a supermarket in order to find out how they compete against each other. Some areas may be more proactive than others; for example, at the time of writing, packaging has become a key competitive area for soups. Students should be able to identify which area of the marketing mix is used as various brands compete against each other, as well as how this competitive activity benefits consumers. In analysing this area, they should learn about the segments of the product market as well as the benefits and drawbacks of having choice.

Discussion point (page 338)

This appears as a question rather than a discussion point. Clearly, premium goods have higher margins than fast turnover goods such as cigarettes or newspapers. Students may refer to the power of branding, status-orientated goods, the importance of lifestyle and the nature of luxury goods; in contrast, they may refer to what they perceive to be necessities, day-to-day goods and rapid-use consumer goods. They may also refer to patterns of purchase.

Check your understanding (page 339)

A value proposition refers to the expectations consumers have about the product or service for which they are charged. The purpose of this exercise is to decide which is the best value proposition by comparing two similar products or services.

Check your understanding (page 340)

1 skimming
2 value-based pricing

3 penetration pricing
4 cost-plus pricing
5 skimming
6 competition-based pricing.

Check your understanding (page 341)

Targeting first-time purchasers of PCs might involve building a strong support package, targeting groups with little incidence of PC use (such as elderly people or the very young) and attempting to build confidence through relationship marketing.

Case study: Blue Train (page 342)

1 Arguments for buying the brand are that:

- it is clearly prestigious and well known
- income levels from the brand can be calculated
- the brand might be transferred to other services
- other links may be made with tour operators.

Arguments against using the brand are:

- occupancy rates
- levels of profit and income
- need to replace rolling stock
- small market segment.

2 This task is largely creative, in that it tries to encourage the students to think about how they could use the brand across a range of packages and travelling opportunities. For example, they could use it to link it to packages on the Orient Express or to target it at train enthusiasts.

Case study: the power of brands (page 343)

1 Brands are important in creating: perceptions in the minds of consumers that may encourage repeat purchase; an appreciation of value for money; and confidence consumers have made appropriate decisions.
2 Although the answers for this may be subjective, and it could be argued that only a few brands could be exciting, clearly some are. Students may talk about selling promotional goods alongside brands, changing a brand image, repositioning a brand, using celebrity support, etc.
3 Though difficult and constantly changing, they may refer (as everybody does!) to Virgin, Marconi Communications, Golden Wonder, Dyson, RM or Tesco.

Check your understanding (page 344)

Being a brand manager is not always easy. This activity is designed to encourage students to think about how brands could be developed over a period of time in a way that injects life into each of the brands. They may refer to re-imaging, repositioning, extending the brand, diversification, etc.

Check your understanding (page 345)

Advertising campaigns do vary according to the objectives for each type of promotion. Students should look for one that is clearly trying to increase the sales of goods or services, and compare it to another that is simply trying to develop public support for its activities. Depending upon the campaigns, similarities may include product descriptions and various artistic merits and emphases, while differences could include product descriptions and an emphasis upon branding or image.

Case study: the top six advertisers, 1998 (pages 345–346)

1 Clearly P&G spends significantly more upon advertising, particularly TV, than any other advertiser. BT and Vauxhall are the largest spenders in the press, and probably use both national media and specialist publications. Advertising is used as a key base for competition in the motor sector. Consumer goods companies seem to be the largest competitors on TV. It would be interesting on this evidence to view the next 6 companies.
2 The other bracket might include direct mail, Internet advertising and bill boards.
3 Each of these companies is in a hotly competitive sector.
4 There may be a number of bases for evaluating the effectiveness of such a spend. These might include:

- sales added
- customer perceptions
- repeat purchases
- brand strength, etc.

Check your understanding (page 347)

The purpose of this activity is to think about why a family is targeted for the nature and type of direct mail delivered through its door. This might include socioeconomic factors, area, composition of household, response to direct mail, etc.

Discussion point (page 348)

The group may discuss a range of limitations they might wish to place on direct mail. For example:

- the number of items delivered
- the ability to withdraw from any form of direct mail
- harassing direct mail
- direct mail that uses unfair methods to encourage you to respond.

Check your understanding (page 349)

In the world of advertising and the media, public relations problems are probably the most difficult to solve. For example, how do you create positive perceptions of M&S's range of clothing or of Rover/MG cars in a short time frame? Students should scan the press looking for what they consider is a public relations problem; it could be an image problem, an issue dealing with ethics such as animals or trade in the developing world, environmental, or to do with people.

Case study: sponsoring the Nationwide Football League (page 352)

1 Sports sponsorship differentiates Nationwide from its competitors, provides it with increased exposure in a positive area, enables it to focus its advertising upon a targeted market and improves the profile of the brand.
2 Sponsorship might make consumers think of a brand in a favourable light and link it with energy and excitement; and it might be used to reposition the brand, to make it seem more memorable and interesting than its competitors.

Check your understanding (page 352)

Although there may be various answers to this, a merchandiser would place:

- milk at the back of the hypermarket so customers would have to come and walk around before buying any, even if they had just popped in for a single carton
- confectionery near the tills as this is an impulse purchase
- clothes at the front of a hypermarket because, when customers enter, they will have the time to browse
- chilled foods together with cook-in-sauces and complementary products.

Check your understanding (page 353)

We are all involved in selling of one kind or another, even if it is just ideas. Students should think of situations where they have 'sold' something to another person, as well as some of the issues involved. They may feel they have a range of responsibilities, such as telling the truth, not over-embellishing arguments, etc.

Check your understanding (page 355)

Many people purchase products or services for the augmented product that accompanies them. For example, the location and service provided by a garage may be as important as the make of car. Students should think of an example that has encouraged them to develop repeat-purchase patterns.

Check your understanding (page 356)

For example, the order would be processed; a purchase order would be sent to a sales department; a warehouse would be contacted; the book would be despatched to the bookseller's head office; it would then be processed and sent to the branch.

Discussion point (page 356)

Physical distribution is often the most underrated element of the marketing mix. Physical distribution is the system that links customers to products and services. It provides a speedy response, helps to meet customer needs and enables customers to have goods in the order size they require. On the other hand, it could be argued that physical distribution adds to the cost, can be inefficient and costly, and involves keeping large inventories.

Case study: distribution to Sainsbury's stores (page 357)

1 Problems delivering in the M25 zone may include traffic problems, low speeds, delivery restrictions, etc.
2 Problems could be overcome by night-time deliveries, better scheduling, using larger vehicles, keeping higher levels of stock, etc.

Check your understanding (page 359)

The advantages of using the Internet are speed, ability to order from your own home, the ability to make choices by visiting other sites and relationship marketing. Disadvantages might include security, not being able to see or sample the goods and postal delays.

Check your understanding (page 360)

This activity enables students to understand some of the decisions made by local retailers in a typical shopping area.

Check your understanding (page 361, a)

In order to find out about the retailing environment of two retailing organisations, students may wish to visit their websites. This is a fairly detailed activity, which the tutor may wish to use as the basis for a long assignment. It enables students to make a direct contrast between the retailing strategies of two organisations.

Check your understanding (page 363)

Examples of good customer service might include response times and knowledge of customer habits and trends, as well as the ability to greet customers and answer their queries. Poor customer service might involve waiting without being informed of the reason for the delay, an inability to deal with queries, a brusque manner, etc.

Check your understanding (page 365)

There are many answers for this, and students may think of a retailer of computers such as Tiny, PC World or Time. However, they might point to help lines, local customer support, online customer help, money-back policies, etc.

Discussion point (page 365)

There is a growing amount of evidence that AVCE students who work part time can use their experience of the workplace to improve the way in which they analyse learning situations. On-the-job training or personal development through a job role is accepted as a key way in which employees develop personally. However, it could also be argued that training also has a critical role in helping staff to improve.

Check your understanding (page 366)

The customer service strategy might include:

- telephone response times
- guaranteed marking periods
- staff dress and attire
- contact times
- handbooks and documentation
- appeals procedures, etc.

SECTION C OHTs

NOTES

OHT 3.10.1: successful marketing

This OHT would be a useful way of introducing the area of marketing. For example, why has marketing today been accepted as a strategic function of all types of organisations? This OHT links in with the list on page 247 of the student book. It shows how a range of different criteria are all related to the same central aim of meeting customer needs.

OHT 3.10.2: marketing defined

The purpose of this OHT is to provide not just the Chartered Institute of Marketing's definition of marketing but also to provide a brief breakdown of key terms in the definition. In order to do so, the tutor may also wish to refer the students to page 249 of the student book.

OHT 3.10.3: business orientation

This OHT is designed to show how marketing orientation has developed over time from production orientation, to sales orientation and then through to marketing orientation. The illustration matches that shown in Figure 10.1 on page 250 of the student book. It illustrates how we have moved from a situation where manufacturers feel they know what is best for customers, through to the period when customers were faced with cheap goods in volume, until we reach today, where many more organisations are market orientated, focusing upon meeting customer needs.

OHT 3.10.4: marketing mix

This illustration shows the four key (and most commonly categorised) elements of the marketing mix. The first element is the product. Once this element is developed, other elements can be focused upon to meet customer needs. The second is the price for the product or service provided, then the distribution (or place) that determines how the goods are available for customers and, finally, promotion, comprising advertising, public relations, personal selling, sales promotion and other key elements.

OHT 3.11.1: five phases of a market research plan

This OHT illustrates the five phases of a market research plan, from the research brief to the plan of work for the data to be collected, the collection of data, analysis and evaluation of data and, finally, the presentation of findings. The OHT is taken from Figure 11.1 on page 271 of the student book. The tutor may wish to develop the five-phase approach to market research as a piece of coursework for the students.

OHT 3.11.2: distinguishing between qualitative and quantitative information

It is important students understand the similar and complementary functions of qualitative and quantitative information. Quantitative information deals directly with hard facts and figures that can be examined statistically, whereas qualitative information deals with descriptions that may include opinions, preferences and other thoughts that are more difficult to analyse statistically. Although this information is difficult to categorise, it can be used after quantitative data has been collected to provide a broader and more detailed understanding of an issue.

OHT 3.11.3: focus groups

Focus groups are an inexpensive method of obtaining qualitative information from consumers. Participants may be product users or simply be selected according to a sampling method from a particular segment. Focus groups may also provide an opportunity to test opinions and perceptions. They may similarly be used to analyse key topics and can be developed to test new ideas.

OHT 3.11.4: your opinion about the performance of a product you regularly purchase

Taken from page 286 of the student book, this case study is designed so the tutor can put feedback from the students directly on to the OHT. Having briefed the students about the case study, the tutor could use this OHT to record feedback about a product that either individuals or groups of students regularly purchase.

OHT 3.12.1: matching the marketing environment to customer needs

This OHT tries to show how marketing attempts to match the knowledge developed from research in the external environment (such as that of markets, customer requirements, competition and of the business environment) to the process of making products or supplying services that closely meet customer needs. Students should think of marketing as something that enables an organisation to respond to external changes by developing the organisation internally to meet customer requirements better.

OHT 3.12.2: PEST model

Using Figure 12.4 on page 306 of the student book, this OHT identifies the four main forces contained in a PEST analysis. Students need to understand how carrying out a PEST analysis enables decision-makers to identify the key factors external to that organisation. The tutor may wish to combine this OHT with a description of the PEST process before asking the students to carry out a PEST analysis themselves using the 'Check your understanding' activity on page 307 of the student book.

OHT 3.12.3: SWOT analysis

This OHT may be used to build up the students' understanding of SWOT analysis, possibly before getting them to look at the long case study on pages 308–311 of the student book. The figure at the top of the OHT shows the four factors that form the basis of a simple SWOT analysis. The next figure identifies those factors that are in the organisation and those that are outside the organisation. Together with the last figure, this shows that strengths and opportunities are positive, and that weaknesses and threats are negative.

OHT 3.12.4: gap analysis

Gap analysis helps to identify variations by comparing recent variations with forecast and achieved figures. The essential purpose of gap analysis is to diagnose the problem, find a solution and use this knowledge to reduce the gap.

OHT 3.13.1: pricing objectives

Based upon the work of D. Shipley, the table shown on this OHT (Figure 13.2 on page 336 of the student book) indicates the principal pricing objectives of a range of organisations. It shows that, from the percentage of firms analysed, a target profit or return on capital employed is the main pricing objective followed by businesses that wish to set prices that are fair and firm for their customers. The tutor may want to follow this up by asking the students to relate these objectives to various pricing techniques.

OHT 3.13.2: skimming

A pricing technique that is commonly used at the launch of a new product is that of skimming. Many consumers, including this author, wait for pricing to reach a certain layer before making a purchase. The tutor could ask the students to think of their own examples of products where skimming has taken place, and could use the spaces on the OHT to reinforce the students' feedback.

OHT 3.13.3: direct mail

This OHT is designed to help the tutor to discuss the pros and cons of direct mail with the students. Direct mail is personally addressed advertising sent through the post, but what are the advantages and disadvantages? The tutor may wish to divide the students into groups and take feedback from each group using the OHT. For example, advantages may include precise targeting of customers, the ability to use offers to entice customers, the development of relationship marketing, the ability to send long messages at low cost. On the other hand, some of the disadvantages are the low response rate, few messages are read, mail that is perceived as junk mail, consumers now receive too much direct mail and that it may be thought of as intrusive.

OHT 3.13.4: selling into and out of the pipeline

Illustrating the processes of developing sales promotions into and out of the pipeline, this OHT helps to distinguish between the two processes. Promotions into the pipeline assist with the sale of products to the trade, in direct contrast to promotions out of the pipeline that assist the trade to sell to the final consumer.

OHT 3.10.1 SUCCESSFUL MARKETING

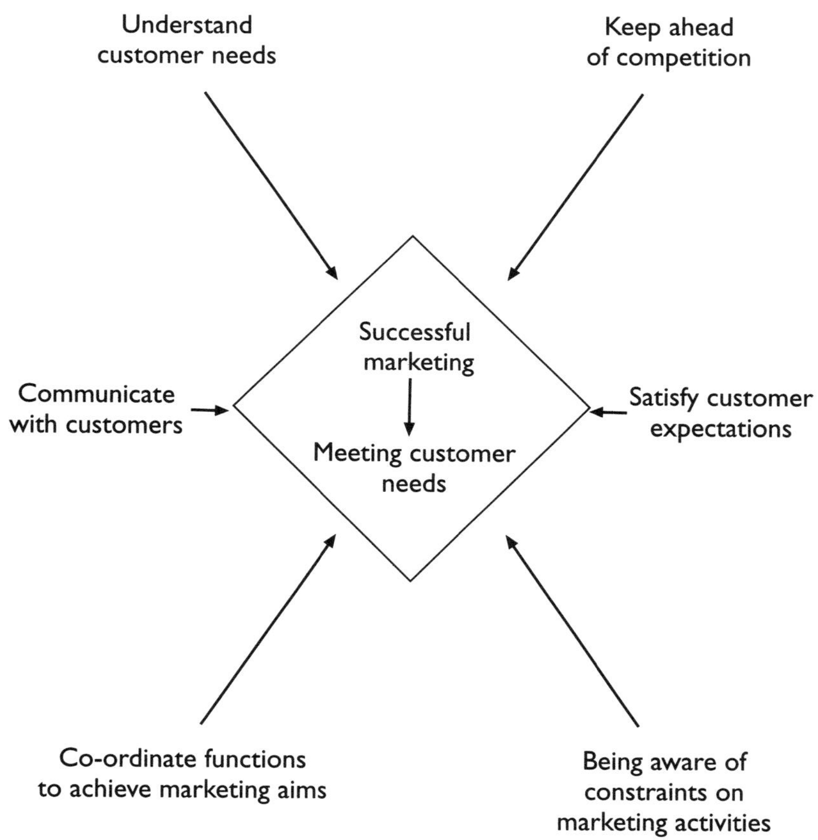

OHT 3.10.2 MARKETING DEFINED

'The *management process* responsible for *identifying*, *anticipating* and *satisfying* customer requirements *profitably*.'

- 'Management process' ⟶ managerial input.
- 'Identifying' ⟶ answering questions and finding out consumer requirements.
- 'Anticipating' ⟶ take into account that consumer requirements change all the time.
- 'Satisfying' ⟶ meeting customer requirements.
- 'Profitably' ⟶ objectives that motivate organisations to supply goods to consumers in a market.

OHT 3.10.3 BUSINESS ORIENTATION

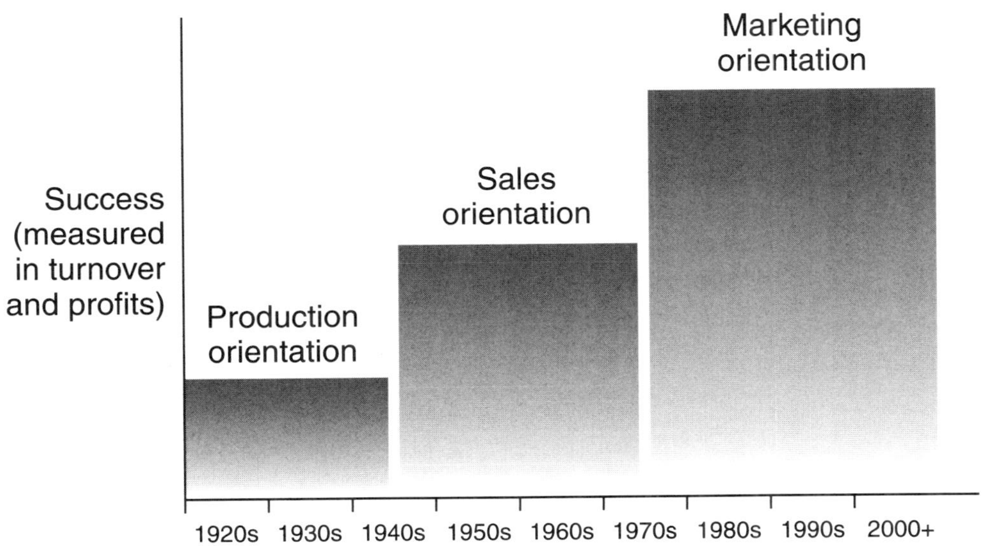

OHT 3.10.4 MARKETING MIX

OHT 3.11.1 FIVE PHASES OF A MARKET RESEARCH PLAN

One	Research brief	*Define the problem to be investigated*
Two	Plan of work	*Specify the data to be collected, the method of collection and the timings*
Three	Collection of data	*The efficiency of each stage should be checked*
Four	Analysis and evaluation of data	*Data storage and retrieval using a marketing information system*
Five	Presentation of findings	*This should be made to management groups and decision-makers, together with conclusions and recommendations*

OHT 3.11.2 DISTINGUISHING BETWEEN QUALITATIVE AND QUANTITATIVE INFORMATION

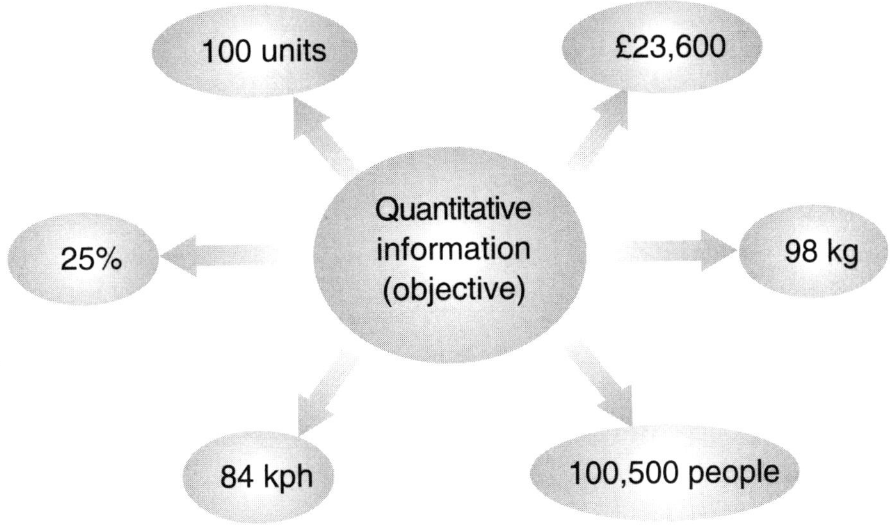

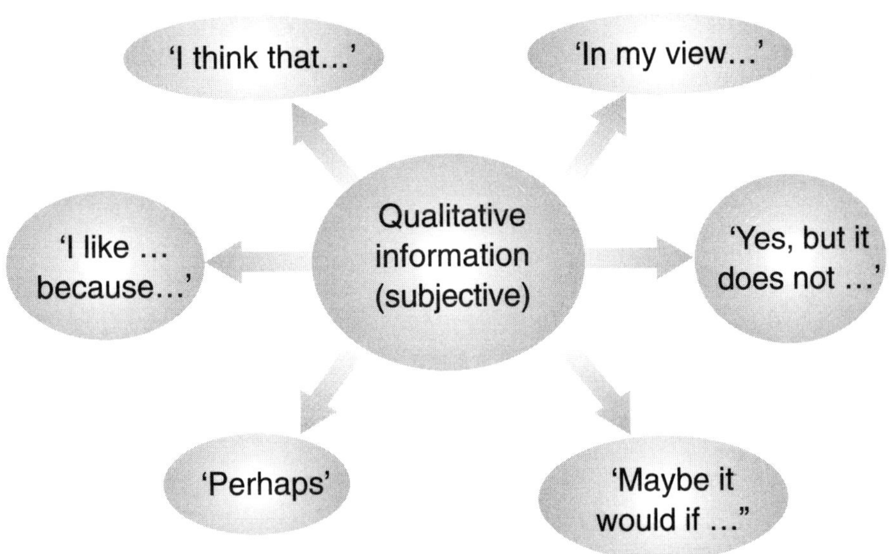

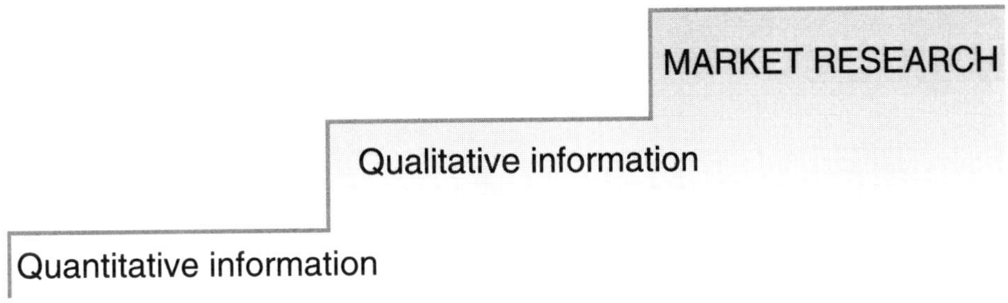

OHT 3.11.3 FOCUS GROUPS

- Inexpensive route to qualitative data.
- Opinions.
- Perceptions.
- Analysis of key topics.
- New ideas.

OHT 3.11.4 YOUR OPINION ABOUT THE PERFORMANCE OF A PRODUCT YOU REGULARLY PURCHASE

Total performance of Product A (including product, sales, support, price, etc.):

Dissatisfied ☐ 1 ☐ 2 ☐ 3 ☐ 4 ☐ 5 ☐ 6 ☐ 7 ☐ 8 ☐ 9 ☐ 10 *Very satisfied*

Compared to one year earlier, is Product A's total performance:

☐ Better ☐ Worse ☐ Same

Why?

What one thing can —— do to improve the performance of Product A in meeting your total needs?

OHT 3.12.1 MATCHING THE MARKETING ENVIRONMENT TO CUSTOMER NEEDS

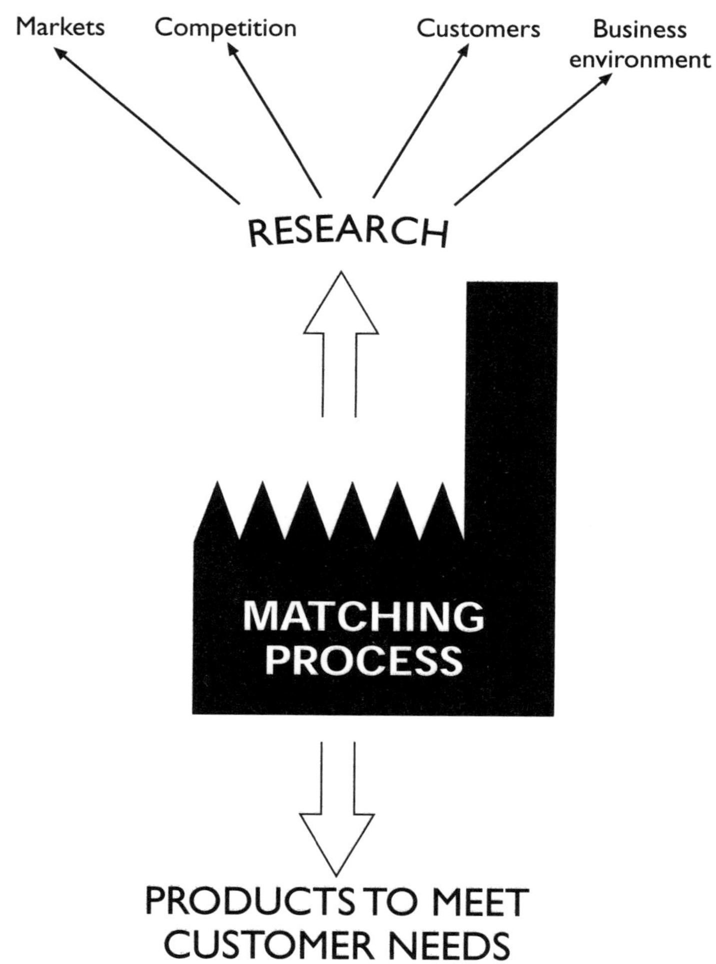

OHT 3.12.2 PEST MODEL

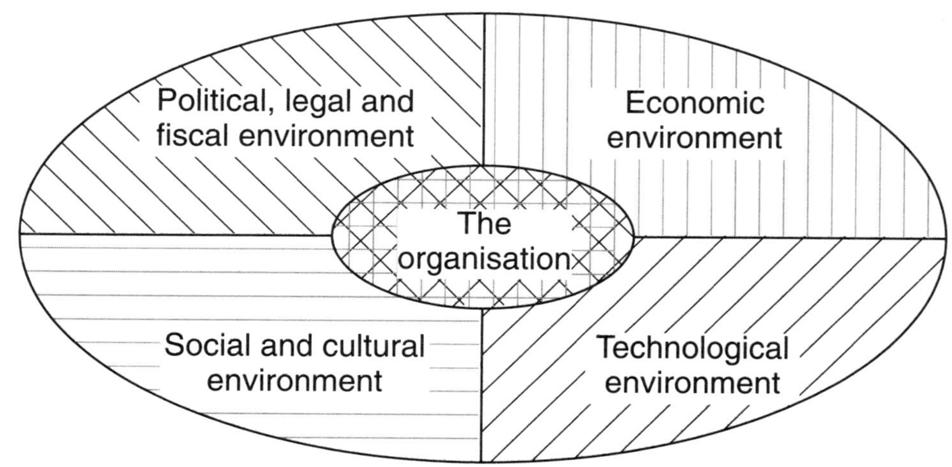

OHT 3.12.3 SWOT ANALYSIS

Product description _

Strengths	**Weaknesses**
Opportunities	**Threats**

Inside the organisation (internal)	**Outside the organisation** (external)
Strengths (positive)	*Opportunities* (positive)
Weaknesses (negative)	*Threats* (negative)

Inside the organisation	**The external environment**
Strengths +	Opportunities +
Weaknesses –	Threats –

OHT 3.12.4 GAP ANALYSIS

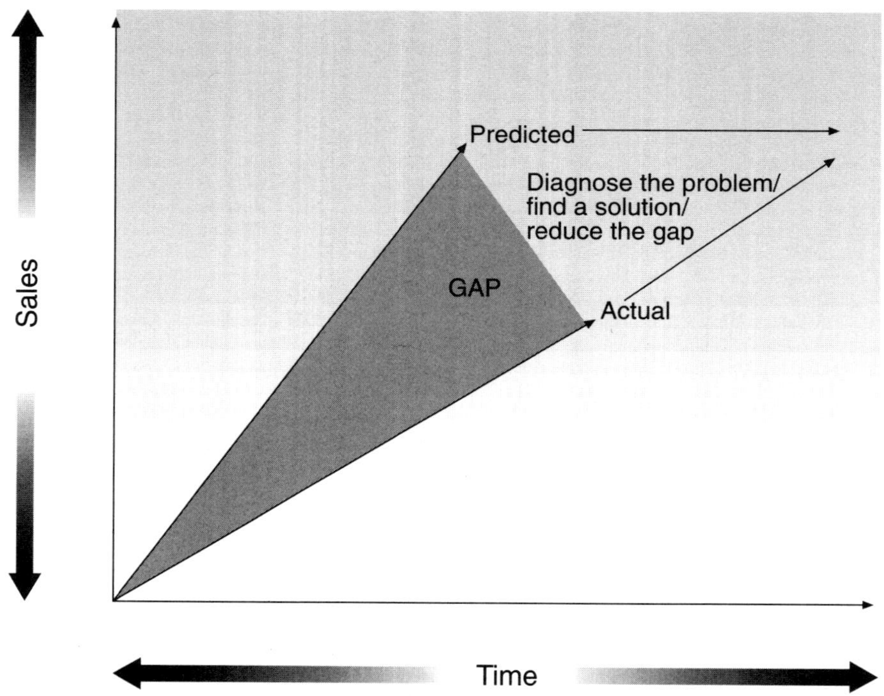

OHT 3.13.1 PRICING OBJECTIVES

Pricing objectives	Percentage of firms
Target profit or return on capital employed	67
Prices fair to firm and customers	13
Prices similar to those of competitors	8
Target sales volume	7
Stable sales volume	5
Target market share	2
Stable prices	2
Other	1

OHT 3.13.2 SKIMMING

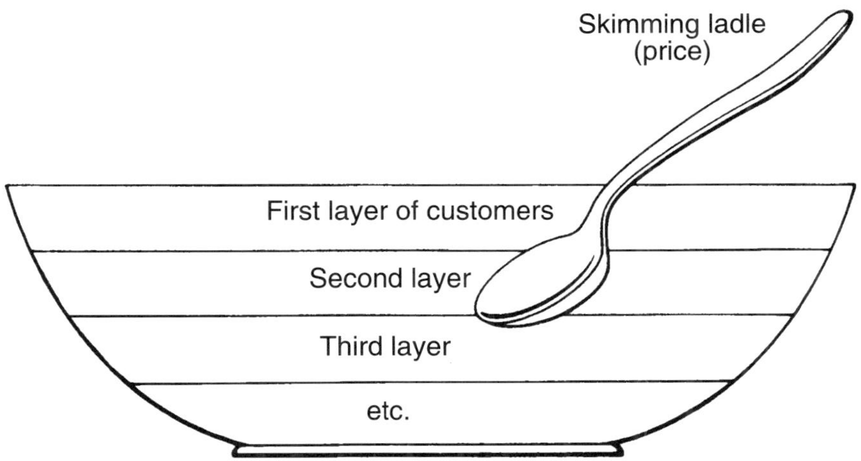

Examples

1 ______

2 ______

3 ______

4 ______

5 ______

OHT 3.13.3 DIRECT MAIL

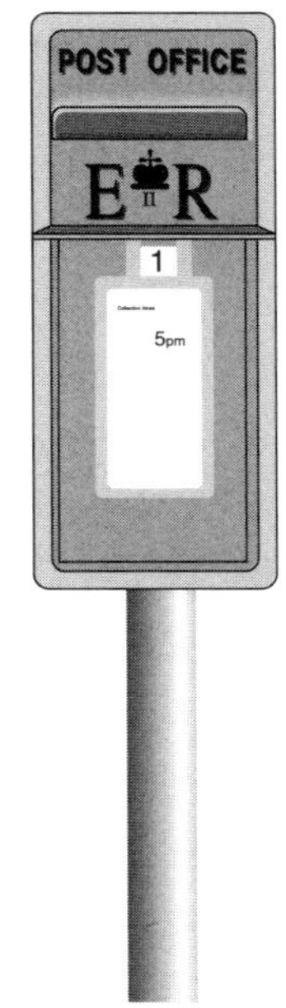

Advantages

1 ______

2 ______

3 ______

4 ______

5 ______

Disadvantages

1 ______

2 ______

3 ______

4 ______

5 ______

OHT 3.13.4 SELLING INTO AND OUT OF THE PIPELINE

Into the pipeline → promotions assisting with the sale of products to the trade

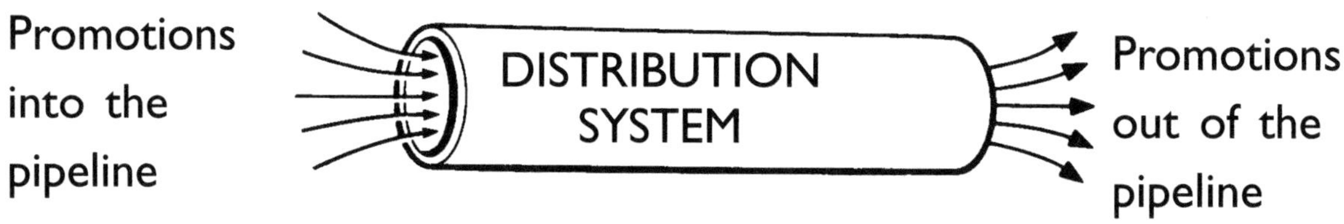

Out of the pipeline → assisting the trade to sell to the final consumer

SECTION D ASSESSMENT

DEVELOPING A MARKETING STRATEGY FOR A NEW OR EXISTING PRODUCT

In order to carry out this assessment, you need to put yourself into the position of a brand manager or product manager for an organisation you know. It helps if you have close personal knowledge of either the organisation or the products, and it would also help if you knew someone who worked for that organisation whom you could interview.

The starting point is to choose a product or service. You may want to choose a confectionery product or, given the rapidly changing nature of technologies, you may wish to choose some form of electronic product or service (e.g. an integrated home entertainment system or some form of Internet provision or trade).

You then need to undertake some comprehensive research to find out more, not just about the product or service you are researching but also about the market it reaches and the competitors for the product or service, as well as the consumers who are targeted by it. Your secondary research should enable you to:

- analyse the external environment for the product or service
- find out more about competitors
- develop an understanding of the marketing mix for the product or service
- analyse existing marketing strategies within this area of competition.

Primary research can then be used to:

- evaluate consumer perceptions of either new or existing product or service ideas
- consider the factors that influence consumer choice
- identify a range of issues that would influence your strategy.

Remember, it is the output and interpretation of these research processes that help to provide the justification for the strategies you wish to undertake. In a rapidly changing and more competitive environment, making decisions is not just about going with a 'hunch', but more about making measured judgements on the basis of concrete evidence that ensures risks are minimised.

AS YOU WORK THROUGH THIS ASSIGNMENT

1 Think about the different models you use as a basis for developing your marketing strategy. For example, are you going to use a SWOT or PEST analysis? What influences are the product life-cycle, the Boston matrix and the work of Ansoff going to have on the decisions you make?
2 Make sure the information you collect has some validity. For example, how has it been collected, what sampling techniques have been used, what consumers have been targeted, etc.?
3 Use appropriate marketing tools to evaluate your marketing strategy.
4 Think carefully about how to evaluate the reliability of all the different marketing tools you have used. For example, has the pricing technique you have used been the most important for your strategy? Remember, you must try to make sure all the different elements of your marketing strategy for this product or service fit together.

CHECKLIST FOR CARRYING OUT YOUR ASSIGNMENT TO A HIGH STANDARD

Tick the boxes

1 I have identified the product or service I have chosen and justified my choice. ☐
2 I have undertaken preliminary research, using secondary materials or the Internet. ☐
3 I have undertaken appropriate reading from the student book and referred to notes. ☐
4 I have created a plan for my secondary research. ☐

5 I have undertaken the secondary research and written up my findings. ☐
6 I have planned my primary research and developed my questionnaires. ☐
7 I have undertaken my primary research and written up my findings. ☐
8 I have used marketing models and tools to develop my strategy. ☐
9 I have related my strategy to my findings. ☐
10 I have produced my report, justifying my approaches. ☐

HOW YOU CAN USE KEY SKILLS WHILE WORKING ON THIS ASSESSMENT

Application of number skills

- While researching primary and secondary data, you should plan and interpret information from various sources.
- You should collect a range of different types of data that may be both quantitative and qualitative.
- You should think about how to use this information as a basis for a marketing strategy.

Communication skills

- You should describe your marketing strategy as part of a group discussion.
- You should develop a persuasive presentation of your strategy.
- You should take on the role of a marketing executive.
- You should show how to communicate complex ideas and thoughts.
- You should write a report.

Information technology skills

- You should collect, store, access and use data from the process of market research for your new product or service.
- You should use a range of text, image, numbers and other data in a presentation you make to your fellow students.

Problem-solving skills

- You should recognise a problem and understand the role you might have to play within an employment situation in solving that problem.
- You should make decisions based upon your understanding of the differences between a range of data.
- You should evaluate and justify your solutions for solving a problem or for making decisions.

Working with others

- You should plan the activity with others and, in doing so, identify responsibilities and set practical working arrangements.
- You should collect information from other people and review your targets with your tutor.

SECTION A DISCUSSION POINT

HOW 'LIBERATED' IS THE MODERN FLEXIBLE WORKPLACE?

Many people cite flexibility and teamwork as presenting the way forward for the twenty-first-century workplace. Gone is the hierarchical, top-down system ruled by an authoritarian boss. In its place is an adaptable, modern workforce.

However, some people believe the new workplace is not all it is cracked up to be, including sociologist Richard Sennett. He argues that flexibility and teamwork are, in fact, nothing less than a sham, an invention dreamt up to increase production and gain greater sway over the workers. According to his view, the modern office is a latter-day workhouse where people talk less, take fewer breaks and perform tasks in isolation. As a result, many employees are tired and fed up.

Richard Sennett's book (*The Corrosion of Character: The Personal Consequences of Work in the New Capitalism*, Norton, 2000) claims that employment systems are undermining people's self-esteem and even their personalities. Flexibility is supposed to allow workers to organise their own schedules without kowtowing to an authoritarian boss.

However, according to Richard Sennett, this is not the case. Flexibility breaks up continuity. The old workplace had 'continuous time' – long-termism, loyalty, dependence and paternalism – which gave lives a shape. What we have now is 'discontinuous time' – dislocation and loose networks altered at managerial whim.

In America, even flexitime isn't necessarily what it claims to be. Invariably it is granted to the most favoured employees, who are usually white, middle-class, daytime workers. Flexitime is not offered to night workers, who are often Hispanics or other disadvantaged groups.

Even working at home now has in-built controls when you are required to phone in and supervisors have the right to open e-mails. 'Workers exchange one form of submission to power – face-to-face – for another which is electronic', writes Sennett. 'The appearance of freedom is deceptive. Time in institutions and for individuals has been unchained from the iron cage of the past, but subjected to new, top-down controls.'

POINTS FOR DISCUSSION

1 What examples of modern flexible work practices are you familiar with? You may want to draw on your own work experience here (e.g. flexitime, job sharing). Describe how each of these flexible systems operate.

2 What are the advantages of flexible practices:

a to employers
b to employees?

3 Do you think work has changed for the better? Have we moved away from top-down work relations, to ones in which employees are trusted more and are given more responsibility? Or is flexibility just a sham to screw more work out of employees?

SECTION B Suggested answers

CHAPTER 14 HUMAN RESOURCES PLANNING

Case study: contradictions in human resource policy (page 373)

1 During the 1990s many companies in this country were reducing the size of their workforces by downsizing. Increasingly, firms were focusing on their core lines and cutting out activities that were regarded as non-essential. It was therefore a time of job insecurity. In contrast, HRM initiatives were all about showing increased concern for employee welfare. It is not surprising that, while HR managers were trying to convince their employees of the benefits of HRM, there was considerable resentment and cynicism on the part of the employees, who did not feel secure about their jobs.

2 Most students acknowledge that HRM is a good idea in theory and that it can have strong positive benefits when put into practice. However, most students also feel that HRM will work effectively only when it is based on a genuine concern for people rather than as another way to improve the bottom line.

3 The early years of the twenty-first century saw an improvement in the job market with unemployment figures falling. There was also a reduction in downsizing initiatives by many companies. If this continues there is room for optimism – although the next downturn in employment may be just around the corner.

4 Students need to follow the business press to find out whether the trend is still continuing. They should check on the latest unemployment figures and see whether the trend is for this to rise or fall.

Check your understanding (page 374)

This activity asks the students to check on whether the trend towards HRM is continuing. They can do this by interviewing employees in companies to find out whether this applies in specific institutions. Alternatively, they could examine reports in the business press about human resource initiatives.

Check your understanding (page 378)

1 Calculate by:

$$\frac{\text{Number leaving}}{\text{Number employed}} \times \frac{100}{1}$$

e.g. in 1991: $\frac{4}{120} \times \frac{100}{1} = 3.333$

2 The wastage rate increases from 1995 onwards. Factors leading to this might have been an increasing average age of the employees so that more were leaving, a decrease in the competitiveness of the wages offered by the advertising agency, changes in key personnel at the agency, internal tensions, increased pressure of work, etc.

3 The students would simply have to break down the workforce into a series of categories (e.g. those with degree qualifications against those without, those with over ten years of working in advertising against those with less time, etc.). The students should then simply calculate a wastage rate for each category.

Case study: Shelbourne School (page 379)

1 The students should use a calculator to work out these figures. These would show that between 1992 and 1995 the figure is 1% or less. In 1996 and 1997 it is about 5% and then it rises to over 10% in 1997–2000.

2 The figures show that the total number of staff in the school was falling, which may have created extra pressures on teachers, leading to increased stress and more people wanting to take early retirement. Many teachers may not have liked the pressures from the new head and from central government requirements. The turbulent atmosphere of change may have

encouraged more teachers to get out. A number of teachers may not have been able to cope with the extra pressures.

3 The answers to this are not clear cut. Increasing wastage rates imply an inefficient use of resources as new staff need to be trained and new relationships within the organisation have to be built up. The wastage rate may also indicate problems and tensions within the organisation so that it is not working effectively to meet its goals. Ideally, you would want people to stay with an organisation and to help a new manager to manage change. However, it is always helpful to have new people coming in with new ideas. The wastage rate may indicate some of the less efficient teachers are leaving.

Check your understanding (page 380)

Working in conjunction with the tutor, students need to gather this information from the school or college office – figures for the total number of tutors/numbers leaving in a given period (and also for ancillary staff). For the football club they need to look at the total number of players typically on the books of the club during the season against the numbers leaving.

Case study: skills shortage in Asia (page 382)

1 Southeast Asia is one of the most rapidly developing parts of the globe. Demand for products and hence for industries is growing at a very fast rate. Consumers in these areas are increasingly seeking sophisticated products with a high input level of intelligence and skill. Currently, the supply of skilled/intelligent employees is not rising as fast as demand.

2 Government policy in this area involves deciding on the level of priority to be given to education and training. Government plays a major role in providing primary, secondary, tertiary and higher education. Education initiatives involving a combination of private and public sector involvement are necessary to ensure people are getting the right sorts of education and training to support economic development.

3 UK companies can develop their own training initiatives that ensure their employees and potential employees develop appropriate skill levels. UK companies can support educational initiatives in local schools, colleges and universities to help develop an appropriately trained workforce.

Check your understanding (page 383)

This task is best done by the tutor allocating various responsibilities to class members to avoid duplication of efforts. The tutor may provide the statistics by dealing directly with the Employment Information Unit.

Check your understanding (page 384, a)

Students again should work on this task in small groups to avoid duplication (e.g. some interviewing human resource planners, others looking through the local press and others dealing with the Employment Information Unit).

Check your understanding (page 384, b)

It is likely that one or more student in the class works for a local supermarket. They can therefore be given the responsibility for providing the information for this task.

Check your understanding (page 385)

The tutor should plan work involving the Employment Information Unit as an integrated whole rather than encouraging the students to contact the EIU on separate occasions.

Check your understanding (page 386)

Maximum number of hours worked in a week is $20 \times 40 = 800$

Number of hours due to sickness $= 2 \times 40 = 80$

$$\text{Sickness rate} = \frac{80}{800} \times \frac{100}{1} = 10\%$$

Case study: age, skills and training at Babcock Engineering (pages 387–388)

1 Students should point out that over half of the employees at Babcock are very close to retirement and that these are the people with the highest skill levels. They could also point out that the youngest employees in the company – 16–21-year-olds – have very poor skill levels yet are receiving very little training.
2 In the near future, Babcock Engineering is going to have to recruit a considerable number of skilled employees. It does not have the internal reserve of skilled employees to replace those who are leaving. This could be a costly exercise.
3 It should be carrying out training courses for existing employees and also be developing links with local colleges to see if they can recruit new apprentices to work for the company.

Check your understanding (page 388, a)

Students can carry out an audit of information about ages, skill levels and training in their place of work. Alternatively, they could do this for their school or college.

Check your understanding (page 388, b)

This task requires the students to interview a member of the personnel/human resource function within an organisation to find out about the plans and approaches the organisation uses to ensure they are training and developing people within the organisation to take on further posts of responsibility, with an eye to filling gaps as and when they arise.

CHAPTER 15 RECRUITMENT AND SELECTION

Check your understanding (page 391)

This is another task that requires an interview with the person/people responsible for recruitment in an organisation.

Check your understanding (page 393)

Students need to draw on their own personal experience and appreciation of the retail function to develop a job analysis, which might include some of the following information.

1 What tasks need to be performed:

- stacking shelves
- bringing items from stores into the selling area
- working on checkouts
- helping customers with queries
- attaching price labels to items?

2 What skills and qualities are required:

- interpersonal skills – ability to greet people in a friendly way and to respond to their queries
- simple numerical skills involved in computation
- ability to handle pressure
- ability to lift and sort goods?

3 How can these skills be acquired:

- training courses involving in-store personnel
- on-the-job training
- working under the supervision of another employee?

Case study: details from a person specification (page 394)

1 The information provided is quite useful in that it would eliminate individuals with fewer than 3 GCSEs or who did not have retailing experience when these candidates are competing with others who have these qualities. However, only one essential detail is provided – the medical certificate. It would be helpful to have more criteria such as ones relating to disposition and personality when selecting people who frequently have to come into contact with customers.
2 Students will benefit from creating a job specification for a job they are familiar with rather than one where they are just guessing at the attributes required.

Check your understanding (page 396)

The tutor needs to provide this material for the students. The tutor should acquire this information from industrial links or by asking students if they can furnish a person specification related to their own work.

Check your understanding (page 397)

1 Students should simply cut out advertisements and stick them neatly on to a large piece of coloured card with arrows pointing to suitable features. They should also write a commentary of strengths and weaknesses on the card.
2 Students should set out a realistic job advertisement for the sort of job they are interested in.

Check your understanding (page 399)

1 Lots of errors. For example, !! in the address and the spelling of collage. Poor grammar. Initial paragraph is too long. CV not included with letter. Letter is too chatty – 'I noticed in the paper'. Is trainspotting as a hobby a suitable reason for applying for a job as a trainee accountant? Why does the job provide a good opportunity?
2 In setting out a letter of application for the Tesco post, the students should take into account the notes provided on pages 397–400 of the student book.

Check your understanding (page 401)

Students need to take account of the suggestions provided on pages 400–401 of the student book in constructing their CVs. Students can then work in pairs to evaluate each other's CVs.

Case study: interview for a trainee manager's job at a local supermarket (page 405)

Possible examples are:

1 Please could you tell us about any previous work experience you have had in retailing (or about other areas of work if this is your first time in retailing)?
2 Could you tell us how you could use your previous experience in your work with us? What did you most enjoy about your previous work?

Check your understanding (page 409)

This activity involves preparation for an interview and will need to be carried out over a two-week period. The group will need to be divided up into job applicants and the interviewing panel. While the interviewing panel decide on the criteria that will be appropriate in selecting candidates and the questions to be asked, room layout, etc., the interviewees will need to create their CVs and think about how they will tackle the interview.

For the evaluation process to be most effective, it is helpful to videotape the interviews.

Check your understanding (page 411)

The tutor should obtain a copy of a commonly used psychometric test from a local company and try it out on the students.

Case study: Employee Recruitment Policy Statement for Melton College (page 414)

Students should discuss the case study in small groups and outline strengths such as the way it seeks to assist a range of groups, for example the handicapped minority groups. Other examples of strengths include the emphasis on induction and monitoring the policy.

Check your understanding (page 415)

Miss –, as a woman, do you think you are capable of doing the job?

This involves direct discrimination as it would not be asked of a male.

Do you think your disability will affect your performance in the job?

Again, involves direct discrimination against the disabled, except in situations where disability would genuinely limit ability to perform a job.

How do you feel about working with people from a different ethnic background from yourself?

Unacceptable because ethnic origin has nothing to do with job performance.

As a woman returner, Mrs –, do you feel you will be able to cope with the new technology in the office?

Again, inappropriate and unacceptable. More appropriate to ask all candidates about their experience of working with the required technology of the company.

As a man, Mr –, you will be working in a department consisting mainly of women. Are you easily distracted?

Again, unacceptable as the same question would not be asked of a woman.

Miss –, don't you think your skirt is rather short?

Again discriminatory and unacceptable as length of skirt has nothing to do with job performance.

Case study: mothers' right to part-time work (page 417)

1 The case states that women have the right to return to their jobs after maternity leave but not the absolute right to work part time. However, the case also states that, under the Sex Discrimination Act 1975, the hours the woman is expected to work need to be justifiable. This suggests employers should not seek to impose unacceptable hours on women in order to force them out of their jobs.
2 Because it is unacceptable to ask people to work such long hours back to back when other arrangements could be made that would suit the employee and the employer.
3 Students should suggest amendments that can be made in the light of their own experience of work.

Check your understanding (page 419)

Students should select an organisation they are familiar with (e.g. one they, a friend or relative works for). They then need to find out the rough proportion of full-time, part-time, permanent and temporary workers. Wherever possible, they should interview an employee from these categories to find out how these forms of employment differ.

Case study: why men and women receive different pay (pages 419–420)

1 The theory is quite helpful in outlining the differences between primary and secondary employment in terms of a dual labour market – one in which there is less competition for jobs than in the other.
2 The theory ignores factors such as historical and traditional differentials, and the impact of discrimination in the marketplace.

Check your understanding (page 423)

Possible arguments for and against flexible working practices might include:

For	Against
Reduces the cost base of the organisation	Can demotivate the workforce
Enables the organisation to concentrate on what it does best	Makes the organisation dependent on outside organisations to carry out non-core functions
Enables the organisation to shop around for cheapest/best sources of contracted services/ activities	Organisation loses direct control of some activities

Check your understanding (page 424)

Students could compare contracts of employment from their own work or, in the case of a full-time contract, from a friend or relative. Alternatively, the tutor may have an example of a full-time contract.

Students should set out criteria for outlining differences and making comparisons between the two contracts (e.g. related to details such as hours worked, holiday entitlement, levels of pay, etc.).

CHAPTER 16 TRAINING AND DEVELOPMENT

Case study: the intelligent organisation takes over (pages 426–427)

1 The 'new economy' is heavily based on intelligence. Highly skilled and competent workers need to have a very high level of education – often to degree level – complemented by extensive 'on-the-job' and 'off-the-job' training.
2 Modern high-tech industries need constantly to update and improve the skills of their employees. This is done at a considerable risk because such employees can always move elsewhere or set up their own businesses.

Check your understanding (page 430, a)

Students need to produce a leaflet which shows they understand the key benefits of training – e.g. to the organisation in driving down costs and increasing output and motivation, and to individuals in making them more employable and able to command better pay and rewards.

Check your understanding (page 430, b)

Students may identify areas where there is a considerable gain to be made in productivity through training (e.g. the information and communications technology sectors) as well as areas where there is a high turnover of labour and people need to come up to the required standard very quickly (e.g. in retailing).

Check your understanding (page 431, a)

Students need to outline a set of criteria against which to judge the induction schemes. Tutors may need to retain induction packs in their resource base should students have difficulty acquiring them. However, many students will have received an induction pack when they have worked part time for an organisation.

Check your understanding (page 431, b)

Students should observe the coaching session, looking for factors that appear to make the session successful. Students should consider the objectives of the session – perhaps by asking the coach what he or she is trying to achieve. The effectiveness of the session can then be judged against these criteria.

Case study: on-the-job training at Nestlé (pages 432–433)

1 The OJT at Nestlé is designed to provide knowledge about the company and to develop skills among the trainees. However, it also has an important focus of encouraging employees to feel they belong to an organisation called Nestlé – that they are part of a much larger team.
2 Students will need to outline what they consider to be the disadvantages of OJT. For example, they might state it focuses too much on a set pattern of working rather than taking a more critical view that could be provided by an external course; that employees are encouraged too much to focus on day-to-day routines rather than to build a broader picture, etc.
3 Nestlé have a training department that designs the courses for trainees, supervisors and managers.
4 Nestlé offer a range of training and development schemes, including learning at work, learning about the company, hands-on experience, induction programmes, ongoing training and development for existing employees, management training, etc.
5 As one of the world's leading food companies, training and development are of paramount importance if the organisation is to retain competitive advantage. The company seeks to develop a common culture based on the Nestlé way of working. All employees need to be up to date with developments in the industry and with the latest technologies. By having this emphasis, Nestlé are able to make sure all their resources are used in an optimal way.

Case study: in-house, off-the-job local and regional training at Nestlé (pages 434–435)

1 As well as developing knowledge and skills in employees, training programmes are designed to promote and develop the culture of the organisation. The emphasis is on helping individuals to feel part of the Nestlé team.
2 There is a healthy emphasis on employee development. This involves finding out about the training and development needs of an individual through a process of dialogue between an employee and his or her immediate manager. Nestlé provide many opportunities for employees to improve themselves in areas that are not strictly related to work.
3 Nestlé carry out local and regional training to complement international training because it is important to recognise local diversity. Also, there will be cost advantages to be gained from fostering grassroots-level training and development.
4 At a managerial level, training courses are regularly held to keep managers up to speed with changes in the dynamic environment in which Nestlé operate, and at a supervisory/employee level there is widespread training in new technologies in a world of rapid technological change.

Check your understanding (page 435)

Students simply need to list and describe the opportunities they have had in one of their part-time jobs for on-the-job and off-the-job training.

Check your understanding (page 436, a)

Many schools and colleges today have Investors in People status or are working towards this award. The students need to arrange an appointment to interview the individual or individuals involved in planning the programme preparing the organisation for the IiP award.

Check your understanding (page 436, b)

Students can prepare a leaflet for those students intending or thinking about joining the course the following year. Producing the leaflet should enable the students to show clearly their understanding of what the course is all about and what its major benefits are.

Case study: Individual Learning Accounts with Lincolnshire TEC (page 439)

1 Students will need to explain how Individual Learning Accounts are part of the process of lifelong learning and are concerned with ensuring everyone has access to learning. They are a form of subsidy to make it worth while for people to take up learning opportunities.
2 Possible problems are that individuals may still be reluctant to pay £25 of their own money, that unless the scheme is properly supervised people may feel disenchanted if they get substandard education and that individuals will need more than £150 worth of education.
3 Students may be able to suggest a range of improvements – particularly if they speak to someone who is on or has used the scheme.

Check your understanding (page 439)

Students may want to ask a tutor to identify a recent development involving education/training as a means to making the country and individuals more competitive. They can then research the initiative through the Internet. They could also evaluate the scheme – perhaps also asking a tutor for his or her view.

CHAPTER 17 PERFORMANCE MANAGEMENT

Case study: an appraisal process (page 442)

1 The evidence tends to indicate that the appraisal scheme has not been very effective. While it involved all the full-time staff, just over a half of the part-timers have been appraised. Those who chose not to take up the appraisal opportunity provide some fairly damning criticisms – that the appraiser/company is

not interested in their views and that nothing was done about previous appraisals. The reasons given for being part of the appraisal process are not very positive ones (i.e. to get more pay and to avoid being penalised).

2 Thus you can see that, in terms of Herzberg's theory of motivation, employees have generally gone into the appraisal scheme for negative reasons.
3 Students should suggest a range of ways of improving appraisal schemes in a general sense (e.g. to gain the commitment of employees so they feel genuinely involved in the initiative).

Check your understanding (page 444, a)

Most students today will have had to evaluate their own educational performance at some stage or another (e.g. in identifying how well they have done in a particular topic and then setting targets for further improvement). On the basis of this self-evaluation process, they should be able to discuss the effectiveness of the self-evaluation process.

Check your understanding (page 444, b)

Peer appraisal involves carrying out an appraisal of someone at the same level as yourself. If students have not had previous experience of this, the tutor could give them a task to do in which they monitor and evaluate each other's performance. They could use their experience of this process to tackle this task.

Case study: peer appraisal in an educational setting (page 445)

1 Students should judge (on the evidence provided) whether they feel peer or top-down evaluation would be more suitable. They could point out the strengths of the peer appraisal scheme, such as the non-threatening atmosphere, and the weaknesses, such as the fact that there is no direct communication with supervisors/line managers. Students may feel the evidence provided in the case study is biased and, therefore, may want to make an evaluation that goes beyond the information provided in the case.
2 Students should draw up a list of the benefits and drawbacks of the two schemes.

Check your understanding (page 448)

Students simply need to identify ways of measuring performance in a specific organisation.

Check your understanding (page 449)

Students need to interview someone involved in the appraisal process (e.g. a tutor, a supermarket worker, etc.) to see whether there is a clear link between appraisal and ongoing training and development. Students should report their finding to the group.

Case study: abuse of the minimum wage (page 450)

1 Many students are working in low-paid occupations. Here, a simple class survey could be carried out to find out wage rates per hour, which can then be compared with the minimum wage.
2 Many students will also be able to cite horror stories of cases where the minimum wage has been abused (e.g. by paying people on the 'black' less than the minimum wage).

Check your understanding (page 451)

Non-monetary rewards are most likely to be effective when employees are doing a job for reasons other than money. For example, nurses and teachers may value status and recognition more than money.

Check your understanding (pages 453–454)

Students will have their own views about where each of these stand in relation to Maslow's hierarchy. Further, where an individual stands in relation to Maslow depends on his or her personal drives, situation and needs.

- The street cleaner will have his basic needs met and probably his safety and security needs. Whether his love needs are met depends on his relationships with others in the work situation. He may have quite a high level of esteem – depending on how others treat him.
- The top footballer is probably able to have all his needs met, including that of self-actualisation, although this depends on the quality of his performance. Some top footballers turn to the bottle!
- The concert violinist has the opportunity for self-actualisation, providing he is in a good orchestra and feels he is fulfilling himself. If this is not the case, he may not earn sufficient money even for basic needs.
- A nurse who enjoys his or her work will probably have all his or her higher-order needs met, providing he or she is working in a well-equipped hospital and is not having too great a demand placed on him or her. However, if the nurse's wages are too low, he or she may not be able to meet some of his or her basic and security needs.
- A call centre operative often works in very stressful situations and is often remote from other employees. He or she may feel a lack of love, esteem and self-actualisation. If on top of that his or her wages are low, he or she will not even have his or her basic needs met.
- The teacher has the potential to have all her needs fulfilled – or very few!

Check your understanding (page 455)

Theory X – 'Only money motivates people'; 'Threatening to take away privileges really works'; 'Bonuses get people to put the effort in.'

Theory Y – 'I appeal to the human side of the individual'; 'I try to find out about people's aspirations'; 'Every employee has different drives.'

Check your understanding (page 456)

After studying the different theories of motivation, students should offer opinions as to which provides the best explanation in the light of their own experience of factors that motivate them as well as others.

Case study: theory and practice (page 457)

1 Herzberg would identify this as involving a dissatisfier's approach. Employees are being moved by the threat of a 'kick in the ass' if their level of sickness rises above a certain level. Herzberg would argue that employees are being 'moved' rather than 'motivated'.
2 In terms of Adams' equity theory, we would have to look at how other people in similar circumstances are treated. If there was not a high level of equity, this could lead to lack of motivation and resentment. People working on the shift may resent the fact that, if some of their colleagues are persistently late, they are having to suffer – they might argue that this is not equitable. Their resentment for the scheme may lead to a withdrawal of motivation and effort. Lawler would see this scheme as involving a clear link between performance and the rewards offered. The lower the sickness rate on a shift, the better the rewards for the members of that shift.

SECTION C OHTs

NOTES

OHT 4.14.1: the characteristics of HRM

This OHT is based on Figure 14.2 on page 374 of the student book. At the start of this unit the tutor will need to explain how new HRM initiatives are different from past ways of dealing with people in the workplace. There are a number of key characteristics which, collectively, can be thought of as creating an HRM approach.

The best way of working through this OHT is for the tutor to expose the characteristics listed on the left-hand side of the OHT and ask the students if they can come up with practical examples of how these might operate in practice. When the students have suggested a few examples, the tutor can show the examples listed on this OHT. The tutor can then work down the OHT to the next characteristic.

OHT 4.14.2: the stages in the HRM process

This illustration is based on Figure 14.3 from page 375 of the student book. The diagram shows the stages in the HRM planning process. The top part of the diagram outlines the processes required to match the demand for human resources with the supply. The tutor should work down the OHT, progressively disclosing and explaining each of the stages.

Once an organisation has worked out what its human resource deficit or surplus is going to be for the period of the plan, it will have to look at alternative policies for acquiring the required levels of resources (e.g. through recruitment, training, etc.).

OHT 4.14.3: wastage rates

This OHT accompanies the section in the student book on pages 377–379, which is concerned with calculating the wastage rates of human resources in an organisation. The OHT is divided into three parts. The top part shows how the wastage rate is calculated. The second part gives some calculations for wastage rates. In the final section, students will have to do some calculations of wastage rates with the support of the tutor.

The answers are:

- 1998: 10%
- 1999: 10%
- 2000: 6.25%
- 2001: 12%

OHT 4.14.4: the impact of the minimum wage

This OHT is based on Figure 14.8 on page 381 of the student book. It shows the impact of imposing a minimum wage that is set at a level higher than the market wage. The net impact is to reduce the quantity of labour that would be employed because employers would not be willing to pay the now higher wage to some of their less productive employees.

OHT 4.15.1: job advertisement

This OHT accompanies the notes about job advertisements on pages 396–397 of the student book. It is a light-hearted approach to getting students to thinking about job advertisements. The job advert is for the vacant post as England Manager. Students can be asked to suggest what they would put in the empty spaces on the advert (i.e. for the outline of: 1 the job; 2 the person; and 3 the fringe benefits). Students should then be asked to identify the features of a good job advertisement that are missing from the advert (e.g. location, address and contact, experience, etc.).

OHT 4.15.2: job selection – the employer's point of view

This OHT should be used in conjunction with OHT 4.15.3 and accompanies the text on pages 397–399 of the student book. This OHT should be used when the students are carrying out an activity involving a selection process. The OHT should be worked through a step at a time as the tutor works down the flow chart.

OHT 4.15.3: job selection – the applicant's point of view

In working down this flow chart, it is helpful for the tutor to ask the students to recount their own experiences of applying for jobs to see how closely these fit with the flow chart provided. This chart provides an excellent accompaniment to activities in which students prepare to interview each other as part of a mock selection process.

OHT 4.15.4: body language

These three illustrations accompany the notes and diagrams on pages 407–408 of the student book. The first illustration outlines an appropriate way of discussing a topic or interviewing someone. Note that both characters are interested and alert, and that they are mirroring each other's body positions. The interviewer is listening to the interviewee and taking notes. Some students may feel the body positions are too stiff and that there is not enough space between the two parties to the interview. The second illustration shows one person crossing herself in a defensive position and looking apprehensive. The other is far too laid back. The third interview shows overaggressive body posturing so that one person is intimidating the other.

OHT 4.16.1: personal development

This OHT is based on Figure 16.2 on page 428 of the student book. It indicates that training is more focused in securing the needs of the organisation, while personal development is concerned with identifying and meeting individual needs. Ideally, the organisation will try to reconcile its own needs and requirements with those of the individuals who work for it through an integrated training and development programme.

OHT 4.16.2: the benefits of training

This OHT has been designed to help the tutor outline the benefits of training, which are explained on page 429 of the student book. The tutor needs, first, to inform him- or herself of the material in the text and then work through the OHT from point 1 to point 5 to give the students a clear understanding of the uses and value of training.

OHT 4.16.3: successful coaching

This OHT accompanies the notes about coaching on page 431 of the student book. While the OHT shows sports coaching, the principles outlined can just as well be applied to coaching within any organisation. The purpose of the OHT is to show the ingredients that need to be in place if successful coaching is to be secured. Of course, if one or more of these ingredients are lacking, coaching may not prove to be very successful.

OHT 4.16.4: Investors in People

This OHT accompanies pages 435–436 of the student book and outlines the key points an organisation must work to if it is to secure IiP status. The tutor, therefore, needs to familiarise him- or herself with the notes in the text before explaining the process to the students. It would be helpful if the tutor also found out from an organisation that has secured or is working towards IiP status how it has been able to show commitment, planning, action and evaluation.

OHT 4.17.1: Super Airways: annual results cycle

This OHT follows pages 441–442 of the student book and is based on Figure 17.1. The diagram helps the tutor to show how an organisation's mission (a generalised aim) is used to determine objectives at each level in the organisation, from company-wide objectives down to individual objectives. It is then a question of monitoring performance results against objectives in order to inform ongoing objective-setting and evaluation of performance.

OHT 4.17.2: possible sources of appraisal for a manager

Some organisations use a process of 360-degrees appraisal for managers. This would mean that managers would be appraised from above, from the sides and from subordinates in an organisation. Of course, there is a range of alternatives (e.g. peer evaluation, subordinate evaluation, etc.).

This OHT is based on Figure 17.5 on page 443 of the student book and will be helpful to the tutor in explaining the appraisal process.

OHT 4.17.3: counter staff performance in a fast-food restaurant

This OHT is based on part of Figure 17.6 on page 447 of the student book. It identifies some of the criteria that someone working in a fast-food restaurant would be judged against in assessing work performance. The tutor should ask the students to bring in any similar materials they have from their own work activities that are used to evaluate their performance. Students should be asked to consider how effective such a performance checklist would be in assessing performance.

OHT 4.17.4: Theory X and Theory Y managers

This OHT outlines a range of statements a manager might make about the way he or she works with others. Students should identify which of the statements are characteristic of a Theory X and which of a Theory Y manager. The activity is based on the notes on pages 453–455 of the student book. Students could also be asked if some of the statements are typical of some of the managers they have worked with and, if it is possible to characterise managers in this way.

OHT 4.14.1 THE CHARACTERISTICS OF HRM

CHARACTERISTIC	EXAMPLES
A reduction in hierarchy and the blurring of the distinction between management and non-management.	The use of quality circles, where employees are part of a team and responsible for their own self-management and regulation. For example, employees in a quality circle in a Jaguar car factory may set their own production targets.
Responsibility for people-management is devolved to line managers. Personnel professionals support and facilitate.	Line managers are responsible for the appraisal of staff and staff development, personnel professionals may offer support through appraisal training for staff and staff managers.
Planning of human resources is part of overall corporate planning.	The mission statements of many organisations today include references to the place of human resources, e.g. – to secure the optimum personal development of company members.
Employees are viewed as individuals with the potential for development, in line with the needs of the organisation.	Many organisations have appraisal systems which focus on the continuing professional development of staff.
Management and non-management are committed to common goals, and have an interest in the success of the organisation.	The increased emphasis on teams in organisations, means that more people are involved in identifying goals and should therefore be more committed to them.

OHT 4.14.2 THE STAGES IN THE HRM PROCESS

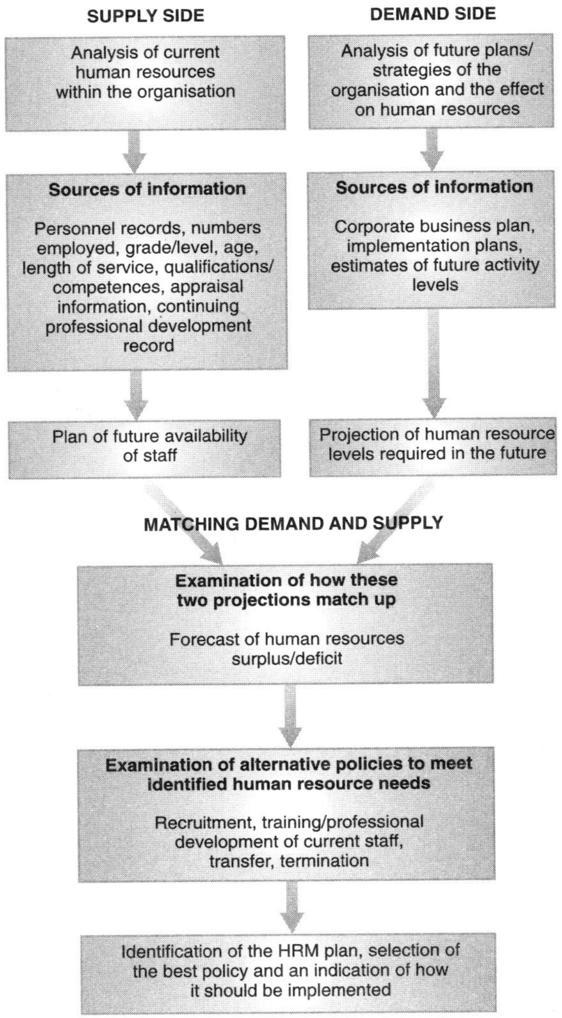

OHT 4.14.3 WASTAGE RATES

$$\text{Wastage rate} = \frac{\text{Number of staff leaving}}{\text{Average staff number}} \times 100$$

	1998	1999	2000	2001
Number of employees	1,000	1,100	1,500	2,000
Number leaving	200	110	50	100
Wastage rate (%)	20	10	3.3	5

	1998	1999	2000	2001
Number of employees	600	650	800	1,000
Number leaving	60	65	50	120
Wastage rate (%)	?	?	?	?

OHT 4.14.4 THE IMPACT OF THE MINIMUM WAGE

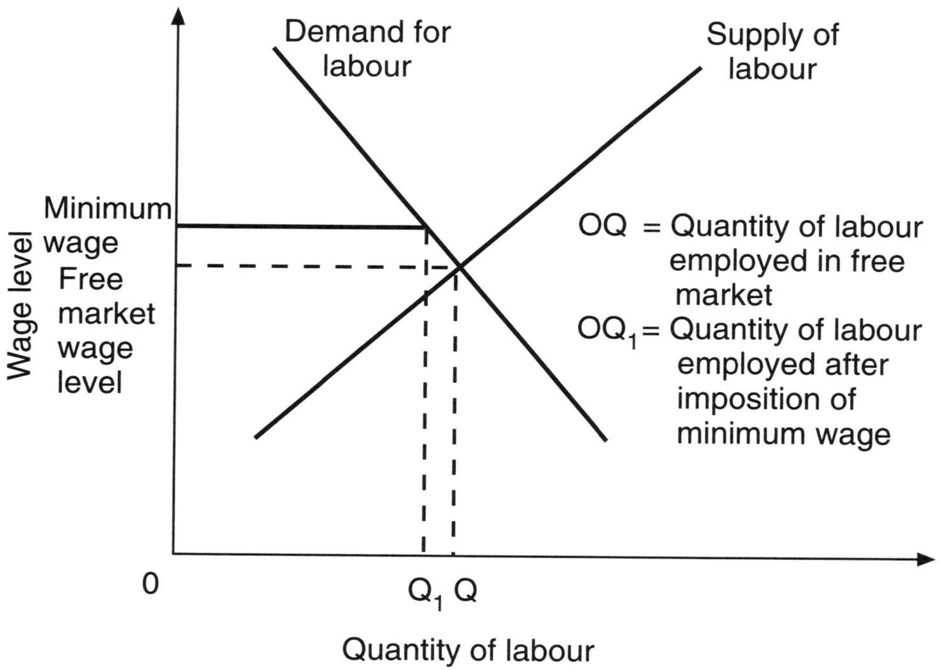

OHT 4.15.1 JOB ADVERTISEMENT

England Manager

£1 MILLION PER YEAR

The job: The Football Association is seeking a manager to lead the England Team to glorious victory in the World Cup

Fill in space

The person:

Fill in space

Salary: £1,000,000 per year

Fringe Benefits:

Fill in space

OHT 4.15.2 JOB SELECTION – THE EMPLOYER'S POINT OF VIEW

1. The need to recruit an extra member of staff is identified.
2. A new job description is set out, or an existing one is updated.
3. The job specification is reviewed and revised.
4. Advertisements are designed and placed in appropriate media.
5. Job details and application forms are sent to applicants.
6. Applications are sorted out and a shortlist drawn up.
7. Interview invitations are sent to shortlisted applicants.
8. Interviews take place (and an oral job offer may be made).
9. Referees are invited to comment.
10. If the references are satisfactory, a written job offer is sent.
11. The offer is accepted.
12. A written contract of employment is signed.

OHT 4.15.3 JOB SELECTION – THE APPLICANT'S POINT OF VIEW

1. Evaluate different career choices, and narrow down your options.
2. Produce and update your curriculum vitae.
3. Ask three people to act as referees.
4. Photocopy your examination and other certificates.
5. See an interesting job advertisement and send for details.
6. Find out more about the organisation.
7. Send a short letter asking for an application form.
8. Fill in the form and write a short letter supporting your application. Send copies of certificates and CV. Keep copies of all these documents.
9. If invited for interview, immediately telephone to confirm the arrangements.
10. Verbal acceptance of job.
11. Write a letter of acceptance and return the contract.
12. Make sure you know when and where you are expected to be on the first day.

OHT 4.15.4 BODY LANGUAAGE

OHT 4.16.1 PERSONAL DEVELOPMENT

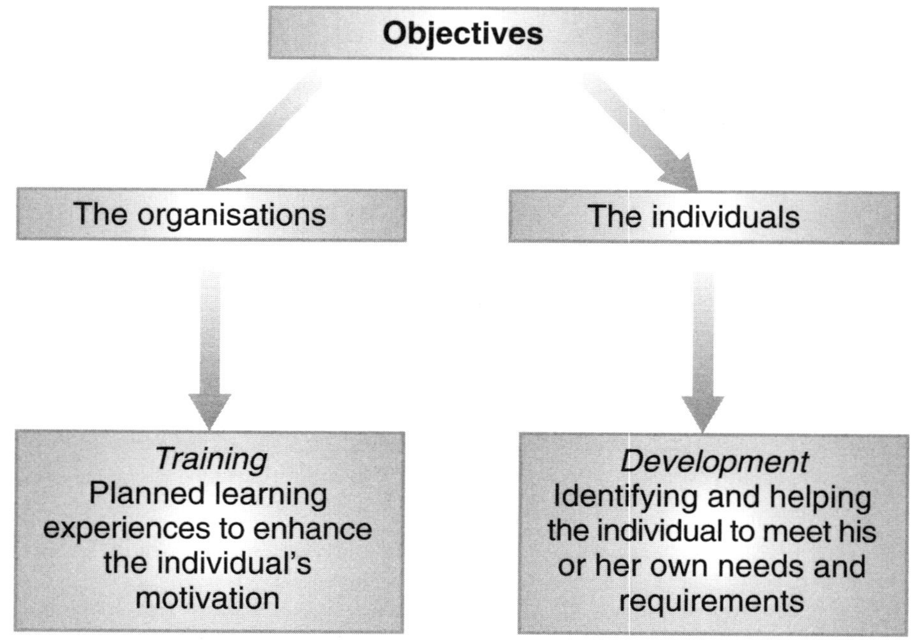

OHT 4.16.2 THE BENEFITS OF TRAINING

Training

1 Improves competitiveness of organisation

2 Reduces costs in the long run

3 Creates right atitudes

4 Improves efficiency

5 Increases motivation and enjoyment

OHT 4.16.3 SUCCESSFUL COACHING

Person wants to be coached

The coach wants to coach the person

Coach has required skills

The organisation values the coaching process

Sufficient time given to coaching

Person being coached wants to learn

OHT 4.16.4 INVESTORS IN PEOPLE

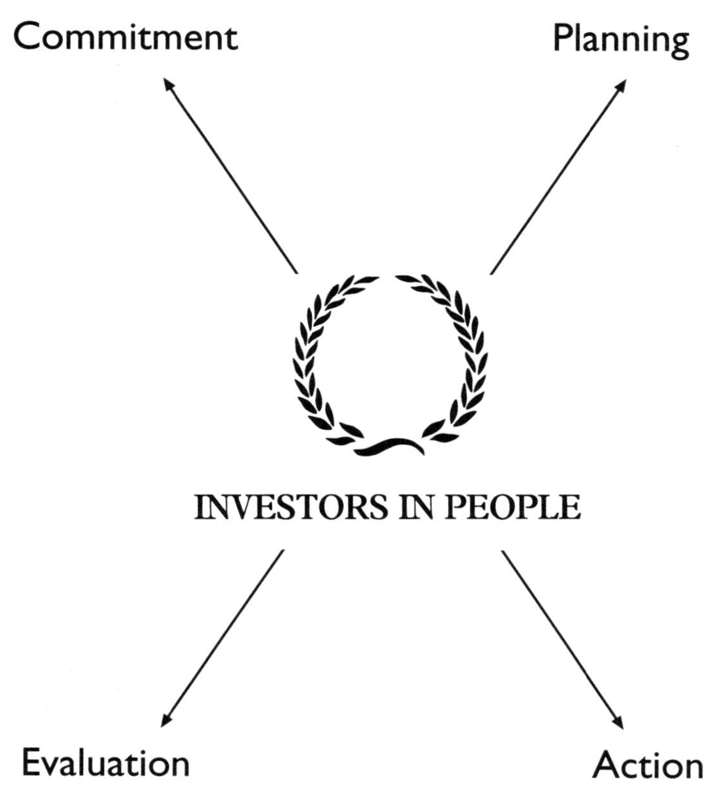

® reproduced with kind permission of Investors in People UK

OHT 4.17.1 SUPER AIRWAYS: ANNUAL RESULTS CYCLE

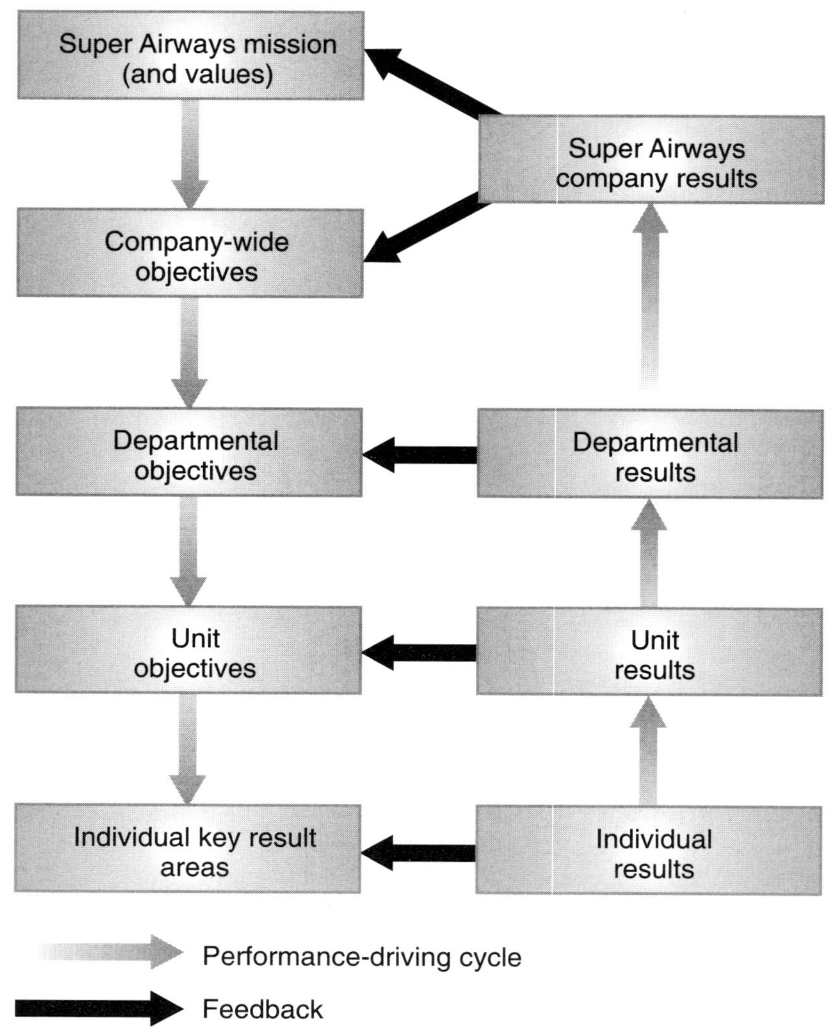

OHT 4.17.2 POSSIBLE SOURCES OF APPRAISAL FOR A MANAGER

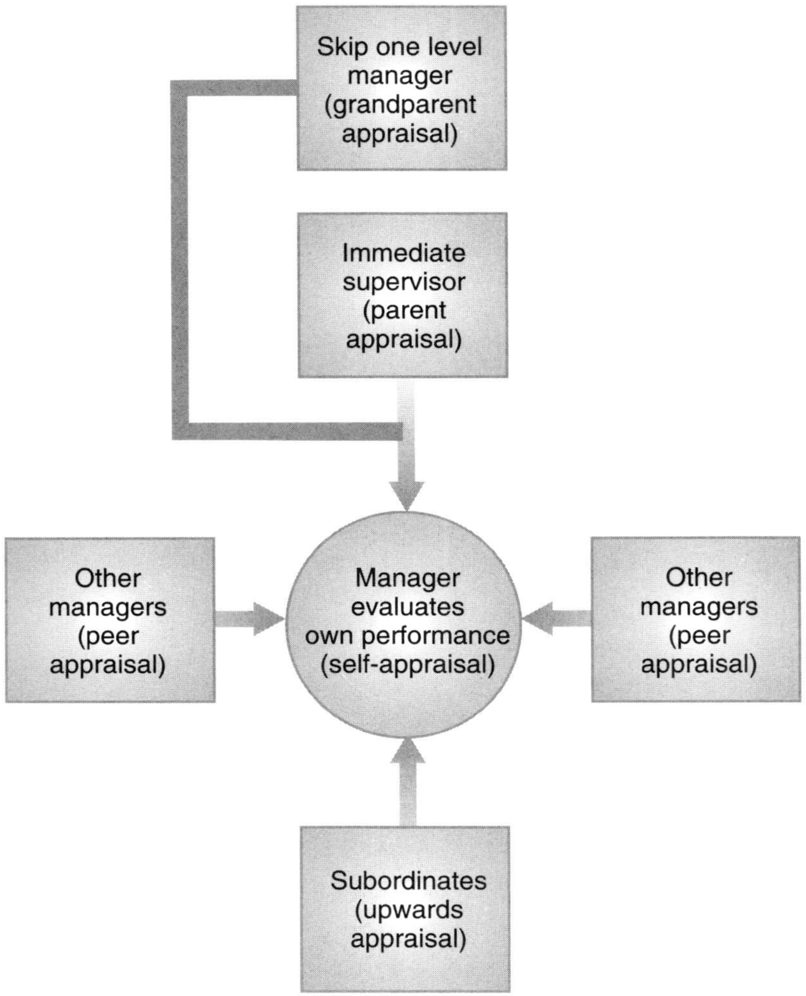

OHT 4.17.3 COUNTER STAFF PERFORMANCE IN FAST-FOOD RESTAURANT

	Yes (✓)	No (✗)
Greeting the customer		
1 There is a smile?	✓	
2 It is a sincere greeting?	✓	
3 There is eye contact?		✗
Taking the order		
1 The counter person is thoroughly familiar with the menu?	✓	
2 The customer has to give the order only once?	✓	
3 Small orders (four items or less) are memorised rather than written down?	✓	
4 There is suggestive selling?		✗
Assembling the order		
1 The order is assembled in the proper sequence?	✓	
2 Grill slips are handed in first?	✓	
3 Drinks are poured in the proper sequence?	✓	
4 Proper amount of ice?	✓	
5 Cups slanted and finger used to activate?		✗
6 Drinks are filled to the proper level?		✗
7 Drinks are capped?	✓	
8 Clean cups?	✓	
9 Holding times are observed on coffee?		✗
10 Cups are filled to the proper level on the coffee?	✓	

OHT 4.17.4 THEORY X AND THEORY Y MANAGERS

SECTION D ASSESSMENT

PRODUCE A REPORT ON HOW ONE LARGE BUSINESS MANAGES HUMAN RESOURCES

This assessment should be carried out using the report format described in the student book on page viii.

You will need to produce an analytical report on how one large business manages human resources. The report will need to give a detailed account of human resources management, showing its importance to the business and including all four of the functions listed below:

1 human resources planning
2 recruitment and selection
3 training and development
4 performance management.

You should identify how these four functions can work together and any areas of conflict that might arise between the four functions.

You should look at one of these four areas in greater depth.

These are the areas you should cover in your report.

1 Give a clear account of the various responsibilities of the human resources function within an organisation. This information is best obtained by visiting an organisation to talk to a human resources manager. This aspect can be covered by your course tutor inviting a human resources manager to visit the school or college to outline the nature of the human resources function in his or her organisation.
2 Examine current labour market trends that affect an organisation. These labour market trends involve both national and local labour market statistics, such as current levels of unemployment, levels of skills shortages in particular categories of work, numbers of trained employees in particular jobs, etc. To obtain higher grades, you need to show how these trends affect the human resource plans of the organisation you have chosen to study. For example, if the organisation is seeking to employ trained information technology specialists, you will need to look at the figures for the demand and supply of such workers nationally over the next few years, as well as examining local figures. Consideration will need to be given to whether shortages will be made up from external recruitment or internal training.
3 Identify and analyse the key recruitment documents employed by organisations. You will need to describe the key stages and processes involved in filling vacancies, and to evaluate the effectiveness of specific documents currently being used for the recruitment process. You will also need to show how these could be improved.
4 Examine the current training and development programme of a business. To achieve higher grades, you will need to show how the programme affects the organisation's performance and will have to identify ways of improving the training and development procedures and methods.
5 Show how training and development initiatives within an organisation are influenced by various theories of motivation (e.g. Maslow, Herzberg, McGregor and Lawler).
6 Show how conflict may arise between the human resource functions within the organisation you are studying. To gain a grade A, you should show how this conflict can be removed or limited to enable the organisation to perform at a high level.
7 Explore a human resource function in depth, giving clear examples of how the work is carried out and the contribution this function makes in helping the organisation to meet its aims and objectives.
8 To obtain a grade A, you will need to outline critically the contribution effective human resources management can make to improving the competitiveness of the business.

CHECKLIST FOR CARRYING OUT YOUR ASSIGNMENT TO A HIGH STANDARD

Tick the boxes

1 I have given a clear account of the key responsibilities of the human resources function in an organisation. ☐
2 I have outlined current labour market trends that affect an organisation. ☐
3 I have shown how these labour market trends affect the human resources plan. ☐
4 I have identified and evaluated the key recruitment documents employed by an organisation and made suggestions for improvement. ☐
5 I have set out the key steps involved in filling vacancies in one organisation and identified possible improvements. ☐
6 I have outlined the current training and development programme of a business. ☐
7 I have shown how this training and development programme affects business performance. ☐
8 I have suggested ways of improving the training and development programme. ☐
9 I have shown the links between training and development programmes and three key motivational theories. ☐
10 I have outlined ways in which conflict can arise between human resource functions and how this conflict can be removed or limited. ☐
11 I have examined one human resource function in depth, showing how it helps the organisation to meet its aims and objectives. ☐
12 I have critically evaluated the contribution of human resource management to the success of a business. ☐

HOW YOU CAN USE KEY SKILLS WHILE WORKING ON THIS ASSESSMENT

Application of number skills

In researching information for your report, you will need to use and interpret statistics and figures for labour market trends at both a national and local level. You will need to carry out operations with these figures to show how labour market trends affect the human resources plans of a specific organisation.

Communication skills

- Producing the report itself. Use the report format suggested on page viii of the student book.
- Contribute to a class discussion, for example, about ways in which effective training and development programmes can help an organisation to meet its objectives and improve performance.
- Researching information for the report. You will need to acquire and interpret a range of source documents, such as recruitment documents, labour market statistics, etc.
- Making a group presentation. You can present your findings when you do your in-depth study of one of the four key human resource functions in an organisation using Powerpoint. The presentation could be to fellow students or to a manager at the organisation you are studying.

Information technology skills

- You should search databases and information on the Internet relating to labour market statistics.
- You could adapt information acquired from the Internet to meet the needs of your report. For example, you could use labour market statistics to support your findings about appropriate human resources planning in your chosen organisation.

Working with others

- You should liaise with members of the organisation you are studying. The organisation you are working with will want to help you – but will want to feel you are organised and are working in a constructive way. This places considerable responsibility on you to make sure you work in a reliable manner.

- Reporting to the organisation you are studying. It is important you give feedback to the organisation you are studying on the progress you are making. It is helpful if you send a copy of your final report to the organisation which has helped you – or even to make a Powerpoint presentation to them.
- Working with others in planning presentations. You will agree roles, procedures, deadlines, and responsibilities with your fellow students.

UNIT 5 – BUSINESS FINANCE

SECTION A DISCUSSION POINT

THE IMPORTANCE OF ACCOUNTING STANDARDS

Can we always trust what we read? Sometimes we hope so. But is this case for all published information? For example, can you believe everything you read in the student's book for this course? When you look at the prospectus for your school or college, is all the information accurate?

The accounts of companies should illustrate both the performance of each business as well as its current financial position. The ways in which accounts are presented within the UK are regulated. For example, they are produced in accordance with:

1 the Companies Act 1985, which decrees that companies produce accounts for publication, and
2 accounting standards. Accounting standards include Statements of Standard Accounting Practice (SSAPs) and Financial Reporting Standards (FRSs). In essence, these standards set out:
   - what information should be included in a company's accounts
   - how this information should be presented.

The Accounting Standards Committee devised SSAPs. In 1991 this committee was replaced by the Accounting Standards Board, which today develops FRSs. The board is gradually replacing SSAPs with FRSs, which are issued when the board identifies a need for control and regulation. These two sets of accounting standards encourage greater clarity so the reader of a set of accounts can fully understand the information represented and can have faith and confidence in how the information has been collected.

POINTS FOR DISCUSSION

1 Why is it necessary to have accounting standards?
2 Could it be argued that accounting standards are an unnecessary straitjacket placed upon accountants who are, anyway, professionals?

SECTION B SUGGESTED ANSWERS

CHAPTER 18 RECORDING FINANCIAL INFORMATION

Case study: putting the sparkle back into Hamleys (page 463)

1 A number of factors might have caused some of the problems experienced by Hamleys. These might include poor decisions made when attempting to diversify, little consistency, high price image within the high street, a lack of a coherent strategy and botched franchise attempts.
2 A number of individuals and organisations will have been affected in a variety of ways, both negatively and positively, by Hamleys' downturn in fortunes. These might include regular customers, employees, managers, suppliers, lenders of money, competitors and local businesses.
3 The new chief executive is repositioning Hamleys by reducing the price of toys to reflect the industry average. A number of changes are also being made to the store to make it a magical experience for visitors and shoppers. Given the unique name and brand of Hamleys, such changes are all in line with making the experience of shopping there better for customers. However, the case does not indicate how it might communicate the changing world of Hamleys to its customers.

Check your understanding (page 465)

- Recording transactions from source documentation (financial)
- Calculating what profit is likely to be over a range of outputs for the launch of new products (management)
- Producing financial statements to show what has happened to the business during the past year (financial)
- Advising a business on its tax liability (financial)
- Creating a budgetary system to improve control over the costs within a business (management)
- Setting the prices of products or services (management)

Case study: The Institute of Chartered Accountants in England and Wales (ICAEW) (page 466)

1 There are a number of reasons why accountants need to be members of a professional body. For example, if they did not need to belong to a body, anybody could call him- or herself an accountant. Professional bodies ensure accountants are properly qualified and able to deal with the increasing range of issues they encounter within the workplace.
2 The main purpose of the ICAEW is to maintain the high standards of professional conduct and competence of its members.
3 The ICAEW supports its members with a coherent range of qualifications, the commissioning of papers for publication, conferences upon a wide range of issues, guidance on ethical matters, dealing with complaints and the monitoring of members' activities.

Check your understanding (page 468)

The purpose of this activity is for the students to choose one of the roles and then try to identify the sort of financial information that person might require. For example, a production director would want information on labour costs (both total and per unit), sales (both actual and forecast – volume and value), overhead costs, material costs, etc.

Check your understanding (page 469)

A competitor would be interested in the profits of other organisations, any changes made in sales, the nature and type of strategic decisions made in recent years, reductions in costs, efficiency details (such as output per worker), etc.

Discussion point (page 470)

There are many arguments for and against the regulation of accounting and other areas, particularly for small and medium-sized enterprises. On the one hand, legislation protects a range of stakeholder interests, ensuring they are not duped through a range of fraudulent activities but, on the other hand, meeting such requirements can be time-consuming and sometimes expensive.

Case study: accounting concepts (page 471)

1 In answering this question, students will refer to one of the accounting concepts appearing within the case study and then explain why it was introduced. For example:
   - the going concern concept assumes the business will continue operations in the foreseeable future. In doing so it does not confuse a potential buyer for the business
   - the accruals or matching concept is an important one as it relates all the business activities and their costs and revenues during a period to that period. Otherwise it would be possible either to overstate or understate profits
   - the consistency concept ensures that activities are dealt with similarly from one period to another
   - the concept of prudence or conservation ensures profits are not underestimated or losses overstated. In doing so it ensures companies both meet their tax liabilities and, at the same time, do not confuse stakeholders.

2 If such basic concepts were not applied to all accounting processes, it would not be possible to make comparisons between businesses or from one time period to another.

Check your understanding (page 472, a)

There are always going to be some risks for the supplier wherever business transactions take place on credit. Risks may include non-payment or late payment. The result of this may also be felt in 'difficult' supplier relationships.

Check your understanding (page 472, b)

Students should collect as many documents as they can. Some will inevitably be receipts, but they might collect some purchase orders from catalogue companies as well as credit card statements.

Discussion point (page 473, a)

Organisations keep fewer documents than they used to. The days of being presented by banks of filing cabinets when you enter offices seem to be over. However, in key areas such as invoices, there will inevitably be some form of paper backup within many organisations, simply because of security. Some organisations, such as insurance companies, claim to be paperless and do scan all documentation as it enters the organisation.

Discussion point (page 473, b)

Discounting does provide large organisations with a competitive advantage over small organisations. As they buy in bulk, they can effectively get better discounts and have a lower cost base. It is difficult for small organisations to deal with this. They may be able to source their products carefully from a wide range of suppliers, or come to an agreement with a supplier over a long period.

Check your understanding (page 474)

1 If the date was omitted from the order, the supplier would not know when the goods had been ordered. It might, therefore, be difficult to deliver the goods within a certain acceptable time frame.
2 Missing the reference to the catalogue number might make the goods difficult to trace and this could again delay meeting the order.

Check your understanding (page 476, a)

The purpose of this exercise is for the students to design at least one document associated with purchasing. In order to do so, they may wish to customise a template within their office package, such as those that exist within Office 2000. The important thing is that students recognise each of the parts of the document as well as how the document would be used.

Check your understanding (page 476, b)

1 For the first of the transactions, the documents that would be used would be a letter of inquiry, a quotation or catalogue, a purchase order, an advice note, an invoice and, shortly afterwards, a statement. The documents should match the templates on pages 473–477 of the student book.

2 The document related to the return of the stumps would be a credit note (see page 475 of the student book). It may also be possible for students to construct a revised statement (see page 479 of the student book).

Check your understanding page (478, a)

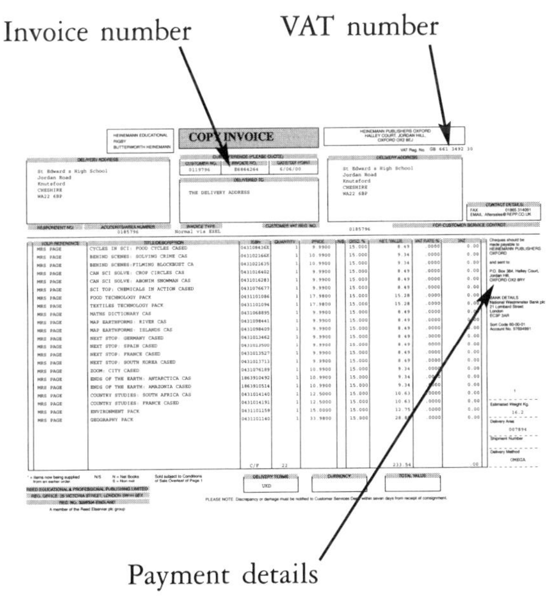

The delivery address might be different from the invoice address where a head office has ordered goods for another part of the business.

Check your understanding (page 478, b)

1 A quotation will refer to a specific inquiry, whereas a catalogue will detail a range of products or services and have a price list.

2 An advice note informs the buyer that goods have been sent and that they will arrive shortly, while a delivery note simply lists the items that have been sent.

3 An invoice is the official request for payment containing the main details of the transaction. It shows the details of the transaction, the amount charged and the terms. The statement is regularly sent to some customers, detailing all the entries in the accounts of these customers.

4 A trade discount may be for a volume purchase or for being a regular customer, whereas a cash discount is for prompt payment.

5 A credit note reduces the invoice price, usually when goods have been returned, while a debit note increases the invoice price.

Check your understanding (page 480)

The purpose of this exercise is for the students to use documents as a basis for a series of dummy transactions among themselves. Clearly, the buyer will have fewer documents to prepare than the seller, so they might go through the exercise twice so that they have a full set. The important element in this activity is that, when they present the documents to the rest of the class, each participant fully understands the nature, purpose and role of each of the documents he or she has just used.

Case study: working as an auto-electrician (page 480)

1 Given her role as an auto-electrician, there are many documents Caroline would need to deal with. For example, an advice note will tell her parts are on the way; delivery notes will accompany goods when they are delivered; invoices will carry details of each transaction; and, when she buys regularly from a supplier, she will receive statements.

2 In order to deal with credit transactions with some of her customers, Caroline needs to set up a basic book-keeping system with ledger accounts that can record amounts owed by her creditors. Caroline ought to supply a price list

quoting the cost of various repairs. She will need invoices to send to her customers, credit notes if there are instances when she has to reduce the invoice prices and, finally, she will need statements to send to her regular customers detailing all the transactions taking place.

3 A computer would be able to keep her accounting records and print the appropriate stationery.

Check your understanding (page 481)

Students need to write a short booklet entitled *How to Write out a Cheque*. In order to do so, the tutor should encourage the students to draw a cheque template and then label each part (refer to page 481 of the student book if any students require guidance). They may be able to obtain illustrative materials from their local bank.

Case study: developing close supplier relationships (page 483)

1 A great deal of information is transferred between M&S and their suppliers. This information includes price and order details, stock information, sales figures, product details and even design information.

2 Exchanging information in such a way enables each organisation to plan for the activities of the marketplace, enabling them to respond flexibly and more efficiently to the needs of customers.

Check your understanding (page 485)

Students should fill in the simple paying-in slip for the two cheques and associated cash amounts. The total comes to £149.65.

Check your understanding (page 486)

The worst-case scenario for a personal financial situation may be not having enough money in a bank account, being seriously overdrawn or having someone fraudulently change your source document to withdraw funds illicitly from your account.

Check your understanding (page 487)

All organisations need security measures for documentation. These might include:

- checking orders are authorised
- making sure copies have been kept and filed
- checking spending limits are not exceeded and appropriate signatures have been used
- checking invoices against orders
- making sure details correspond to goods delivered
- keeping documents secure.

Students should also find out more about documentation procedures within their own school or college.

CHAPTER 19 CONSTRUCTING ACCOUNTS

Discussion point (page 490)

It is important that everybody within a business knows, to some extent, what is going on and how well or badly the business is doing. For example, at the simplest level, they will want to know if the business is profitable, simply from their point of view as stakeholders to the business. They may also have to make judgements on the basis of financial information, particularly if they work in marketing or operations.

Case study: Association of Accounting Technicians (page 490)

1 There are a number of reasons why non-accountants might want their own professional body. For example, they might want to attend conferences and exchange information with others involved in similar work. They may want some of the advantages of being an accountant without having the full qualification. AAT examinations also provide part-qualified status and exemptions from a range of other qualifications.

2 AAT members may be involved with book-keeping, other work in an accountancy environment and credit control.

Check your understanding (page 504)

Example 1

Dr — **Rent paid account** — **Cr**

Date	Narrative	£	Date	Narrative	£
15 January	Bank	3,000	31 January	Balance c/d	3,000
		3,000			3,000
1 February	Balance b/d	3,000			

Example 2

Dr — **Sales account** — **Cr**

Date	Narrative	£	Date	Narrative	£
31 January	Balance c/d	13,000	1 January	T. Robinson & Co.	13,000
		13,000			13,000
			1 February	Balance b/d	13,000

Example 3

Dr — **Bank account** — **Cr**

Date	Narrative	£	Date	Narrative	£
1 January	Capital	4,300	6 January	Rent paid	2,100
7 January	Loan	5,000	15 January	Motor vehicle	2,300
31 January	Balance c/d	4,200	21 January	Drawings	700
		9,300			9,300
			1 February	Balance b/d	4,200

Case study: Sage Line 50 (pages 505–506)

1 Clearly from the description, Sage Line 50 has all the ingredients of a double-entry book-keeping system. For example, it has a sales ledger, purchases ledger, nominal ledger and cash book – the key elements of a double-entry system. However, the package is clearly much more integrated with other functions, and links to management accounts and the generation of documentation.

2 The advantages of using such a package include savings in time, improved efficiency, a backup system, better interpretation of statements and the generation of reports.

Check your understanding (page 506)

The purpose of this activity is for the students to find out how financial data is recorded and used within their school or college. The tutor may wish to ask a school bursar or a college administrator or accountant to talk to the students about the system.

Discussion point (page 508)

In order to minimise errors made within a book-keeping system, it may be necessary to carry out a number of procedures. These might include double-checking of documentation, regular audits, improved monitoring of work, a regular checking of printouts, etc.

Check your understanding (page 509)

The trial balance of R. James as at 31 December 2000

Single-column trial balance	£
Purchases	12,400
Sales	(65,700)
Stock 1 January 2000	7,100
Salaries	14,400
Wages	2,500
Interest paid	3,200
Rent paid	4,000
Light and heating	3,500
Land and buildings	45,000
Machinery	14,000
Motor vehicles	8,000
Debtors	18,000
Bank	7,500
Cash	2,000
Creditors	(18,400)
Drawings	8,000
Bank loan	(15,000)
Capital	(50,000)
	Zero

The trial balance of R. James as at 31 December 2000

Double-column trial balance	£	£
Purchases	12,400	
Sales		65,700
Stock 1 January 2000	7,100	
Salaries	14,400	
Wages	2,500	
Interest paid	3,200	
Rent paid	4,000	
Light and heating	3,500	
Land and buildings	45,000	
Machinery	14,000	
Motor vehicles	8,000	
Debtors	18,000	
Bank	7,500	
Cash	2,000	
Creditors		18,400
Drawings	8,000	
Bank loan		15,000
Capital		50,000
	149,600	149,600

Check your understanding (page 512)

1 **The trading account of M. Patel for the year ended 31 December 2001**

	£	£	£
Sales			34,800
Less: Returns inwards			500
Net sales			34,300
Opening stock (1 January 2001)		3,900	
Purchases	15,300		
Carriage inwards	400		
	15,700		
Less: Returns outwards	700		
Net purchases		15,000	
		18,900	
Less: Closing stock		4,100	
Cost of sales			14,800
Gross profit			19,500

2 **The trading account of J. Gallian for the year ended 31 December 2001**

	£	£	£
Sales			15,000
Less: Returns inwards			650
Net sales			14,350
Opening stock (1 January 2001)		4,789	
Purchases	10,125		
Carriage inwards	324		
	9,801		
Less: Returns outwards	550		
Net purchases		9,251	
		14,040	
Less: Closing stock		3,200	
Cost of sales			10,840
Gross profit			3,510

Check your understanding (page 514, a)

Six probable assets of a small corner-shop might include:

- land and buildings
- shop fitments
- vehicle
- stocks
- bank account balance
- cash.

Six probable liabilities of a small corner-shop might include:

- capital
- mortgage
- creditors
- tax due
- bank loan
- drawings.

There are few discernible changes between those of a corner-shop and those of a public house, but students might specifically refer to particular types of stocks.

Check your understanding (page 514, b)

Assets are items or amounts owned by the business, which are used by the business within the trading or commercial process.

The inverse order of liquidity of the assets in the list would probably be:

1 the baker's premises
2 the baker's oven
3 a bakery van
4 supplies of flour
5 bread in the shops
6 money owed to the bakery by firms
7 money in the bakery's bank account
8 cash in the tills.

Check your understanding (page 515)

The following are likely to be considered as the current assets of a newsagent:

- cash in the tills
- money in the bank
- money owed by customers for newspaper bills
- stocks of newspapers in the shop (given the 'sale or return' nature of newspapers, there is a degree of uncertainty about whether these are ever registered as current assets).

Check your understanding (page 516)

The trading and profit and loss account of G. Archer for the year ended 31 December 2001

	£	£
Sales		81,250
Opening stock	12,700	
Purchases	18,325	
	31,025	
Less: Closing stock	10,300	
Cost of sales		20,725
Gross profit		60,525
Less: Expenses		
Electricity	1,451	
Stationery	1,526	
Business rate	1,845	
Loan interest	3,955	
Advertising	2,150	
Sundry expenses	1,205	
Total expenses		12,132
Net profit		48,393

The balance sheet of G. Archer as at 31 December 2001

	£	£
Fixed assets		
Land and buildings		161,000
Machinery		4,900
Motor vehicles		18,300
		184,200
Current assets		
Stocks	10,300	
Debtors	12,100	
Bank	4,250	
Cash	325	
	26,975	
Less: Current liabilities		
Creditors	4,300	
Working capital		22,675
		206,875
Less: Long-term liabilities		
Bank loan	10,000	
Mortgage	20,000	
		30,000
Net assets		176,875
Financed by:		
Capital		137,832
Add: Net profit		48,393
		186,225
Less: Drawings		9,350
		176,875

CHAPTER 20 INTERPRETING FINANCIAL INFORMATION

Check your understanding (page 523)

Four stakeholder groups to an organisation might include suppliers (need information about solvency), shareholders (want to know about their investment and profitability), lenders of finance (solvency) and managers (information about a range of issues so they can improve the way they manage the business).

Case study: Deloitte & Touche (page 523)

1 The process of auditing developed as a result of one company, GWR, valuing the experience provided by an independent accountant, who audited its accounts. As more companies came into being, a demand developed for people who were able to understand some of the financial problems and issues associated with these businesses.
2 Independent auditors can provide an impartial and objective view of a business's accounts, and are not influenced by internal decision-making or strategic influences.

Check your understanding (page 526)

The appropriation account of Workhard Ltd for the year ended 31 December 2001

	£	£
Net profit		300,000
Less: Corporation tax		75,000
Profit after tax		225,000
Less: Dividend		
Ordinary shares	50,000	
Preference shares	30,000	80,000
		145,000
Less: Transfer to general reserve		50,000
		95,000
Add: Retained profit from previous year		125,000
Balance of retained profit		220,000

Check your understanding (page 528)

The trading, profit and loss and appropriation account of Twyford Ltd for the year ended 31 December 2001

	£	£
Sales		123,400
Opening stock	7,300	
Purchases	12,500	
	19,800	
Closing stock	3,400	
Cost of sales		16,400
Gross profit		107,000
Less: Expenses		
Electricity	4,100	
Advertising	3,200	
Business rate	800	
Salaries	16,000	
Directors' salaries	18,000	
Loan interest paid	4,400	
Debenture interest paid	1,000	47,500
Net profit		59,500
Less: Corporation tax		14,875
Profit after tax		44,625
Less: Proposed dividend		
Ordinary shares	5,000	
Preference shares	1,000	6,000
		38,625
Less: Transfer to general reserve		3,000
		35,625
Add: Retained profit from previous years		4,900
Balance of retained profit carried forward		40,525

The balance sheet of Twyford Ltd as at 31 December 2001

	£	£	£
Fixed assets			
Land and buildings			124,000
Motor vehicle			16,000
			140,000
Current assets			
Stocks		3,400	
Debtors		7,000	
Bank		15,000	
Cash		1,000	
		26,400	
Less: Current liabilities			
Creditors	4,000		
Proposed dividend			
Ordinary	5,000		
Preference	1,000		
Corporation tax	14,875	24,875	
Working capital			1,525
			141,525
Less: Long-term liabilities			
10% debenture		10,000	
Bank loan		25,000	
			35,000
Net assets			106,525
Financed by:			
Authorised share capital			
50,000 ordinary shares (£1)			50,000
10,000 preference shares (£1)			10,000
			60,000
Issued share capital			
50,000 ordinary shares (£1)		50,000	
10,000 preference shares (£1)		10,000	
			60,000
Reserves			
General reserve		6,000	
Balance of retained profit		40,525	46,525
			106,525

Check your understanding (page 530)

	2000	2001	2002
Stock turnover	4.61	4.21	3.8

Over this period, the stock turnover has been falling steadily. The implication is there has been a reduction in efficiency, shown by higher average stock levels, even though cost of sales has increased.

Check your understanding (page 531, a)

- Debtors' collection period $= \dfrac{402{,}200{,}000}{13{,}820{,}821} = 29.1$ days
- Asset turnover $= \dfrac{5{,}044{,}600{,}000}{1{,}780{,}600{,}000} = 2.833$
- Proprietary ratio $= \dfrac{1{,}780{,}200{,}000}{1{,}788{,}600{,}000} = 0.995$

The debtors' collection period is a good indicator of how well debts are collected from customers. Improving collection methods may improve efficiency and cash flow. The figure of 29.1 days is a short collection period for any company although, given the nature of their activities, most sales from Boots are in the retail sector for cash. It could be argued that sales figures broken down into sector components would be a better indicator. The asset turnover ratio refers to the efficiency of net assets in generating sales. The figure shown seems quite high, but would need to be compared to figures from previous years, as well as those of other competitors within the sector. The proprietary ratio is beyond the minimum and there is a close balance between the owners' funds and the tangible assets of the organisation.

Check your understanding (page 531, b)

Finding out about debt collection and credit control would be a useful exercise for the students, particularly if they know someone involved in some form of debt collection. It would be interesting for them to find out how cash, or sometimes the lack of it, affects the ability of individual businesses to control their activities.

Case study: calculating the current ratio (page 533)

1 The current ratio of the business is 3:1 (i.e. 3000/1000).

2 If trade creditors increased by £1,500, the ratio would be 1.2:1 (i.e. 3000/2500). As 2:1 is a prudent ratio, and given this level of debtors, they might decide to reduce stocks or make the business more liquid by encouraging debtors to pay earlier.

Check your understanding (page 534)

It is fairly straightforward for the students to access the accounts of an organisation using the Internet. The current ratio and acid test ratio will provide valuable information about the liquidity or solvency situation of the chosen organisation, and the students might want to compare this information with an organisation's competitors.

Case study: BT's nine-month results to 31 December 1999 (page 537)

1 A number of stakeholder groups might be interested in the results, including shareholders, suppliers of credit, lenders of finance, managers, employees and anyone else involved with the company.
2 The figures show a fall in profitability with reduced earnings per share. They clearly spell a difficult period for the company.
3 Shareholders are likely to be dispirited about the figures and will be trying to find out why profitability has fallen, as well as what decisions can be taken to reach former profit levels.

Case study: comparing the performance of two organisations (page 540)

1 Performance ratios:

	Alpha	*Beta*
Stock turnover	15.5	5
Debtors' collection period	1.52	58.96
Asset utilisation	4.8	4
Asset turnover performance	4.36	2.22
Solvency ratios		
Working capital	£25,000	£260,000
Current ratio	1.5:1	3.88:1
Acid test ratio	0.3:1	2.66:1
Profitability ratios		
Gross profit percentage	22.5%	53.84%
Net profit percentage	12.5%	23.07%

2 Alpha keep lower stock turnover and have higher stock turnover. Both companies are profitable, but Beta have a long debt-collection period and are less efficient. Their working capital is also too large and suggests they are not making best use of their resources.
3 From the information, as Alpha's sales are clearly mainly cash and they have a larger stock turnover, they are likely to be the food retailer. Beta are a successful engineering company, but could improve their performance if they were more efficient.

Case study: a fresh face leading Boots (page 541)

1 As a retailing leader, as with other market sector leaders, the only way is often down! As a cash cow within a mature market with few areas of growth, Boots have sat back on their laurels and let things happen. The effect has been they have fallen out of fashion with the City.
2 Investors will look for Boots to become more dynamic and develop new business opportunities in new market sectors.

Check your understanding (page 543)

Having already compared the performance of two organisations, students might like to make their own comparisons. This is not always easy to do as the accounts of every organisation are presented slightly differently and some are not always easy to understand. Hence, the students may need some guidance.

CHAPTER 21 CASH FLOW MANAGEMENT AND BUDGETING

Case study: the Society of Practitioners of Insolvency (page 547)

1 The main reasons for insolvency cited are poor management and financial constraints. For example, if a business is

badly managed, there may be little forward planning in the area of cash management and it may not use any form of credit control procedures.

2 The guide emphasises that every business faces a cash crisis without good planning. It poses some key questions for businesses, as identified within the study. The questions are really fundamental to basic business planning and will help an organisation to cope with events happening in the future.
3 The questions nearly all deal with planning ahead and monitoring actual events against those planned. They emphasise the need to review constantly the progress of a business.

Check your understanding (page 548)

We all budget to a greater or lesser extent, but few of us legitimise the process by writing down our forecasts and monitoring our forecasts against events. Students may feel their own finances might be helped by a process of planning and may point to something large they might be saving for, such as a car or a holiday. They might also point to some responsibility they might have for planning within a sports club, etc.

Check your understanding (page 550)

Each school or college will have a financial plan. In fact, colleges should have a set of published accounts. With this exercise, it might again be possible for the college accountant or school bursar to come to talk to the group about financial planning and his or her role within the process.

Case study: Spreadware Budgeting (page 552)

1 Computer software enables revisions to be made easily to budgets and also provides a basis for analysis of budgets. The software enables variances to be detected and forecasts to be compared to actual data, and the information is available immediately to prescribed users on their desktops.
2 Variances enable action to be taken quickly when plans are not following the forecast pattern. Forecasts are really important for a business, as it is only by thinking ahead that crises can be avoided or planned for.
3 An organisation that becomes far too data-centred may become less proactive and more reactive.

Check your understanding (page 554)

	Jan	Feb	Mar	Apr	May	June	July	Aug	Sept	Oct	Nov	Dec
Exten			3,000		75,000		1,200				2,000	
Repla	1,600											
H&S	5,000					5,000						
Total	6,600	–	3,000	–	75,000	5,000	1,200	–	–	–	2,000	–

Case study: Planware (page 555)

1 Computer packages, particularly those that incorporate spreadsheets, allow planning to take into account lots of 'what if' situations by changing some of the variables.
2 Those requiring the information would generally be senior managers of the business or budget controllers/financial managers. They might also be useful for any budget holder, such as middle managers and heads of department.

Check your understanding (page 560)

Cash flow statement of Dallington Roofing for the six months to June

	January	February	March	April	May	June
Receipts						
Sales	7,000	7,000	7,000	7,000	7,000	7,000
Total	7,000	7,000	7,000	7,000	7,000	7,000
Payments						
Materials	1,600	1,600	1,600	1,600	1,600	1,600
Wages	3,500	3,500	3,500	3,500	3,500	3,500
Rent	1,000	1,000	1,000	1,000	1,000	1,000
VAT paid	1,500					
Equipment			2,350			
Total	7,600	6,100	8,450	6,100	6,100	6,100
R – P	(600)	900	(1,450)	900	900	900
Bal b/f	3,000	2,400	3,300	1,850	2,750	3,650
Bal c/f	2,400	3,300	1,850	2,750	3,650	4,550

Check your understanding (pages 562–564)

1

The cash flow forecast of C. Moon for the six months to June

	January £	February £	March £	April £	May £	June £
Opening balance	500	1,400	(1,300)	(1,600)	500	1,100
Sales	2,300	1,400	5,300	6,100	4,700	1,400
Net inflow	2,800	2,800	4,000	4,500	4,200	2,500
Payments	1,400	4,100	5,600	5,000	3,100	900
Closing balance	1,400	(1,300)	(1,600)	(500)	1,100	1,600

Christine is going to suffer from a cash shortage during the months February to April. To help her through this period, she should apply for an overdraft facility on her business bank account. The overdraft should be authorised for at least £2,000. Her maximum net shortfall is currently forecast at £1,600 in March but circumstances may worsen or forecasts may not be accurate. It is important she arranges the overdraft with a margin of error in mind.

2

The cash flow forecast of S. Huang for the six months to June

	January £	February £	March £	April £	May £	June £
Opening balance	250	550	1,450	2,050	1,650	1,550
Sales	1,400	1,600	1,500	1,000	900	700
Net inflow	1,650	2,150	2,950	3,050	2,550	2,250
Payments	1,100	700	900	1,400	1,000	900
Closing balance	550	1,450	2,050	1,650	1,550	1,350

3

The cash flow forecast of Andrew Nut for the six months to June

	January £	February £	March £	April £	May £	June £
Opening balance	28,500	14,250	8,300	5,050	13,300	15,300
Cash sales	2,750	3,550	4,000	7,000	8,500	7,150
Credit sales	0	0	2,750	3,550	4,000	7,000
Inheritance	0	0	0	8,000	0	0
Net inflow	31,250	17,800	15,050	23,600	25,800	29,450
Payments	0	6,500	7,000	7,300	7,500	6,100
Wages	1,000	1,000	1,000	1,000	1,000	1,000
Machinery	15,500	0	0	0	0	0
Rent	500	500	500	500	500	500
Other	0	1,500	1,500	1,500	1,500	1,500
Net outflow	17,000	9,500	10,000	10,300	10,500	9,100
Closing balance	14,250	8,300	5,050	13,300	15,300	20,350

4

The cash flow forecast of Albert Spanner for the six months to June

	January £	February £	March £	April £	May £	June £
Opening balance	17,400	16,850	13,300	11,100	10,450	11,415
Cash sales	500	1,000	1,550	1,750	2,050	2,100
Credit sales	0	0	1,500	3,000	4,650	5,250
Total sales	500	1,000	3,050	4,750	6,700	7,350
Loan	0	0	0	0	4,000	0
Net inflow	17,900	17,850	16,350	15,050	21,150	18,765
Purchases	0	0	3,200	3,350	4,185	5,500
Wages	800	800	800	800	800	800
Machinery	0	2,500	0	0	3,500	0
Rent	250	250	250	250	250	250
Other	0	1,000	1,000	1,000	1,000	1,000
Net outflow	1,050	4,550	5,250	5,400	9,735	7,550
Closing balance	16,850	13,300	11,100	10,450	11,415	11,215

5

The cash flow forecast of Anna Djurkovic for the six months to June

	January £	February £	March £	April £	May £	June £
Opening balance	1,000	2,910	11,755	5,150	6,045	6,660
Cash sales	3,000	3,400	3,300	3,500	3,300	3,800
Loan	0	8,000	0	0	0	0
Net inflow	4,000	14,310	15,055	8,650	9,345	10,460
Motor car	0	0	7,000	0	0	0
Salary	1,000	1,000	1,000	1,000	1,000	1,000
Raw materials	0	1,200	1,200	1,200	1,200	1,200
Loan repayment	0	250	250	250	250	250
Loan interest	0	15	15	15	15	15
Electricity	0	0	50	0	0	50
Telephone	0	0	0	0	80	0
Water rates	0	0	0	0	0	300
Car expenses	0	0	50	50	50	50
Post	90	90	90	90	90	90
Rent	0	0	250	0	0	250
Net outflow	1,090	2,555	9,905	2,605	2,685	3,205
Closing balance	2,910	11,755	5,150	6,045	6,660	7,255

6

The cash flow forecast of Robin Chilton for the six months to June

	January £	February £	March £	April £	May £	June £
Opening balance	1,350.00	(7,712.50)	(5,025.00)	(2,387.50)	(362.50)	2,325.00
Sales	8,000.00	8,000.00	8,000.00	8,000.00	8,000.00	8,000.00
VAT on sales	1,400.00	1,400.00	1,400.00	1,400.00	1,400.00	1,400.00
Net inflow	10,750.00	1,687.50	4,375.00	7,012.50	9,037.50	11,725.00
Materials	3,500.00	3,500.00	3,500.00	3,500.00	3,500.00	3,500.00
Wages	2,500.00	2,500.00	2,500.00	2,500.00	2,500.00	2,500.00
Equipment	10,000.00	0	0	0	0	0
Rent	100.00	100.00	100.00	100.00	100.00	100.00
Water rates	0	0	50.00	0	0	50.00
VAT on payments	2,362.50	612.50	612.50	612.50	612.50	612.50
VAT to C&E	612.50	0	0	0	0	0
Net outflow	18,462.50	6,712.50	6,762.50	7,375.00	6,712.50	6,762.50
Closing balance	(7,712.50)	(5,025.00)	(2,387.50)	(362.50)	2,325	4,962.50

Check your understanding (pages 568–569)

Sales budget

	July	Aug	Sept	Oct	Nov	Dec	Jan	Total
Forecast number of units	100	100	500	1,300	10,000	20,000	0	32,000
Selling price (£)	2.5	2.5	2.5	2.5	2.5	2.5	2.5	
Sales turnover	250	250	1,250	3,250	25,000	50,000	0	80,000

Finished stock and production budget

	July	Aug	Sept	Oct	Nov	Dec	Jan	Total
b/f quantity	100	100	1,800	18,300	20,000	20,000	0	100
Production	100	1,800	10,000	10,000	10,000	0	0	31,900
Sales	100	100	500	1,300	10,000	20,000	0	32,000
c/f quantity	100	1,800	11,300	20,000	20,000	0	0	0

Raw materials – dried

(kg)	July	Aug	Sept	Oct	Nov	Dec	Jan	Total
b/f quantity	50	900	5,000	5,000	5,000	0	0	50
Purchases	900	5,000	5,000	5,000	0	0	0	15,900
Issues	50	900	5,000	5,000	5,000	0	0	0
c/f quantity	900	5,000	5,000	5,000	0	0	0	0

(lb)	July	Aug	Sept	Oct	Nov	Dec	Jan	Total
b/f (£)	60	1,080	6,000	6,000	6,000	0	0	60
Purchases (£)	1,080	6,000	6,000	6,000	0	0	0	19,080
Issues (£)	60	1,080	6,000	6,000	6,000	0	0	19,140
c/f (£)	1,080	6,000	6,000	6,000	0	0	0	0

Raw materials – other

(kg)	July	Aug	Sept	Oct	Nov	Dec	Jan	Total
b/f quantity	0	0	0	0	0	0	0	0
Purchases	50	900	5,000	5,000	5,000	0	0	15,950
Issues	50	900	5,000	5,000	5,000	0	0	15,950
c/f quantity	0	0	0	0	0	0	0	0

(lb)	July	Aug	Sept	Oct	Nov	Dec	Jan	Total
b/f (£)	0	0	0	0	0	0	0	0
Purchases (£)	30	540	3,000	3,000	3,000	0	0	9,570
Issues (£)	30	540	3,000	3,000	3,000	0	0	9,570
c/f (£)	0	0	0	0	0	0	0	0

Stock – packaging

(kg)	July	Aug	Sept	Oct	Nov	Dec	Jan	Total
b/f quantity	0	34,900	33,100	23,100	13,100	3,100	0	0
Purchases	35,000	0	0	0	0	0	0	35,000
Issues	100	1,800	10,000	10,000	10,000	3,100	0	35,000
c/f quantity	34,900	33,100	23,100	13,100	3,100	0	0	0

(lb)	July	Aug	Sept	Oct	Nov	Dec	Jan	Total
b/f (£)	0	3,490	3,310	2,310	1,310	310	0	0
Purchases (£)	3,500	0	0	0	0	0	0	3,500
Issues (£)	10	180	1,000	1,000	1,000	310	0	3,500
c/f (£)	3,490	3,310	2,310	1,310	310	0	0	0

Direct labour (£)

	July	Aug	Sept	Oct	Nov	Dec	Jan	Total
Direct labour (£)	20	360	2,000	2,000	2,000	0	0	6,380

Distribution cost (£)

	July	Aug	Sept	Oct	Nov	Dec	Jan	Total
Distribution cost (£)	20	20	100	260	2,000	4,000	0	6,400

Premier Christmas Pudding Co.: cash budget for 7 months to January 2002

	July £	Aug £	Sept £	Oct £	Nov £	Dec £	Jan £	Total £
Sales	0	250	250	1,250	3,250	25,000	50,000	80,000
Payments								
Dried fruit	1,080	6,000	6,000	6,000	0	0	0	19,080
Other ingredients	30	540	3,000	3,000	3,000	0	0	9,570
Packaging	3,500	0	0	0	0	0	0	3,500
Labour	20	360	2,000	2,000	2,000	0	0	6,380
Distribution	20	20	100	260	2,000	4,000	0	6,400
Overhead	3,000	3,000	3,000	3,000	3,000	3,000	3,000	21,000
Total	7,650	9,920	14,100	14,260	10,000	7,000	3,000	65,930
Receipts – payments	–7,650	–9,670	–13,850	–13,010	–6,750	18,000	47,000	14,070
b/f	15,930	8,280	–1,390	–15,240	–28,250	–35,000	–17,000	15,930
c/f	8,280	–1,390	–15,420	–28,250	–35,000	–17,000	15,930	

Premier Christmas Pudding Co.: budget trading and profit and loss account for the 7 months to January 2002

	July £	Aug £	Sept £	Oct £	Nov £	Dec £	Jan £	Total £
Sales	250	250	1,250	3,250	25,000	50,000	0	80,000
Opening stocks								
Pudding @ £1.20	120	120	2,160	13,560	24,000	24,000	0	120
Dried fruit	60	1,080	6,000	6,000	6,000	0	0	60
Packaging	0	3,490	3,310	2,310	1,310	310	0	0
Total	180	4,690	11,470	21,870	31,310	24,310	0	180
Direct costs								
Dried fruit	1,080	6,000	6,000	6,000	0	0	0	19,080
Other	30	540	3,000	3,000	3,000	0	0	9,570
Packaging	3,500	0	0	0	0	0	0	3,500
Labour	20	360	2,000	2,000	2,000	0	0	6,380
Total	4,630	6,900	11,000	11,000	5,000	0	0	38,530
Closing stock								
Puddings	120	2,160	13,550	24,000	24,000	0	0	0
Dried fruit	1,080	6,000	6,000	6,000	6,000	0	0	0
Packaging	3,490	3,310	2,310	1,310	310	0	0	0
Total	4,960	11,470	21,870	31,310	24,310	0	0	0
Cost of sales	120	120	600	1,560	12,000	24,310	0	38,710
Gross profit	130	130	650	1,690	13,000	25,690	0	41,290
Distribution cost	20	20	100	260	2,000	4,000	0	6,400
Overhead	3,000	3,000	3,000	3,000	3,000	3,000	3,000	21,000
Net profit	–2,890	–2,890	–2,450	–1,570	–8,000	18,690	–3,000	13,890

NB: The gross profit of one pudding would be:

	£	£
Sales	2.50	100
Labour cost	0.20	
Packaging	0.10	
Materials	0.90	
Total cost	1.20	48
Gross profit	1.30	52

Check your understanding (page 570)

It could be argued that many of the costs itemised in the list could be controlled by a marketing manager. The costs illustrated more likely to be controlled by a marketing manager in this instance would include advertising, stationery and training costs. A short explanation should accompany each to serve as justification.

Case study: MBB Tools Ltd (page 573)

1 Managers across a range of departments found budgeting process difficult to implement. As a result, certain departments noticed they had expenditures higher than were initially planned. Blame seems to have been apportioned to the managers rather than to the inflexibility of the system.
2 The problems could have been avoided by giving the system an opportunity to work.

SECTION C OHTs

NOTES

OHT 5.18.1: distinguishing between financial and management accounting

This overhead is useful for distinguishing between financial and management accounting. It is important that, from an early stage, the students are able to make this distinction. The OHT is taken from Figure 18.1 on page 465 of the student book and the tutor may wish to combine using this OHT with the 'Check your understanding' activity on the same page.

OHT 5.18.2: internal and external users of information

There are many people, both within and outside a business organisation, who use information. The word 'stakeholder' seems suddenly to have become a popular word in our vocabulary in recent years, earmarking anyone affected in one way or another by the actions or decisions taken within an organisation. Referring to page 467 of the student book, this OHT itemises each of the stakeholders, breaking them down into either internal or external users of information.

OHT 5.18.3: accountancy practice

This OHT attempts to illustrate that accountants are under an obligation to use best accountancy practice in the preparation of accounts, which must be designed to give a 'true and fair view' of a business's trading performance and financial position. In meeting the needs of this best practice, within 10 months of the end of an accounting period, a public limited company must submit:

- a balance sheet
- a profit and loss account
- a cash flow statement
- notes to the accounts describing the company's accounting policies
- an auditor's report.

OHT 5.18.4: invoice

This OHT provides an illustrative invoice that may be used to show various elements, such as the order number, carriage, E & OE, trade discount, VAT, the invoice number and the VAT registration number.

OHT 5.19.1: the accounting process

Having looked at various types of documents, it is important the students understand how the documents fit into recording processes and what books are then used for recording within a book-keeping system. Linking in with pages 491–492 of the student book, there are really two elements to this OHT. On the left-hand side, the OHT shows that documents are posted to ledgers, from which a trial balance is extracted before the writing up of final accounts. The right-hand side breaks this process down into different types of source documents, ledgers and final accounts.

OHT 5.19.2: the double-entry system

This is a particularly important OHT and one that will, we hope, help explain some of the really difficult issues for students to grasp when coming to terms with the rather fuzzy logic of double-entry explanations. It illustrates that an account is debited when receiving value – recording an asset or recording an expense. Conversely, an account is credited when losing something of value – recording a liability or recording an income item.

OHT 5.19.3: computerised accounting packages

This OHT simply itemises some of the benefits of using computerised accounting packages, and fits in with pages 504–506 of the student book. For example, some of the advantages include better control, improved accuracy, the supply of reports, being able to access account balances quickly, the production of reports and the ability to provide managers with a view of how the business is functioning.

OHT 5.19.4: assets equal liabilities plus capital

This simple OHT illustrates the formula that underlies all accounting activity – that assets equal liabilities plus capital. Referring to pages 513–516 of the student book, this could be used when introducing the concept of the balance sheet.

OHT 5.20.1: memorandum and articles of association

This OHT provides some comparisons between the content of a company's memorandum of association and a company's articles of association. For example, the memorandum will have the name of the company, its address, objectives or activities and amount of capital, all of which help to form a view of the business from the outside. On the other hand, designed to assist with the internal operation of the business, the articles will deal with more practical matters, such as how the accounts are kept, recording procedures for the accounts and the rules for issuing and transferring shares, as well as the directors' powers.

OHT 5.20.2: performance ratios

This OHT summarises the performance ratios from the student book. The student book was written with considerable emphasis on reinforcement through practice, particularly in the area of accounting – not only because this is externally assessed but also because students traditionally find this area more difficult than others. Each of the last three OHTs for this section, although simple, is designed to help the tutor to go through all the ratio areas with the students to improve both their knowledge and their understanding of ratio analysis.

OHT 5.20.3: solvency ratios

This OHT summarises the solvency ratios that appear on pages 538–539 of the student book.

OHT 5.20.4: profitability ratios

This OHT summarises the profitability ratios that appear on page 539 of the student book.

OHT 5.21.1: the money-go-round

The money-go-round (illustrated on page 546 of the student book) summarises many of the problems for businesses. In the money-go-round, capital and sales revenue come into a business, but is there enough left over after paying all the costs for expansion and development? There are clearly many different potential versions of the money-go-round, but students need to realise that the effective management of a business organisation involves using financial planning to deal with what is likely to happen in the future.

OHT 5.21.2: a budget timetable

Students need to realise that a budgetary process involves, at some level, almost everyone within a business organisation. One way of linking the process into all elements of planning is the budget timetable for control centres.

OHT 5.21.3: cash flow timing

The area of timing in a cash flow process is something students may become confused about. It is also an area in which it is easy to make mistakes. This OHT may be used to help the students understand the process of timing and to use it correctly within their cash flow exercises. For example, goods paid for three months after a sale in January would mean payment is received in April, etc.

OHT 5.21.4: cash flow statement

The statement in Figure 21.12 on page 560 of the student book may be used as an exemplar for students about to start the exercises on pages 562–564. There are various ways of doing a cash flow forecast, and the tutor may have preferences for a different format. Whichever method is used, it is important to be consistent.

OHT 5.18.1 DISTINGUISHING BETWEEN FINANCIAL AND MANAGEMENT ACCOUNTING

Financial accounting	Management accounting
Subject to accounting regulations to ensure that reports/statements follow a standard approach	Reports are only for internal use so no restrictions are necessary
Provides a broad overview of the whole business using totals	Information extracted relates to parts of the organisation where it is used to help with a particular decision
Provides information to a particular date	Will look at future performance as well as at past performance
Produces general statements and reports	Produces reports with a specific decision in mind
Quantifies information in monetary terms and values	May have non-financial information such as stocks

OHT 5.18.2 INTERNAL AND EXTERNAL USERS OF INFORMATION

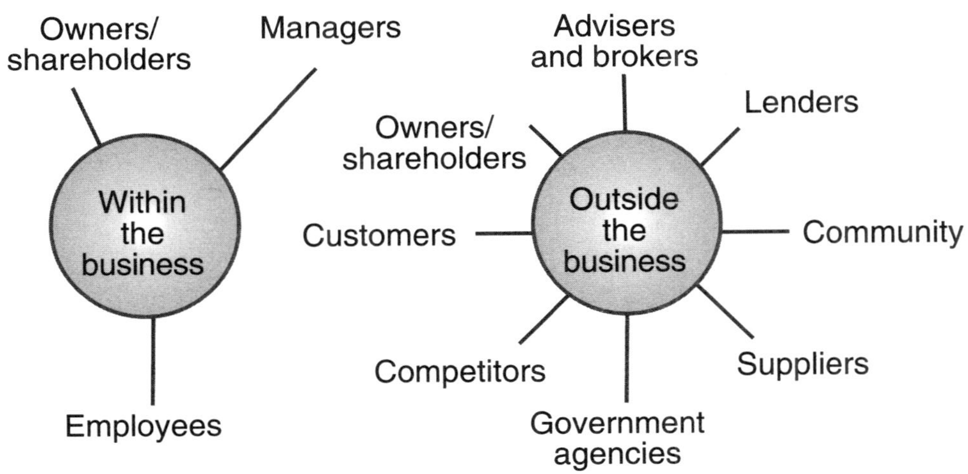

OHT 5.18.3 ACCOUNTANCY PRACTICE

10 months

↓

1. Balance sheet
2. Profit and loss account
3. Cash flow statement
4. Notes to the accountants
5. Auditor's report

OHT 5.18.4 INVOICE

INVOICE

J. P. P. Evans & Co.
Birmingham Road
DUDLEY
West Midlands
B34 7BB

Tel 0121-378-1666 Email evans@server.co.uk Fax 0121-379-1676

VAT Reg 0633 4742 15

Invoice to:

Customised Caravans
Scotland Road
Stanwix
CARLISLE
CA3 8JB

Order No: KL 2322
Date: 12th May 2001
Account: PBB33
Invoice No.:

Quantity	Cat. no.	Description	Price per unit £	Total £	Discount	Net £
10	B345	Tins Henna Red paint	7.00	70.00	0	70.00

Total	70.00
Cash Discount	0.00
	70.00
VAT	8.75
Total	78.75

Terms:
Net monthly
E & OE

OHT 5.19.1 THE ACCOUNTING PROCESS

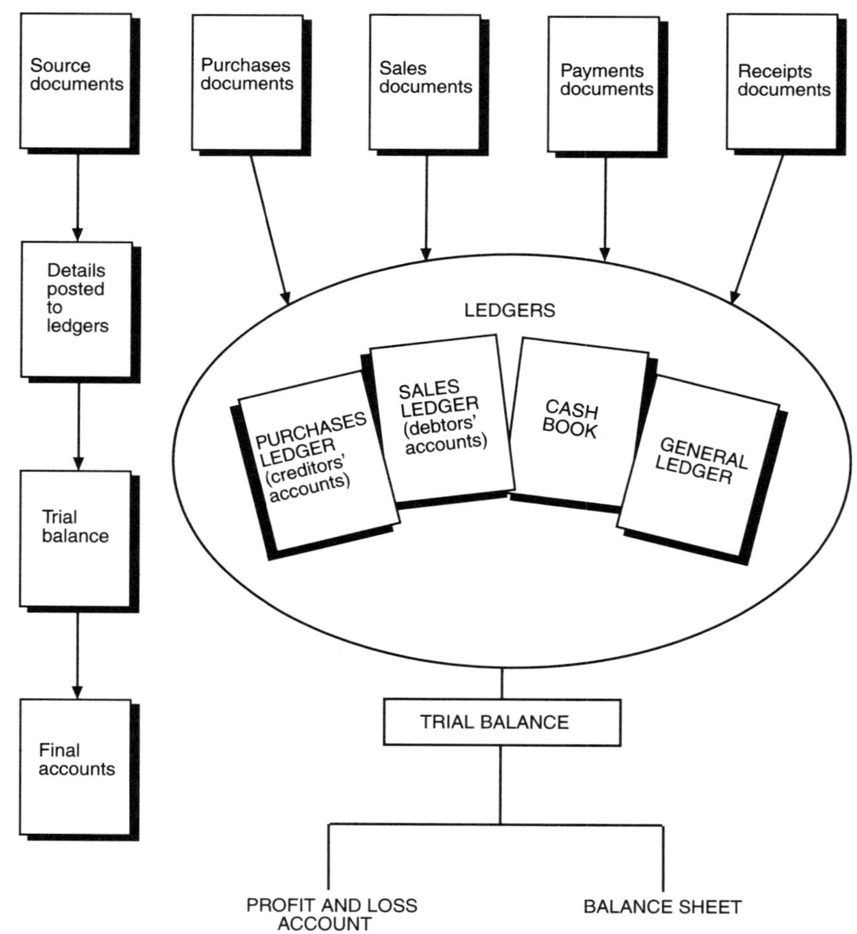

OHT 5.19.2 THE DOUBLE-ENTRY SYSTEM

Account 1

Dr **Cr**

Date	Narrative	£	Date	Narrative	£
	Receiving value, recording an asset or recording an expense				

Account 2

Dr **Cr**

Date	Narrative	£	Date	Narrative	£
				Losing something of value, recording a liability or recording an income item	

OHT 5.19.3 COMPUTERISED ACCOUNTING PACKAGES

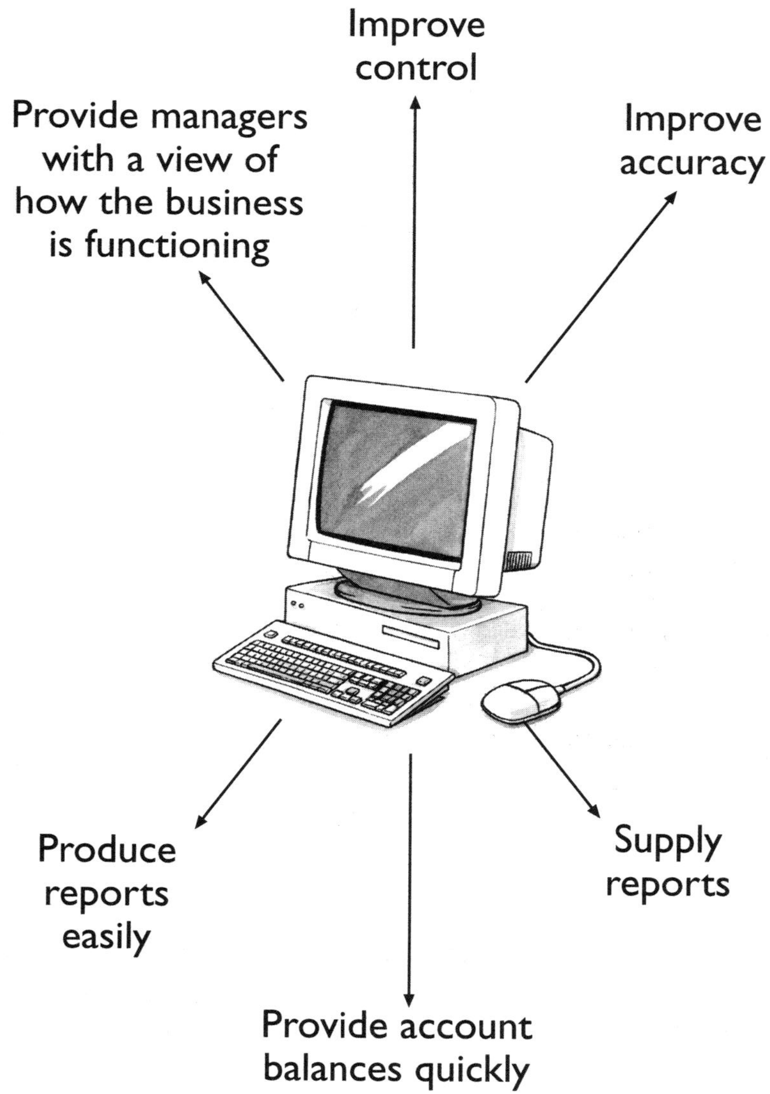

OHT 5.19.4 ASSETS EQUAL LIABILITIES PLUS CAPITAL

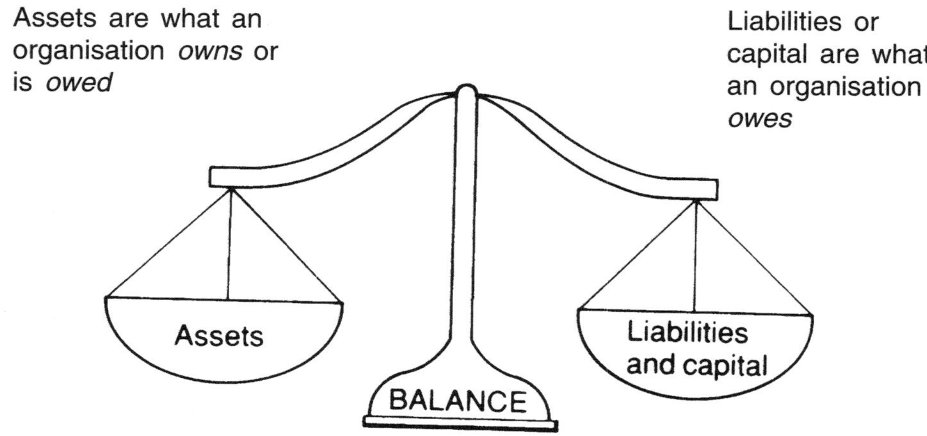

OHT 5.20.1 MEMORANDUM AND ARTICLES OF ASSOCIATION

Memorandum (when viewed from outside)	Articles (rules governing inside working of company)
• Name of company • Address • Objectives/activities • Capital	• Details of how accounts are kept • Recording procedures • Rules for issuing and transferring shares • Powers of directors

OHT 5.20.2 PERFORMANCE RATIOS

1 Stock turnover (times per year) = $\dfrac{\text{Cost of sales}}{\text{Average stock}}$

Where:

Average stock = $\dfrac{\text{Opening stock + Closing stock}}{2}$

Number of days' stock held on average = $\dfrac{\text{Average stock}}{\text{Cost of sales}} \times 365$ days

2 Debtors' collection period = $\dfrac{\text{Debtors}}{\text{Average daily sales}}$

3 Creditors' payment period = $\dfrac{\text{Creditors}}{\text{Average daily purchases}}$

4 Asset utilisation = $\dfrac{\text{Sales}}{\text{Fixed assets}}$

5 Asset turnover performance = $\dfrac{\text{Sales}}{\text{Net assets}}$

Net assets for the purpose of ratio analysis is:

Fixed assets + Current assets – Current liabilities

6 Proprietary ratio = $\dfrac{\text{Ordinary shareholders' funds}}{\text{Tangible assets}}$

OHT 5.20.3 SOLVENCY RATIOS

1 $\text{Working capital} = \text{Current assets} - \text{Current liabilities}$

2 $\text{Current ratio} = \dfrac{\text{Current assets}}{\text{Current liabilities}}$

3 $\text{Acid test ratio} = \dfrac{\text{Current assets} - \text{Stocks}}{\text{Current liabilities}}$

4 $\text{Gearing ratio} = \dfrac{\text{Long-term loans (including debentures and preference capital)}}{\text{Ordinary shares and reserves}}$

5 $\text{Interest cover} = \dfrac{\text{Profit before interest and tax}}{\text{Interest paid in the year}}$

OHT 5.20.4 PROFITABILITY RATIOS

1 $\text{Gross profit percentage} = \dfrac{\text{Gross profit}}{\text{Sales}} \times \dfrac{100}{1}$

2 $\text{Net profit percentage} = \dfrac{\text{Net profit}}{\text{Sales}} \times \dfrac{100}{1}$

3 $\text{Operating profit percentage} = \dfrac{\text{Profit before interest and tax}}{\text{Sales}}$

4 $\text{Return on equity} = \dfrac{\text{Net profit (after tax and preference dividend)}}{\text{Sales}} \times \dfrac{100}{1}$

5 $\text{Return on capital employed} = \dfrac{\text{Net profit + Interest on debentures}}{\text{Ordinary shares + Reserves + Preference shares + Debentures}} \times \dfrac{100}{1}$

6 $\text{Dividend yield} = \dfrac{\text{Ordinary share dividend}}{\text{Market price per share}} \times \dfrac{100}{1}$

7 $\text{Earnings per share} = \dfrac{\text{Net profit after tax and preference dividend}}{\text{Number of ordinary shares}}$

8 $\text{Earnings/dividend yield} = \dfrac{\text{Earnings per ordinary share}}{\text{Market price per share}} \times \dfrac{100}{1}$

9 $\text{Price/earnings ratio} = \dfrac{\text{Market price per share}}{\text{Earnings per share}}$

10 $\text{Dividend cover} = \dfrac{\text{Net profit after tax and dividends}}{\text{Ordinary dividends}}$

OHT 5.21.1 THE MONEY-GO-ROUND

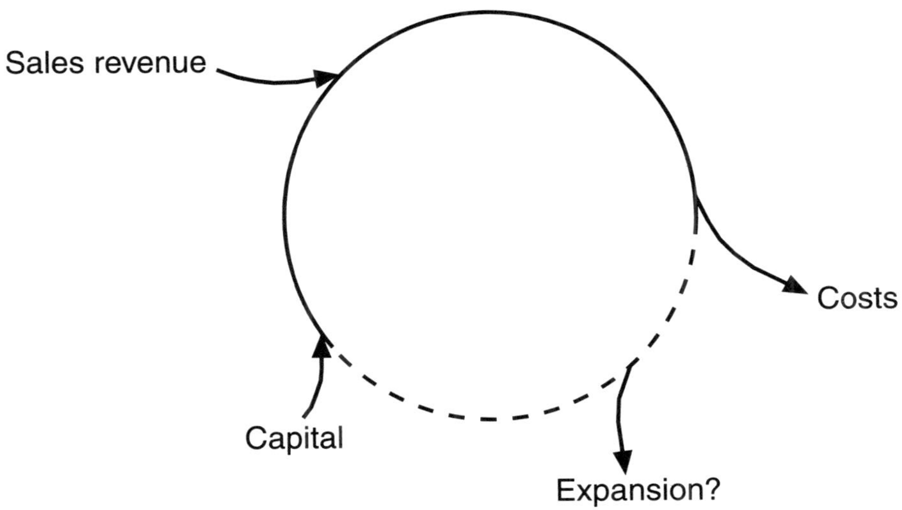

OHT 5.21.2 A BUDGET TIMETABLE

Budget timetable for year 1 April 2001 to 31 March 2002

Date	*Narrative*	*Responsibility*
1 Sept	Board of directors to review long-term objectives and strategies and specify short-tem goals for the year	Directors
22 Sept	Budget guidelines and standard forms issued to line managers	Accounts
6 Oct	Actual results for year are issued to line management, so that comparisons can be made with current budget and last year's actual results	Accounts
20 Oct	Budget submissions are made to the management accountant	Line management
27 Oct	First draft of the master budget is issued	Accounts
3 Nov	First draft of the budget is reviewed for results and consistency – line managers to justify their submissions	MD and individual directors
6 Nov	New assumptions and guidelines issued to line management	Accounts
10 Nov	Budgets revised and resubmitted	Line management
20 Nov	Second draft of master budget issued	Accounts
27 Nov	Final review of the draft budget	Managing director and financial director
1 Dec	Final amendments	Accounts
11 Dec	Submission to the board for their approval	Financial director

OHT 5.21.3 CASH FLOW TIMING

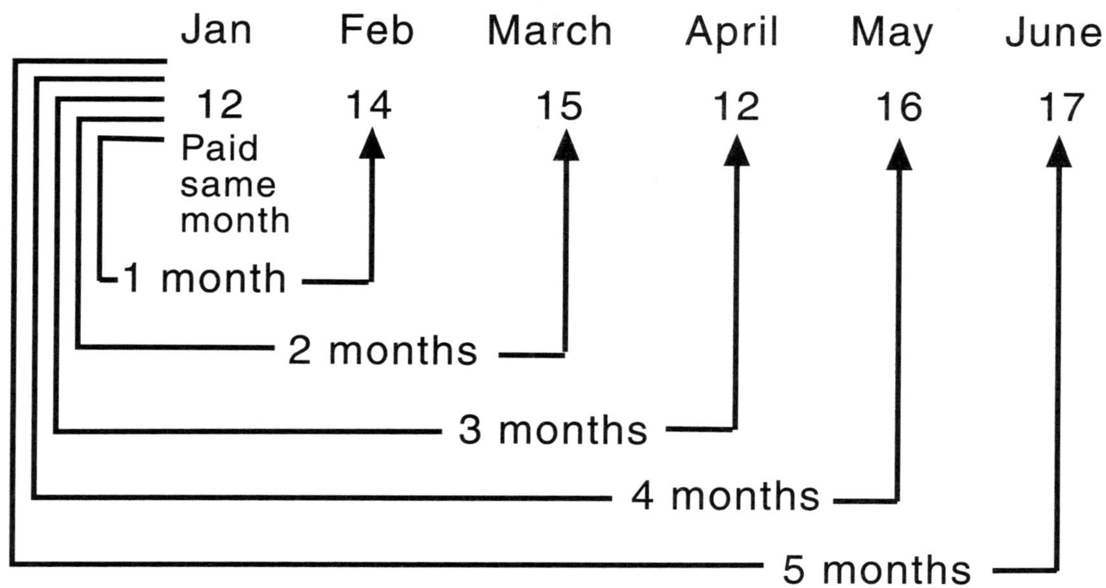

OHT 5.21.4 CASH FLOW STATEMENT

	March	April	May	June	July	August	Total
Receipts							
Sales	5,000	5,000	5,000	5,000	5,000	5,000	30,000
VAT on sales	875	875	875	875	875	875	5,250
Total	5,875	5,875	5,875	5,875	5,875	5,875	35,250
Payments							
Equipment	1,000						1,000
Rent	500	500	500	500	500	500	3,000
Wages	2,000	2,000	2,000	2,000	2,000	2,000	12,000
Materials	2,000	2,000	2,000	2,000	2,000	2,000	12,000
VAT on payments	525	350	350	350	350	350	2,275
VAT paid to C&E				1,400			1,400
Total	6,025	4,850	4,850	6,250	4,850	4,850	31,675
Receipts – payments	(150)	1,025	1,025	(375)	1,025	1,025	3,575
Balance b/f	1,000	850	1,875	2,900	2,525	3,550	1,000
Balance c/f	850	1,875	2,900	2,525	3,550	4,575	4,575

SECTION D THE BALANCE SHEET ISSUE

One of the problems with producing any set of accounts is ensuring consistency of format and design, so that having approached a problem in one way, the students know they can use a similar template or approach for the next exercise. In the student book the balance sheet design is as follows:

The balance sheet of .... as at ....

	£	£	£
Fixed assets			XXX
Current assets	XXX		
Less: Current liabilities		XXX	
Working capital			XXX
Less: Long-term liabilities			XXX
Net assets			XXX
Financed by:			
Capital	XXX		
Add: Net profit (or deduct loss)		XXX	
		XXX	
Less: Drawings		XXX	XXX
			XXX

Note that the long-term liabilities are deducted from the total of fixed and current assets. However, Edexcel (in their specimen external assessment) show the balance sheet as follows:

The balance sheet of .... as at ....

	£	£	£
Fixed assets			XXX
Current assets	XXX		
Less: Current liabilities		XXX	
Working capital			XXX
Net assets			XXX
Financed by:			
Capital	XXX		
Add: Net profit (or deduct loss)		XXX	
		XXX	
Less: Drawings		XXX	XXX
			XXX
Add: Long-term liabilities			XXX
			XXX

Note that Edexcel have opted for adding the long-term liabilities to the outcome of capital (add net profit and less drawings). Without entering into a debate, which would be easy to do, let us agree that both methods are correct – but it is important that, whichever method is used within the classroom, students should be prepared or be able to deal with the alternative Edexcel way of doing things in their assessment.

SECTION E TEST

Time: 2 hours.

1 You work for Proud House Ltd selling high-class electrical novelty products to the high street. During the day you sell the following to R. Jones:

- 5 novelty lamps @ £18.35 each
- 2 bookends @ £4.35 each
- 1 hatstand @ £15.50.

Fill in the receipt below, entering the appropriate details. Use the current date and charge VAT at 10%. *(8 marks)*

Proud House Ltd	Receipt no. 4576..........
High Street *Luton* *LU13 1UP*	
Customer	**Date**
	£
	VAT ______
	Total ______

2 Match the document with the appropriate description: *(8 marks)*

a providing details of availability and of terms being offered
b unconditional order in writing drawn upon a bank
c copy of the customer's account in the sales ledger
d sent with the goods
e contains all the relevant details of a transaction
f used for paying cheques and cash into an organisation's bank account
g reduces the amounts appearing on invoices
h form upon which customers can advise their bank to make regular payments on their behalf

1 statement
2 paying-in slip
3 credit note
4 quotation
5 standing order
6 delivery note
7 cheque
8 invoice

a	
b	
c	
d	
e	
f	
g	
h	

3 Describe two security checks that could be undertaken that could be applied to a range of documents: *(4 marks)*

____

____

____

____

4 What is EDI? Describe two advantages of using EDI. *(6 marks)*

____

____

____

____

5 Imagine you work in the cashier's department. In the morning post, there are a number of remittances. These include:

- a cheque for £17.22
- a cheque for £19.45.

In addition, the following cash payments are received during the day:

9 × £10 notes
10 × £5 notes
22 × £1 coins

Prepare a suitable paying-in slip for all the above to be paid into the bank. Use today's date and sign.

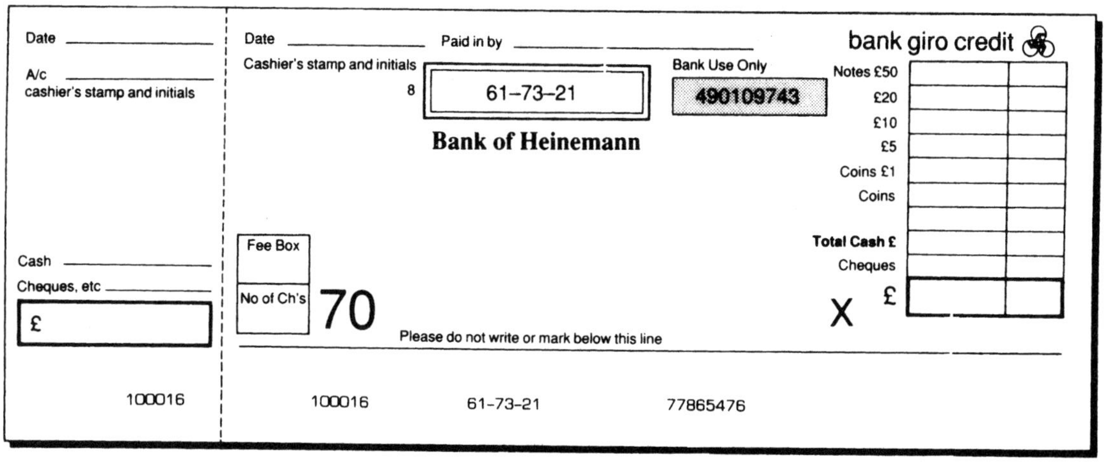
Date
A/c
cashier's stamp and initials
Cash
Cheques, etc
£
100016

Date
Paid in by
Cashier's stamp and initials
8
61–73–21
Bank of Heinemann
Bank Use Only
490109743
bank giro credit
Notes £50
£20
£10
£5
Coins £1
Coins
Total Cash £
Cheques
£
Fee Box
No of Ch's
70
X
Please do not write or mark below this line
100016 61–73–21 77865476

(10 marks)

6 Complete the following sentences using the words listed below: *(10 marks)*

- E & OE
- inquiry
- pro-forma invoice
- advice note
- quotation
- order form
- invoice
- VAT registration number
- statement
- payment

1 A buyer wishing to find out details from a seller will start off by sending a letter of ....

2 When the seller has made up the order he or she will send the buyer an ....

3 For tax purposes, a .... will be printed on an invoice.

4 A seller will send a buyer a .... indicating the types of goods and the prices and terms under which they will be prepared to supply.

5 A .... would be sent by a seller dealing with a buyer for the first time.

6 The letters .... printed on an invoice give the seller the right to amend an incorrectly filled-in invoice.

7 .... can be made by cheque.

8 There are several copies of an ...., one of which is packed with the goods.

9 An .... will be used when placing an order for goods.

10 A .... gives a record of all transactions made within a certain period of time.

7 Rank the following assets of a clothes shop in order of liquidity: *(9 marks)*

- The premises directly owned by the owner.
- Cheques in the till that have been received for the day's trading.
- Clothes in the shop that are most likely to be sold in the next fortnight.
- Clothes in the shop that will take longer to sell.
- The fixtures and fittings of the shop.
- Money owed to the shop that will be repaid within the next month.
- The cash in the till.
- Money owed to the shop over the next year.
- Money the owner currently has in the bank that can be withdrawn on demand.

8 Min Patel started his business on 1 April 2000. He has asked you to help him draw up his end-of-year accounts, and you have

agreed to give up a Saturday morning to go into his business unit and assist him.

Min's business involves buying high-tech gadgets and then selling them to up-market mail-order companies. The business started quite simply when Min visited Thailand on holiday last year, where he was impressed by the electronic goods he saw. He bought a range of items and, when he got home, he wrote to several companies offering the gadgets for sale and asking them to quote him some prices. He then started buying the items, storing them and selling them on to the catalogue companies.

When you look at Min's books you find his paperwork is in quite a mess. He has tended to put everything into a box file and then to forget about it. Nothing is up to date. You have, however, managed to identify the following facts.

1 Min started his business with £2,000 in his business bank account.
2 Last year Min sent out invoices for:
   - 1,000 item Xs at £10 each
   - 500 item Ys at £9 each.

   From this you can work out his sales figures.
3 Over the year, Min has received invoices for £4,000, for goods he has purchased. All these invoices have been paid and he therefore has no creditors.
4 Min's costs have been as follows:
   - rent of unit – £30 per month
   - postage – £40 per month
   - electricity – £23 per month
   - other expenses – £589 for the year.
5 Each month, Min has drawn £400 out of the business account for his own use.
6 Over the year, Min has purchased a motor van for £1,100 and fixtures and fittings for £500.
7 At the end of the year, Min has £1,100 worth of goods in stock.
8 Min's bank balance at the end of the year stands at a healthy £3,395.

Tasks

1 How much capital did Min's business have on 1 April 2000?
2 Work out Min's sales figures for the year.
3 Work out the total of Min's expenses for the year.
4 Identify the two fixed assets purchased during the year.
5 Each month, Min draws £400 out of the business account for his own use. Explain why this £400 per month is not a business expense.
6 Complete Min's trading and profit and loss account for the year.
7 Produce a balance sheet for the end-of-year date.

MARKING SCHEME FOR THE TEST

1 Allocate marks where indicated – total eight marks.

Proud House Ltd		Receipt no. 4576..........
High Street		
Luton		
LU13 1UP		
Customer R. Jones (*1 mark*)	**Date** 21 January 2001 (*1 mark*)	
		£
5 novelty lamps @ £18.35 each	(*1 mark*)	91.75
2 bookends @ £4.35 each	(*1 mark*)	8.70
1 hatstand @ £15.50	(*1 mark*)	15.50
	(*1 mark*)	115.95
	VAT	11.59 (*1 mark*)
	Total	127.54 (*1 mark*)

8

2 One mark for each correct answer – total eight marks.

a = 4
b = 7
c = 1
d = 6
e = 8
f = 2
g = 3
h = 5

16

3 One mark should be allocated for each security check as well as one mark for a full and adequate description of each check – total four marks. For example:

- Orders should be authorised and copies of orders should be sent to the receiving department and accounts department for the checking of prices.
- Invoices should be checked against the original order to ensure the correct goods have arrived, that prices are correct, etc.
- All documents should be filed and kept safely where they can be referred to.
- Certain transactions should be sanctioned and approved, requiring the authorisation of others.

20

4 Two marks should be allocated for the definition of EDI. Two marks should be allocated for each lengthy and full description of an advantage of using EDI – total six marks.

Electronic Data Interchange (EDI) is the exchange of business transactions that would otherwise be undertaken by purchase orders, invoices and other documents, through a standardised computerised format. It is therefore a form of electronic, paperless, contracting between two organisations.

Its advantages include:

- speeding up business transactions between suppliers and their customers
- shortening the lead time between sending and receiving an order
- providing a more responsive and market-focused environment for the customer
- reducing the burden of paperwork
- reducing labour and production costs, etc.

26

5 One mark should be allocated in each correct area – total ten marks, including one for presentation.

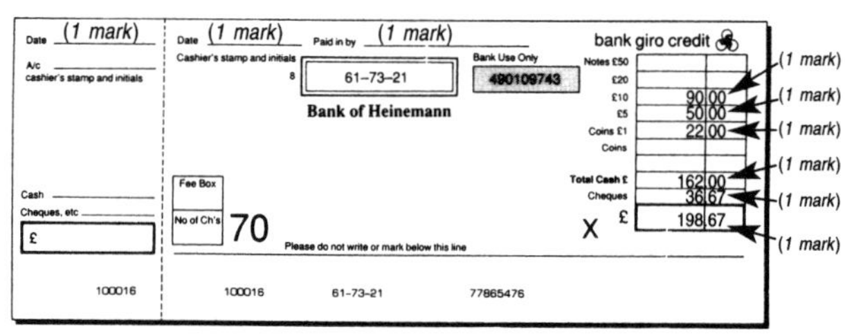

36

6

1 inquiry
2 advice note
3 VAT registration number
4 quotation
5 pro-forma invoice
6 E & OE
7 payment
8 invoice
9 order form
10 statement

(*10 marks*)
46

7 One mark for each correct position.

(*9 marks*)

1 Premises.
2 Fixtures and fittings.

3 Clothes in the shop that will take longer to sell.
4 Clothes in the shop that are most likely to be sold in the next fortnight.
5 Money owed to the shop over the next year.
6 Money owed to the shop that will be repaid within the next month.
7 Cheques in the till that have been received for the day's trading.
8 Money the owner currently has in the bank that can be withdrawn on demand.
9 The cash in the till.

55

8

1 On 1 April 2000, Min's bank account had capital of £2,000 in it.

(*2 marks*)

2 Min's sales figures are as follows:

Item Xs	£10,000
Item Ys	£4,500
Total	£14,500

(*2 marks*)

3 Min's expenses for the year were:

Rent	£360
Postage	£480
Electricity	£276
Other	£589
Total	£1,705

(*2 marks*)

4 Two fixed assets purchased during the year were the motor van and fixtures and fittings. (*2 marks*)

5 The £400 represents the drawings out of the business (i.e. Min is taking it out of the capital of the business, rather than as a wage). It should therefore be seen as a drawing on future profits. (*2 marks*)

6 **The trading and profit and loss account of Min for the year ended 1 April 2001**

	£	£
Sales		14,500
Less:		
Opening stock	–	
Purchases	4,000	
Less: Closing stock	1,100	
Cost of sales		2,900
Gross profit		11,600
Less: Expenses		
Rent	360	
Postage	480	
Electricity	276	
Other	589	
Total expenses		1,705
Net profit		9,895

(*12 marks, including 1 for the title*)

7 **The balance sheet of Min as at 1 April 2001**

	£	£	£
Fixed assets			
Motor van		1,100	
Fixtures and fittings		500	
		1,600	
Current assets			
Closing stock	1,100		
Debtors	1,000		
Bank	3,395	5,495	
		7,095	
Capital		2,000	
Add: Net profit			9,895
		11,895	
Less: Drawings			4,800
		7095	

(*14 marks, including 1 for the title*)

91

UNIT 6 – BUSINESS PLANNING

SECTION A DISCUSSION POINT

WHAT MAKES SOMEONE GOOD IN BUSINESS?

Many of you will be at a stage in your lives when you will be asking yourselves the question: 'Am I the type of person to start up my own business, and could I succeed?' At this stage in your development, it is important you try to appraise your own strengths and weaknesses.

Many studies have been made of small business managers over the years. Most of these have looked at the traits and characteristics that appear common to most people who have been successful in small businesses. A key element in many of the studies has been to look at the characteristics that distinguish people who open and run their own business from those of the sort of person who works for someone else.

One of the findings has been that many people who start their own business have mixed feelings about authority. As a result, they may not have been comfortable working under someone. They may also have a strong 'need for achievement' – and also for status. This is a motivational factor and is an important element in people feeling successful. And, of course, people who start their own business have to be prepared to take risks, and be a plunger, high-risk taker and a bit of a gambler.

As a result, the characteristics that appeared most frequently among 'successful' business managers were as follows:

- *Drive* – vigour, initiative, persistence and health.
- *Thinking ability* – the ability to be original, creative, critical and analytical.
- *Competency in human relations* – emotional stability, sociability, good personal relations, consideration, cheerfulness, co-operation and tact.
- *Communication skills* – verbal comprehension, and oral and written communications.
- *Technical knowledge* – understanding of the physical process of producing goods or services, and the ability to use the information purposefully.

POINTS FOR DISCUSSION

1 Prioritise each of the successful business characteristics shown in the list above, indicating those you feel are the most important and those that are least important.
2 Explain why many of the characteristics needed for someone to be successful as an entrepreneur in small business are different from those needed for people who work for someone else.

SECTION B SUGGESTED ANSWERS

CHAPTER 22 MARKETING ANALYSIS AND MARKETING PLANNING

Case study: personal computer repairs (page 581)

1 Jane should have supplied her bank with a range of information, but has not done so. The letter might help, but the bank will want to know about the history of the business and the background to the ideas Jane has, her background and experience, the aims and objectives of the business, how much Jane has herself invested in the business, details of market research, as well as any distinctions she wants to make about her own business, what the business owns and owes, forecast financial projections and final accounts, any other form of accounting forecasts (such as details of costs and revenues), together with a break-even point, etc.

2 Most of the data would have been obtained by looking at other small businesses, by talking to other people and by spending a great deal of time working out her financial projections.

3 There are many questions she is seeking answers to. For example:

- How many people will use her service?
- What sort of support are they looking for?
- How much are they willing to pay?
- Are they likely to be regular customers or occasional users of the service?
- Will there be quiet periods in the year?

Check your understanding (page 582)

Jill's likely sales revenue in 2002 is £20,200. This is 40% of £50,000, which is then expanded by 10%. The bank is probably likely to take the prudent view of the market and look at it as being worth £320,000. Some 10% of sales is just £32,000.

Discussion point (page 583)

This sounds more like an essay than a discussion point, but is clearly a 'hot' topic that will be extensively debated over the next few years. Sellers are less likely to be face to face with buyers as all these changes take place, but may well have a better relationship with them. Relationship marketing is likely to become much more important, with better personalised communications between the two.

Case study: soft drinks (page 586)

1 Many businesses are faced with these important strategic decisions. It is not easy to make the right decision all the time. There are a number of types of further information the manufacturer would require before making any of the decisions listed. For example, they might want to know about distribution costs, any barriers to entry to the markets indicated, investment costs, competitors in each market, the strategies of other companies likely to enter each market, information about tastes and consumer preferences, etc.

2 The dangers with hastily making a decision are that entry to the market hits a range of snags and that both the financial and marketing forecasts have not been accurate. There is always the problem of unforeseen circumstances.

3 Joint ventures are usually the safest, as the organisation entering the market is then working with a business with good local knowledge.

Check your understanding (page 587)

This is probably best conducted as a group exercise, and the answer is also endless. Essentially, before making a decision to enter a market, an organisation will want as much information as possible to counter any problems it might have. For example, Robin will want information about market demographics, costs of distribution, any regulations or legal compliances, areas of the market that expand faster than others, less fast than others, market segments, actions of competitors, etc. There are a number of barriers. For example, there could be exchange rate issues, import regulations, barriers in the market, etc. Problems might include brand dependency on competitors, maturity of the marketplace, distribution issues, loyalty of retailers, etc.

Check your understanding (page 588)

Students are expected to make up a basic spreadsheet, which they can then use for forecasting purposes. It may refer to sales forecasts or cash flow.

Check your understanding (page 589, a)

This is a simple exercise where, from a basic table, students are expected to draw a pie chart to present the figures. They should use the formula on page 588 of the student book to help them calculate each segment angle. For example, the angle for home would be:

$$\frac{15}{40} \times 360 \text{ degrees} = 135 \text{ degrees}$$

Check your understanding (page 589, b)

There are many elements of information capable of being elicited from the bar chart. Marketing managers seem to be dominated by men, as do chief executives. However, there seem to be more female brand managers and marketing executives. It is quite simple to make comparisons from this sort of bar chart, which is visual and easy to interpret.

Check your understanding (page 591)

This is a simple piece of market research, which, given the huge amount of selling in the PC market in recent years, should not be difficult to carry out. The tutor may wish to break the analysis down into four or five of the major brands, with the 'have another' category covering the remaining brands.

Case study: cream teas over the Web (page 593)

1 This is a novel business idea, which seems to be developing well. There are a number of influences on the purchasing behaviour of consumers using the Web. For example, these might include: security issues, experience of surfing or buying on the Web, demographic profile of the surfer, the sorts of things he or she looks for in a website, etc.
2 Clearly, each of these factors is important in influencing the success of The Thin End Patisserie. For example, as it becomes safer to buy and give credit card details online, it should attract more people to do so. Experience of surfing and using the Web is a clear factor, as is the link between this experience and the type of customer likely to use The Thin End.

Discussion point (page 594)

Incomes are only one factor in determining the demand people have for goods and services. They are, however, a key and important factor. Some people, of course, look as if they earn a great deal and have many goods and services but depend heavily upon borrowing to support their lifestyle, while others are prudent, never spend all their income and forfeit investment decisions because they look towards retirement and old age.

Discussion point (page 595)

As a basic theory of motivation, a great deal can be learnt about the motivations individuals have before they make purchases, and this can be aligned to marketing messages. For example, messages may be targeted at being able to satisfy people's basic needs. Alternatively, they may be aimed at people's need for status and esteem.

Check your understanding (page 596)

This is an interesting and useful activity in which to engage. Students may be able to use the Web to find much of the information they require. It will help them to understand that markets are not static, with constant interaction between each of the competitors in the marketplace.

Case study: competition between the 'majors' in petrol retailing (pages 597–598)

1 The competitors in the petrol retailing market are constantly changing and there have been some huge worldwide mergers in recent years. Students may refer to large companies such as Texaco, Shell and BP, but also refer to the increasing influence supermarkets have in the area of retailing.
2 The Shell Shop, and many of the aged adverts we can still remember, probably started the revolution so that, today, we get a retailing experience as well as the opportunity to buy petrol. Students may also refer to loyalty cards, 24-hour-a-day opening and other elements of competitive activity.
3 With a homogeneous product on offer, differentiating through competitive activity is not easy. Students may refer to personal service, car washing and steam cleaning, the importance of branding, location, etc.
4 More competition would be encouraged by more retail opportunities to earn more money on non-petrol sales and higher profit margins at the pump. Competition is likely to be discouraged by reduced margins, the increasing monopoly power of the majors and many of the issues that have caused uncertainty in the UK petrol market in recent years.

Check your understanding (page 599, a)

The owners of such a site might have a range of objectives, such as the number of 'hits' or 'users', to change the way people search for food or even book a table, to provide an opportunity for customers to browse for food, to receive revenue from participating restaurants, to increase their reliance upon the website, etc.

Check your understanding (page 599, b)

If the marketing plan does not work, then no other plan will meet its specifications. The marketing plan will refer to the wider objectives of the organisation, its financial projections, the number of sales made, the operations of the business, etc.

Check your understanding (page 602)

The success of this activity will largely depend upon the support received from the local business people chosen. The best way to carry out the activity may be to volunteer to help for the day, and to go to spend a whole day working with them.

Case study: flower selling (page 602)

1 Researching a market is not easy, and is certainly likely to involve a great deal more than simply a local survey. They need to find out as much as possible about buying patterns in the flower market. This they might do by talking to other florists or, perhaps, by looking for more detailed information on the market such as that which may have been published by a market research company. Only after they have gone through an extensive research of secondary material is it worth thinking about undertaking some primary research related to their local area and circumstances.
2 Their primary research might ask a range of questions, such as:

- How often do you shop in the market?
- What do you look for when shopping?
- Are purchases by impulse or are they planned?
- What sort of flowers do you buy?
- How do you like them presented/wrapped? etc.

3 They may put questions to particular target groups, such as young men in a particular age range, middle-aged men between certain ages, teenagers, etc.
4 Predicting demand for turnover is difficult and has direct implications for the nature and type of flowers they buy, as well as stocks, particularly given they are a fresh commodity. Having carried out their questionnaire, they might try to find out the average takings of each of the stalls in the market. They may also try to extract some figures from the data they have collected.

Check your understanding (page 603)

This question tries to establish what it is

about a particular product that identifies it from its competitors. The product may be anything from a newspaper, to clothes, to watching a football match. When analysing the tangible and intangible benefits, it is important for the students to think about how the features of the product distinguish it from its competitors.

Discussion point (page 604)

We all know the reasons for advertising, but does it affect the ability of consumers to make rational and measured decisions about their purchases? There is an extensive debate that advertising persuades people to buy products because they feel deprived without them (AIDA). If this is the case, then, when consumers buy, the messages held within their retentive mind are those that are likely to influence them either as adopters or as repeat purchasers. The core issue is whether there are real alternatives to many of the goods that are extensively advertised. If the answer is 'no', then really it could be argued that advertising is wasteful because it simply divides or helps to share the spoils from various markets.

Case study: Cricket 2000 (page 604)

1 These types of computer games are based upon real effects and an element of virtual reality. They provide excitement through the simulated graphics and the element of ownership players feel as they work through the game.
2 Many factors will have determined the price point of £29.99, particularly for a limited format such as PlayStation. Skimming tends to be a pricing strategy for these types of high-tech goods, which start with a high-price adopter point.

Case study: targeting working women (page 605)

1 Magazines relate to various categories of usage, including specialist titles and demographically focused status-based titles. This narrow band of readership makes them more likely to be successful and responsive to advertising messages.
2 Measuring advertising effectiveness is important but not always easy. To determine whether or not advertising is meeting its objectives, it is possible to evaluate any changes in sales performance in response to a campaign or to provide a post-sale evaluation from a targeted group.

Check your understanding (page 606)

This is a simple, generally focused activity in which the tutor needs to encourage the students to compare and contrast two products or services that have been developed to reach consumers. It is better if these products or services are competing. Students may find one is more product based, available in more outlets and aims at a mass market. In contrast, they may find another has more benefits (e.g. with service elements), has a more exclusive image and higher price, and is aimed at a limited market.

CHAPTER 23 PRODUCTION AND RESOURCE REQUIREMENTS

Check your understanding (page 609)

There are many reasons why consumers have preferences, but the notion of value added underlines their motivations, even if it is as simple as using a shop regularly for its opening times. Students should identify all the elements they like about a good or service they buy in answering this question. As they do so, they should think about why or how the value added by their chosen supplier makes them choose them in preference to someone else.

Case study: adding value in the airline business (page 609)

1 The emphasis in this case study is about adding value and its relationship to all that is received by each customer. Value reflects, in this sense, the total amount of any benefit received by each customer from the airline for any of the services they provide. The assumption is that, if the value proposition is better, the customers will make preferential choices about the airline.

2 Almost everything an airline does to satisfy customer needs is part of the value-added process. To add more value, an airline needs to think about how to provide more facilities and services for its customers.
3 Added value is particularly important in service industries, but can apply to anything (e.g. a car franchise that lends cars to its clients when theirs are being serviced is adding value to the service it provides; a kettle that boils faster than another is adding more value, etc.).

Discussion point (page 610)

In the increasingly competitive business environment of today, it has become more typical for all sorts of organisations to mix production with a service. For example, a large manufacturing company may choose their suppliers of tools because they know they will deliver them within 24 hours of an order, replace them when faulty and are prepared to wait 28 days for payment.

Discussion point (page 612)

The movement towards leaner and fitter organisations does not necessarily mean small is beautiful. However, it does mean modern organisations are aware of many of the issues associated with diseconomies of scale, and are willing to take decisions to ensure they are not badly influenced by too many of the negative effects of being large.

Case study: British Book Printers plc (page 613)

1 The figures illustrate many different examples of economies of scale. For example, output over the period from 1998 to 2001 has doubled, but the number of machines has increased only from 8 to 13, and the number of employees has increased only from 175 to 194. At the same time as output has expanded, the product portfolio has tripled, and costs of manufacture per publication have fallen dramatically.
2 Many different sorts of economies are likely to have taken place. For example, division of labour has probably improved the productivity of each of the employees, technical economies have enabled goods to be produced in higher volumes at lower costs and bulk buying has probably reduced the cost base.

Check your understanding (page 614)

There are usually many different mergers and integrations at any one time. For example, there have been some recent mergers of large oil companies (horizontally) and financial service organisations. The press might describe some of the motivations behind each of the mergers, such as a reduction in the number of branches or outlets, improved efficiency, response to other competitors, etc.

Discussion point (page 614)

Overtrading is the common trap many organisations fall into simply by taking on too much business they cannot afford to finance. However, if businesses do not take risks, they may find they cannot compete. Expansion moves them from a niche producer or an SME into the realms of a completely different type of business unit or organisation. It also provides them with many other revenue-earning opportunities. What most business organisations have to accept, however, is that there is an appropriate size of production for the type of business they are in.

Discussion point (page 615)

There should always be a close link between the production decisions and marketing decisions of organisations. A production manager would prefer to have a long run of similar products being produced at any one time. A marketing manager would prefer small runs of a variety of products but would also want sufficient quantities of stocks to be held so that customer needs could be met quickly at any one particular time.

Case study: Tactician maps and analyses (page 617)

1 This sort of software is particularly good in helping production planners to extrapolate information about their customers and for use in production planning. By being able to extract meaningful data, it is possible to improve production timing volumes, reduce stocks,

and gear the production capability of an organisation much more closely around customer needs.

2 The system would require access to customer databases, information from marketers, customer trend surveys and any other information that can be used as a basis for tactical decision-making.

Case study: Electronic Miniature Products Ltd (EMPL) (pages 620–621)

1 In answering this question, it is important that the students explore the alternative routes to find the lowest costs between each location:

	A	B	C	D
Oil transport costs	200	490	400	–
Raw material transport costs	290	150	–	800
Labour costs	1,300	1,400	1,300	1,500
Finished goods	400	200	–	1,000
Removal costs	1,000	1,000	1,000	–
Effects of government grants	(319)	(324)		
Total cost per 1,000 miles	2,871	2,916	2,700	3,300

2 The lowest cost location is C.

3 Current location D 492 × 3,300= 1,623,600
New location C 492 × 2,700 = 1,328,400
Estimated saving £295,200

4 A number of other factors might influence the decision, such as local factors, position of suppliers, availability of factory units and storage space, skills of local workers, etc.

5 These are only forecasts. A rail strike would soon change the equation, as would a change in the source of supply of raw materials. Each of the factors affecting the location decision could change in the short term.

Discussion point (page 623)

The quality versus price issue is always going to be around. Some would argue that, in recent years, the two consumer markets that have flourished have been that at the very bottom of the market with very cheap goods, and that at the top with branded premium goods. There is no doubt, however, that given all the deflationary effects in the UK economy in recent years, consumers have had it better than they have had for a long time, with much more quality being offered at low prices.

Check your understanding (page 623)

Students are expected to identify three high-quality premium products and three that are of poor quality. The tutor may, as this activity is debriefed, try to bring out the notion of perceptions as provided by branding. Students may feel something is high quality but it may not be any different from a significantly cheaper product but have a high price tag and all that goes with that because of the brand it carries.

Case study: Murphy Company (page 625)

1 QUALITY QUEST is a quality initiative aimed at total quality management and involving everybody in the Murphy organisation.

2 At the end of the day, whatever the business does, it must satisfy the customer. A business developing a total quality approach will be improving the way it both thinks and acts in the interests of its customers.

Check your understanding (page 626, a)

Being a member of a quality circle or improvement group is something almost everyone in the workplace is having to face at one time or another. The purpose of this activity is to be constructive not destructive. Participants should think about things that would help to improve the course and, in doing so, make them better prepared to move on to the next phase of their education.

Check your understanding (page 626, b)

The practical suggestions about quality standards are an important element in students' thinking about this task. For example, it may be possible to apply the process of standard setting to their own course procedures. There are many drawbacks for organisations facing ISO 9000, not least the bureaucracy and being limited in flexibility and response by paperwork and procedures.

Check your understanding (page 629)

Traffic planning has often involved a great deal more thought than might be imagined. It is easier to identify instances of flow and batch when one thinks about town centres and inner-city areas. There may also be some heavy traffic blackspots the students might think could be improved with better logistical planning.

Case study: falling productivity (pages 631–632)

1 A number of lessons could be drawn from the survey. Falling productivity is clearly a negative thing and leads to rising labour costs and high prices. In effect, it makes a company's products less competitive than they used to be.
2 There are many implications for resource requirements. In order to avoid falling productivity, organisations should invest more in capital, improve their research and development processes and constantly evaluate how well their resource base matches those of competitors and meets the needs of customers.
3 Many of the elements mentioned in the study suggest a spiral, such as an ageing plant, the age mix of the workforce, the growth of alternative sectors, etc.

Check your understanding (page 633)

As students undertake this exercise, it is important they take a theoretical approach to marketing which they then apply to a practical circumstance. It helps if they encourage the manager they interview to discuss marketing as a strategic and tactical discipline used by the company.

CHAPTER 24 FINANCIAL ANALYSIS AND PLANNING

Check your understanding (page 636)

The information in the example clearly indicates it is probably best not to increase sales at the lower price point as, although it will increase market share, it will not generate enough to replicate what was made at the previous margin. There is a great deal of information that might be useful before making this decision. For example, what are competitors doing, how have customer trends changed in the previous 12 months, what are customer perceptions of price, etc.? This is a linear model, and the assumption is that there is a direct relationship between price and turnover.

Case study: a changing industry (page 637)

1 This whole industry is associated with controversy and emotion. Many feel that, as pubs change character, we are somehow destroying our heritage. On the other hand, many people felt the traditional view of the pub had never moved on, with many pubs smoky, anti-family and uncomfortable places in which to eat. External influences will have included changing customer tastes, the poor location of many pub buildings and an uncertain competitive environment, with many pub chains often putting unfair pressures on pub managers to perform.
2 Some pubs do well, but why? In this author's area (a traditional rural area), many pubs have closed, and those that are doing well are doing so because they have specialised in good food or have opened up smoke-free dining rooms for families.
3 It looks as if many of the changes are now strategic, with pubs becoming part of a branded concept appealing in different ways to carefully targeted groups. All this activity will require a great deal of investment, and will inevitably lead to a different view of the pub as we know it.
4 Variables that might influence forecasting include number of customers, demographic make-up of customer groups, quality of dry and wet stock supplies, opening up of competition, etc.
5 It cannot be easy to plan as a pub operator, but the themed pubs have, in some instances, been particularly successful.

Check your understanding (page 638)

Most households draw upon a range of sources of finance for a variety of purposes from time to time. Interest-free credit, for example, may simply be for 12 months, but a mortgage will invariably last for 25 years. Students may identify a correlation between the size of the purchase and the time required. For example, the house and car cost more and so take longer to pay back. The microwave or purchases bought on the credit card are less expensive and, being more consumable, they are paid for relatively quickly.

Discussion point (page 641)

This is the classic question. For some reason, despite all the odds being stacked against them, small firms still continue to exist. There are a number of reasons for this. Some markets are better served by small firms, particularly where a personal service is required, such as in hairdressing, taxi businesses or solicitors. Other small firms exist because they haunt parts of a market that are not deemed to be profitable by larger organisations. Often these businesses are niche businesses that operate by searching for openings that are non-standard to large organisations.

Case study: the birth of The Body Shop (page 642)

1 The lesson Anita learnt was clear: you have to play their game. By 'power dressing' she was meeting the expectations the bank manager would have of someone wanting a loan.
2 Information included in the business plan would have included a description of the business and its personnel, the aims and objectives of the project, a description of the resources required for the business, a forecast set of accounts (including a profit and loss account and balance sheet), a cash flow forecast and, possibly, a break-even analysis.

Check your understanding (page 643)

Overdrafts are quick and easy to arrange and are suited flexibly to meet the needs of the user. However, they are an expensive form of finance and it is all too easy to depend too heavily upon them.

Case study: RealCall float (page 644)

1 There are a number of reasons it required investment capital. Clearly, the business is going through a process of expansion it needs to finance, which includes further development of the company's products.
2 Funding has come through moving from a private limited company to a public limited company and through a flotation on the Stock Exchange.
3 They could have raised money through a loan from a merchant bank, have raised short-term cash through factoring or sold and leased back some of their assets.

Check your understanding (page 646)

The most appropriate sources might include:

- school photocopier – hire purchase
- hospital wing – public-private partnership
- computer system – lease
- factory expansion – loan
- cash flow problem – overdraft.

Check your understanding (page 647)

Long-term assets might be school buildings, motor vehicles, desks and classroom equipment, reprographic equipment, office fixtures and fittings. Short-term items might include paper and stationery, exercise books, pens, pencils, etc.

Check your understanding (page 648)

	500	1,000	1,500	2,000	2,500	3,000
	£	£	£	£	£	£
Sales @ £9	4,500	9,000	13,500	18,000	22,500	27,000
Minus:						
Variable costs @ £5	2,500	5,000	7,500	10,000	12,500	15,000
Contribution	2,000	4,000	6,000	8,000	10,000	12,000
Minus:						
Fixed costs	4,000	4,000	4,000	4,000	4,000	4,000
Profit	(2,000)	0	2,000	4,000	6,000	8,000

Check your understanding (page 649)

The break-even point in units is as follows:

$$= \frac{£18{,}000}{£25 - £13} = \frac{£18{,}000}{£12} = 1{,}500 \text{ units}$$

Break-even sales value = £1500 × £25 = £37,500

The units and sales value necessary to achieve the selected operating point are as follows:

18,000 (fixed costs) + 18,000 (selected profit)/£12 contribution

The sale of 3,000 units will meet the profit target with a turnover of £75,000.

Check your understanding (page 650)

The tutor might ask the students if any of them has a business idea and, if they have, to try to estimate the costs and to work out its break-even position.

Task 1 (pages 651–652)

1 Break-even point in customers and value: fixed costs are £103,800 per annum. With an average spending value for each customer at £70 and variable costs per customer at £20, the contribution from each customer is £50. The break-even point in number of customers is therefore £103,800/50 and this comes to 2,075 customers. With each paying an average of £70, their value is £145,320.

2 To make a gross profit of £35,000, the number of customers will be:

$$\frac{£35{,}000 + £103{,}800}{50} = 2{,}776 \text{ customers}$$

3 Break-even chart:

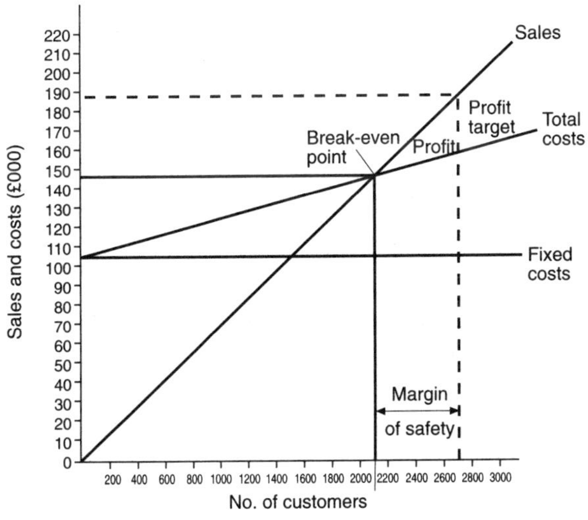

4 John might want a range of other information, such as the seasonality of visits, local competitors, prices charged by competitors, ways of reducing fixed and variable costs, etc.

Task 2 (pages 652–653)

1 Contribution for the European holidays:
£160 – £120 = £40 per holiday

Total contribution =

(160 × 200) – (120 × 200) = £8,000

Contribution for the American holidays:

£650 – £400 = £250 per holiday

Total contribution:

(650 × 200) – (£400 × 200) = £50,000

2 Profit = total contribution – total fixed costs:
£58,000 – £450,000 = £392,000 loss

3 European holidays revised contribution per unit calculation:

£144 – £120 = £24 per holiday

Total contribution

(144 × 350) – (120 × 350) = £8,400

American holidays revised contribution per unit calculation:

£585 – £400 = £185 per holiday

Total contribution

(585 × 350) – (400 × 350) = £64,750

Revised profit calculation:

£73,150 – £450,000 = £376,850 loss

4 Revision of first calculation:

£58,000 – £405,000 = £347,000 loss

Revision of second calculation:

£73,150 – £405,000 = £331,850 loss

Task 3 (pages 653–654)

1 £24,000 – £17,000 = £7,000 contribution

£755,980/7,000 = 108 contracts

With an average contract size of £24,000, the break-even point in turnover is £2,592,000.

2 Break-even chart:

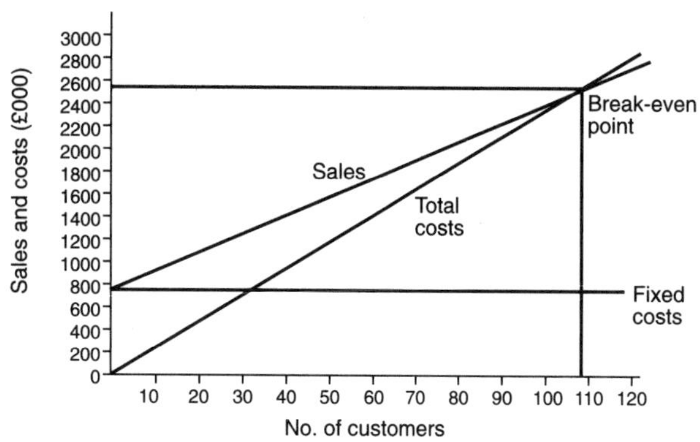

3 Total costs calculation:

£755,980 + (£130 × £17,000) = £2,210,000

Profit calculation:

(£130 × £24,000) – £755,980 + (£130 × £17,000) = £154,020

or total contribution – fixed costs = profit

(£7,000 × £130) – £755,980 = £154,020

4 Number of units = total contribution/contribution:

£1,055,980/£7,000 = £150.85 rounded up to 151

5 Total costs calculation:

£805,980 + (£165 × £17,000) = £3,610,980

Profit calculation:

(£165 × £24,000) – (£805,980 + £165 × £17,000) = £3,960,000 – £3,610,980 = £349,020

6 Profit calculation:

(£175 × £24,000) – (£755,980 + £175 × £17,000) = £4,200,000 – £3,730,980 = £469,020

Task 4 (pages 654–655)

1 The fixed costs account for 96% of the costs of a flight. Variable costs account for merely 4% of the total. Virgin should therefore concentrate on sales maximisation in order to pass a high break-even point (which is forced by high fixed costs).

2 Contribution calculation:

(£350 – £4 = £346)

Break-even calculation:

$$\frac{£96{,}000}{£346} = £277$$

3 Calculations for standard service:

80% occupancy = 300

Profit at occupancy 300

£346 × £300 – £96,000 = £7,800

4 Increasing occupancy rates is a way airlines fill surplus capacity. Because of the high fixed cost element of the cost structure, an airline needs to operate as closely to capacity as possible.

5 Richard Branson has shown considerable flair and good economic timing with the introduction of Mid Class on his 747s. This new sector is either a jumped-up economy or scaled-down business class, depending on whether you are upgrading or trading down. Costing £688 return, London–New York, it offers excellent value for the business traveller. The service offers better seats and more leg-room. The food is the same as that served in economy but, since Virgin have always scored highly for their meals, this is hardly an inconvenience. Importantly, Virgin have no rivals yet for their new service. The business-class fare for the similar trip works out at £2,122 return and looks exorbitant. The new service was introduced out of the need for Virgin to fill their plane seats. Operating at near capacity is the only way a smaller airline can compete with British Airways. Branson knows that Virgin cannot compete on price alone: bigger airlines benefit from economies of scale, so Virgin attempt to provide a differentiated service.

Check your understanding (page 656)

It is possible for a firm to be highly profitable but run out of cash. It is also possible for a business to make losses but be liquid. Cash is the tangible ability to meet liquid debts as and when they arise in the organisation. Profits, in contrast, reflect the outcomes from the trading position of the business organisation over a period of time.

CHAPTER 25 EVALUATING YOUR BUSINESS PLAN

Case study: investing in the new economy (pages 659–660)

1 There are many '.coms' in the news at the moment. They represent the many changes

that have taken place in the structure of the UK economy in recent years. The tutor should ask the students to talk about the example they have chosen.

2 It would be interesting to see if a pattern arises of similar types of products and services being developed through the .coms the students identify. The tutor may wish to put them into categories, such as books and stationery, fashion products, etc.
3 Again, this may depend upon the age and profile of the company. During 2000–2001, confidence in the .coms plummeted, and this spelt out many warnings for investors in companies wishing to use the Internet to develop their business opportunities.
4 Given all that has been happening, the tutor should encourage the students to think about the long-term prospects of the chosen company.
5 Before investing it would be useful to know about changes in the marketplace, the use of the Internet made by customers looking for alternative ways of shopping, the cost base of .com companies and their history in attracting business away from traditional distribution routes.

Check your understanding (page 664)

Gross and net profit margins are clearly an important way of evaluating the effectiveness of one business in comparison to another. Although it is sometimes difficult to find out comparable margins from other business, the tutor should encourage the students to surf the Net to find out details from other companies.

Case study: the growth in Tesco's operating profits (pages 664–665)

1 Profit margins have dropped from 6.5% in 1992 to 4.69% in 1997–1998, despite an increasing market share.
2 Both earnings per share and dividends per share have increased over the period, which means Tesco now represent a better investment.

Case study: estimating market share (page 666)

The purpose of this case study is to help the user to identify the market share and value of sales he or she might obtain if he or she entered that market. It may be helpful if, having gone through the various questions in this study focusing upon one market, the students report their findings back to the class.

SECTION C OHTs

NOTES

OHT 6.22.1: consumer and organisational markets

A key element in analysing markets is distinguishing between the operation of consumer and organisational markets, and organisational markets are far too often taken for granted. Referring to page 583 of the student book, this OHT reinforces the fact that, within consumer markets, advertising creates demand amongst consumers that pulls products into the market. On the other hand, organisational markets depend heavily on the work of an efficient salesforce to push products into a market.

OHT 6.22.2: PEST framework

A key element in business planning is being able to undertake a PEST analysis to provide an accurate view of an organisation's external environment. This OHT itemises many of the PEST factors and may be used as a checklist while students undertake their own PEST analysis for their own business planning processes.

OHT 6.22.3: presenting information

Having obtained statistical data, students need to become adept at being able to present it in a way that can be understood by others. This OHT illustrates a simple activity on page 589 of the student book. Given the nature of the activity and the opportunity to use a spreadsheet and graphics, this may be used as an opportunity for the students to use their IT skills to present the data in an interesting way.

OHT 6.22.4: Maslow's hierarchy of needs

Maslow's is a defining work that has implications for so many different areas involving people. It is a perceptive interpretation of people's motives, which builds into a series of levels. Referring to pages 594–595 of the student book, the OHT illustrates the different levels. In order to encourage the students to interact, the tutor should get them to talk about the products or services that could be related to each level in the hierarchy.

OHT 6.23.1: the creation of added value

Businesses that add more value are more likely to be successful. The left-hand side of this OHT shows the value of sales to customers. From this is deducted the value of goods and services bought from other firms. This then provides a figure for the gross value added by the business organisation. From this is deducted money that needs to be set aside for paying back debts from the past, finally arriving at the figure for net value created by the business in a particular time period. The added value will then be distributed to the government in taxes, in dividends to shareholders and in interest to investors.

OHT 6.23.2: returns to scale

Organisations have to make appropriate decisions about the appropriate scale of production. If output increases faster than the rate of inputs, average unit costs will be falling and a company is said to be benefiting from increasing returns to scale. Beyond the point at which average unit costs are at their lowest, the increase in output will be less than the increase in input so that average unit costs are pushed up and the company is suffering from decreasing returns to scale. This OHT refers to key decisions about the amount to produce illustrated on pages 611–613 of the student book.

OHT 6.23.3: British Book Printers plc

The purpose of this case study was to encourage students to justify their interpretation using and quoting from this data. The figures clearly indicate increasing returns to scale and provide a useful opportunity for students to justify that economies are taking place.

OHT 6.23.4: managing stock levels

This OHT illustrates a perfect situation for managing stock levels. Stocks never fall below the set minimum level or go above the set maximum stock level. Stocks are replenished just at the point at which the minimum stock level is about to be breached.

OHT 6.24.1: methods of finance used by different types of organisations

Different types of organisations tend to depend upon different methods of finance. This OHT refers to page 639 of the student book and illustrates the dependency of different organisational types upon various forms of finance.

OHT 6.24.2: bank accounts: a) personal; and b) business

The bank accounts of personal customers differ from those of business customers. Whereas the account of a personal customer will show a regular input of income per month and a regular pattern of expenditure, this does not happen to a business customer, who is dependent upon debtors to pay their bills. As a result, it is easy to understand why business customers often slip into an overdraft situation and need an overdraft as a flexible form of short-term finance.

OHT 6.24.3: profit table

This table illustrates how an organisation's profitability can be identified at different units of production. It helps to show the relationship between profit and volume and provides a useful basis for the students to understand the operation of break-even analysis. It also provides a useful introduction for students, who can then go on to undertake the 'Check your understanding' activity on page 648.

OHT 6.24.4: break-even chart

Taken from Figure 24.7 on page 649 of the student book, this OHT provides a good example of a break-even chart, illustrating the break-even point, margin of safety and selected operating profit. Students can use this chart as a basis for drawing their own.

OHT 6.25.1: evaluating the business plan

This OHT illustrates two key elements in evaluating the business plan. On the one hand, the plan must meet the needs of the owners of the business, who will evaluate it as they attempt to implement each part of the plan. On the other, the plan must meet the needs of external scrutineers, such as people who have lent money and want to know that repayments can be made.

OHT 6.25.2: the chip-vending machine

This OHT shows the chip-vending machine developed by William Bartfield from Leeds. The tutor may wish to use this as a creative opportunity for the students to think of their own ideas for a product of their own choice. The tutor could ask them to draw an illustration such as that of Bartfield to show how it would work.

OHT 6.25.3: setting profitability targets

This OHT shows how profitability targets can be set. Using the data from page 663 of the student book, students can appreciate that, as sales increase, there are also targets for gross and net profit.

OHT 6.25.4: Tesco's operating profits and share earnings

Based on the case studies on pages 664–665 of the student book, this OHT enables the tutor to introduce the case studies to the class and to refer to key elements of the data.

OHT 6.22.1 CONSUMER AND ORGANISATIONAL MARKETS

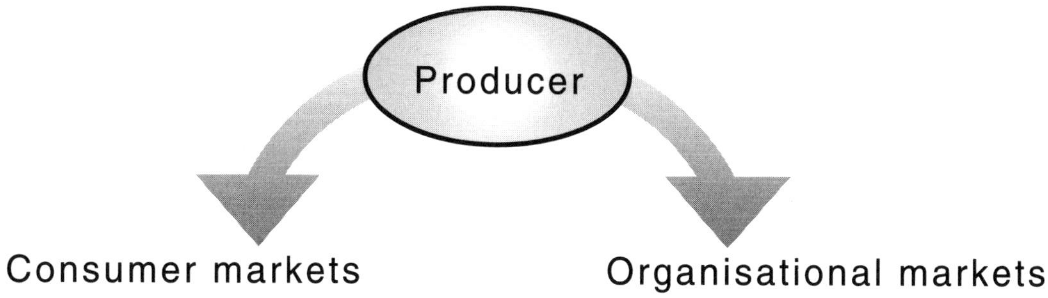

Advertising draws goods into consumer markets by creating expectations among consumers

Organisational markets depend upon direct selling

OHT 6.22.2 PEST FRAMEWORK

- *P Political/legal/fiscal*
  - privatisation
  - taxation
  - duties/levies
  - change of government
- *E Economic*
  - inflation
  - budget
  - energy prices
  - unemployment
- *S Social/cultural*
  - demographic changes
  - lifestyle changes
  - changes to education
  - environmental changes
- *T Technical*
  - new technologies
  - changing material technologies
  - new products
  - energy-saving substitutes.

Check your understanding

A company's sales are made up from the statistics shown in Figure 22.7.

	Sales (million)
Home	15
USA	4
Australia	3
EU	8
Middle East	10
Total	40

Figure 22.7 Company sales (£ million)

Draw an accurate pie chart to present these sales figures. Label the chart.

OHT 6.22.4 MASLOW'S HIERARCHY OF NEEDS

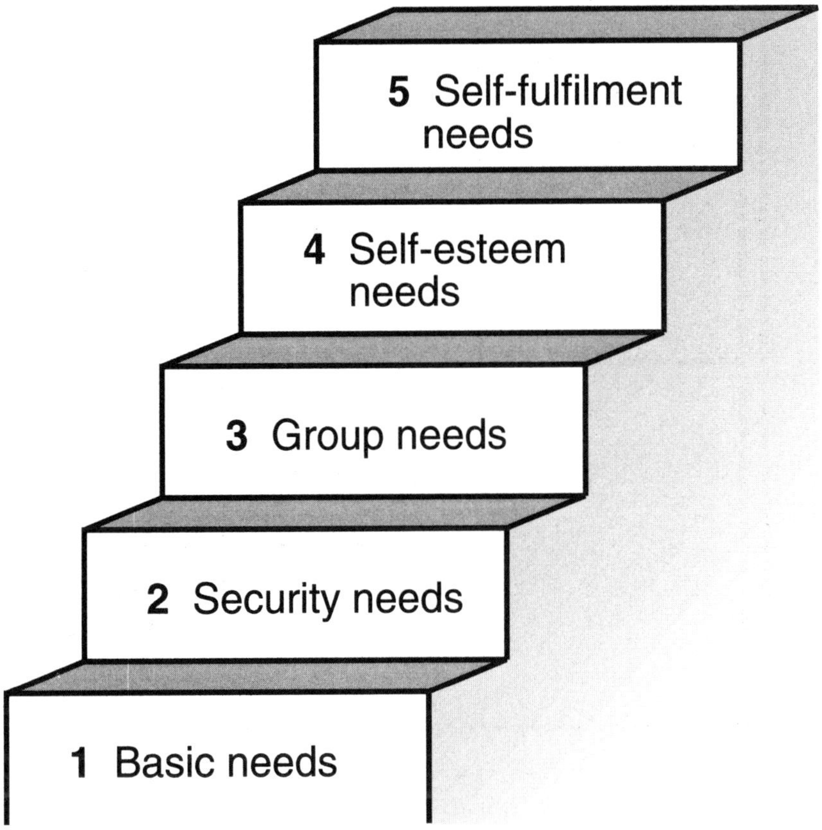

Think about the products or services that could be related to each level

OHT 6.23.1 THE CREATION OF ADDED VALUE

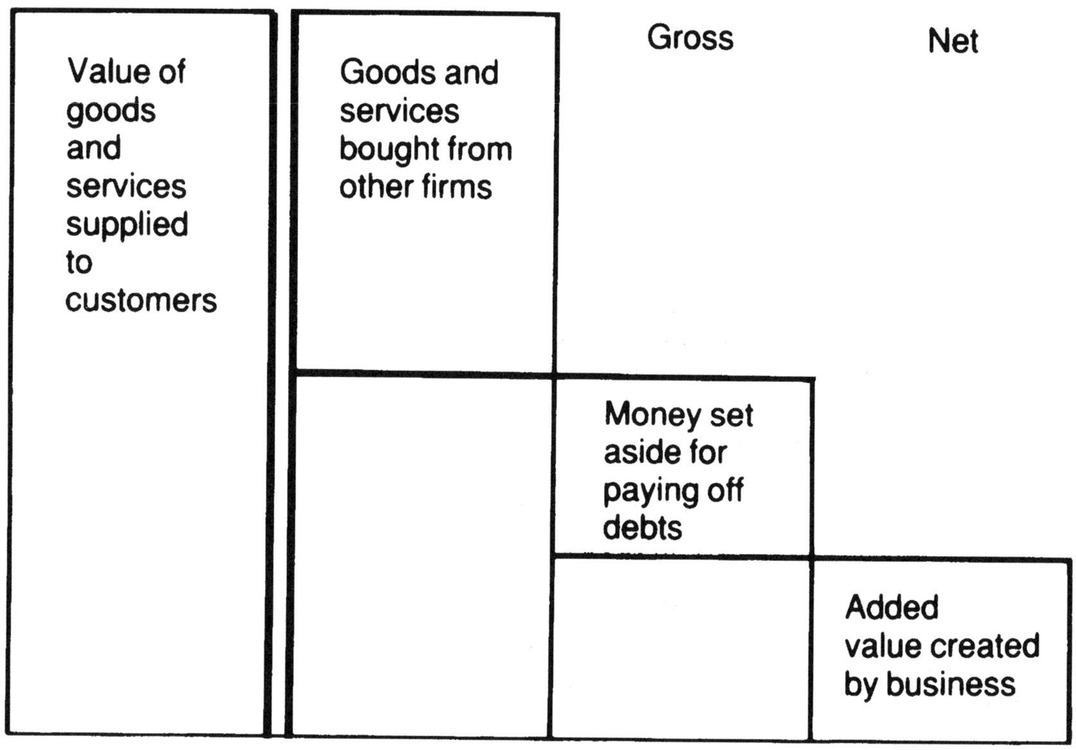

OHT 6.23.2 RETURNS TO SCALE

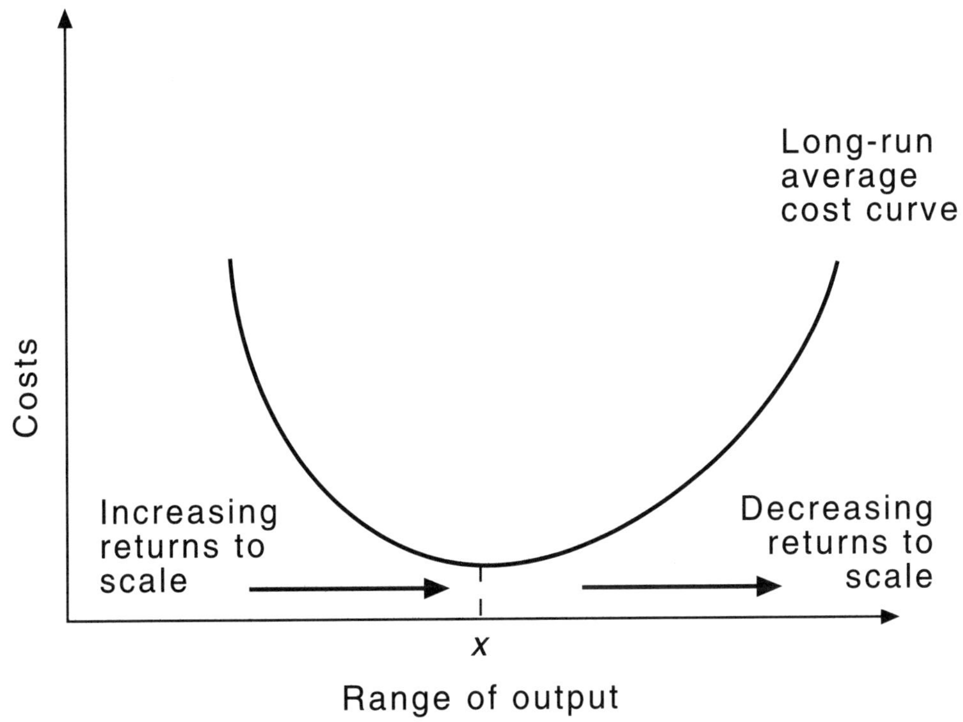

OHT 6.23.3 BRITISH BOOK PRINTERS plc

Case study: British Book Printers plc

In recent years, British Book Printers plc has grown through a rapid expansion programme to become one of the biggest book printers in London and southeast England. The statistics shown in Figure 23.4 have been extracted from the most recent financial statements.

	1998	1999	2000	2001
Yearly output ('000)	300.00	450.00	525.00	615.00
Number of machines	8.00	10.00	12.00	13.00
Number of employees	175.00	182.00	190.00	194.00
Number of products	14.00	27.00	38.00	51.00
Cost of manufacture per publication (£)	3.20	3.10	2.90	2.00

Figure 23.4 British Book Printers plc: growth in recent years

1 To what extent do these figures illustrate economies of scale?

2 What sort of economies are likely to have taken place within this company?

OHT 6.23.4 MANAGING STOCK LEVELS

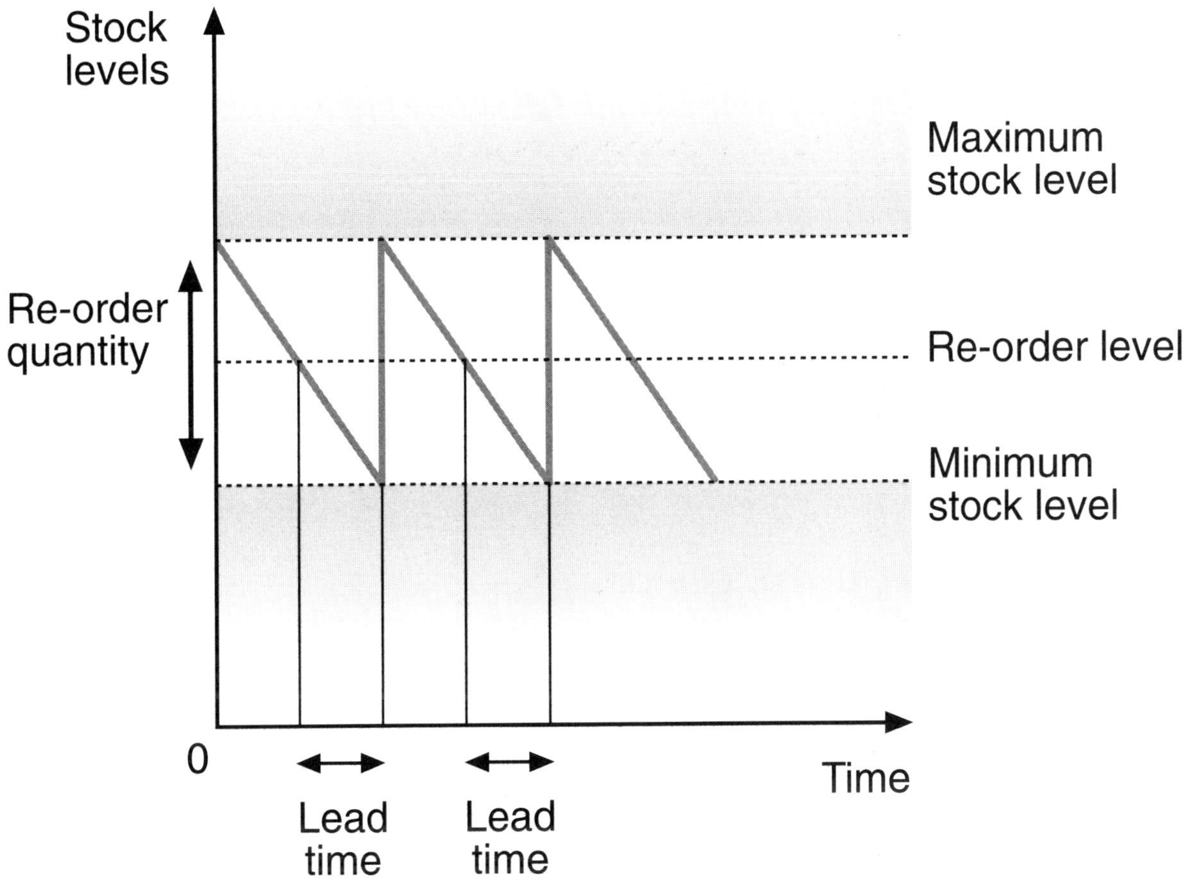

OHT 6.24.1 METHODS OF FINANCE USED BY DIFFERENT TYPES OF ORGANISATIONS

	Sole traders	Partnerships	Private limited companies	Public limited companies	Non-profit organisations
Personal funds	✓	✓	✓	✓	✓
Shares			✓	✓	
Mortgage	✓	✓	✓	✓	
Grants	✓	✓	✓	✓	✓
Gifts					✓
Loans	✓	✓	✓	✓	✓
Profit retention	✓	✓	✓	✓	✓
Trade credit	✓	✓	✓	✓	✓
Overdraft	✓	✓	✓	✓	✓
Leasing and hire purchase	✓	✓	✓	✓	✓
Trade credit	✓	✓	✓	✓	✓
Factoring	✓	✓	✓	✓	✓

OHT 6.24.2 BANK ACCOUNTS: A) PERSONAL; AND B) BUSINESS

a)

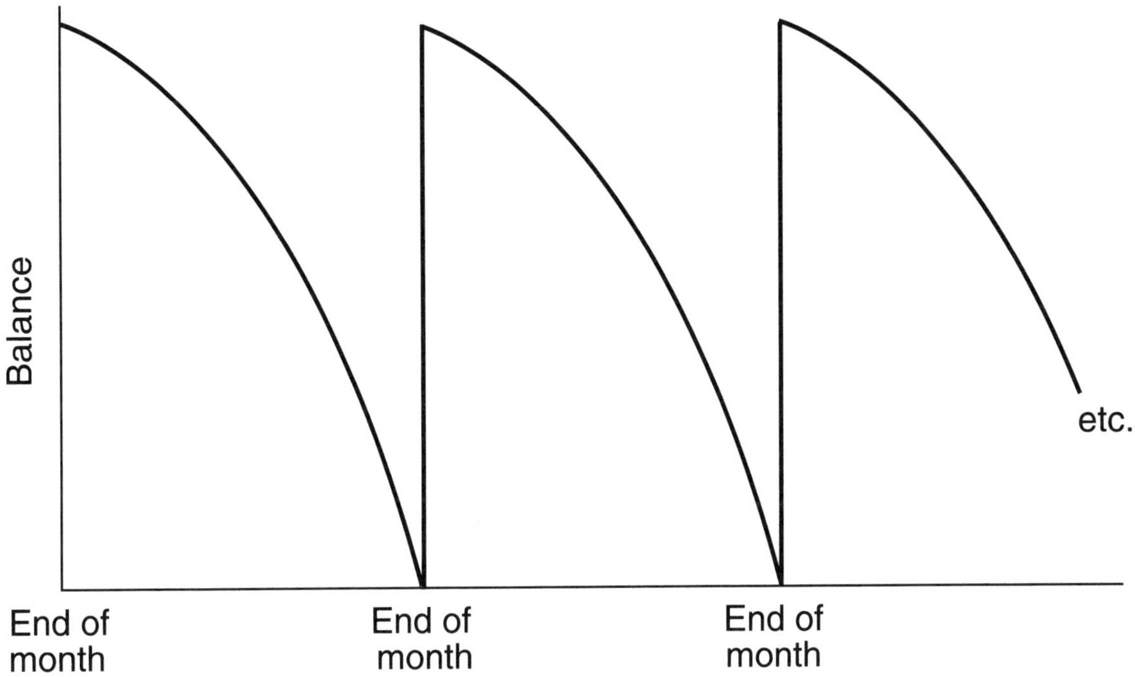

b)

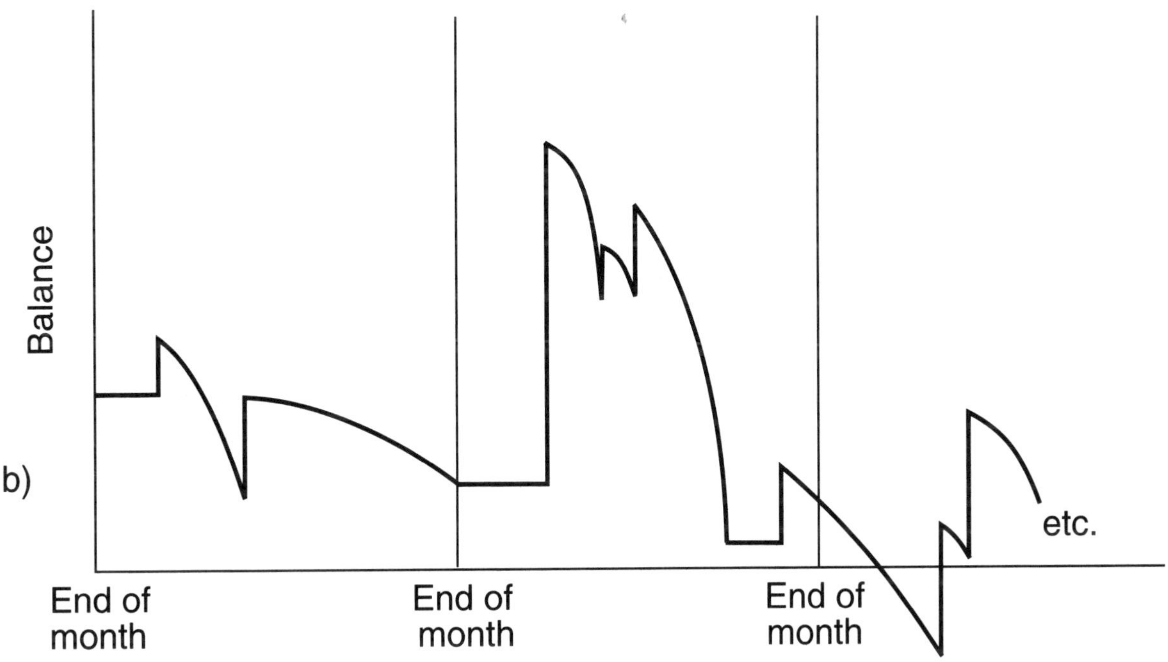

OHT 6.24.3 PROFIT TABLE

Units of production	Fixed costs (£)	Variable costs (£)	Total costs (£)	Revenue (£)	Profit (loss) (£)
1,000	9,000	15,000	14,000	12,000	(2,000)
2,000	9,000	10,000	19,000	24,000	5,000
3,000	9,000	15,000	24,000	36,000	12,000
4,000	9,000	20,000	29,000	48,000	19,000
5,000	9,000	25,000	34,000	60,000	26,000
6,000	9,000	30,000	39,000	72,000	33,000
7,000	9,000	35,000	44,000	84,000	40,000
8,000	9,000	40,000	49,000	96,000	47,000
9,000	9,000	45,000	54,000	108,000	54,000
10,000	9,000	50,000	59,000	120,000	61,000

OHT 6.24.4 BREAK-EVEN CHART

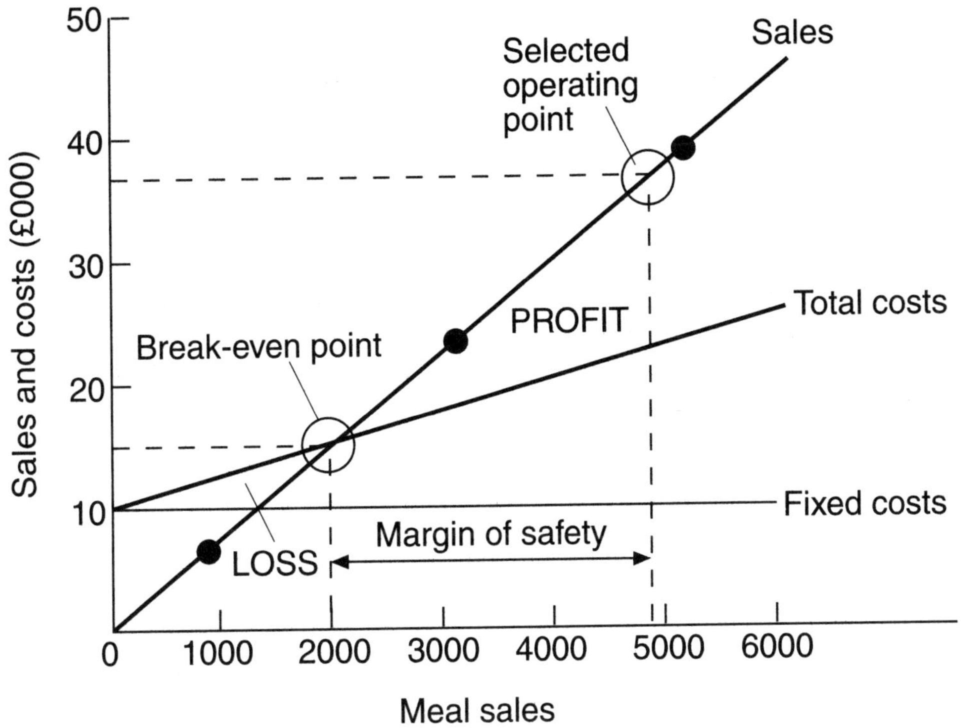

OHT 6.25.1 EVALUATING THE BUSINESS PLAN

THE BUSINESS PLAN

Internal scrutineers
The owners of the business (e.g. the sole owner, partners, shareholders)

External scrutineers
People who have lent money to the company (e.g. banks, debenture holders, etc.)

OHT 6.25.2 THE CHIP-VENDING MACHINE

Draw a diagram to illustrate one of your own ideas

OHT 6.25.3 SETTING PROFITABILITY TARGETS

	January	*February*	*March*
Income			
Sales	3,000	4,000	5,000
Purchases	2,000	2,000	2,000
Gross profit	1,000	2,000	3,000
Gross profit (%)	33	50	60
Expenditures	1,000	1,000	1,000
Net profit	0	1,000	2,000
Net profit (%)	0	25	40

OHT 6.25.4 TESCO'S OPERATING PROFITS AND SHARE EARNINGS

Case study: The growth in Tesco's operating profits

Since the early 1990s Tesco have undergone considerable growth, particularly in market share, which has risen from 10.4% in 1992–93 to 15.2% in 1997–98. The changes in key profit figures are shown in Figure 25.3.

Evaluate the success of Tesco in terms of profit margins.

Year	Turnover (£m)	Operating profit (£m)	Market share %
1992–93	7,581	496	10.4
1993–94	8,600	521	10.7
1994–95	10,101	617	12.0
1995–96	12,094	724	13.7
1996–97	13,887	774	14.5
1997–98	17,400	817	15.2

Figure 25.3 Tesco: changes in profit figures, 1992–98

Case study: Tesco share earnings in the late 1990s

Figure 25.4 shows earnings per share and dividends per share at Tesco. Earnings per share is the profits divided by the number of shares. Dividends per share is the profit distributed to shareholders divided by the number of shares.

Why might an investor be pleased to have put money into Tesco?

Year	Earnings per share (pence)	Dividends per share (pence)
1992–93	18.3	7.10
1993–94	18.8	7.75
1994–95	20.1	8.60
1995–96	21.9	9.60
1996–97	23.5	10.35
1997–98	26.6	11.60

Figure 25.4 Tesco: earnings per share and dividends per share, 1992–98

SECTION D ASSESSMENT

PRODUCING A BUSINESS PLAN FOR A NEW PRODUCT OR SERVICE

Many people from time to time have an idea for a business or a product they think they could develop and make successful. Few, however, develop their idea and turn it into a practical business proposition. This piece of coursework enables you to develop the tools and skills necessary to do so. The difference is that, instead of having the idea first, we are asking you to develop your ideas as part of your coursework practice. In fact, if your ideas are really good, and you are happy with your business plan, you might even want to use it after you have left school or college.

You need to produce a business plan for a new product or service of your choice. To do this, you may wish to work in a group and allocate roles. The business plan should include everything you need. This means it should:

- contain a market analysis for the product or service you choose
- include a marketing plan
- have a production plan, supported with a quality-assurance plan
- contain a financial plan, including a spreadsheet or similar document produced using it
- contain some form of evaluation that enables you to comment upon the effectiveness of all the procedures and activities you have gone through in producing your business plan.

Planning is an important element in business. The entrepreneurs of all businesses have to plan ahead, often in an uncertain business environment. Although planning will not eliminate risk, it will help to reduce it. Producing a business plan is a key skill in business, and one many find difficult to acquire. If a business requires finance, particularly from a bank or other large creditor, it is essential that a well-researched business plan is developed beforehand.

You may wish to construct your plan based upon a business you have first-hand experience of, or the plan could simply be based upon an idea you have about which you wish to find out more.

AS YOU WORK THROUGH THIS PIECE OF COURSEWORK

- Relate your work to everything you have covered in your AVCE course in Business.
- Conduct an external audit for your plan, using a PEST framework.
- Think about the aims and objectives you will have for your business idea. Try to make this practical and realisable.
- Conduct both secondary and primary market research. Try to make sense of the data, and use a range of tools to make predictions of demand for your product or service.
- Use IT packages to analyse and display the findings you have obtained from the data.
- Look at all the competitors, both direct and indirect, to the service or product you intend to provide. Try to think how your approach is likely to be better than that of the competitors.
- Look not just at the product but at all the other service elements you intend to provide for your customers.
- Think carefully about how you price the product or service.
- Consider the sort of business you want to set up. For example, would you want it to be a sole trader, partnership or limited company?
- Think about key issues for your business, such as size and location. Is it possible to obtain details about suitable business premises?
- Try to consider the quality levels you intend to provide and how these relate to those provided for competitor products or services. What might these quality standards involve?
- Consider all the resources you need in order to make your business work. How

would you obtain the finance for all these resources?

- Produce your financial analysis and financial plan. You should identify sources of finance for your business, produce a cash flow forecast, forecast trading and profit and loss accounts, as well as a forecast balance sheet. You will also be helped by developing some form of break-even analysis. (Make sure the figures for the break-even analysis roughly match your other forecasts.)
- Think about how you would evaluate your business if it were to operate for 12 months. How would the actions of your business idea have to relate to the objectives of the business for you to feel it has been successful?

HOW YOU CAN USE KEY SKILLS WHILE WORKING ON THIS ASSIGNMENT

Application of number skills

- As part of your marketing, production and finance plan, you can draw upon and interpret complex numerical data.
- As you work through the planning process, you should have to interpret a range of financial calculations, present your findings and justify your interpretation.

Communication skills

- You should make decisions as you plan your business idea.
- You should use knowledge from other areas of the course and apply it to marketing, production, quality assurance and financial plans.
- You should be able to contribute your ideas to a group discussion.

Information technology skills

- A great deal of the data you identify for your business plan will come from a range of IT sources.
- You should plan and use different sources to search for and select information for your business idea.
- Information extracted from different contexts has to be analysed in relation to the business plan.
- You should use data to create text, a spreadsheet and other ways of demonstrating data.
- IT can be used for calculations and images.

Problem-solving skills

- As you work through your plan, you should consider alternative strategies.
- Alternative solutions should be developed for problems presented by the business idea.
- You could make comparisons between two different solutions.

Working with others

- A great deal of the time working through the plan will involve you liasing with others.
- You need to set targets to produce the plan.
- Responsibilities need to be allocated and managed.
- As you work through the plan, the group should monitor its progress.
- You should review and evaluate your work with others.

Induction: Starting Work with People with Learning Disabilities

Supporting the Certificates in Working with People who have Learning Disabilities

ALICE BRADLEY

British Library Cataloguing in Publications Data

A CIP record for this book is available from the Public Library

ISBN 1 902519 80 9

BILD Publications is the imprint of:
British Institute of Learning Disabilities
Campion House
Green Street
Kidderminster
Worcestershire
DY10 1JL

Telephone: 01562 723010
Fax: 01562 723029
E-mail: enquiries@bild.org.uk
Website: www.bild.org.uk

Please contact BILD for a free publications catalogue listing BILD books, training materials and journals.

BILD Publications are distributed worldwide by:

BookSource
50 Cambuslang Road
Cambuslang
Glasgow G32 8NB

Telephone: 0845 370 0068
Fax: 0845 370 0068

INDUCTION:
Starting Work with People with Learning Disabilities

Contents

Introduction

Introduction

Welcome to ***Induction – Starting Work with People with Learning Disabilities,*** a study workbook for people starting a new job with people with learning disabilities, and for staff who have been in service for some time, but haven't had their experience recognised.

If you are in a new job in care, you may be feeling apprehensive – after all, there is a lot to learn and understand. During your first few weeks and months, your employer will provide a detailed induction programme covering:

- working safely
- your organisation and its policies
- your role as a worker
- the needs of people with learning disabilities.

This workbook aims to provide you with the information you need for induction. As you work through the book, you'll find out about the lives of the people with learning disabilities and the service you work for, as well as reading about aspects of care.

You can use this workbook:

- for your own personal study, or
- as part of an accredited learning programme, with a certificate to show what you have successfully learned (see page 10).

Who will find this workbook useful?

This workbook is aimed at:

- new workers
- workers who have been in service for some time, but haven't had their experience recognised
- managers who supervise new staff
- training managers in services for people with learning disabilities.

New Workers in a Learning Disability Service

This workbook is particularly designed for you if you are undertaking induction training. It will help you to understand:

- the needs and expectations of service users – a term used to describe the people with learning disabilities who use your services
- your responsibilities when working in a social care setting.

This workbook does not cover induction training on safe working practice – your employer will normally provide this training, which covers:

- moving and handling
- fire safety
- first aid
- infection control
- safe food handling.

The health and safety training, together with the training in this workbook, will complete your induction.

The next three parts, 'Managers who supervise new staff', 'Training managers' and 'Relationship to Care Qualifications' are for managers and training managers. You can either read through them for interest or skip to the section headed Confidentiality and Consent on page 8.

Managers who supervise new staff

Many services organise the induction of new staff using a variety of learning situations and experiences including training sessions, peer support, supervision and the use of open learning materials.

This workbook provides information and activities that you may find helpful in supporting new staff in your service. It will be a useful resource to use in supervision sessions and for staff mentoring new employees as it covers the induction standards relating to understanding:

- the principles of care
- the worker role
- the experiences and particular needs of the service user group
- the effects of the service setting on service provision.

New workers will also need to cover all aspects of maintaining safety at work to complete their induction.

Training managers

This workbook covers the induction requirements for new support staff in learning disability services relating to:

- the TOPSS induction standards (excluding those relating to Maintain Safety at Work)
- The Induction – Learning Disability unit of the *Certificate in Working with People who have Learning Disabilities* at Level 2.

If staff wish to use the learning they have completed in this workbook for accreditation towards the Certificate, they need to be registered with one of the awarding bodies and studying on a recognised programme of study. They will also need to complete a portfolio of work for assessment. Further information on this can be obtained from BILD or the awarding bodies (see the resources section at the back of this workbook).

This workbook will be a useful resource for planning and delivering induction programmes. It can also be given to individual members of staff to supplement training sessions, to consolidate learning and assist learners in providing a portfolio of evidence, particularly for those seeking accreditation for their learning.

Relationship to Care Qualifications

NVQ and SVQ Qualifications in Care

The induction standards are closely linked to the NVQ/SVQ Level 2 care units and have a similar portfolio of evidence format. Many staff progress onto either levels 2 or 3 care qualifications on completion of an induction and foundation in care programme.

The Certificates in Working with People who have Learning Disabilities

The Certificate in Working with People who have Learning Disabilities at level 2 contains two units which cover all or part of the following TOPSS standards for Induction – Learning Disability:

- understand the principles of care
- understand the organisation and the worker's role
- understand the experiences and the particular needs of the service user group.

Learners on an induction programme recognised by one of the awarding bodies will be able to submit a portfolio of work for assessment. If it reaches the required standard they will receive a certificate identifying the units achieved. For further details about the BILD accredited programme contact the BILD learning administrator on 01562 723025.

Learners considering progressing towards the certificates will need to complete the Foundation in Care units after induction, and then go on to complete further mandatory and optional units which reflect the service user group and organisational setting they work in.

Confidentiality and Consent

This workbook encourages you to relate what you're learning to your work situation. As part of this you will need to reflect on the way you work with people with learning disabilities.

Before involving a service user in any activities from this book you'll need to obtain their consent. Discuss this with your line manager before going ahead. A few activities are based on discussions or observations of colleagues or service users, and when you write these up you need to be aware of the need for confidentiality. Rather than using someone's real name, use an alias (a false name) or an initial to identify the person. Discuss your organisation's confidentiality policy with your line manager before completing any of the activities.

Labels and terms

People have debated long and hard about how we should describe people with learning disabilities. Ideally we should call people by their names, since everyone is different, with their own personality, characteristics, strengths and failings.

However there are times when labels, no matter how much we dislike them, are used for all of us: students, parents, teenagers, claimants, senior citizens, patients.

What labels have people used about you in the past? Which ones were you proud or pleased to have? Which ones did you dislike?

Throughout this workbook I use the term *learning disability*, which is the most commonly used term in health and social care settings. The terms 'mental handicap' and the American term 'mental retardation' are inappropriate, and people with learning disabilities don't consider them acceptable. People First, an organisation run by people with learning disabilities, uses the term *people with learning difficulties*. This is also the term often used in schools and colleges.

As you work through this workbook you'll find the term service user is used to refer to people with learning disabilities – after all, they are the users of the service you work for.

It's likely that you are a paid member of staff, so I've generally used the terms *workers* or *practitioners*. However, much of what I say also applies if you are a volunteer or informal carer.

I have tried to avoid sexism by using *he* or *she*, unless it sounds clumsy or when I am referring to a particular man or woman.

I use the word *service* to refer to the workplace situation, whether it is residential, day care, based in the community or elsewhere. I also use the word *organisation* to refer to the agency that runs your service. Any other terms that may not be clear are explained as they arise.

How to use these materials

We all vary in how we study and learn. Some people prefer to study in short bursts, spreading their learning over a long period. Others prefer more sustained periods of concentration. Some of us like to study early in the day, others don't start until late in the evening. No one way of studying is better than another. What matters is that you find the way which suits you.

These materials are interactive – as well as reading, you'll be:

- thinking about things
- giving your own ideas and opinions
- talking to colleagues
- trying out some activities.

You'll learn plenty of good ideas and theory in this workbook, but unless you can apply them to your work, they are not very useful. So I regularly encourage you to apply these good ideas and theories to your work, and include **Key Points** at the end of each section. These bring together the key ideas in the book.

Whichever way you prefer to study, there are some things you can do to make your study more effective and enjoyable. Try these:

- Keep a pen or pencil with you while reading this workbook. Write comments in the margins or underline bits you find interesting or thought provoking

- Find a place for study where you will be undisturbed, and where you can safely leave your work
- Plan a timetable with set periods of time to study
- Break the unit down into manageable chunks that you know you can complete it in a set time
- Keep your written work and any information you collect in a loose-leaf ring binder
- Discuss your study regularly with your line manager and colleagues. This will help you to think about how you can use the ideas from this workbook in your day to day support of people with learning disabilities.

Accreditation for your study

You probably want to receive accreditation for your study from this workbook. If so, you will need to study on an induction programme provided by an organisation recognised by one of the awarding bodies for the Certificates in Working with People who have Learning Disabilities.

BILD is one of the organisations recognised by the two awarding bodies, City and Guilds and National Open College Network. For more information about the BILD Certificate Programme, which provides in house training, external training accreditation and distance learning, please contact the learning administrator on 01562 723025.

How this workbook is organised

There are five sections in this workbook:

1 You and your job

This will give you the opportunity to think about the job you do, your role in relation to others in the workplace and the aims and objectives of the service you work in. It also explores the main principles of care. By the end of section one, you should understand more about your own role as a practitioner.

2 Confidentiality

This looks at why confidentiality is important in the workplace and asks you to think about how this relates to your situation. The aim is to help you understand and apply the principles of confidentiality.

3 About Learning Disability

What do we mean by the term 'learning disability'? What are the causes? This section will help you understand more about the nature of learning disability.

4 Lessons from History

This section deals with the effect of beliefs and attitudes on people with learning disability, on society and on services as times have changed.

5 Challenging Behaviour

This section explores the meaning of the term 'challenging behaviour' and looks at why such behaviours happen. The aim of this section is to enable you to understand the origins of challenging behaviour.

I suggest you do the workbook activities as you work through the materials. You'll also find workplace activities at the end of each section. Doing these activities will help you to absorb the information and improve your work as a practitioner.

Good luck and enjoy the workbook!

SECTION 1:
You and Your Job

You and Your Job

Introduction

This first section covers:

- your job title and job description
- your role and responsibilities at work and those of your colleagues
- the aims and objectives of your service
- the main principles of 'care'.

Working through the section should give you a clearer understanding of your own job and your responsibilities. You should also get a better idea of how your contribution in the workplace helps your service work towards its ideals.

Your Job Title and Job Description

Your job title

Some job titles describe the job very well. For example, bus driver, secretary, electrician, teacher. With others, it is almost impossible to know what the person actually does, eg, systems analyst, operational researcher.

Job titles in learning disability can fall into either group, although they usually give you some idea of what the job involves. For example, what can you tell about the job from the following titles?

"I'm a group worker."	**"I'm a care assistant."**
"I'm a home support worker."	**"I'm employed as a job coach."**

These titles tell you something about the job, but not much. Two people with different titles may in fact do very similar work and two people with the same job title may have very different work responsibilities.

What is your job title and how well does it describe what you do?

....

....

....

Your job description

Your *job description* gives much more detail. Like job titles, job descriptions vary greatly from place to place. Some are very specific, others are much more general.

Get a copy of your job description and read it through to remind yourself of what it says. Now do the next activity.

Activity 1

Find your job description and any other information you have about your job. (If you do not have your job description, ask your direct line manager for a copy.) Read through the information carefully – there will be words and phrases that relate to different aspects of your work. These will refer to:

- ☆ *the kinds of activities you will be doing with service users, and possibly families*
- ☆ *your responsibilities*
- ☆ *who you will be accountable to.*

Re-read your job description and decide which words and phrases relate to the different aspects of your job. List the key words and phrases below in the appropriate place.

Which words and phrases tell you about	***Write the words and phrases here***
The kind of activities you are expected to do with service users?	
Where you are expected to work in (the different places or settings)?	
Your responsibilities in the workplace?	

Which words and phrases tell you about	*Write the words and phrases here*
Who you are responsible or accountable to?	....
	....
	....
	....
Your colleagues?	....
	....
	....
	....
Any other important parts of your job (please list them)?	....
	....
	....
	....

Follow up. *Discuss what you have written with your line manager. This will help you to understand your new job more clearly.*

Understanding Aims and Objectives

The words 'aims' and 'objectives' are used in many services. But what do they mean and do they help you do the job any better?

In some services the two words are used together and taken to mean the same thing. In others, they are separated and a difference is made between them. It is more helpful for aims and objectives to be understood separately, because they really have different meanings, although they are closely linked.

☞ *Key points*

An aim is a general statement of what a service hopes to achieve in its work with people with learning disabilities. *Objectives* are clear, precise statements that describe what a service will do to achieve its overall aims.

For example:

"Our aim is to ensure that all of our service users become as independent as possible, able to look after themselves, make their own decisions and take full control of their own lives."

"We aim to provide quality services for all service users, to offer them choice and opportunity in all areas of life so that they can take their place alongside other people in society."

"Our aim is very simple. We want to get more people with learning disability into the mainstream workforce."

I wouldn't argue with these statements but they don't really tell me much about the actual work of the service. This is where objectives come in. Whereas aims are general statements, usually expressing aspirations, objectives are more precise statements of what the service hopes to achieve. Although they don't tell us exactly how things will be achieved, they do bring us a step closer.

Take a look at the aim and then the objectives below and see how they differ:

"The AIM of this service is to enable people with learning disabilities to develop their capacity to the fullest extent possible, to take their place alongside other people in society and to live satisfying and fulfilling lives as part of their own communities."

Our OBJECTIVES are:

- *To provide a wide range of educational, social and personal growth activities appropriate for the age, interest and ability of each individual*
- *To ensure that all activities are undertaken in community settings alongside other ordinary citizens*
- *To make full use of local community resources*
- *To match all activities to the assessed needs of each individual*
- *To work in partnership with service users and their families or carers."*

You will see that objectives provide a much clearer picture of the service, what it hopes to achieve and how it intends to do this. Unlike an aim, which is general, an *objective* is much more specific and sets out briefly how the aims will be met.

Understanding More about Your Own Role and Your Responsibilities

You play a crucial role in ensuring your service achieves its aims and objectives and in helping people with learning disabilities make major changes to their lives. This is an exciting and important responsibility.

In fact, I should really talk about *responsibilities* in the plural, because your job as a practitioner will involve many different things. Some responsibilities are straightforward, some more complex.

There will probably be times when you're not sure yourself exactly what your responsibilities are. The next activity will help you to think about this.

Activity 2

Answer the following questions as they relate to your own work. Write a brief answer under each question.

A new service user is about to join your service. Who will you go to find out about your responsibilities in relation to this person?

....

....

....

Marjorie, a service user you work with, has a private and personal problem and you are not sure how to deal with it. Who will you go to for advice?

....

....

....

You answer the telephone to someone from a housing association who asks for information about one of the service users. Who will you consult to see whether this information should be passed on?

....

....

....

A family member is unwilling for her son, Ron, to take part in an activity she sees as 'too dangerous' but Ron is keen to take part. Can you support Ron in his decision or will you have to seek advice? If so, who will you go to?

....

....

....

The brother of one of the service users has made a complaint against you which you feel is unjustified. Who will help you resolve the problem?

....

....

....

You are aware that a colleague is treating some of the service users harshly. Who can you talk to about this?

....

....

....

Follow up. *Once you have completed this activity discuss it with your line manager or the person responsible for your induction.*

Understanding Other People's Roles and Responsibilities

How many people are employed by your service? Do you know, or do you have to stop and count because there are so many? And how well do you understand your colleagues' roles and responsibilities? Think about two people you work with by doing the following activity.

Activity 3

First, think about one person from your staff group, who has a different job from yours, but is not your line manager. Imagine you were introducing this person to a new member of staff or a visitor to your service and explaining his or her role and responsibilities. In the space below, write what you would say.

My colleague's role

His/her job title: ....

His/her role (one sentence): ....

....

....

....

His/her responsibilities: ....

....

....

....

Next, do the same for your line manager.

My line manager's role

His/her job title: ....

His/her role (one sentence): ....

....

....

His/her responsibilities: ....

....

....

....

Follow up. *Use this activity to talk to your colleagues about their work, find out as much as you can about what they do and how their job relates to your own.*

A 'Professional Relationship'

In your work you probably come into contact with different people at different times. These could include service users, their relatives, colleagues, visiting professionals and people in the community. This contact means that you have a responsibility to 'be professional' or 'behave in a professional manner'.

A 'professional relationship' means many different things, depending on the people involved and the circumstances. It relies a great deal on your own *judgement* and *sensitivity*. Nobody can tell you what 'behaving professionally' means in every situation, but these guidelines will help.

Having a professional relationship with service users means:

- respecting and valuing all service users – even if you find it difficult to like some of them
- trying not to let your own feelings and prejudices get in the way of your work
- listening to people and trying to understand their perspective
- recognising and upholding the rights of every service user
- responding appropriately and sensitively to people's needs and demands, while helping them to recognise and accept their responsibilities
- working *with* them and not doing everything *for* them or taking over all responsibilities
- not patronising people or criticising them in public or behind their backs
- recognising people's rights to control their own lives in a responsible way that does not affect the freedom of others.

☞ *Key points*

A professional relationship with service users means good communication, respect, upholding rights, valuing all service users equally and working in partnership with them.

Having a professional relationship with the relatives and friends of service users means:

- recognising and nurturing the partnership which exists between you
- recognising and respecting their expertise in relation to the service user
- listening to them and taking account of what they say
- being aware of the conflicts which may exist between their opinion and perspective and those of the service user.

☞ *Key points*

A professional relationship with relatives and friends of service users means good communication, respecting their expertise, understanding their perspective, providing appropriate support and working in partnership.

Having a professional relationship with colleagues and other professionals means:

- learning about and respecting other people's roles and responsibilities
- being prepared to listen to and try to understand opinions and ideas that are different from your own
- not taking part in any situation you recognise as 'unprofessional'
- having the courage to tackle any situations where you know people have behaved unprofessionally – something that can be difficult
- recognising that you are a member of a team of people with different strengths and talents and being confident in your own worth and ability while not undermining anyone else
- doing your best to work as a member of the team
- dealing immediately and directly with any injustice done to you or any colleague.

☞ *Key points*

A professional relationship with colleagues means respect for their roles, expertise and opinion; teamwork; openness; good communication and common objectives.

Understanding Policies and Procedures

All organisations have policies and procedures that set out the right way to carry out particular tasks. *Policies* tell staff what should be done and *procedures* set out in more detail how they should be done.

So, for example, your organisation will have a policy on confidentiality. This will explain to staff, service users and family carers the reasons for confidentiality and the organisation's commitment to maintaining confidential information. These procedures will also explain and show to staff and others how they are to deliver the policy in their daily work. For example, the procedures will tell you:

- what information you can give to others
- how you must store records and files
- what to do in case of a breach of confidentiality.

Policies and procedures are usually kept in the staff handbook. Every member of staff should have a copy, or should know where a copy is kept. Supervisors and managers need to be sure that every member of staff is aware of all the policies and procedures relating to their work. As a new member of staff it is your job to find out about policies and procedures and to check with your manager if there is anything you don't fully understand.

☞ *Key points*

During your induction discuss with your line manager any policies or procedures which relate to your work. It is your responsibility to be sure you fully understand all of them.

Activity 4

In the space below write in where you would go to find a complete list of all your organisation's policies and procedures.

In the space below write the name of the person you would go to for further information or advice about any policies or procedures.

In the space below note down two policies that relate directly to your new job.

1.

2.

Understanding the Purpose of Supervision

One of the most important aspects of your development as a practitioner is having time to reflect on what you are doing and learn from it. Sharing this experience with someone else can help give you insights into your own abilities, strengths and needs. This is the purpose of *supervision.*

Supervision is normally carried out by your immediate line manager, but, in some circumstances, may be done by someone else. The way it is done varies from workplace to workplace, but it is something which should be happening regularly in every service.

The word 'supervision' can be off-putting, but the idea behind it is good. Supervision has a number of useful purposes:

- it gives you the opportunity to discuss matters that are important to *you*
- it is a time when you can ask for advice about, or help with, problems
- it gives you the opportunity to make suggestions about how things might be changed or developed
- it focuses on *you, your work and your needs*
- it is a useful time to discuss your own development as a practitioner, career prospects and opportunities for training
- it helps to build better *teamwork* because everyone has their own chance to talk things through in private
- it helps *staff morale* because you know there is someone to listen and help deal with problems before they get out of hand.

Activity 5

In your own words answer the two questions below. When you have completed this activity discuss it with the person responsible for your induction.

What are the three main reasons for supervision in your service?

☆ ....

☆ ....

☆ ....

Describe briefly two examples of supervision situations that you have found helpful in your work with people with learning disabilities.

☆ ....

☆ ....

☆ ....

☆ ....

Understanding the Main Principles of Care

The kind of work you do is often described as 'care work' or 'social care'. Many people feel that this is not a very good description because it implies that people with learning disabilities are dependent and need the care and protection of others. They also feel that it denies their adult status and their right – and ability – to control their own lives. Most people prefer to use the word 'support', rather than 'care'. What do you think?

However, the term 'care' is the one used in official documents and policy, so it is the one used in this unit.

In working with people with learning disabilities, there are certain basic principles and values that sum up everything we believe and guide everything we do. In the final part of this section you'll be focusing on these: the main principles of care.

The main principles of care (or support work) covered here are:
- empowerment
- choice
- dignity
- respect
- individuality
- privacy.

Empowerment

As things stand today, very few people with learning disabilities are empowered. They are most often on the receiving end of other people's decisions and plans. Much of their lives, if not all, is controlled by others. They very seldom have the power to decide their own lifestyle. Someone else usually makes these decisions for them: service providers, families, care workers or support workers.

You have a vitally important role in the empowerment of people with learning disabilities. You cannot empower them – people can only empower themselves – but you can help them to work towards empowerment. Empowerment cannot happen overnight, especially for people who have been disempowered all their lives. It is a process which happens step by step and it will take people with learning disabilities a long time to achieve.

☞ *Key points*

Empowerment means a shift in the balance of power so that people with learning disabilities can make their own decisions and take control of their own lives.

The empowerment of service users is the most fundamental of the main principles of care or support work.

Choice

Every day we make many choices. Some of them are quite small and others can be very important. Day to day choices are often about the clothes we wear, the food we eat, how we spend our money and who we spend time with. Other choices we may make include where to work, who to live with, where to live and where to go on holiday. You probably take these choices for granted, but for people with learning disabilities these choices are often made for them.

People with learning disabilities can make many choices for themselves. Part of your job is to help service users by making sure they have enough information to make choices and to support them when they speak up for themselves. Having choice over a particular part of your life means you have control. Part of your role is to encourage the people you work with by supporting their opportunities for choice.

☞ *Key points*

Choice means having access to a wide range of options, deciding for yourself which ones suit you best and having your choice respected.

Dignity

People with learning disabilities have the same rights as every other citizen in our society. This fundamental principle means that people with learning disabilities should never be treated in an inhuman or degrading way, but should always be treated courteously as people of value. You should always seek to maintain the dignity of each individual service user you work with.

☞ *Points for practice*

Dignity means that we recognise and value people with learning disabilities as equal human beings with the same rights as every other citizen.

Respect

The way that you and your colleagues behave towards the people with learning disabilities you support affects the way that other people see them and the way they see themselves. You should show consideration to individual service users and demonstrate through your actions and attitudes that all service users are worthy of respect.

☞ *Key points*

Respect means that we behave towards every person with the consideration they deserve, valuing their opinions, views and achievements, no matter how different these are from our own.

Individuality

After just a few days of starting work with people with learning disabilities it should be clear to you that each service user is an individual in their own right with their own particular likes, dislikes, strengths and personalities. Services and member of staff should always focus on individual needs rather than the needs of a group. You and your colleagues should have the needs of individual service users as a top priority in your daily work.

☞ *Key points*

Individuality in the work context means that we respond to and work with each person as an individual with his or her own unique personality, needs, perspective and strengths.

Privacy

Privacy is a basic human need. We all need to do some things alone and have time to ourselves to do as we please. Our personality, interests and circumstances determine our need for privacy.

You need to respect people's need for privacy and their dignity at all times. If your work involves supporting service users with their personal care you will need to take particular care to ensure privacy for the individual.

☞ *Key points*

We respect service users' privacy by ensuring that everyone is treated at all times and in all ways in a manner which safeguards their dignity and does not expose them to any situations which might humiliate or embarrass them or cause them personal or emotional discomfort.

These are the main principles of care which must underpin all work with people with learning disabilities.

Activity 6

In your own words explain in one or two sentences the main principles of care:

Empowerment

Dignity

Choice

Cultural differences

There may be people who use your service who are from different ethnic backgrounds from your own. This means that some service users and their families may interpret the principles of care in a different way to you.

For example, you might work with people from cultural backgrounds who:

- Live very closely with extended family members
- Have lots more people in their family
- Have different expectations of the role of men and women from the majority of people in the UK
- Have arranged marriages
- Have different ideas of what 'ability' and 'disability' mean

- Expect sons and daughters to live with the family until marriage
- Expect sons and daughters to be more dependent on the family until they leave home, regardless of their age
- Have strict religious requirements
- Have particular dietary requirements.

For service users from minority ethnic groups, and their families, the cultural expectations in the service may be very different from their own. There might be potential for conflict.

Part of your job is to be aware of these differences and know how they may affect your work. Use the next activity to think this through. You might like to discuss this with some colleagues while doing it.

Understanding Prejudice, Discrimination and Equal Opportunities

People in social care work – as well as in society at large – are concerned about prejudice, discrimination and equal opportunities. Throughout history, people with disabilities have been treated differently to non disabled people. Today disabled people are still discriminated against. Other people are also discriminated against, perhaps because of their race, sex, sexuality, age or religion.

You need to understand issues of prejudice, discrimination and equal opportunities, so that they inform the work that you do with people with learning disabilities.

Prejudice

Prejudice means that we have preconceived opinions that are not based on reason and this may cause us to act in an unjust way on the basis of these ideas. Prejudice can mean that we believe other people are different from us and use this to justify unfair or intolerant behaviour. In your day to day work supporting people with learning disabilities you need to be alert to prejudiced attitudes which could lead to unacceptable behaviour.

Discrimination

If we behave in a discriminatory way it means that we are treating people in a less favourable way because we see them as different from ourselves. Discrimination can be against an individual or a group, and can include racism, ageism and sexism. Can you think of any other reasons that individuals or organisations can use to discriminate against people?

Equal opportunities

If individuals and organisations support equal opportunities it means that they recognise that all people are of equal value and share the same rights. They should be treated fairly and provided with similar chances and experience. At work this means that each individual is treated as of equal status regardless of any disability or other difference.

Activity 7

This activity covers all of section one from this workbook, so please re-read the section before starting.

1. A professional relationship

Think about the professional relationship you have with service users and colleagues. Write down one example that shows how this works in practice. Use the space below:

2. Supervision

Next time you have supervision, use the list of purposes on page 23 to prepare for it. What difference does this make to your session?

3. The Main Principles of Care

Give two recent examples of how you put these principles into practice in your own work.

Example 1

Example 2

....

....

....

SECTION 2: Confidentiality

Confidentiality

Introduction

This section looks at the *principles of confidentiality*. I'll be asking you to consider how they apply in your own work situation.

What is meant by 'confidentiality'?

You are in a trusted position in your kind of work and have access to very personal information about individuals and their families, all of which is confidential.

☞ *Key points*

Confidentiality means respecting personal information about individual service users and their families and carers, and keeping this information private. It also means not disclosing this information unless an appropriate person, or people, give you permission to do so.

Why is confidentiality important?

Stop for a minute and think just how much you know about service users' personal lives. Imagine how you would feel if someone had this sort of information about you: your personal history – possibly even details of your birth – your family background, assessments showing what you can and cannot do, personal medical information ... and so on. You would feel exposed and very much at the mercy of that person, wouldn't you?

Do the next activity to remind yourself why confidentiality must be maintained at all times.

Activity 8

Read the list below – it gives some of the reasons why confidentiality is important. Add any others you can think of. In your opinion, which reason is the most important and why? Which is the least important and why?

Write your answers next to the reasons and add any other reasons you feel are important.

Confidentiality is important in my job because:

☆ *Everyone has a right to privacy and dignity*

☆ *Information in the wrong hands can cause problems*

☆ *It is an important part of doing a professional job*

☆ *I agreed to it when I got this job*

☆ *I might be disciplined if I disclose information to the wrong people*

☆ *It shows that I respect service users.*

Add your own reasons here:

1. ....

2. ....

3. ....

Understanding your organisation's policies and procedures in relation to confidentiality

Every organisation takes confidentiality very seriously and should have policies and procedures that tell staff what is required of them. The Data Protection Act has guidelines your organisation needs to follow when collecting and storing confidential information.

Use the next activity to help you check your knowledge of your organisation's policies and procedures on confidentiality.

Activity 9

Read through your organisation's policies and procedures on confidentiality at least twice. In the space below, list the main points.

☆ ....

☆ ....

☆ ....

☆ ....

☆ ....

☆ ....

Good practice in relation to confidentiality

If policies and procedures are to work well within a service, people have to know them and use them. The next activity will help you think about this in more depth.

Activity 10

1. Where are your organisation's policies and procedures on confidentiality normally kept and how do you get hold of them if you need them?

2. If you were unclear about something written in these documents, who would be the best person to explain it to you?

3. If the father of a service user complained to you about a breach of confidentiality, what would you do about it?

4. If you felt that a colleague had breached confidentiality, how would you handle this?

5. If you had, by mistake, passed on information that was confidential, what would you do, and who would you talk to?

6. If there was a serious breach of confidentiality in your service, what disciplinary procedures would be taken, and by whom?

....

....

Follow up. *When you have completed this activity discuss it with your line manager. If there is any question you are unsure about make sure you get a clear answer from your manager.*

Confidentiality is about much more than just records and documents, of course. It also refers to information given verbally, or overheard by accident. *Good practice* in relation to confidentiality in the workplace means:

- Putting confidential papers away safely after using them
- Using the most private means of conveying information that is private and personal. For example, not using faxes or e-mails which can be read by anyone
- Having private conversations, both face-to-face and by telephone, in places where you cannot be overheard
- Making sure that you do not leave information on a computer screen open for all to see
- Not discussing matters which are personal to a particular service user, or making reference to them, in groups, either of staff or of service users
- Taking it for granted that something personal is confidential unless the person concerned tells you otherwise
- Guiding service users away from talking about private or personal matters in public
- Not relaying to relatives anything that service users may have told you about private matters, but instead suggesting to service users that they should keep these things within the family
- Not encouraging service users to give you personal or private information
- Being careful about how you phrase confidential information when you have to pass it on to someone else
- Not discussing confidential information with colleagues, assuming that they also know about it
- Respecting confidences.

Allowing other people access to information and premises

Another important aspect of confidentiality is checking people's identity before they have access to information or premises. Documents relating to policies and procedures should give guidance on this.

There are several reasons why this is important:

- Passing on information without authorisation is against the rights of an individual
- It shows lack of respect for the privacy and individuality of service users and their families
- There are legal requirements relating to keeping information confidential
- Disclosing information can result in intrusion into an individual's private affairs
- Information can be passed on to other people who should not have access to it
- It will reflect badly not only on the person who discloses the information, but also on the service
- It can make service users the subject of gossip and can often cause unwarranted rumours.

You can probably add to this list.

The activity below will help you think about your own organisation's guidelines for checking identity.

Activity 11

Read through the list below. Tick 'yes' if this is mentioned in your organisation's guidelines, 'no' if it is not.

Guidelines for allowing people access to premises

Always check the identity of anyone seeking entry to the premises.

Yes ○ *No* ○

If you find someone wandering around, ask if you can help and direct or accompany this person to the office.

Yes ○ *No* ○

Do not allow visitors to wander around unaccompanied unless they have the authority to do so.

Yes ○ *No* ○

If you see anyone acting suspiciously, call the manager or a senior member of staff.

Yes ○ *No* ○

Guidelines for allowing people access to information

Never disclose information about service users without checking with your line manager

Yes ○ *No* ○

Never disclose information about service users over the telephone

Yes ○ *No* ○

Never disclose private or personal information about a service user in a meeting on or off the premises unless given permission to do so by the person and your line manager

Yes ○ *No* ○

Follow up. *Take time to discuss your answers to this activity with your line manager and refer back to your organisation's policies or procedures if you are unsure about what you should do.*

Limits and Boundaries of Confidentiality

There may be times when confidentiality needs to be breached, even if these are rare. Read the list below and see whether confidentiality should be breached in these situations or not. For each question in the list, write brief notes underneath.

Activity 12

Irene, one of the service users, tells you that she is afraid of her father, but will not tell you why. Should you pass this information on to your line manager?

Abdul, one of the service users in your group, says something which makes you think he might be being abused at the hostel where he lives. Should you discuss this with anyone?

Your line manager has suggested that you pass on some information which you feel should be kept private. Should you do as instructed?

Clifton, who attends your day centre, is multiply disabled and highly dependent for personal care needs. Should you pass on information about his personal habits and responses to staff at the leisure centre he attends once a week?

Innis has finished at the leavers' unit and is moving on to college. His siblings have a history of petty crime and you are concerned that he might be drawn into this lifestyle as he gets older. Should you pass this information on to college staff?

Follow up. *There are no easy answers to these questions. So much depends on circumstances and what would happen if you did or did not pass on information. However, remember two things:*

1. You need to weigh the rights of the individual against the danger that will result if you don't disclose the information.

2. Always seek guidance from managers, or senior colleagues if managers are not available.

SECTION 3: About Learning Disability

About Learning Disability

Introduction

So far this course has concentrated on you, your job and the organisation you work for. This section concentrates on:

- the term 'learning disability' and the way it is used
- some of the causes of learning disability.

Learning Disability

Are you particularly good at any of these activities:

Art? Cooking? Driving? Making friends? Gardening? Swimming?

Are you particularly bad at any of them? Chances are that you're good at some things, not so good at others and not interested in some, just like everybody else.

If you have ever had a really bad time trying to learn something and felt like a failure, you know what it's like to experience difficulties in learning. It has happened to all of us in some way or another. People with learning disabilities have marked difficulty in learning most things. But, like the rest of us, they are better at some things than others.

The definition of 'learning disability' used in this course is:

Learning disability is a term used to describe significant difficulties in learning things which society expects of people at certain stages in their life.

You know from your own experience that people who use learning disability services are as different from one another as any other group of people. They may all experience difficulties in learning, but even these are not the same. Some learn more slowly than others, while some find certain things easy to learn and others almost impossible!

You may have heard the term 'a continuum of ability' or a 'continuum of disability'. This is an idea which is used to explain different degrees of ability or disability.

A continuum is like an imaginary line with one extreme at one end and one extreme at the other. For example, you could have a continuum of interest in the National Lottery, like this:

←-·-→

People who are fanatical and buy lots of tickets every week	**People who don't care and hardly know it exists**

In between these two extremes you have many other people who have varying degrees of interest in the National Lottery. Where would you place yourself along this continuum? Mark this spot with an X.

If you imagine a continuum of learning disability, the most extreme learning disability would be at one end and mild learning disability would be at the other.

Some people find the idea of a continuum of learning disability useful in helping them to understand different degrees of ability and learning disability. Of course, the continuum does not really exist. It is only a way of thinking about different abilities.

There are other ways of describing different degrees of learning disability which you may have come across in the course of your work: mild, moderate, severe and profound.

Mild learning disability usually means that someone has obvious difficulties in learning most things, especially formal educational skills, but can acquire the skills of everyday living.

Moderate learning disability usually means that someone has considerable difficulty in learning most things and will probably need help in mastering the skills of everyday living.

Severe learning disability usually means that the person's learning difficulties will be substantial, that his or her language abilities will be limited and that he or she will probably need support with many daily living skills.

Profound learning disability usually means that someone will have extreme difficulty in all learning. He or she will have limited communication, may have both physical and intellectual impairment and will be highly dependent on others for personal care.

However, you will see that this way of referring to people is extremely negative. Many of us are very uneasy about categorising people, feeling that it depersonalises and devalues people.

People with learning disabilities themselves, like the rest of us, dislike being labelled and always described in terms of their shortcomings and dis- abilities – especially as these are judgements that are based on what is supposedly 'normal' in our society. Their argument, like those of people with other kinds of disability, is that dis- ability is not within the individual, but created by a society with fixed ideas of what is and is not acceptable.

Nevertheless there are those who think that categorising disability in this way can be helpful in understanding people's needs and in getting them the services they require and are entitled to. This is a discussion you will probably return to on many occasions in your work with people with learning disabilities.

Some of the Causes of Learning Disability

There are many reasons why learning disability occurs. Impairments which cause or contribute to learning disability can happen before, during or after birth:

- Before birth or pre-natal: these are known as "congenital" causes and include Down syndrome or Fragile X syndrome
- During birth or peri-natal causes such as oxygen deprivation resulting in cerebral palsy
- After birth or post-natal causes such as illness, injury or environmental conditions; for example, meningitis, brain injury or children being deprived of attention to their basic needs and undernourished, neglected or physically abused.

Just how important is it to know the causes of a person's learning disability? Does it make them a different person from the one we know? And is it more important than knowing how they feel, what they are good at or what they want to achieve in life?

Advantages of knowing the cause of a learning disability

- Some types of learning disability are thought to be associated with particular learning characteristics, eg specific problems in understanding visual information, or understanding spoken language. Knowing this can help us change our approach when supporting someone.
- Some people have difficulty with relationships, for example, people with autism. Knowing this can help us learn the best way of supporting them.
- Some syndromes or impairments are associated with medical conditions; knowing this will enable us to help people avoid situations which may be dangerous, or help us deal with emergencies.

Disadvantages of knowing the cause of a learning disability

- We may become more aware of the disability and forget the value and humanity of the individual
- We might use the learning disability as a reason for doing or not doing certain things
- We might stereotype people and think of them as a group rather than as individuals with their own unique qualities, for example, people with Down syndrome are friendly, outgoing and love music.

You will be able to add to these lists from your own experience.

Activity 13

This workplace activity will help you apply what you have learned and discussed in this section. Read the section on confidentiality on page 33 before you start this activity.

Spend some time with two people who use your service. Find out from talking with them and spending time with them:

1. *What they enjoy doing*
2. *What new things they are learning*
3. *How they deal with new unfamiliar situations*
4. *Do they like being referred to as a person with a learning disability?*

Write some of your findings below

Person 1

1. What they enjoy doing

2. What new things they are learning

3. How they deal with new unfamiliar situations

4. Do they like being referred to as a person with a learning disability?

Person 2

1. What they enjoy doing

2. What new things they are learning

3. How they deal with new unfamiliar situations

Now answer these two questions:

1. In your own words, what do you think the term learning disability means?

2. Think about the two people you worked with for this activity. What does it mean for them to be seen as having a learning disability?

Follow up. *Discuss this activity with a senior colleague. Find out from them or from service users about any self-advocacy groups in your area for people with learning disabilities. If you can, find out what the local self-advocacy group does.*

SECTION 4:
Lessons from History

Lessons from History

Introduction

If you have been working with people with learning disabilities for some time, you will have experienced many changes both in the words we use and in the way services have developed. You might have been used to the words 'mental handicap' and you might have worked in a 'training centre'. Now you use the term 'learning disability' and you may work in a 'social education centre' or a 'day centre'. Or maybe you have moved from a hospital work setting to a community setting.

This section looks at what we can learn from the history of learning disability in society.

Being 'different'

Sometimes people of different ethnic origins, or who are asylum seekers or who belong to a particular religious group are seen as 'different'. For one reason or another, they do not fit the stereotype of what some people consider 'normal' and they are on the receiving end of prejudice and discrimination as a result.

People with learning disabilities are among those who, for a long time, have been seen as different. Throughout history they have been seen in different ways:

- sometimes as objects of pity, unable to do anything for themselves and less fortunate than other human beings
- as 'eternal children': people who never grow up, despite their real age, and who behave in life as if they were forever children
- as a menace to society, a threat that ordinary people must be protected from
- as 'sub-human', labelled in schools as educationally sub-normal or severely sub-normal. They have been labelled as 'mentally backward' and 'mentally handicapped'.

These ways of thinking, and the labels that go with them, have been degrading and dehumanising to people with learning disabilities. They have also had other effects:

- Shaping the thinking of the public at large
- Giving rise to the idea that such people have to be 'cared for' by 'experts' who know how to deal with them

- Creating an artificial distinction of 'us' and 'them', ie, 'normal' human beings and the others
- Establishing a false idea of 'normality'
- Promoting segregation and discrimination
- Shaping the kinds of services available
- Denying people their basic human rights.

Institutionalisation and its effects

One of the most harmful effects of this sort of thinking has been to exclude people with learning disabilities from mainstream society and shut them away in large institutions. Some survivors of institutionalisation have harrowing tales to tell. Listen to James, who was 70 years old when he moved out of an institution and was 78 when he told his story:

"I remember it very well. My mother died and I was only a little child of four. They came to take me away – I think it was because I kept running on to the road and it was dangerous. It was a long journey and they took me to that place. (In fact, James was taken to a very large institution 250 miles away from his home.) *It was frightening for a little child. But I soon learned to keep quiet and do what I was told. That way you didn't get into trouble. It was a terrible place, a terrible place – I cannot ever tell you all the things that happened there. I'm never going back there again. Never!"*

Ellen also remembers her days in various institutions:

"I was no good in school. I couldn't learn properly. Then I was a bit wild. They locked me up. They told me they had to lock me up for my own good. I really hated it. I use to scream and cut my arms. They moved me to another place. It was worse. I still cut myself. Then they moved me to another place but it wasn't so bad as the one before. Then I got out when I was 60. They were very good there – they helped me to get out – they said 'Would you like to live in the community?' and I said 'Yes please' but I was a bit scared. Now I love it here and I'll never, never go back even if they ask me."

We know that 'institutionalisation' – the effect of living in an institution such as a long stay hospital – has long-term consequences for people:

- Causing them to behave in ways other people consider strange, eg talking to themselves, always being on the move or repeating words and actions over and over again

- Finding it difficult to get used to new situations
- Not being able to move away from set routines or set patterns of behaviour
- Not being able to relate appropriately to people in different situations, eg hugging people inappropriately
- Being extremely anxious and afraid in unfamiliar situations
- Asking permission for everything, eg 'Can I go to the toilet?'

Nowadays we know more about the effects of institutionalisation on individuals and on society. We are trying to work towards inclusive societies where everyone is valued and has equal opportunities for growth and development according to their own strengths and needs. You'll be exploring these developments in more detail later in the course. One thing I'm sure about: we still have a very long way to go!

Activity 14

This activity covers the main points of section four and I suggest you re-read this section before starting.

You may find it helpful to talk to a colleague and a service user about their experiences of living or working in a long stay hospital. Discuss this with your manager before going ahead.

1. People with learning disabilities have been treated differently to other groups of people in our society. Give one example of a negative description of people with learning disabilities that was used in the past.

2. Explain how this description might have affected the way people with learning disabilities were treated.

3. Where was the nearest long stay hospital for people with learning disabilities in your area?

4. How do you think the people with learning disabilities who lived in such a hospital were affected?

SECTION 5:
Challenging Behaviour

Challenging Behaviour

Introduction

This final section covers:

- the meaning of the term 'challenging behaviour'
- the relationship between challenging behaviour, emotions, communication and personal power
- some of the factors which influence behaviour.

The Meaning of the Term 'Challenging Behaviour'

This is probably a term you are familiar with. It has replaced older terms, such as 'behaviour problems' or 'difficult behaviour'. There are good reasons for this change.

Challenging behaviour is precisely that: it is behaviour which is a challenge to us and the situation or circumstances a person finds himself or herself in. It is an individual's way of saying, 'I don't like (or want) this and I want to change it (or stop it).' There are always good reasons for the challenge!

Because people with learning disabilities often have communication difficulties, they can find it difficult to challenge things verbally. They may not have the confidence to challenge people they see as 'authority figures'. Those with profound and multiple disability will often be unable to remove themselves from a situation they dislike or may be unable to make themselves understood.

These are some of the behaviours we often find challenging:

- constant movement such as rocking or rushing around and refusing to stop
- people harming themselves by biting, hitting or banging parts of themselves
- continuous masturbation
- talking non-stop and over what others are saying
- continuous shouting, screaming or laughing
- hitting, pinching, pushing or biting anyone who comes near
- chewing or tearing objects and clothes.

Activity 15

Think of your own work situation. You may have come across behaviour you have found challenging. Describe briefly two examples of behaviour which you have found challenging when working with service users. Do not include behaviours which are just irritating, only those which could be termed 'challenging behaviours'.

☆

☆

Why did you find these behaviours challenging?

What do you think people using them were challenging?

Follow up. *When you have completed this activity discuss what you have written with your supervisor or a senior colleague.*

Communication, Emotional Life and Personal Power

There are many reasons why people use behaviours which we find challenging. Let's look at the relationship between challenging behaviour and:

- communication
- emotional life
- personal power.

Communication

People with learning disability often have difficulties with communication. In particular:

- They may not have the words they need to use
- They may be unable to use sentences which are long enough to explain what they want to say
- They may have difficulty with pronunciation
- They may be unable to speak
- They may not fully understand the meaning of a conversation because it is too quick or complicated
- They may feel intimidated and 'clam up' in stressful situations.

In addition, we often have problems understanding what they are trying to tell us:

- We misunderstand a situation or jump to conclusions
- We do not give the person time to communicate adequately
- We assume that the person cannot express himself
- We say everything for the person
- We often ignore someone's attempts to communicate.

Given all these possibilities for breakdown in communication, it's not surprising that an individual finds some other, much more powerful way of communicating!

You can help to improve communication with service users by using verbal and non-verbal communication that is suitable for the particular person. As you get to know individual service users you will find out from them and from your colleagues the types of verbal and non-verbal communication that person finds most helpful.

You may find it useful to think about:

Your verbal communication

Does the tone, loudness and clarity of your voice make it easy to understand what you are saying?
Is the length of each sentence or utterance OK, or are you making things too long and complicated?
Are the words you are using ones that the service user understands?

Your non-verbal communication

Are you too close or too far away from the service user?
What does your posture, and how you sit or stand, communicate?
Does your facial expression communicate the same message as your words?
If you use touch and physical contact as part of your communication, are you sure what this is communicating?

Emotional life

Emotions can be difficult to express at the best of times. If you have a learning disability which makes communication difficult, the situation becomes even more of a problem. Add to this the fact that it is not always easy to sort out your feelings and you can see why emotional life and challenging behaviour are closely linked.

Challenging behaviour can be a way of expressing feelings such as boredom, loneliness, frustration or anger. It can mean:

- *'Why can't you understand how I'm feeling?'*
- *'I'm really raging about this and I can't do anything about it!'*
- *'I don't know WHAT I feel!!'*
- *'I haven't seen Alan all day – I miss him.'*
- *'Please don't let Mason anywhere near me – he scares me.'*
- *'Have you any idea what happened at home today – it really upset me!'*
- *'Don't ignore me – I have feelings too, you know.'*
- *'Why won't anyone talk to me – I need some company.'*

Personal Power

People with learning disabilities are seldom in control of their own lives, even in very basic ways. Challenging behaviour can be a reaction against their feelings of powerlessness and a demand for something to be done about it. The person may be telling us:

- *'Don't do everything for me – I want to try for myself.'*
- *'I want some time alone when I can just sit and do nothing.'*
- *'I'm bored – I need to do something more interesting.'*
- *'I don't like this – take it away.'*
- *'Don't anticipate everything I'm going to say.'*
- *'I don't like Janice, I'd rather be with Elsa.'*
- *'I'm an adult – you don't have to make my decisions for me.'*
- *'I'm an adult and this is much too childish for me.'*

Factors that influence behaviour

Many things influence the way we behave, including:
- personal factors
- environmental factors
- cultural features
- previous abuse
- loss.

Personal factors

Personal factors affect the way everybody behaves. Think about three or four people you know, the differences in their personalities, the way they react to good or bad news and the way they spend their time. I'm sure they all react differently. The same is true of people with learning disabilities.

Like ours, their behaviour is affected by:
- their personality, eg introverted or outgoing, optimistic or pessimistic
- health and wellbeing, eg feeling 'under the weather', having a medical condition such as epilepsy or diabetes, being pre-menstrual
- sexual needs and frustrations, eg being ignored by someone they feel attracted to, having unfulfilled sex needs
- established patterns of behaviour, eg being in the habit of reacting negatively, or violently, so that it has become second nature
- self esteem, eg feeling worthless, or used to being belittled.

There are other personal factors which might also influence the behaviour of people with learning disabilities:
- the extent of the impairment, eg people with severe impairment who have little control over their own lives and severe communication problems will probably experience much more frustration than the rest of us
- some people with learning disabilities will be at an earlier stage in their development than non-disabled people and their behaviour will reflect this.

Environmental factors

Our environment also affects our behaviour. Environment can be divided into the physical environment and the social environment.
The *physical environment* includes:
- surroundings such as the size of the room, the lighting, the space and the furniture
- noises from such things as radios, heaters and toilets
- equipment used for activities and physiotherapy
- comfort factors such as seating and temperature
- how much choice you have
- the level of stimulation around you.

The *social environment* includes:

- the number of people around and passing through the room
- the person or people in your private space
- how people respond to you or ignore you
- who you spend time with and how many different people pass through your life in a day, a week, or a month
- the unpredictability of other people's behaviour, eg someone suddenly shouting, or talking very loudly or grabbing hold of you.

Cultural features which might affect behaviour

Our experiences of our own culture and of other cultures can also influence our behaviour. For example:

- We can experience conflict and confusion when we find ourselves in a situation where cultural norms and expectations are different from those we are used to, eg when we go on holiday to other countries
- Different cultures react differently to noise levels
- Family size and family groups vary from culture to culture
- Expectations of the roles of men and women also vary
- The level of independence expected of people at different times in their lives differs from culture to culture.

Behaviour and loss

Loss is associated with sadness and often confusion and depression, all of which influence the way an individual behaves. This may include:

- loss through bereavement
- loss through someone moving away
- loss through a change in personal circumstances, eg Pat has moved from the family home into a hostel; Samuel has moved from the centre into a job
- loss through a change in circumstances in the service eg Ewan has moved on from the induction group to the vocational group and no longer works with Steve.

Previous abuse

Physical, sexual or mental abuse has a profound effect on any individual. Some people will try to suppress the feelings associated with abuse, while others will have the memories at the forefront of their minds. The extent to which this influences behaviour will vary from person to person. One person will show withdrawn and uncommunicative behaviour, another may react violently, while a third may have unpredictable mood swings.

Final Comments

All of these factors can influence our behaviour in different ways, according to the kind of people we are and how much we've had to put up with. We can all think of situations where someone has suddenly shouted, 'That's the last straw – I can't take any more!' or something similar.

It is seldom one factor which causes challenging behaviour. More likely, it's a combination of things which move someone beyond their level of tolerance. Understanding this can help you learn about the 'triggers' which set off challenging behaviour and ways in which these might be avoided.

Activity 16

Use this workplace activity to help you see how the ideas in section five can help you in your day-to-day work. Refer back to the section as you work on the activity.

During your work over the next few weeks, make a note of one example of challenging behaviour. Try to find a quiet time to reflect on the situation and use the notes below to help you decide how you and your colleagues might avoid a similar event in the future. Remember the issue of confidentiality when completing this activity.

Notes

Describe the incident briefly.

Where and when did it happen?

Can you remember what you or your colleagues did or said before it happened?

Can you remember what you or your colleagues did or said after it happened?

Was anyone else involved apart from you and the service user? If so, how?

What do you think caused the behaviour (think about the people, the environment, what was happening and being said at the time)?

Can you think of anything that you or your colleagues might do to avoid this behaviour happening again?

Follow up. *You will learn more about working with service users who challenge as you go on in your work. Discuss this activity with a colleague or your manager.*

SECTION 6: Resources

Resources

You may find it helpful to look at one or two of the following books or websites or contact the organisations for more information.

Publications

Department of Health (2001) *Valuing People: A new strategy for Learning Disability for the 21st Century* London The Stationery Office.

The Scottish Executive (2000) *The Same As You Review of Services*, The Stationery Office

Hughes, A and Coombs P. (2001) *Easy Guide to the Human Rights Act 1998: Implications for people with Learning disabilities* Kidderminster, BILD Publications.

Johnstone, D. (1998) *An Introduction to Disability Studies* London, David Fulton Publishers.

Emerson, E. et al (2000) *Learning Disabilities: the Fundamental Facts* London, The Foundation for People with Learning Disabilities.

Philpot, T. and Ward, l. (1995) *Values and Visions: Changing ideas in services for people with learning disabilities* London, Butterworth Heinemann.

Thompson, T. and Mathias, P. (1998) *Standards and Learning Disability* Edinburgh Harcourt, Brace and Co.

Fraser, W, et al (1998) Hallas': *The Care of People with Intellectual Disabilities* London, Butterworth Heinemann.

Atkinson, D. et al (1997) *Forgotten Lives: Exploring the History of Learning Disability.* Kidderminster, BILD.

Atkinson, D. et al (2000) *Good Times, Bad Times: Women with Learning Difficulties Telling their Stories* Kidderminster, BILD.

Brechin, A and Walmesley, J. (1990) *Making Connections: Reflecting on the lives and experiences of people with learning disabilities* London, Hodder & Stoughton.

Websites

www.bild.org.uk

www.doh.gov.uk/learningdisabilities Department of Health or England and Wales website.

www.arcuk.org.uk ARC (Association of Residential Care) an umbrella organisation of residential providers.

www.bris.ac.uk/Depts/NorahFry A research centre part of the University of Bristol with an interest in supporting the rights of people with learning difficulties.

www.mencap.org.uk MENCAP provides services for people with learning disabilities.

www.ndt.org.uk National Development Team an independent development agency.

www.united-response.co.uk a provider of housing for people with learning disabilities and mental health problems.

www.doh.gov.uk/london/learningdisabilities contains information of strategic network for London learning disabilities services.

www.scotland.gov.uk/ldsr the Scottish Executive site with details of the national review of services for people with learning disabilities in Scotland.

www.wales.gov.uk Welsh Assembly site

Organisations

People First
Central England People First
PO Box 5200
Northampton
NN1 1ZB
Tel: 01604 721666
Website: www.peoplefirst.org.uk
Central England People First will be able to give you information on People First organisations in your area.

City and Guilds Affinity (Awarding body)
1 Giltspur Street
London EC1A9DD
Tel: 0207 294 2800
Email: enquiry@city-and-guilds.co.uk
Website www.city-and-guilds.co.uk

National Open College Network (Awarding body)
9 James Court
Friargate
Derby DE1 1BT
Tel: 01332 268080
Email: nocn@nocn.org.uk
Website: www.nocn.ac.uk

BILD Services

Information Services provides up to date reading lists on over 40 subjects and literature searches on request. For more information contact 01562 723010.

Learning Services provides in house training, distance learning, conferences and workshops. The BILD Certificates Programme can provide accreditation for staff through studying this and other units for more information contact 01562 723025 email learning@bild.org.uk

BILD Publications provides books, training materials and accessible materials for people with learning disabilities. For a free publications catalogue, and for more information, contact BILD on 01562 723020.

Other books from BILD

The following titles may also be of interest to you. To order any of these titles, please ring BookSource on 0845 370 0068, adding 10% for post and packing. For a free BILD publications catalogue, and for more information, please call BILD on 01562 723020.

Good Times, Bad Times:
Women with Learning Difficulties telling their stories

Edited by Dorothy Atkinson, Michelle McCarthy, Jan Walmsley, Mabel Cooper, Sheena Rolph, Simone Aspis, Pam Barette, Mary Coventry and Gloria Ferris.

Includes easy-to-read version

"People think that when you've been in them kind of places, they think we're stupid, they think we don't know nothing, but we're not! Just because I can't read or write very well, that doesn't stop me doing things, do it?" ***Jean Andrews***

Women with a learning disability give voice to their thoughts, and feelings on a range of topics that matter to them most, including work, relationships and children.

The book also records how women with and without a learning disability worked together to make their voices heard. It is essential reading for anyone involved in working in learning disability services.

2000 ISBN 1 902519 18 3 £10.00

Forgotten Lives:
Exploring the History of Learning Disability

Edited by Dorothy Atkinson, Mark Jackson and Jan Walmsley

"This book is so informative, funny and moving that I cannot imagine anyone not liking it or learning something from it." **Nursing Times**

This publication explores a long-neglected topic: the history of people with a learning disability. *Forgotten Lives* draws on a variety of different perspectives, including first hand acounts from people with a learning disability, documentary evidence, photographs and archive sources.

1997 ISBN 1 873791 84 4 £20.00

Easy Guide to the Human Rights Act
Andrea Hughes and Phil Coombes

The *Easy Guide to the Human Rights Act* outlines the key elements of this important legislation and shows how the Act can be applied in daily life. The guide includes real life stories and examples to illustrate various abuses of human rights, as well as suggestions for good practice and contact details for more information. A free poster accompanying the guide lists the most important human rights and abuses, and can be used in day centres, residential homes, offices and clubs.

2001 ISBN 1 9021519 75 2 £10.00